THE
THEATER
EXPERIENCE

FIFTH EDITION

THE THEATER EXPERIENCE

EDWIN WILSON

Hunter College and Graduate Center
The City University of New York

McGraw-Hill, Inc.

New York   St. Louis   San Francisco   Auckland   Bogotá
Caracas   Lisbon   London   Madrid   Mexico   Milan
Montreal   New Delhi   Paris   San Juan   Singapore
Sydney   Tokyo   Toronto

THE THEATER EXPERIENCE

3 4 5 6 7 8 9 0 HAL HAL 9 0 9 8 7 6 5 4 3 2 1

ISBN 0-07-070683-2

Library of Congress Cataloging-in-Publication Data

Wilson, Edwin.
   The theater experience / Edwin Wilson. — 5th ed.
     p.   cm.
   Includes bibliographical references and index.
   ISBN 0-07-070683-2
   1. Theater.   I. Title.
PN1655.W57   1991   90-47630
792—dc20

This book was set in Palatino by Waldman Graphics, Inc.
The editors were Peter Labella and Susan Gamer;
the designer was Joan E. O'Connor;
the production supervisor was Diane Renda.
The photo editor was Inge King.
New drawings were done by Fine Line Illustrations, Inc.
Arcata Graphics/Halliday was printer and binder.

Cover photo by Martha Swope (*Jerome Robbins' Broadway*).
Photo of the author by Wayne Geist.

Acknowledgment notes appear on pages 473-478,
and on this page by reference.
Credits for color photographs are on pages 478-479.

ABOUT THE
AUTHOR

Teacher, author, and critic, Edwin Wilson has worked in many aspects of theater. Educated at Vanderbilt University, the University of Edinburgh, and Yale University, he received a Master of Fine Arts degree from the Yale Drama School, as well as the first Doctor of Fine Arts degree awarded by Yale. He has taught at Hofstra, Vanderbilt, and—since 1967—at Hunter College and the CUNY Graduate Center. At Hunter he has served as chair of the Department of Theatre and Film and head of the graduate theater program. At CUNY he directs the Center for the Advanced Study in Theater Arts (CASTA).

As a writer, Edwin Wilson has been since 1972 the theater critic of the Wall Street Journal. In addition to *The Theater Experience*, he is a coauthor of *Living Theater* and *Theater: The Lively Art* also published by McGraw-Hill, and he was responsible for the volume *Shaw on Shakespeare*. He is a member of the New York Drama Critics Circle, of which he has served as president. He has also been on the Tony Nominating Committee and was four times a member of the Pulitzer Prize Drama Committee. He has been president of the board of directors of the Theatre Development Fund, which (among other activities) runs the half-price TKTS booth in Times Square; and he is on the boards of the John Golden Fund and the Susan Smith Blackburn Prize.

Before turning to teaching and writing, Edwin Wilson was assistant to the producer for the film *Lord of the Flies*, directed by Peter Brook, and the Broadway play *Big Fish, Little Fish*, directed by John Gielgud. He produced several off-Broadway shows and coproduced a Broadway play directed by George Abbott. He also directed in summer and regional theater, serving one season as resident director of the Barter Theater in Virginia.

To my wife,
Catherine

CONTENTS

ix

LIST OF
SYNOPSES OF PLAYS

PREFACE

Preparing a new edition of *The Theater Experience* invariably becomes a balancing act. On the one hand, we wish to preserve those qualities and features from previous editions which have met with wide approval. On the other hand, there is a desire to improve the book: to make it more responsive to students' needs and more up-to-date than ever before. I hope this fifth edition has successfully met both objectives—that we have retained the best elements of the previous four editions while eliminating outdated material and adding new information that will make this the best edition yet.

Features that we have incorporated from previous editions include a nonhistorical approach to theater, an accessible writing style, frequent analogies to everyday experience, a coherent organization, abundant photographs and illustrations tied directly to the text, and a series of informative appendixes.

One important change has been to tighten the text. Upon reviewing the previous editions, I recognized that I often gave two or three illustrations or examples in making a point where one would do. There were other redundancies as well that have been eliminated. The result, I hope, is a clearer, more concise text. In addition, references have been updated throughout the book.

Another significant change is the rearrangement of the parts of the book. As always in the past, we open with a section on the audience. For Part Two, however, rather than turning to the playwright and the script, we take up the performers and the director. The actor-audience exchange is the heart of theater, and for many people the theater's excitement and immediacy are epitomized by the work of actresses and actors onstage. The hope, therefore, is that this early placement of acting and directing will engage the student's interest at the start of his or her studies. In Parts Three and Four, we turn to the playwright and the script—first to structure and characters, and then to genre. Part Five remains, as before, about the design elements.

In Part Six—Bringing the Elements Together—there is another important change. Because both the playwight Arthur Miller and the director Elia Kazan have written autobiographies in recent years, describing their collaboration on the original production of *Death of a Salesman*, the decision was made to substitute this play for *A Streetcar Named Desire* in the final chapter. Firsthand accounts of the way the production was put together provide a vivid picture of the theater's collaborative process.

A word here about the sequence of chapters in the book: it has become increasingly clear that the book can easily be taught out of sequence and frequently is. Teachers adopt their own approach and ask students to study chapters or parts according to their own preferences. This appears to work admirably, with a minimum of disruption or loss of continuity. Some teachers, for example, assign Chapter 20 toward the beginning of the course rather than at the end. I have always been pleased that teachers approach the book in such a creative and individual way.

A long-standing trademark of *The Theater Experience* has been its use of carefully selected and clearly reproduced photographs and illustrations. As in previous editions, these are drawn from a range of productions—Broadway theaters, smaller not-for-profit theaters, regional theaters, college theaters. Ninety percent of the illustrations are new to this edition, and once again they are closely tied to material in the text. As with the third and fourth editions, sixteen pages in full color have been included.

Because the book stresses the encounter between audience and performers, it is assumed that anyone using it will make attendance at performances an integral part of the course. Though the text deals with specific plays, its approach can easily be adapted to a current production readily available to students. Any Shakespearean play, for example, can prove beneficial, as can any Greek play, any work by Ibsen, or a more modern piece.

In order to supplement the plays that students see and read as a part of the course, this edition, like the third and fourth editions, includes a series of plot summaries, set apart from the text in boxes. The plays thus summarized include *King Oedipus, King Lear, Tartuffe, Ghosts, The*

Cherry Orchard, Death of a Salesman, A Streetcar Named Desire, A Raisin in the Sun, and *Waiting for Godot;* all the synopses are listed on page xiii.

The Theater Experience is intended as a text for the introductory theater course offered by most colleges and universities. Generally, such a course is aimed at students who are not intending to major in theater, and the book has been written with that in mind. While it is neither a history nor a "how to" book, there is an abundance of solid information in it. It can serve equally well as the text for a prerequisite course leading to advanced work in theater or for the theater component in a combined arts course. Students who plan to concentrate on theater can begin in no better way than by examining the actor-audience exchange, learning the spectator's side of the equation as well as the creator's.

Before *The Theater Experience,* most theater texts adopted either a historical or a genre aproach to the subject. Historically oriented texts begin where western theater began—with the Greeks. Texts adopting a historical approach generally devote half of the book to a chronological treatment of theater, with subsequent chapters on the actor, designer, and director, among others. In the genre approach, chapters on tragedy, comedy, farce, and so forth, are substituted for the history. In both of these, theater tends to be treated as a frozen artifact divided into discrete units of history or genre: tragedy, Restoration drama, the Spanish golden age, and so on.

In his book *The Empty Space,* Peter Brook speaks of the "immediate theater." In a sense, all theater is immediate—an experience given and received. Treated as a set entity, a remote body of knowledge divorced from the lives of those who view it, theater loses any chance of immediacy. The aim of this text is to analyze and explain what theater is about—what goes on in theater and what it means to the viewer. For audience members, the experience begins when they come into the theater, confront the environment, and, following that, encounter the performance. This encounter, between those who create theater and those who view it, is at the heart of theater. Thus, the crucial role of the audience—its importance in the dynamic exchange between creators and viewers in theater—is dealt with throughout this text.

Every effort has been made to relate theater to experiences already familiar to the student. Certain elements in theater have analogues in daily life, and wherever possible these are used to provide a key, or bridge, to the theater experience. Interior design, for example, can be used to create an atmosphere or ambience in a restaurant, or a room can be viewed as a form of "scene design." In this way a familiar experience becomes the basis for understanding the more specialized art of stage design. In this, as in every other feature of *The Theater Experience*—approach, writing style, and organization—the aim has been to provide both teachers and students with a book that is not only informative and incisive but also pleasurable.

✳ ACKNOWLEDGMENTS ✳

I first developed the ideas in this book while teaching a course in Introduction to Theater at Hunter College of the City University of New York. To my colleagues and students at Hunter, I express my deep appreciation.

I particularly wish to thank three colleagues who have contributed specific material: Stuart Baker, who was responsible for Appendixes 4 and 5; Alvin Goldfarb, who wrote the special sections on the theories of tragedy and comedy; and Mira Felner, who wrote "A Note on Women and Greek and Elizabethan Theater." I am grateful to J. K. Curry, who was responsible for the index; and to Scott Walters, who prepared the Instructor's Manual for the fifth edition. Special thanks, also, to Emilie Smith Kilgore of Stages Theater.

McGraw-Hill and the author wish to express their thanks for the many useful comments and suggestions provided by the following reviewers: William Akins, Arizona State University; Byrne Blackwood, Southwest Missouri State University; David Burr, Rhode Island College; Joseph Capello, Broward Community College; Sharon Carnegie, University of Southern California; Lorraine Commeret, University of Northern Iowa; Tony Distler, Virginia Polytechnic University; Robert Gilmore, Southwest Missouri State University; Lou Hackleman, Indiana State University; Glen Harbaugh, Indiana State University; John Jellicorse, University of North Carolina; Betty Jean Jones, University of North Carolina; Joe Karioth, Florida State University, Kae Koger, University of Massachusetts–Amherst; Paul Lifton, North Dakota State University; Jim Ludwig, Bradley University; Alice Mcelhaney, Southwest Missouri State University; Sherry McFadden, Indiana State University; Geraldine Maschio, University of Kentucky; Mildred Mulliken, Broward Community College; Doug Paterson, University of Nebraska; Ellis Pryce-Jones, University of Nevada at Las Vegas; George Roesler, Inver Hills Community College; Chuck Vicinus, University of Toledo; Albert Wehlburg, University of Florida; Bob Welk, University of Nebraska; Laura Wescott, Indiana State University; and Ben Wilson, University of Nebraska.

I express special appreciation to the artist Al Hirschfeld, who has allowed us to use his incomparable drawings for the part openings.

Through all five editions of *The Theater Experience* I have had the extreme good fortune to work with two people: the exceptional, imaginative photograph editor, Inge King; and the talented, highly creative designer, Joan O'Connor. I also wish to thank, for their support and tireless efforts, editing supervisor Susan Gamer and editor Peter Labella.

Edwin Wilson

THE
THEATER
EXPERIENCE

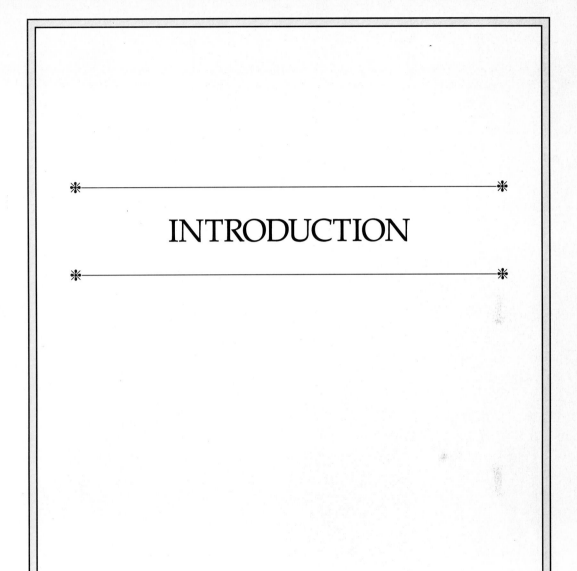

INTRODUCTION

THEATER: A UNIQUE EXPERIENCE.
Performers onstage before an audience combine with the words in the script and with scenery, lighting, and costumes to create a special moment of theater. When we go to the theater, we experience a series of such moments. The scene shown here is from Summer and Smoke *by Tennessee Williams, with Christopher Reeve and Laila Robins in a production at the Williamstown Theater.*

The impulse toward theater is universal. It has occurred wherever human society has developed: in Europe and Asia, throughout Africa, and among Native Americans. In virtually every culture recorded in history or studied by anthropologists, we find rituals, religious ceremonies, and celebrations that include elements of theater.

One element is a presentation by *performers* in front of an *audience*—a ceremony, for example, conducted by religious leaders before members of a community.

Another element is the wearing of *costumes*, such as those worn by priests or tribal chiefs. In some rituals or ceremonies, animals or gods are impersonated by people in costume.

Storytelling is a third element. In many cultures there are strong traditions of storytellers who recite myths or legends from the past, or teach lessons by means of stories, to a group of listeners. In doing this, the narrator impersonates the characters in the story, sometimes actually changing his or her voice to imitate the character.

THE IMPULSE TOWARD THEATER IS UNIVERSAL.

Cultures throughout the world have rituals, ceremonies, and dances that include theatrical elements such as masks, costumes, and impersonations of people, animals, or spirits. Shown here is a Salaam ceremonial dance in Tanzania, Africa, featuring elaborate costumes and headdresses as well as ritualized dance movements.

Exactly how and at what point these rituals, ceremonies, or stories move into the separate realm of theater is a matter of conjecture, but disputes among authorities over these questions need not concern us here. It is enough to know that theater as a distinct art form has emerged in many different cultures. In India, for instance, theater became well established nearly 2000 years ago. In Greece, a fully developed theater had emerged even earlier, almost 2500 years ago.

Wherever theater has become a separate art form, it has had certain essential qualities: an action or a story (the play) is presented by one group (the performers) to another group (the audience). Theater is thus an experience—a shared, indivisible event that includes both those who perform and those who observe. Like other experiences—riding a bicycle, attending a football game, falling in love—theater requires a personal presence: in this case, the presence of the audience.

✳ THEATER AS A TRANSITORY ART ✳

A theater performance changes from moment to moment as the audience encounters a series of shifting impressions and stimuli. It is a kaleidoscopic adventure through which the audience passes, with each instant a direct, immediate experience.

The transitory nature of theater—a quality it shares with all the performing arts—sets it apart in a significant way from literature and the visual arts. A painting, a piece of sculpture, a novel, and a book of poems are fixed objects. When they leave the artist's hands (or in the case of a book, when they leave the printer's shop), they are complete. They exist as finished products, and their tangible, unchangeable quality is one reason we value them, in the same way that we value historic buildings or antique automobiles. In a world of change and uncertainty, they remain the same. We can go back to them again and again; and, if they have been preserved, they will always be there and always be the same. The Winged Victory from the island of Samothrace in Greece is the same majestic figure that was fashioned 2200 years ago. When we view the statue, we are looking at the same torso facing into the wind, with wings spread behind, that the Greeks viewed at the time it was created.

The essence of literature and the visual arts is to catch something at a moment in time and freeze it. With the performing arts, however, this is impossible, because these arts are not objects but events. Music provides a good illustration. Music may have timbre, pitch, and volume, but none of these registers on the listener except as it moves through time. A note in a melody cannot be held forever as a line in a drawing is forever fixed. Instead, music is created by the perpetual shift of notes, through repetition, variation, and an accumulation of effects. Similarly,

3

**THE PERMANENCE
OF THE VISUAL ARTS.**
*In the Winged Victory of Samothrace on display
at the Louvre museum in Paris, France, the
torso enfolded in flowing robes and the out-
stretched wings appear just as they did when the
sculpture was first created on the island of
Samothrace in Greece around 200 B.C.—over
2,000 years ago. If they are preserved, painting
and sculpture—unlike performing arts such as
theater, dance, and music—are permanent, un-
changing works of art.*

theater occurs through time. A cumulative series of sights, sounds, and impressions creates theater.

Objects—costumes, props, scenery, a script—are a part of theater, but none of these constitutes the art. Bernard Beckerman explains the difference:

> Theater is nothing if not spontaneous. It occurs. It happens. The novel can be put away, taken up, reread. Not theater. It keeps slipping between one's fingers. Stopping, it stops being theater. Its permanent features, facets of activity, such as scenery, script, stage, people, are no more theater than the two poles of a generator are electricity. Theater is what goes on between the parts.[1]

The distinction between reading a novel and attending a theatrical performance reminds us that drama is sometimes looked on as a branch of literature. The confusion is understandable. For one thing, plays are often printed in book form, like literature; for another, many novels and short stories contain extensive passages of dialogue that could easily be scenes in a play.

Although scenes of dialogue in a novel resemble drama—and plays appear in book form—there is an important difference between the two forms. Unlike a novel, a play is written to be performed. In some respects a script is to a stage production as a musical score is to a concert, or an architectural blueprint is to a building: it is an outline for a performance.

Playwrights understand this distinction quite well. They know that what occurs onstage may be different from what we imagine when we read a script. Certainly the *experience* will be different. The physical production—the environment, scenery, and costumes—will affect the performance, and so will the performers. The *ways* in which actors and actresses interpret their roles—such things as facial expressions, gestures, and vocal inflections—have much to do with a play's ultimate effect on the audience.

Because of this, some playwrights go to great lengths in their stage directions to tell performers how to play their parts. Look, for example, at the stage direction given by the American playwright Eugene O'Neill (1888–1953) in the third act of *Long Day's Journey into Night*. When the scene begins, we discover that Tyrone (the father) and Edmund (his son) have been drinking. As they approach their home, they are fearful that Mary, the mother, has begun taking drugs again, as she has done in the past. The following are O'Neill's instructions:

> Tyrone comes in through the front parlor. Edmund is behind him. Tyrone has had a lot to drink but beyond a slightly glazed look in his eyes and a trace of blur in his speech, he does not show it. Edmund has also had more than a few drinks without much apparent effect, except that his sunken cheeks are flushed and his eyes look bright and feverish. They stop in the doorway to stare appraisingly at her [Mary]. What they see fulfills their worst expectations. But for the moment Mary is unconscious of their condemning eyes. She kisses her husband and then Edmund. Her manner is unnaturally effusive. They submit shrinkingly. She talks excitedly.[2]

Drama can be studied in a classroom for imagery, character, and theme, just as we study a novel; but study of this sort takes place *before* the event. It is a form of preparation for the experience; the experience is the performance itself. Obviously, we have more opportunities to read plays in book form than to see them produced; but when we read a play, we should always attempt to visualize the other aspects of a production in our mind's eye. We should constantly be aware that theater is performance.

One special quality of a theater performance is its immediacy. In the theater we live in what the playwright Thornton Wilder (1897–1975)

THEATER IS ACTION.
In contrast to sculpture, painting, or literature, theater is a dynamic art, changing from moment to moment as performers interact with one another. In this scene from a production of Shakespeare's Coriolanus *at the Old Globe Theater, Chuck Cooper (left), in the role of Aufidius, fights with Byron Jennings as Coriolanus.*

called the *perpetual present tense.* Contained in the present is the fresh remembrance of the past and the anticipation of what is to come. Robert Edmond Jones (1887–1954), an American scene designer and critic, describes it this way:

> All that has ever been is in this moment; all that will be is in this moment. Both are meeting in one living flame in this unique instant of time. This is drama; this is theater—*to be aware of the now.*[3]

As Jones suggests, the theater experience has a quality all its own; it is like other experiences—the other arts in particular—but it is also unique.

The nature of the theater experience and the elements which make up that experience will be the subject of this book.

A performance is the result of many forces coming together— some tangible, some intangible—including the physical presence of the performers, the colors and shapes of the costumes and scenery, and the ideas and emotions expressed in the words of the playwright. The elements of theater are varied and complex, and to understand theater we must study them separately.

Altogether, we will examine the following basic elements of theater:

1   The audience: its function, its general makeup, and the background which each spectator brings to a performance.

2   The performances of the actors and actresses and the director's supervision of the production.

3   The work of the playwright in creating dramatic structure and dramatic characters.

4   The purpose of a theater piece and the point of view adopted by those who create it. Is the work intended as an escape from daily cares or to provoke thought? Is it serious or comic?

5   The environment in which a production occurs—in a small space or a large one, indoors or outdoors—together with the visual effects created by costumes, lighting, and scenery, and also with sound.

At every point during a performance, these elements intersect; they fuse and combine to produce theater. In addition to studying the elements separately, we will look at the ways in which they join together to form the whole.

When an audience comes to witness a performance, an exchange takes place between performers and spectators; the two groups engage in a form of communication or a celebration. At its best, theater affords members of the audience an opportunity to be transported outside themselves or to look deep inside themselves. In the following pages we will attempt to discover what makes this profound and magical experience possible.

PART ONE

❋ ──────────────────────────────── ❋

THE AUDIENCE

THE ACTOR-AUDIENCE CONNECTION

The audience forms an indispensable element in the theater equation because theater occurs only when spectators are present to interact with performers and identify with the characters being portrayed. The drawing by Al Hirschfeld on the following pages shows a scene from August Wilson's The Piano Lesson. *Charles S. Dutton (center right) plays a brother who wants to sell a piano that is a family heirloom while his sister, played by S. Epatha Merkerson (center left), is determined to keep it. Audience members identify strongly with individual characters and with family conflicts such as those found in* The Piano Lesson.

1

THE ROLE
OF THE AUDIENCE

THE KEY ROLE OF THE AUDIENCE.
The audience and the performers are the two basic elements in the theater equation: both are essential for a theater event to take place. Here we see an audience entering the Vivian Beaumont Theater at Lincoln Center to see a performance of the musical Anything Goes.

In the theater season of 1927–1928 in New York City, there were nearly 80 Broadway theaters operating in the area around Times Square. That season, a total of 302 productions opened on Broadway.

Ten years later the number of theaters had been reduced to 44, and the number of productions opening was down to 80. One of the reasons for this drop in the number of theaters and productions was the depression of the 1930s and the economic hardships it caused both to institutions and to individuals. In the case of the theater, however, there was another important cause: the challenge from radio and movies.

For nearly 2,500 years, theater was virtually the only means by which drama was presented to audiences. Beginning around 1900, however, a succession of mechanical and electronic devices appeared which many people argued would make theater obsolete and replace it entirely.

In the early part of the twentieth century, silent movies became popular; in the 1920s, radio appeared. With radio, it was pointed out, people did not even need to leave their homes to hear a good suspense story or an amusing comedy.

Soon after—in the late 1920s and early 1930s, when talking movies arrived—it was argued that theater had no real chance of survival. The talkies, after all, combined sight and sound; they could do everything theater could. In fact, because motion picture cameras are able to move around to show vast outdoor panoramas and action, such as chases on horseback or by car, movies could do things theater could not do.

More was to come. After World War II, television arrived—first black-and-white and then color. This seemed the ultimate challenge, one it would be impossible for theater to meet: plays with first-rate performers, in full color and with good sound, could now be seen free in the home. How could theater match that?

The amazing thing about the drop in Broadway productions noted above is not how sharp it was but, given the many challenges theater has faced, the fact that live theater has survived at all. It has survived, however; in fact, it has met each one of the threats it has faced and continued very much intact. In recent years there has been a shift in emphasis from Broadway to off-Broadway and the regional theater, but overall the theater is as healthy as it has been in some time. In the United States, for example, there is an amazing diversity of theater activity—not only in New York, with Broadway, off-Broadway, and off-off-Broadway theaters; but throughout the country, with permanent professional companies in major cities and college and university theaters in every state. (The full range of theaters in the United States will be described in Chapter 3.)

✳ THE ACTOR-AUDIENCE RELATIONSHIP ✳

How has theater been able to meet so many challenges and not only survive but emerge in some ways stronger than ever? There are several answers, but the most important of all has to do with the "live" nature of theater. Theater is an event in which the performers are in the presence of the audience.

But not destroyed

The Special Nature of Theater: A Contrast with Film

The special nature of theater will be more apparent if we contrast a drama seen in a theater with one shown on film or television. In many ways the two forms are alike. Both present a story told in dramatic form—a reenactment of scenes played by performers who speak and act as if they were the people they represent. The same actress can play Juliet in *Romeo and Juliet* by William Shakespeare (1564–1616) on both stage and screen. Not only the dramatization and the acting but also other elements, such as scenery and costume, are often similar on stage and screen. In fact, many films and television specials have been based on stage productions: *The Odd Couple; A Chorus Line; Annie; 'Night, Mother; Children of a Lesser God;* and numerous Shakespeare plays. Unquestionably one can learn a great deal about theater from watching a play on film or television—and can have some of the same experiences.

Despite this, there is a fundamental difference of which we become aware when we contrast theater with movies. This does not have to do with technical matters, such as the way films can show outdoor shots made from helicopters or can cut instantaneously from one scene to another. The most significant difference between films and theater is the *actor-audience relationship.* The experience of being in the presence of the performer is more important to theater than anything else. No matter how closely a film follows the story of a play, no matter how involved we are with the people on the screen, we are always in the presence of an image, never a person.

Film vs Theater

We all know the difference between an image of someone and the flesh-and-blood reality. How often we rehearse a speech we plan to make to someone we love or fear. We run through the scene in our mind, picturing ourselves talking to the other person; but when we meet face to face, it is seldom the same. We freeze and find ourselves unable to speak; or perhaps the words gush forth incoherently. Seldom does the encounter take place as we planned.

The American playwright Jean-Claude van Itallie (1936–) explained the importance of the actor-audience relationship in the theater, and how theater differs from films and television, when he wrote:

15

Theater is not electronic. Unlike movies and unlike television, it does require the live presence of both audience and actors in a single space. This is the theater's uniquely important advantage and function, its original religious function of bringing people together in a community ceremony where the actors are in some sense priests or celebrants, and the audience is drawn to participate with the actors in a kind of eucharist.[1]

The Chemistry of Actor-Audience Contact

Cranmer
Conspiracy =
to breath together
(go to P. 17)

The drama critic Walter Kerr elaborated on the idea of what it means for the audience and actors to be together:

> It doesn't just mean that we are in the personal presence of performers. It means that they are in *our* presence, conscious of us, speaking to us, working for and with us until a circuit that is not mechanical becomes established between us, a circuit that is fluid, unpredictable, ever-changing in its impulses, crackling, intimate. *Our* presence, the way we respond, flows back to the performer and alters what he does, to some degree and sometimes astonishingly so, every single night. We are contenders, making the play and the evening and the emotion together. We are playmates, building a structure.
>
> This never happens at a film because the film is already built, finished, sealed, incapable of responding to us in any way. The actors can't hear us or feel our presence; nothing we do, in our liveness, counts. We could be dead and the film would purr out its appointed course, flawlessly, indifferently.[2]

Like films, television seems very close to theater; sometimes it seems closer than film. Television programs often begin with such words as "This program comes to you live from Burbank, California." But the word *live* must be qualified; in one sense, television distorts the meaning we have customarily assigned to this term. Before television, *live* in the entertainment or theatrical world meant "in person": not only was the event taking place at that moment, it was taking place before the spectator's eyes. *Live television* means that the event is taking place at that moment but not in the presence of the viewer. In fact, it is generally far removed from the television audience, possibly half a world away. With television we see an image on a small tube; we are free to look or not to look, or even to leave the room. The effect of a personal encounter, so vital to theater, is missing.

The fascination of being in the presence of a person is difficult to explain but not difficult to verify. No matter how often fans have seen their favorite stars in the movies or heard rock singers on television, they will go to any lengths to see them in person. As another example, at one time or another each of us has braved bad weather and shoving crowds to see celebrities at a parade or a political rally. The same pull of personal contact draws us to the theater.

TELEVISION: A DIFFERENT EXPERIENCE FROM THEATER.
When people like the young man in this photograph see films or television programs, they see images—or pictures—of performers on a screen rather than the performers themselves. The experience, therefore, is once removed from personal contact.

At the heart of the theater experience, therefore, is the actor-audience relationship: the immediate, personal exchange whose chemistry and magic give theater its special quality. At a stage performance the actresses and actors can hear laughter, can sense silence, and can feel tension in the audience. In short, the audience can affect, and in subtle ways change, the performance. At the same time, members of the audience watch the performers closely, asking a number of conscious or unconscious questions: Are the performers talented? Have they learned their parts well? Are they convincing in their roles? Will they do something surprising, or make a mistake? Each moment, in every stage performance, the audience is looking for answers to questions like these.

It is important to understand, too, that for the audience, theater is a group experience—as the following section will discuss.

✳ THE GROUP EXPERIENCE ✳

Some of the arts—painting, sculpture, literature—provide solitary experiences. The viewer or reader contemplates the work alone, at her or his own pace. This is true even in a museum, where many people may flock to look at a single painting: they are with each other, but they respond as individuals, one at a time. In theater, however, as in the other performing arts, the group experience is indispensable. The performing arts share this trait with other communal events such as reli-

ACTOR-AUDIENCE CONTACT.
In theater, the audience is always involved, sometimes at a distance, sometimes more closely—as in the case of the audience members shown here watching a scene from a production of Tamara, *which moves from room to room in a house.*

gious services, sports, and celebrations. Before the event can take place, a group must assemble—at one time in one place. When people are gathered together in this way, something mysterious happens to them. Though still individuals, with their own personalities and backgrounds, they take on other qualities as well, qualities which often overshadow their independent responses.

Psychology of Groups

Gustav Le Bon, a forerunner of social psychology and one of the first to study the phenomenon of crowds, wrote that a collection of people "presents new characteristics very different from those of the individuals composing it. The sentiments and ideas of all the persons in the gathering take one and the same direction, and their conscious personality vanishes."[3] Le Bon went on to say that the most striking peculiarity of a crowd is that although the people who compose it are different as individuals, once they have been transformed into a crowd, they develop a "collective mind which makes them feel, think, and act in a manner quite different from that in which each individual of them would feel, think, and act were he in a state of isolation."[4]

In his book *Social Psychology*, Lawrence S. Wrightsman points to a number of studies confirming the idea that a crowd or group can influence the thoughts and actions of individuals. "Groups can be swayed by a 'groupthink' process," he writes.[5] Elsewhere he affirms that "the awareness of others watching us has an impact on virtually every component of behavior."[6]

Not all crowds are alike. Some are aggressive, such as an angry mob that decides to riot or a gang of young people who terrorize a neighborhood. Others are docile—the passengers on an airline flight, for example. A crowd at a football game is different from a congregation at a religious observance; and a theater crowd is distinct from all these. In spite of being different, however, the theater audience shares with all such groups the special characteristics of the collective mind.

As an example, when sitting alone in a theater, we are reluctant to clap and laugh out loud. In a group, however, we feel free to do so. One explanation for this is what the behaviorist B. F. Skinner calls *reinforcement.*

> If it is always the individual who behaves, it is nevertheless the group which has the more powerful effect. By joining a group the individual increases his power to achieve reinforcement. . . . The reinforcing consequences generated by the group easily exceed the sums of the consequences which could be achieved by members acting separately. The total reinforcing effect is enormously increased.[7]

This subject is complicated, of course, and Skinner deals with only one aspect of it. Also, this is not the place to try to fathom the mysteries of crowd behavior. It is important, however, to note the existence of the "group mind" and, beyond that, to emphasize the importance of group behavior to theater. Becoming part of an audience is a crucial element of the theater experience. For a time we share a common undertaking; we are members of a group focused on one activity—the performance of a play. Not only do we laugh or cry in a way we might not otherwise; we also sense an intangible communion with those around us.

When a collection of individuals respond more or less in unison to what is occurring onstage, their relationship to one another is reaffirmed. If there is a display of cruelty at which we shudder, or sorrow by which we are moved, or pomposity at which we laugh, it is reassuring to have others respond as we do. For a moment we are part of a group sharing a common experience; and our sorrow or joy, which we thought might be ours alone, is found to be part of a broad human response.

THEATER IS A GROUP EXPERIENCE.

In the theater, the size, attitude, and makeup of the audience affect the overall experience. The theater can be large or small, indoors or outdoors, and the audience can be people of similar tastes and backgrounds or a collection of quite varied individuals. At Unto These Hills, *produced each summer in Cherokee, North Carolina, the performance is outdoors and the audience is a mixture of young and old from many parts of the country.*

How Audience Makeup Affects the Theater Experience

Although being part of a group is an essential element of theater, groups vary, and the makeup of a group will alter a theatrical occasion. Some audiences are general—for instance, the thousands who attend outdoor productions such as *Unto These Hills,* a play about the Cherokee Indians presented each summer on the Cherokee Reservation in western North Carolina, and the Shakespeare festival in Ashland, Oregon. General audiences include people of all ages, from all parts of the country, and from all socioeconomic levels. Other audiences are more homogeneous, such as spectators at a high school play, a children's theater production, a Broadway opening night, a political play, or a performance given in a prison.

Still another factor affecting our experience in the theater is our relationship to the other members of the audience. If we are among friends or people of like mind, we feel comfortable and relaxed, and we readily become part of the group experience. On the other hand, if we feel alien—for example, a young person with an older group, a radical with conservatives, or a naive person with sophisticates—we will be estranged from the group as a whole. The people with whom we attend the theater—their relative homogeneity and our relation to them—strongly influence our response to the total event.

✳ THE SEPARATE ROLES OF ✳ PERFORMERS AND SPECTATORS

In recent years numerous attempts have been made to involve members of the audience in the action of the play, with performers coming into the audience to make contact with spectators—shaking hands, touching them, arguing face to face. Spectators, too, have been encouraged to come onstage and join the action. At certain performances of the Living Theater, a group that flourished in the late 1960s, the stage sometimes became so crowded with spectators that a space had to be cleared so that the performers could continue with the play.

How Should the Audience Be Involved?

The attempt to involve audience members directly springs from a worthwhile impulse: the desire to make theater more immediate and intense. But when taken to an extreme, it ignores the manner in which art functions.

Art is not life but a reflection of life—a special creation that abstracts or mirrors life. Often, as we shall see in Chapter 2, it comes closer than our everyday observations to portraying the truth of life; but it remains a separate creation. One essential element of this process is a degree of separation between the object or event an artist creates—a painting, a sculpture, a dance, a musical performance, a theater production—and the audience that observes it.

Imagine trying to get the full effect of a large landscape painting when standing a few inches from it: one would see only the brush strokes of a single tree or a small patch of blue sky. We need distance in order to take in and appreciate works of art. This separation, which is called *aesthetic distance,* is necessary in theater just as it is in the other arts.

In the same way that a viewer must stand back from a painting to get its full effect, so in the theater spectators must be separated from the performance in order to see and hear what is happening onstage and thus absorb the experience. Whatever happens, it is essential in theater that the roles of actor and observer remain distinct, and it is important for members of the audience to understand the different ways in which the two parties function. If an audience member goes onstage

21

and takes part in the action, or otherwise becomes involved in the proceedings, at that point he or she reverses roles and becomes a performer, not a spectator.

There are activities employing theatrical techniques in which everyone concerned does participate; such activities point up the contrast between *observed* and *participatory* theater. In this book we are concerned with observed theater; but it is helpful to be aware of participatory theater, which will be discussed in the following section.

Audience Participation through Direct Action

The question of actor-audience separation has been complicated in recent years by the rapid growth of theatrical activities in which ordinary people play roles and improvise dramatic scenes. Most theater events offer the experience of an audience observing what happens onstage. But a theater event can be set up as a workshop or laboratory in which everyone present is expected to take part. Both types of theater involve participation, but of different kinds, and it is important to make a distinction between the two.

In observed theater, the audience participates vicariously or empathically with what is happening onstage. *Empathy* is the experience of mentally entering into the feelings or spirit of another person—in this case, a character onstage. Sometimes an audience will not be in tune with the characters onstage but will react violently against them. In either situation, though, members of the audience are participating. They might shed tears, laugh, pass judgment, sit frozen in their seats, or literally tremble with fear. But they participate through their imaginations while separated from the action: sitting in a seat or, in the case of street theater, standing around the edge of the playing area. (We will discuss this type of participation in more detail in Chapter 2.)

The theater of direct participation works differently. Those who take part are not actors in the usual sense, and there is no attempt to follow a written script. Rather, the emphasis is on education, personal development, and therapy: fields in which theater techniques have opened up new possibilities. In schools, for example, creative dramatics, theater games, and group improvisations have proved invaluable in aiding self-discovery and developing healthy group attitudes. By acting out hypothetical situations or giving free rein to their imaginations, children build self-confidence, discover their creative potential, and overcome their inhibitions. In some cases creative dramatics teaches lessons which are difficult to teach by conventional means.

In addition to creative dramatics, a wide range of other activities— sociodrama, psychodrama, and drama therapy, for example—incorporate theatrical techniques. For adults as well as children, these activities are coming to the forefront as educational and therapeutic techniques.

DRAMA THERAPY.
Theater techniques can be used for purposes of education and therapy. A group called the Geese Company, for example, visits prisons and has convicts reenact scenes from their past in an attempt to come to a better understanding of themselves. In the scene here, the actress Pamela Daryl (right) is listening to a prisoner unburdening painful memories of childhood in a drama therapy session.

In sociodrama, the members of the participating groups, such as parents and children, students and teachers, or legal authorities and ordinary citizens, explore their own attitudes and prejudices. One successful approach is *role reversal.* A group of young people, for instance, may take the part of their parents while the adults assume the roles of the children; or members of a street gang will take the roles of the police, and the police will take the roles of the street gang. In such role playing, both groups become aware of deep-seated feelings and arrive at a better understanding of one another.

Psychodrama uses some of the same techniques as sociodrama, but it is more private and interpersonal; in fact, it can become so intense that it should be carried out only under the supervision of a carefully trained therapist. In psychodrama, individual fears, anxieties, and frustrations are explored. A person might reenact a particularly traumatic scene from childhood, for example.

The various fields of participatory theater are fascinating, and their full potential has only recently begun to be explored; but the purpose

**PARTICIPATORY THEATER:
A DIFFERENT EXPERIENCE.**
*In participatory theater, audience members,
rather than simply observing, become part of
the action. A group that develops audience-
participation theater pieces is Antenna Theater
of San Francisco. Here two audience members
have been asked to put on Walkman tape recorders and take part in a piece called* Adjusting
the Idle.

here is to draw a distinction between participatory drama and observed
drama. In participatory drama, theater is a means to another end: education, therapy, group development, or the like. The aim is not public
performance, and there is little emphasis on a carefully prepared, expertly performed presentation before an audience; in fact, just the reverse is true. In observed drama, on the other hand, there must always
be a separation between the performers and the audience. This is the
"aesthetic distance" referred to earlier.

At times in the contemporary theater, as has been noted, spectators
go on stage to be part of the action; at other times, performers come
into the audience to engage in repartee with a spectator. If the spectator
takes part, he or she is no longer an observer but a participant.

Our concern in this book is primarily with those who observe theater.
By definition, the experience of the observer is not one of direct, physical contact. How, then, does this experience occur? If we are not involved physically, how can those of us who are spectators be so affected
by what happens on a stage? What can cause us to laugh out loud, to
cry, to become enraged, to become so frightened that we break out in
goose bumps? The answer is the human imagination—the power of the
mind and heart—and in Chapter 2 we will see how this operates.

✳ SUMMARY ✳

1 During this century, theater has been challenged by a succession of technological developments: silent movies, radio, talking movies, and television. It has survived these challenges partly because of the special nature of the actor-audience relationship.

2 The relationship between actor and audience is a "live" relationship: each is in the other's presence, in the same place at the same time. It is the exchange between the two which gives theater its unique quality.

3 Theater—like the other performing arts—is a group experience. Also, the makeup of the audience has a direct bearing on the effect of the experience.

4 Participants and spectators play different roles in the theater experience, the latter's role being to observe and respond.

5 There is a difference in theater between participating by direct action and participating by observation. In the former case, nonactors take part, usually for the purpose of personal growth and self-development. In the latter case, a presentation is made by one group to another, and the spectators do not participate physically in the experience.

✳ TOPICS FOR DISCUSSION ✳

1 Theater has survived, and thrived, despite the development of movies, radio, and television. Do you think this implies that it will continue to thrive no matter what new forms of entertainment may appear in the future? Or can you imagine some futuristic form which would probably render theater obsolete?

2 The "chemistry" between performers and audiences is central not only in theater but in the other performing arts—music and dance. With painting, sculpture, architecture, and literature, the chemistry is different. How would you describe these two kinds of chemistry? Which, if either, of the following points of view would you agree with, and why? (a) "Theater is much richer than, say, painting or architecture, because of the actor-audience relationship." (b) "Painting, sculpture, literature, and architecture are 'purer' arts than theater because they depend on a relationship different from the actor-audience relationship."

3 From personal experience, describe both a group encounter and a solitary encounter with some form of art. How did these experiences differ? Were there any ways in which they were alike?

4 The requirements for involvement in participatory theater are different from those for professional performance in the theater. How would you describe what is required of people taking part in participatory theater?

2

THE IMAGINATION
OF THE AUDIENCE

THE IMAGINATION OF THE AUDIENCE.
In the play Prelude to a Kiss *by Craig Lucas, a young woman (Lisa Zane) is kissed by an older man (Frank Hamilton) at her wedding, and the two people exchange souls. The husband (Mark Arnott) must then communicate with the spirit of his wife in the body of the elderly man. In the theater the audience is called on to use its imagination to accept many things: ghosts, spirits, witches, or—in the case of this production at the South Coast Repertory Theater—two people exchanging souls.*

For those who take part in it, theater is a direct experience: an actress walks onstage and impersonates a character; a carpenter builds scenery; a scene designer paints it. For these people the experience is like that of someone who cuts a finger or is held in an embrace: the pain or the warmth is felt directly and physically.

Members of the theater audience experience a different kind of pain or warmth: a sensation that is no less immediate, but separate. As spectators in the theater, we are presented with a number of stimuli—we sense the presence of other audience members; we observe the movements and gestures of performers and hear the words they speak; and we see costumes, scenery, and lighting. From these we form mental images or make imaginative connections which provoke joy, laughter, anger, sorrow, or pain. As was noted in Chapter 1, however, all this occurs without our moving from our seats.

✳ THE DRAMATIC IMAGINATION OF SPECTATORS ✳

We naturally assume that those who create theater are highly imaginative people and that their minds are full of vivid, exciting ideas which may not occur to the rest of us. If we conclude, however, that we in the audience have a limited theatrical imagination, or no theatrical imagination at all, we do ourselves a great injustice. As we saw earlier, theater is a two-way street—an exchange between actors and audience—and this is nowhere more evident than in the creation of *illusion*. Illusion may be initiated by the creators of theater, but it is completed by the audience.

In the eerie world of *Macbeth*, by William Shakespeare, when three witches appear out of the mist or when Banquo's ghost interrupts Macbeth's banquet, we know it is fantasy; witches and ghosts like those in *Macbeth* do not appear in everyday life. In the theater, however, we take such fantasy at face value. In Shakespeare's own day, a convention readily accepted by Elizabethan audiences was that women's parts were played by boy actors. Shakespeare's heroines—Juliet, Desdemona, Lady Macbeth—were acted, not by women, as they are today, but by young boys. Everyone in the audience at an Elizabethan theater knew that this was the case but accepted without question the notion that a boy actor was presenting an impression or an imitation of a woman. In a symbolic sense, the boy *was* the female character portrayed.

The main character of the expressionistic play *The Adding Machine* by Elmer Rice (1892–1967) is called Mr. Zero. The play, written in 1923, depicts the loss of identity and individuality in the machine age and still seems prophetic today. Mr. Zero, however, is not a real name from a telephone directory, nor is it meant to be. Rather, it is symbolic of the character: he is nothing—a cipher, zero. His friends do not have ordi-

**IN THEATER,
FANTASY BECOMES REAL.**
*We know that ghosts—such as the one that
appears to Hamlet—are not real people, but
through the power of the imagination, they become completely believable. In this scene from
the Stratford Festival in Ontario, Canada, Brent
Carver as Hamlet (right) encounters the ghost
of his father, played by David Schurmann (left).*

nary names either—they are Mr. One, Mr. Two, Mr. Three, and so
forth—and we accept this symbolism. An example in *The Adding Machine*
of our acceptance of the fantastic in theater occurs when Mr. Zero dies
and goes to heaven; he is shown in the afterlife carrying on conversations with two people who have worked with him in his office for many
years.

Along with fantasy, theater audiences accept drastic shifts in time
and space. Someone onstage dressed in a Revolutionary uniform says,
"It is the winter of 1778, at Valley Forge," and we do not question it.
What is more, we accept rapid movements back and forth in time. *Flashbacks*—abrupt movements from the present to the past and back again—
are a familiar technique in films like *Back to the Future, Peggy Sue Got
Married,* and *Stand by Me,* but they are also commonplace in modern
drama.

A similar device often used in drama is the *anachronism.* This means
placing a person or an event outside the proper time sequence: for
example, having characters from the past speak and act as if they were
living today. Medieval mystery and morality plays frequently contained
anachronisms. The medieval play *Abraham and Isaac,* for instance, is set
in the time of the Old Testament, but it contains several references to
the Christian trinity, obviously a religious concept that was not devel-

29

SUSPENSION OF REALITY.

In the musical City of Angels *scenes from a movie, shown onstage in black and white, are juxtaposed with scenes from real life, shown in color. The audience accepts both types of make-believe: the film version and the staged version. Here we see a wife in real life (Kay McClelland, left) in a song performed at the same time by a secretary in a scene from the movie (Randy Graff, right).*

oped until centuries later. The medieval audience accepted the shift in time as a matter of course, just as we do in theater today.

Eugène Ionesco (1912–), a Romanian-born French dramatist, fills his plays with bizarre and fantastic concepts. In his play *Rhinoceros*, a man turns into a rhinoceros. Another play, *A Stroll in the Air*, features a man who rises from the stage floor each time he speaks; at times he walks several feet off the ground. In Ionesco's *Amédée*, a corpse, dead many years, continues to grow; it is in the next room, and during the play it pushes through the wall of the apartment onstage.

In the theater, our imagination allows us to conceive of people and events we have never seen or experienced and to transcend our physical circumstances to the point where we forget who we are, where we are, or what time it is. How is this possible? It happens because in the theater our imagination works for us just as it does in everyday life.

❋ TOOLS OF THE IMAGINATION: ❋ SYMBOL AND METAPHOR

We can understand this process better if we look closely at two tools of our imagination, usually considered poetic devices, that are actually potent forces in real life: symbol and metaphor.

Functions of Symbol and Metaphor

SYMBOLS   In general terms, a *symbol* is a sign, token, or emblem that signifies something else. A simple form of symbol is a sign. Some signs stand for a single uncomplicated idea or action. In everyday life we are surrounded by them: road signs, such as an S-shaped curve; audible signals, like sirens or fog horns; and a host of mathematical and typographical symbols: −, +, $, 1/4, %, &. We sometimes forget that language itself is symbolic. In written language, the letters of the alphabet are only lines and curves on a page. And words are an arrangement of letters which by common agreement represent something else. The same four letters mean different things depending on the order in which they are placed: *pear, reap, rape.* These three words set different imaginative wheels in motion and signal a response which varies greatly from word to word.

In the commercial world, the power of the symbol is acknowledged in the value placed on a trademark. As an example, in 1972 Standard Oil Company of New Jersey changed its name: before doing so, it had done 5 years of computer research to find what it considered the best name; after finally coming up with "Exxon," the company spent $125 million changing its stationery, its service station signs, etc. The term *status symbol* is a frank recognition of the importance of personal possessions in conferring status on the owner. The kinds of cars people drive, the way they dress, the furnishings of their homes: these indicate what kind of people they are—at least, that is the theory.

Flags are symbols: lines, shapes, and colors which in given combinations become immediately recognizable. At times, symbols exhibit an incredible emotional power; and flags are a good example, embodying a nation's passions, fears, and ambitions. Proof of this was the national debate in the United States in 1989 and 1990 when the Supreme Court ruled that burning the flag was protected by the Constitution. President Bush and many others were outraged and called for a constitutional amendment outlawing the burning of the flag—it was the one thing, they argued, that should not be protected by safeguards of free speech.

Like flags, some symbols signify ideas or emotions that are far more complex and profound than the symbol itself. The cross, for example, is a symbol of Christ and, beyond that, of Christianity as a whole. Over the Fourth of July weekend in 1986, the renovated Statue of Liberty in New York harbor was unveiled in a series of elaborate celebrations on its hundredth anniversary. The statue is a significant symbol to millions of Americans, especially to immigrants who first saw it when they entered New York harbor on their way to finding a new home and a new life. In June 1989, students and other citizens protesting repression in China made a replica of the Statue of Liberty in Tienenman Square which became a symbol of their bid for freedom and was one of the first things destroyed when troops invaded the square and quashed the demonstration.

(Wide World)

THE POWER OF SYMBOLS.
Symbols and metaphors, though not real in a literal sense, have enormous power to influence our lives, and in that sense become "realer than real." The potent effect of symbols was demonstrated in June 1989, when Chinese students erected their version of the Statue of Liberty in Tiananmen Square in Beijing, only to have it torn down a few days later when troops converged on the square, killing students and other demonstrators.

The famous psychologist Carl Jung made a distinction between symbols and simple signs such as product trademarks. Jung reserved the term *symbol* for an emblem, a word, or a picture that has a special, even mystical, meaning. Examples are religious symbols and symbols suggested in dreams or by the unconscious. As the mind explores such a symbol, Jung said, "it is led to ideas beyond the grasp of reason." He explained: "Because there are innumerable things beyond the range of human understanding, we constantly use symbolic terms to represent concepts that we cannot define or fully comprehend."[1]

Whatever form a symbol takes—language, a flag, or a religious emblem—it can embody the total meaning of a religion, a nation, or an idea.

METAPHORS A similar transformation takes place with *metaphor*, another form of imaginative substitution. With metaphor we announce that one thing *is* another, in order to describe it or point up its meaning more clearly. (In poetry, you will remember, a simile says that one thing is *like* another; metaphor simply states directly that one thing *is* another.) Calling the government the "ship of state," for example, is a metaphor. The Bible is filled with metaphors. The psalmist who says, "The Lord is my shepherd," or who says of God, "Thou art my rock and my fortress," is speaking metaphorically. He does not mean literally that God is a shepherd, a rock, or a fortress, but that God is *like* these things.

Like symbols, metaphors are part of the fabric of life, as the following common expressions suggest:

"Everything's coming up roses."

"That's gross."

"He's out to lunch."

"She's off the wall."

"It's a real rip-off."

"What's the bottom line?"

These are metaphors; we are saying one thing but describing another. Everyone knows, for instance, that the statement "Everything's coming up roses" does not mean that a field of flowers is suddenly springing up. The person saying it might be standing on a concrete pavement in the dead of winter. Still, the meaning is unmistakably clear: everything is working well; things are looking up. We can see from this, and from the other examples above, that metaphor, like symbol, is part of everyday life.

The "Reality" of the Imagination

Some people believe—or think they believe—only the tangible and objective. They want an object they can see, touch, and measure; for them, anything which defies this test has an air of fakery about it. In modern society, this has been a widely held attitude.

Our use of symbol and metaphor, however, shows how large a part imagination plays in our lives. Advertisers use packages, musical jingles, and logos to sell products. Soldiers go to battle inspired by a flag or slogan; and millions of automobiles in the United States can be brought to a halt, not by concrete walls, but by a small colored light changing from green to red. Imagine attempting to control traffic, or virtually any type of human activity, without symbols. Beyond being a matter of convenience, symbols are necessary to our survival.

The same holds true for metaphor. Frequently we find that we cannot express fear, anxiety, hope, or joy—any of the deep human feelings— in descriptive language. That is why we sometimes scream. It is also why we have poetry and use metaphors.

Even scientists, the men and women we are most likely to consider realists, turn to metaphor at crucial times. They discuss the "big bang" theory of creation and talk of "black holes" in outer space. Neither description is "scientific," but both terms communicate what scientists have in mind in a way that an equation or a more strictly logical phrase could not.

Dreams provide another example of the power of the imagination. You dream that you are falling off a cliff; then, suddenly, you wake up and find that you are not flying through the air but lying in bed. Significantly, however, the dream of falling means more to you than the objective fact of lying in bed.

Although people have long recognized the importance of dreams in human affairs, in the modern period interest in dreams has been intensified as a result of the monumental work of Sigmund Freud on the subconscious. Despite variations and corrections of his theories, no one today disputes Freud's notion of the importance and "reality" of dreams, nightmares, or symbols in the human mind.

Even when a product of the imagination cannot be verified by outside observation or proved scientifically, it nevertheless exists in the mind and in that sense is entirely real. A young woman who is feeling alienated and alone may be told that she cannot feel lonely, because she is not alone: she is sitting elbow-to-elbow in a football stadium or on a crowded bus. But in her mind she *knows* she is alone. And she is.

Theater functions in precisely the same way. Though not real in a literal sense, it can be painfully real in an emotional or intellectual sense. The critic and director Harold Clurman (1901–1980) named one of his books on the theater *Lies Like Truth*. Theater—like dreams or fantasies—can sometimes be more truthful about life than a mundane, objective description. This is a paradox of dreams, fantasies, and art, including theater: by probing deep into the psyche to reveal inner truths, they can be more real than outward reality.

Theater as Metaphor

Theater operates on the level of symbol, metaphor, and dreams. Mr. Zero, for example, is a symbol. So are virtually all dramatic characters, and so is much scene and costume design. In later chapters we will study in detail the ways in which theater makes use of these elements of the imagination.

Beyond its use of symbols and metaphors, however, one could say that a theater performance as a whole is a metaphor for a segment of life. When an actress stands onstage dressed as Joan of Arc, she does not say, "I am going to act *like* Joan of Arc," as in a simile; rather, by her presence she proclaims, "I *am* Joan of Arc." In the same way, the theater program does not say, "A room designed to look like the Dauphin's palace." It says simply, "The Dauphin's palace." Everything we see in a theater—an entire performance, including the action and the scenery—can be viewed as a giant metaphor.

When the metaphor succeeds, we see before us a complex creation which mirrors life. It takes us inside our subconscious and lets us either laugh at ourselves or learn to look at our deepest fears. At such moments we suspend disbelief; theater is undeniably real, even though we are not part of its action at all but are simply sitting still. Such is the power of the imagination.

✳ THE IMAGINARY WORLDS OF THEATER ✳

Realism and Nonrealism

In theater, the audience is called on to accept many kinds of imaginary worlds. These imaginary realms are often divided into *realistic* and *nonrealistic* theater. At the outset, it is essential to know that in the theater the term *realistic* denotes a special application of what we consider "genuine" or "real." A realistic element is not necessarily more genuine or truthful than a nonrealistic element. Rather, in the theater, *realistic* and *nonrealistic* denote different ways of presenting reality.

REALISTIC ELEMENTS OF THEATER   A realistic element in the theater is one that resembles *observable* reality. It is a kind of photographic truth. We apply the term *realistic* to those elements of theater that conform to our observation of people, places, and events. Realistic theater follows the predictable logic of everyday life: the law of gravity, the time it takes a person to travel from one place to another, the way a room in a house looks, the way a person dresses. With a realistic approach, these conform to our normal expectations. The act of imagination the audience is called on to exercise in realistic theater is the acceptance of the notion that what is seen onstage is not make-believe but real life.

We are quite familiar with realism in films and television. Part of the reason is mechanical. The camera records what the lens "sees." Whether it is a bedroom in a house, a crowded city street, or the Grand Canyon, film captures the scene as the eye sees it.

Theater has always had realistic elements, too. Every type of theater that is not pure fantasy has realistic aspects. For example, characters who are supposed to represent real people—even larger-than-life heroes and heroines—must be rooted in a human truth that audiences can recognize. During the latter part of the nineteenth century, in keeping with a number of social and political changes that were occurring at the time, realistic elements became increasingly predominant. The emphasis in theater was not to be on fairy tales or make-believe, on kings or knights in armor in faraway places, but on what was happening to ordinary people in familiar surroundings. Dialogue would not be poetry or elevated prose but normal conversation, and the actors would behave like people we know and recognize from life around us.

In Europe, realistic theater became a dominant form in the late nineteenth century when three playwrights—Henrik Ibsen (1828–1906) of Norway, August Strindberg (1849–1912) of Sweden, and Anton Chekhov (1860–1904) of Russia—produced a number of strongly realistic plays. Together they set the pattern for the next century in this type of theater. Their dramas presented characters with life histories, motives, and anxieties that audiences could immediately identify as truthful from their own experiences or observations. The housewives in Ibsen's plays, the quarreling couples in Strindberg's, and the dispossessed families in Chekhov's: here were characters who spoke, dressed, and behaved as one expected people to; and because the characters and situations were so easily recognizable, they seemed truer.

This kind of theater resembles life so closely that one assumes it must *be* life. When we are readily able to verify what we see before us from our own observations and experience, we are likely to accept its authenticity more quickly. Because of this direct appeal, realistic theater has become firmly established in the past hundred years, and it seems likely to remain so.

NONREALISTIC ELEMENTS OF THEATER   Nonrealistic elements of theater consist of everything that does not conform to our observations of surface reality—poetry instead of prose, ghosts rather than believable people, abstract forms for scenery, and so forth. Once again, we have a counterpart in films and television. Movies like *Ghostbusters* and *ET* employ special effects to give us otherworldly creatures, rides through outer space, or encounters with prehistoric monsters.

In the theater, the argument for nonrealism is that the surface of life— a real conversation or a real room in a house—can never convey the whole truth, because so much of life occurs in our minds and imaginations. If we are deeply depressed and we tell a friend that we feel "lousy" or "awful," we do not even begin to communicate the depth of our feelings. It is because of the inadequacy of ordinary words that people turn to poetry and because of the inadequacy of other forms of daily communication that they turn to music, dance, art, sculpture, and the entire range of symbols and metaphors discussed earlier.

In theater, symbolic expression takes the form of nonrealistic techniques. The chorus in a Greek play can express ideas, feelings, and emotions which could never be included in a strictly realistic presentation. The feeling of being haunted by the past can never be as vividly portrayed in a simple description as it can by a figure like the ghost of Hamlet's father, or Banquo's ghost appearing before Macbeth. The opportunity for the presentation of these inner truths—of the reality that is "realer than real"—is what nonrealistic theater offers.

THE CONTRAST BETWEEN REALISTIC AND NONREALISTIC THEATER.
The scenes shown here illustrate the difference between two approaches to theaer. Top: a scene between Larry Fishburne and Ella Joyce from August Wilson's Two Trains Running *is realistic in all its details—the furniture and other objects in the room, the clothes of the characters, and so forth. Every aspect duplicates its counterpart in real life. Below: The figures in a tableau from Robert Wilson's production of* the CIVIL warS, *by contrast, does not resemble everyday reality in any way—the figure on the horse, the bird, and the arrangement of the elements all have a stylized, artificial quality that is poetic and symbolic rather than realistic.*

A wide range of techniques and devices in the theater fall into the category of nonrealism. A good example is the *soliloquy*, in which a solitary character speaks to the audience, expressing in words a hidden thought. In real life, we might confess some of our inner fears or hopes to a priest, a psychiatrist, or our best friend, but we do not announce such fears out loud for the world to hear as Hamlet does when he says, "To be, or not to be . . . ." Another example is *pantomime,* in which performers pretend to be using articles that do not actually exist, such as drinking a cup of coffee or opening an umbrella. Many aspects of musical comedy are nonrealistic. People in the streets do not break into song or dance on the pavements as they do in musicals like *Guys and Dolls* and *West Side Story.* Nor do people burst into song in someone's living room or in a classroom. One could say that any activity or scenic device which transcends or symbolizes reality tends to be nonrealistic. (For a detailed contrast between realism and nonrealism, see Appendix 1.)

COMBINING THE REALISTIC AND THE NONREALISTIC   In discussing the realistic and nonrealistic elements of theater, it is a mistake to assume that these two approaches are mutually exclusive. They are simply a convenient way of separating those parts of theater which correspond to our observations and experiences of everyday life from those which do not.

Most performances and theater events contain a mixture of realistic and nonrealistic elements. In acting, for example, the performance of a Shakespearean play calls for a number of nonrealistic qualities or techniques. At the same time, any performer playing the part of a Shakespearean character must convince the audience that he or she represents a real human being. To take a more modern example, in *The Glass Menagerie,* by Tennessee Williams (1911–1983), and in Thornton Wilder's *Our Town,* one of the performers serves as a narrator and also participates in the action. When the performer playing this part is speaking directly to the audience, his actions are nonrealistic; when he is taking part in a scene with other characters, they are realistic.

Distinguishing Stage Reality from Fact

Whether theater is realistic or nonrealistic, it is different from the physical reality of everyday life. In recent years there have been attempts to make theater less remote from our daily lives. Plays have been presented which were largely transcripts of court trials or congressional hearings. This was part of a movement called the *theater of fact,* with reenactments of material gathered from actual events. Partly as a result of this trend, theater and life have become deeply intertwined. Television has added to this with *docudramas,* dramatizing the lives, for example, of rape victims, ex-convicts, and ordinary people who become heroic.

Such confusion and interaction between life and art have been heightened, of course, by the emergence of television and film documentaries, which cover real events but are also edited. A few years ago there was a heated debate about television news programs which showed "simulated" news footage that had been re-created rather than actually filmed. In addition, today we have "staged" political demonstrations and hear of "staged news." When news becomes "staged" and theater becomes "fact," it is difficult to separate the two.

These developments point up rather vividly the close relationship between theater and life; nevertheless, when we see a performance—even a re-creation of events which have actually occurred—we are always aware on some level that we are in the theater. No matter how authentic a reenactment may be, we know that it is a replay and not the original event. Most of us have seen plays with a stage setting so real we marvel at its authenticity: a kitchen, for instance, in which the appliances actually work, with running water in the faucets, ice in the refrigerator, and a stove on which an actor or actress can cook. What we stand in awe of, though, is that the room *appears* so real when we know, in truth, it is not. We admire the fact that, not being a real kitchen, it looks as if it were.

We are abruptly reminded of the distinction between stage reality and physical reality when the two lines cross. If an actor unintentionally trips and falls onstage, we suddenly shift our attention from the character to the person playing the part. Has he hurt himself? Will he be able to continue? A similar reaction occurs when a performer forgets lines, or a sword falls accidentally during a duel, or a dancer slips during a musical number.

We remember the distinction, also, at the moment when someone else *fails* to remember it. Children frequently mistake actions onstage for the real thing, warning the heroine of the villain's plan or assuming that blows on the head of a puppet actually hurt. There is a famous story of a production of *Othello* in which a spectator ran onstage to prevent the actor playing Othello from strangling Desdemona. Another instance of audience involvement was a production by the Street Theater of Ossining, New York, of *Street Sounds* by the black playwright Ed Bullins (1935–   ). The play opens with two black policemen beating a 15-year-old black youth. At one performance, a spectator ran onstage in the midst of the beating to stop the actors playing the policemen. In each of these cases, the distinction between fantasy and reality disappeared for the spectator, who mistook the imagined event for a real one.

There have been situations in which people considered a symbol or a fantasy as the fact itself. J. A. Hadfield reports that this was frequently the case with the dreams of primitive people. A "primitive man . . . considered that if in his dream he saw himself in a neighboring hostile village, he had actually been in that village, and if he saw the villagers in his dream preparing for battle, this would be quite enough for him to report the fact, and his tribe would immediately prepare to meet the onslaught."[2]

When people are mentally unbalanced, the disturbance sometimes manifests itself as an inability to separate the real from the imagined. Most people, however, are always aware of the difference. The result is that our minds manage two seemingly contradictory feats simultaneously: we know on the one hand that an imagined event is not objectively real, but at the same time we go along with it completely as fantasy.

We accept all kinds of theater, the most realistic as well as the most fantastic, because of a "willing suspension of disbelief." This is the term the poet and critic Samuel Taylor Coleridge (1772–1834) used to explain the phenomenon of our accepting so completely the products of our imaginations, particularly as they occur in art. The aesthetic distance mentioned earlier makes this possible. Having separated, at the outset, the reality of art from the reality of everyday life, the mind is prepared to go along with the former without reservation.

In this chapter we have looked at what goes on inside the minds of spectators at a play: how they use their imaginations to conjure up images that deeply affect their ideas and emotions. When we turn from the inside to the outside, there are other factors, surrounding the theater event, that also have a bearing on how we view the experience and how well we understand it. These include the circumstances under which a play was created and the expectations we have when we attend a performance; and they will be the subject to which we turn next, in Chapter 3.

❋ SUMMARY ❋

1 For the observer, theater is an experience of the imagination and the mind, which seems capable of accepting almost any illusion as to what is taking place, who the characters are, and when and where the action occurs.

2 Our minds are capable of leaps of the imagination, not just in the theater but in our everyday lives, where we employ symbol and metaphor to communicate with one another and to explain the world around us.

3 The world of the imagination—symbols, metaphors, dreams, fantasies, and various expressions of art—is "real," even though it is in-

tangible and has no objective reality. Frequently it tells us more about our true feelings than any form of logical discourse.

4 Theater makes frequent use of symbols and metaphors—in writing, acting, design, etc.—and theater itself can be viewed as a metaphor.

5 In theater, audiences are called on to imagine two kinds of worlds: the realistic and the nonrealistic. The first depicts things onstage that conform to observable reality; the second is in the realm of dreams, fantasy, symbol, and metaphor. Frequently in theater, realism and non-realism are mixed.

6 In order to take part in theater as an observer, it is important to keep the ''reality'' of fantasies and dreams separate from the real world. By making this separation, we open our imagination to the full range of possibilities in the theater.

❈ TOPICS FOR DISCUSSION ❈

1 Suppose that someone put on an ''authentic'' production of one of Shakespeare's plays, with all the women's parts played by boys. Do you think it might be interesting, provocative, and effective? Or, given today's conditions, do you think it would be unacceptable or even rather absurd?

2 As was noted in this chapter, realistic and nonrealistic elements of theater are not an ''either-or'' matter: any theatrical event might be pictured as located somewhere along a continuum or spectrum with ''realism'' at one extreme and ''nonrealism'' at the other. Do you tend, on the whole, to find more satisfaction in plays that fall closer to one end of the spectrum than the other? If so, explain why. If not, can you explain why the distinction between realism and nonrealism does *not* seem to affect you particularly?

3 ''Aesthetic distance'' helps audiences separate reality from fact in the theater; or, to put it another way, aesthetic distance prevents us from confusing reality and fact. In participatory theater, as we saw in Chapter 1, aesthetic distance is to some degree removed or modified; still, even in participatory theater, audiences do not become bewildered: they remain aware of what is real and what is not. Does this imply (*a*) that aesthetic distance is not simply—or even primarily—physical? Or does it imply (*b*) that something else may operate—in conjunction with aesthetic distance or instead of it—to let us distinguish reality from nonreality in the theater? Defend your choice. If you have chosen *b*, describe whatever else you think might be operating.

3

BACKGROUND AND EXPECTATIONS OF THE AUDIENCE

BACKGROUND INFORMATION AFFECTS THE THEATER EXPERIENCE. *Audience members have personal experiences which help them understand and identify with the plays they see.* The Heidi Chronicles *by Wendy Wasserstein is about a single woman who grew up in the 1960s and 1970s and who now teaches art history. Anyone who is single, or is a woman, or grew up in the same period, or is a woman trying to balance the demands of a career with her personal life will understand the attitudes, fears, hopes, and dreams of the play's heroine, shown here performed by Joan Allen. Before being presented on Broadway, the play was awarded the Susan Smith Blackburn Prize, given annually to the best new play by a woman writer.*

When audiences attend a theater event, they bring more than their mere presence; they bring a background of personal knowledge and a set of expectations that shape the experience. Several important factors are involved:

1 The knowledge and personal memories of individual members of the audience.

2 Their awareness of the social, political, and philosophical world in which the play was written or produced: the link between theater and society.

3 Their specific information about the play and playwright.

4 Individual expectations concerning the event: what each person anticipates will happen at a performance. As we will see, misconceptions about what the theater experience is or should be can lead to confusion and disappointment.

✳ BACKGROUND OF INDIVIDUAL SPECTATORS ✳

A background element which every member of the audience brings to a theater performance is his or her own individual memories and experiences. Each one of us has a personal catalog of emotional scars, childhood memories, and private fantasies, and anything we see onstage which reminds us of this personal world will have a strong impact on us.

When we see a play that has been written in our own day, we bring with us a deep awareness of the world from which the play comes because we come from the same world. Through the books we read, through newspapers and television, through discussions with friends, we have a background of common information and beliefs. Our shared knowledge and experience are much larger than most of us realize, and they form a crucial ingredient in our theater experience.

The play *A Raisin in the Sun* by Lorraine Hansberry (1930–1965) tells the story of a black family in Chicago in the late 1950s whose members want to improve their lives by finding better jobs and moving to a new neighborhood. But they face a number of obstacles put in their way by society. Any black person—or, for that matter, any person who belongs to a minority or to a group that has lacked opportunities—can identify with the situation quite easily. Such a person will know from personal experience what the characters are going through.

We can also relate to characters and events onstage when we see plays set in other times and places. The story of Antigone, for example, was treated by Sophocles in Greece in the fifth century B.C. and more

THE BACKGROUND OF INDIVIDUAL AUDIENCE MEMBERS.

An example of a particular experience which would influence the way an audience member might view a production would be someone from the business, legal, or financial community who saw Other People's Money. *This play was based on the freewheeling financial dealing of the 1980s, and anyone familiar with that world would have a special appreciation of the actions of the characters.*

recently, during World War II, by the French playwright Jean Anouilh (1910–1987). The young woman Antigone adamantly opposes her uncle, Creon, the ruler of the state, because he is a political pragmatist who makes compromises; she is an idealist who believes in higher principles. Anyone, especially a young woman, who has ever tried to oppose corruption or complacency in an entrenched political regime will find much to recognize in Antigone. A person like this will feel a special affinity for the character, and the performance will have a more personal meaning for that person than for someone who has no direct experience of the situation.

Any activity onstage that reminds us of something in our own lives will trigger deep personal responses which become part of the equation of our theater experience.

A RAISIN IN THE SUN (1959)

LORRAINE HANSBERRY (1930–1965)

CHIEF CHARACTERS:
Lena Younger—Mama
Walter Lee Younger—her son
Ruth Younger—Walter's wife
Travis Younger—Ruth and Walter's son
Beneatha Younger—Walter's sister
Joseph Asagai—Beneatha's friend
George Murchison—Beneatha's friend
Karl Lindner—representative of white neighborhood

SETTING: The Youngers' apartment in a poor section of Chicago, sometime after World War II.

BACKGROUND: The Youngers are a hard-working black family with dreams of improving their lives. The father had worked hard all his life. Now that he is dead, his only legacy is a $10,000 life insurance policy which the family is about to receive. He and Mama always wanted to own a house but could never afford one.

ACT I, SCENE 1: It is Friday morning, and Ruth wakes the family. All of them are looking forward to the arrival of the insurance check, which promises an escape from poverty. After their son Travis goes to school, Walter tells Ruth that he has a chance to buy a liquor store with some friends. Walter wants Ruth to persuade Mama to give him the insurance money for this new venture, but Ruth is not supportive. Walter's sister Beneatha, an aspiring doctor, enters and tells him that the insurance money is Mama's, not theirs. After Walter goes to work, Mama enters. Her grandmotherly concern for Travis is a source of conflict between her and Ruth. Ruth talks to Mama about Walter's liquor store: Ruth believes that Walter needs a purpose in life which the store could provide, but Mama, a God-fearing woman, doesn't like the idea of selling liquor. Mama wants to put some money aside for Beneatha's education and to buy a house in a nice neighborhood with the remainder of the money. Ruth suddenly becomes ill, and Mama expresses concern for her condition.

SCENE 2: The following morning, Saturday, is cleaning day. As Mama works at home, Walter goes out to talk with his friend Willy about buying the liquor store. Ruth comes back from the doctor very upset and tells Mama that she is pregnant. Beneatha's friend Asagai arrives with an African outfit for her to wear. Beneatha is always trying new things, like playing the guitar and pursuing her African roots. Asagai is from Africa; he is an intellectual taken with Beneatha, but his attentions frighten her because she wants to find her own identity. Meanwhile, the insurance check arrives and Mama becomes upset. It acts as a reminder that instead of the warm, loving husband whom she has lost, now all she has is a piece of paper. Walter enters excitedly talking about buying the liquor store, and Ruth storms out. Mama tries to tell Walter that she understands his frustration, but she explains to him that Ruth is pregnant and wants an abortion.

ACT II, SCENE 1: Later the same day. Ruth is ironing when Beneatha enters, ready for a date with George, a wealthy, successful black man. Walter is obviously jealous of George's success. Mama enters and tells everyone that she has made a down payment on a house with part of the insurance money. Ruth and

Travis are happy with the news, but Walter is depressed. He believes that this is another setback to his dream of owning the liquor store. When the family discovers that the house Mama plans to buy is in an all-white section, they wonder how they will be accepted.

SCENE 2: Friday night a few weeks later. The house is strewn with packing crates in anticipation of the move to the new house. Walter has not gone to work for three days; he is spending his time in a bar. This dismays Mama, who has always worked for her children and now fears that she may be destroying her son. She therefore decides to give Walter $6,500—the remainder of the insurance money—to invest as he chooses. She tells Walter that he should finally become the head of the family. He excitedly begins to talk to his son about his dreams.

SCENE 3: Saturday, a week later—moving day. Ruth tells Beneatha that her relationship with Walter is better because he seems to have a new lease on life. Walter enters, followed by Mr. Lindner, a middle-aged white man who has come to discourage the black family from moving into their new house. Walter throws him out, and when Mama comes back, they tell her about this "welcoming committee" from the new neighborhood. Mama is greatly moved when the others give her some presents for the new house. In the midst of the celebration, Walter's friend Bobo enters with the bad news: their "friend" Willy has run off with all their money. Walter breaks down and tells the family that he had invested the whole $6,500 with Willy. Mama is distraught, remembering all the suffering

and sacrifices the family had made for the money.

ACT III: An hour later. The mood is despairing. Beneatha fears that this is the end of all her plans. She attacks Walter bitterly, and he exits. Mama starts unpacking because now they must stay in the old house. Walter returns and tells them he has called Lindner to make a deal. Mama is against it: "We ain't never been that poor." Walter is about to sell out to "The Man" when his pride stops him; he tells Lindner that they have decided to move into the new house because his father earned it. The family members bustle into activity. After everyone else has left, Mama stands alone for a short while, and then exits into the future.

(Sara Krulwich/NYT Pictures)

Even when we identify closely with the characters or situation in a play, in dramas from the past there is much that we cannot understand unless we are familiar with the history, culture, psychology, and philosophy of the period when it was created. This is because there is a close connection between any art form and the society in which it is produced.

Theater and Society

Artists are sometimes charged with being "antisocial," "subversive," or "enemies of the state," and such accusations carry the strong suggestion that they are outsiders or invaders rather than true members of a culture. To be sure, art frequently challenges society and is sometimes on the leading edge of history, appearing to forecast the future. More often than not, however, such art simply recognizes what is already present in society but has not yet surfaced. A good example is the abstract art which emerged in Europe in the early part of the twentieth century. At first it was considered a freakish aberration: an unattractive series of jagged lines and patches of color with no relation to nature, truth, or anything human. In time, however, abstract art came to be recognized as a genuine movement whose disjointed and fragmentary lines reflect the quality of much of modern life.

Art grows in the soil of a specific society. It must, in order to take root. With very few exceptions—and those soon forgotten—art is a mirror of its age, revealing the prevailing attitudes, underlying assumptions, and deep-seated beliefs of a particular group of people. Art may question society's views or reaffirm them, but it cannot escape them; the two are as indissolubly linked as a person and his or her shadow. When we speak of art as being "universal," we mean that the art of one age has so defined the characteristics of human beings that it can speak eloquently to another age; but it should never be forgotten that every work of art first emerges at a given time and place and can never be adequately understood unless the conditions surrounding its birth are also understood.

Greek Theater and Culture

A study of theater in significant periods of history confirms the close link between art and society. In ancient Greece, for example, civilization reached a high point during the time of Pericles, the latter part of the fifth century B.C. This was the golden age of Greece—when politics, art, architecture, and theater thrived as they never had before, and rarely have since. As the Greeks of that period gained control over the world around them and took new pride in human achievements, they developed ideals of beauty, order, symmetry, and moderation which permeated their entire culture, including theater.

THE SYMMETRY OF A GREEK TEMPLE.

The formalism and sense of order of Greece in the fifth century B.C. are reflected in the temple of Athena Nike, on the acropolis in Athens. All art, including theater, reflects the attitudes and values of the society in which it is created.

By the fifth century B.C., standard forms of drama had emerged in Greece, both for tragedies (such as *King Oedipus*) and for comedies. Playwrights introduced some innovations, but essentially they adhered to prescribed conventions. One of these conventions required a limited number of scenes in each play, usually five scenes interspersed with choral sections. The drama usually took place in one locale—often in front of a palace—and covered a limited amount of time. Another practice reflected the society's sense of balance and order. Bloody deeds occurred in the myths on which most Greek plays were based, but in the Greek plays that have survived these deeds almost never took place in sight of the audience; murders, suicides, and other acts of violence occurred offstage. The Greek notion of moderation is also reflected in another feature of most Greek tragedies: any character in a play who acted in an excess of passion was generally punished or pursued by avenging furies.

Elizabethan Theater and Culture

Another example of the strong link between theater and society—one which stands in contrast to the classical Greek period—is the Elizabethan age in England. Named after Queen Elizabeth I, who reigned from 1558 to 1603, this period saw England become a dominant force in the world. Under Elizabeth's rule England was forged into a unified country; trade and commerce flourished, and with the defeat of the Spanish

Armada in 1588, an age of exploration for England was in full bloom. England was expanding on all fronts and feeling self-confident in the process; these characteristics were reflected in the drama of the period.

From medieval drama the Elizabethans inherited stage practices that made it possible to shift rapidly from place to place and from one time period to another. Using these techniques, as well as others they perfected, Shakespeare, Christopher Marlowe (1564–1593), and their contemporaries wrote plays that are quite different from the more formal drama of the Greeks. A single play might move to a number of locations and cover a period of many years. Rather than being restrictive, the plays are expansive in terms of the numbers of characters and action, and there is no hesitancy whatsoever about showing murder and bloodshed onstage. At the end of an Elizabethan play, corpses frequently cover the stage in full view of the audience.

A Note on Women and Greek and Elizabethan Theater

In considering the link between theater and society, it is worth noting that in both Greek and Elizabethan theater, despite important female characters in the dramas themselves, there were no female playwrights or performers. This is a result of the place women were accorded in these two cultures.

Classical Greek theater was intrinsically linked to the well-being of the state. Its themes reflected the political necessity for order and control and were intended to serve a didactic purpose, ensuring the continuation of democratic government. In Athenian society, where women were excluded from all political roles and were not even considered citizens, it followed logically that they could not participate in the theater's creative processes. In fact, we do not even know if women were permitted to attend performances. It is interesting to note that the most persuasive evidence given by classical scholars for women's presence at theatrical events is that men were allowed to bring their male slaves; if slaves could attend, why not free women? We do know that women often acted in wandering mime troupes. These popular entertainers sang, danced, juggled, and performed acrobatics and brief comic sketches. Because of the bawdy nature of these acts, women mimes were often thought to be of low moral character. This unfortunate label was to remain with women performers for hundreds of years and is at least partly responsible for an exclusionary attitude which eliminated the contribution of women from legitimate theater activity.

In Elizabethan England, despite the presence of a powerful female monarch, theater practices continued to reflect long-standing prejudices against women. Although, during the reign of Elizabeth, actors were raised above vagabond status, actresses were still considered little better than prostitutes—a result of medieval and Puritan thinking. Women were thus barred from performing on the legitimate stage, and female roles were played by young boys who did much to effect feminine beauty and grace. It was not until 1660 that women were allowed to appear on the stage of licensed theaters in England.

Modern Theater and Culture

Moving to a more contemporary period, we find once again a tie between theater and society. Modern society, especially in the United States, is heterogeneous. We have people of many races, religions, and national backgrounds living side by side. Moreover, the twentieth century has been marked by increasingly swift global communications. By means of radio and television, events that occur on one side of the world are instantaneously flashed to other parts. By these means, too, people are constantly made aware of cultures other than their own.

When cultures and societies are brought together, we are reminded of the many things people have in common but also of the differences among us. At the same time that we are brought together by global

(Gerry Goodstein)

THEATER REFLECTS SOCIAL ISSUES.
In the United States in our time, a crisis that affects many people is the AIDS epidemic. Concern with this issue is reflected in the theater in such works as Falsettoland. *Shown here is a scene from a production at Playwrights Horizons in New York City, with Stephen Bogardus (left) and Michael Rupert (right).*

communications, other aspects of life have become increasingly fragmented in recent years. A number of institutions that held fairly constant through many centuries—organized religion, the family, marriage—have been seriously challenged in the past hundred years.

Discoveries by Charles Darwin about evolution raised fundamental questions about views of creation held at that time: Were human beings special creatures made by God, or were they subject to the same process of evolution that other forms of life had gone through? People of the nineteenth century feared that if human beings had evolved, they might not occupy the unique place in the universe that had always been assumed for them. Shortly after Darwin published his findings, Karl Marx put forward revolutionary ideas on economics that challenged long-held beliefs about capitalism.

At the end of the nineteenth century, Sigmund Freud cast doubt on the ability of human beings to exercise total rational control over their activities. Later, Albert Einstein's discoveries about relativity questioned well-established views of the universe. The cumulative effect of these discoveries was to make human beings much less certain of their place in the cosmos and of their mastery of events. Life now appears to be much less unified and ordered than it once seemed.

These two developments—the bringing together of cultures by population shifts and communication, and the challenges to long-held beliefs—are reflected in today's theater. It is a theater of *eclecticism* (the embracing of different strains) and of fragmentation. The typical theater company today performs a wide range of plays. In a single season, the same company may present a tragedy by Shakespeare, a farce by the Frenchman Molière (1622–1673), a modern drama by the Spanish writer Federico García Lorca (1898–1936), and a new play by an American playwright. Moreover, the dramatists of today write on many subjects and in a wide range of styles.

I spoke earlier of Greek and Elizabethan society. More properly, these should be referred to as *Athenian* society and *London* society, because the culture in which the arts developed was concentrated in those two cities. In Athens and London in those time periods, society was homogeneous; that is, people had a similar racial and religious background. Theatergoing in each society was a uniform experience. In the modern world, by contrast, the variety and types of drama reflect the complex and heterogeneous nature of society.

The three periods we have looked at are examples of the close relationship between a given society and the art and theater it produces. One could find comparable links in every culture. It is important to remember, therefore, that whatever the period in which it was first produced, drama is woven into the fabric of the time.

BACKGROUND INFORMATION ❋ ON THE PLAY OR PLAYWRIGHT ❋

In some cases it is not only the historical period surrounding the play about which we need additional knowledge but also the play itself. A good example would be difficult passages or obscure references which it is helpful to know before we see a performance of the play.

As an example, we can take a segment from Shakespeare's *King Lear:* the scene in the third act when Lear appears on the heath in the midst of a terrible storm. Earlier in the play Lear had divided his kingdom between two of his daughters, Goneril and Regan, who he thought loved him but who he discovered had deceived him. Gradually they had stripped him of everything: his possessions, his soldiers, even his dignity. Finally they send him out from their homes to face the wind and rain in open country. As the storm begins, Lear speaks the following lines:

> Blow, winds, and crack your cheeks! Rage! Blow!
> You cataracts and hurricanoes, spout
> Till you have drenched our steeples, drowned the cocks!
> You sulphurous and thought-executing fires,
> Vaunt-curriers of oak-cleaving thunderbolts,
> Singe my white head! And thou all-shaking thunder,
> Strike flat the thick rotundity o' the world.

Even if we do not understand every reference, we realize that Lear is invoking the heavens to bring on a terrifying storm. The sounds of the words alone—the music of the language in its combinations of vowels, rhythm, and inflections—convey the sense of a raging storm. But how much more the passage will mean if in addition we understand the meanings of key words and phrases. Let us examine the passage more closely: In the first line, the expression "crack your cheeks" refers to pictures in the corners of old maps showing a face puffed out at the cheeks, blowing the wind.[1] Shakespeare is saying that the face of the wind should blow so hard that its cheeks will crack. In the second line, "cataracts and hurricanoes" refer to water from both the heavens and the seas. In line three, the word "cocks" refers to weathercocks on the tops of steeples; Lear wants there to be so much rain that even the weathercocks on the steepletops will be covered with water. In line four, "thought-executing" means as quick as thought; in other words, fires should ignite instantaneously. "Vaunt-curriers" of line five suggests that lightning is followed by thunderbolt; first the fire comes and then a bolt which can split an oak tree. Line seven, "strike flat the thick rotundity o' the world," conveys the image of a storm so powerful that the round earth will be flattened. If we are aware of these meanings,

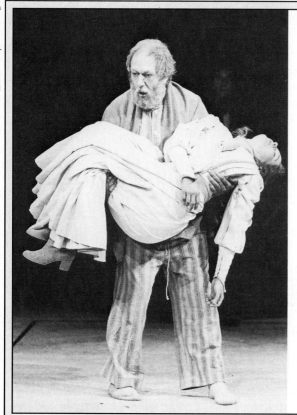

**BACKGROUND INFORMATION
ON A PLAY OR PLAYWRIGHT.**
*When we view a play from another time or coun-
try or a play on a subject with which we are not
familiar, the experience is greatly enhanced if we
have knowledge of what the playwright was
trying to do and of the context in which the play
was written. For example, if we understand
Shakespeare, and the references in the poetry of
his play* King Lear, *we will appreciate a performance of the play more than we would otherwise. In this scene from a production by the
Royal Shakespeare Company in Stratford,
England, Michael Gambon plays King Lear and
Alice Krige is his daughter Cordelia.*

we can join them with the sounds of the words and the rage which the
actor expresses in his voice and gestures to get the full impact of the
scene.

In the contemporary theater, playwrights frequently employ special
techniques which will confuse us if we do not understand them. The
German playwright Bertolt Brecht (1898–1956), who lived and wrote in
the United States during the 1940s, wished to provoke his audience into
thinking about what it was seeing. To do this, he interrupted the story
with a song or a speech by a narrator. The theory is that when a story
is stopped in this manner, the audience has an opportunity to consider
more carefully what it has seen and to relate the drama onstage to other
aspects of life. If one is not aware that this is Brecht's purpose in inter-
rupting the action, one might conclude that he was simply a careless
or inferior playwright. In this, as in similar cases, knowledge of the play
or playwright is indispensable to a successful theater experience.

EXPECTATIONS: THE VARIETY OF
EXPERIENCES IN MODERN THEATER

A misconception held by spectators who have not been to the theater very often is the expectation that all theater experiences are alike; they are not. Audiences go to the theater for different purposes. Some, like those who enjoy the escape offered by movies and television, are interested primarily in light entertainment. Audiences at dinner theaters or Broadway musicals do not want to be faced with troublesome problems or serious moral issues. They may be tired after a hard day and may want some relief from their jobs and from tensions at home. Consequently they seek an "escape" from everyday cares; they look for something which will be amusing and perhaps will include music, dancing, and beautiful costumes.

There are other audiences, however, who want to be stimulated and challenged, both intellectually and emotionally. To these audiences, a situation comedy or a light musical will seem frivolous or sentimental.

It must be remembered, too, that many people like both kinds of theater. The situation and the audience member's frame of mind are the determining factors. At times a person may seek light entertainment; at other times, meaningful drama.

In understanding a theater event, it is important to understand the social context in which it occurs and the demands of the audiences. A theater event can entertain, offer an escape, provoke thought, inspire, educate, challenge, and delight. Often several of these purposes are combined. A production might be intended, for instance, to amuse but also to teach a lesson. Another production may challenge the audience to think and, beyond that, to take action.

Not only do performances vary in terms of the type of theater they offer; they also take place in a variety of settings, and this too has an effect on the nature of the experience. Fifty years ago "the theater" was synonymous with one kind of experience: Broadway. In the last several decades this has changed dramatically—further evidence of how the diversity in theater reflects the overall diversity in contemporary life. To see the changes in the kinds of places theater is presented, it will be helpful to look at developments in the United States over the past half-century.

Broadway Theater

Broadway is the name given to the professional theater in New York City: it refers specifically to plays performed in the large theaters in the district near Times Square. From 1920 until the early 1950s, most new plays written in the United States originated there, and productions in

BROADWAY THEATER.
Productions in the major theaters in New York City—collectively known as Broadway—are marked by elaborate scenic elements, first-rate acting, and scripts with wide appeal: either new plays or revivals. The scene here is from a production of Cat on a Hot Tin Roof *by Tennessee Williams, which starred the screen and stage actress Kathleen Turner (right), and Daniel Hugh Kelly opposite her.*

other areas were usually copies of Broadway productions. Broadway itself was confined and standardized; it consisted of an area in Manhattan roughly six blocks long and a block and a half wide. The thirty or more theaters located in these few blocks were the same size, seating between 700 and 1,400 people, and had the same style of architecture as well as the same picture-frame stage.

Productions sent on tour from Broadway to the rest of the country were exact replicas of the original. Scenery was duplicated down to the last detail, and New York performers often played roles they had played on Broadway. Nonprofessional theaters copied Broadway as well; acting versions of successful plays were published for colleges, schools, and community theaters, providing precise instructions for the movements of the performers and the placement of scenery onstage.

The Broadway concept gave the theater a yardstick of excellence and produced outstanding work; but in the period just after World War II the realization grew that there were large numbers of people in the United States from whom Broadway was remote—not just geographically, but spiritually.

Because our society is diverse and complex, and because theater reflects society, it is difficult to see how any one form of theater today—however profound—can speak equally to all of us. As if in response to the complexity of the modern world, in the years immediately after World War II people began searching for new forms in theater and for alternative locations in which to present drama.

Resident Professional Theaters

A significant development, which began in the 1950s and has since spread across the country, is the resident professional theater movement, sometimes known as *regional theater*. In a number of cities around

REGIONAL PROFESSIONAL THEATERS.
All across the United States and Canada, resident professional theaters have become established in the past quarter-century and are now an important aspect of the total theater scene. Shown here is a production of Shakespeare's Measure for Measure *at the Oregon Shakespeare Festival in Ashland, Oregon.*

(Hans Kranzler)

CHAPTER 3 • BACKGROUND AND EXPECTATIONS OF THE AUDIENCE

the United States, theater companies have been formed, and theater facilities have been built, for the continuing presentation of high-quality professional productions to local residents. The performers, directors, and designers are generally high-caliber artists who make theater their full-time profession.

A few of these theaters are repertory in the European tradition. In *repertory*, several plays are performed on alternate nights rather than a single play's being performed night after night for the length of its run. For example, in repertory a Molière play may appear on Monday night, a Beckett play on Tuesday, a Shakespearean play on Wednesday, and so forth. Two successful repertory theaters in the United States are the American Conservatory Theater in San Francisco and the American Repertory Theater in Boston.

Many other cities have developed theaters that present a series of plays over a given time, with each play being performed for about 4 to 12 weeks. Among the best-known of these theaters are the Arena Stage in Washington, D.C., the Long Wharf in New Haven, the Actor's Theater in Louisville, the Mark Taper Forum in Los Angeles, the Alley Theater in Houston, the Goodman Theater in Chicago, the Milwaukee Repertory Theater, and the Seattle Repertory Theater. A season of plays in these theaters will usually consist of a mixture of new plays and classics, and audiences are encouraged to buy a season subscription.

In addition to resident companies, there are now a number of permanent summer theater festivals throughout the United States and Canada. Among the best known are the Shakespeare festivals at Stratford, Ontario; San Diego, California; and Ashland, Oregon.

College and University Theaters

In the last few decades, college and university theater departments have become increasingly important too, not only in teaching the theater arts but in presenting plays. In some localities, college productions are virtually the only form of theater offered. In other areas they are a significant supplement to professional theater programs.

The theater facilities in many colleges are excellent. Most large colleges and universities have two or three theater spaces—a full-size theater, a medium-size theater, and a smaller space for experimental dramas—as well as extensive scene shops, costume rooms, dressing rooms, and rehearsal halls. Productions are usually scheduled throughout the school year.

The quality and the elaborateness of these productions vary. In some localities productions are extremely elaborate, with full-scale scenery, costumes, lighting, and sound. Colleges vary, too, in the level of professionalism in acting. Many colleges use only performers from the undergraduate theater program. If the college has a master's degree program,

COLLEGE AND UNIVERSITY THEATER.
A vital segment of theater today consists of the many productions mounted each year by theater departments and programs in colleges and universities across the country. Many of these achieve a high degree of professionalism; they also provide excellent training for people wishing to pursue a career in theater, as well as interesting theater viewing for audiences. The scene here is from Albee's Who's Afraid of Virginia Woolf? *at Ohio State University.*

it will utilize both graduate and undergraduate performers. Colleges or universities may bring in outside professionals to perform along with student actors. Most college and university theaters offer a variety of plays, including classics and experimental plays rarely done by professional theaters.

Alternative Theaters

In New York City the *off-Broadway theater* began in the 1950s as an alternative to Broadway, which was becoming increasingly costly. Off-Broadway theaters were smaller than Broadway theaters—most of them under 200 seats—and were located outside the Times Square area in

CHAPTER 3 • BACKGROUND AND EXPECTATIONS OF THE AUDIENCE

places like Greenwich Village. Because off-Broadway was less expensive than Broadway, it offered more opportunity for producing serious classics and experimental works.

Off-Broadway itself, however, became expensive and institutionalized in the 1960s and 1970s. As a result, small independent groups wishing to produce plays had to develop another forum. The result was *off-off-Broadway*.

Under an arrangement with the actors' union, Actors Equity Association, professionals were allowed to perform for little or no salary for short runs in workshop productions, and for minimal salaries in longer-running productions. *Off-off-Broadway* shows are produced wherever inexpensive space is available—churches, lofts, warehouses, large basements—and are characterized by low-priced productions and a wide

(Paula Court)

ALTERNATIVE THEATER.
Aside from Broadway and other professional theaters, there are many smaller theaters—off-off-Broadway and in cities across the United States—that present experimental, avant-garde productions, as well as productions for special populations such as minorities and those with definite political agendas. Shown here is a scene from an avant-garde play, Symphony of Rats, *a joint production of the Ontological-Hysteric Theater and the Wooster Group, written and directed by Richard Foreman.*

variety of offerings. It is in these theaters, too, that experimental work takes place (see Chapter 12). Such experiments include productions in which performers create their own work and in which theater is combined with painting, dance, or television.

An important development in the American theater is that an equivalent of the off-off-Broadway movement has sprung up in other major cities across the United States—Washington, Atlanta, Chicago, Minneapolis, Los Angeles, San Francisco, Seattle—where small theater groups perform as alternatives to large organizations.

One virtue of these small theater groups is that they can present productions of interest to special groups. The kinds of plays they offer include classics, new plays, and experimental work. Other theaters aim their productions at particular groups—for example, feminist theater, black theater, radical political theater.

In addition, all across the country there are cabaret and dinner theaters in which the atmosphere of a nightclub or restaurant is combined with that of a theater; in an informal setting, guests eat and drink before watching a performance.

Still another growing theater movement is theater for children. Theaters across the country have developed programs of theater training and full-scale productions for young people. Some children's theater operations, like those in Minneapolis and Nashville, occupy impressive building complexes and produce an extensive season of plays.

Today there is theater for almost everyone, in many kinds of places, under widely varying conditions, and for very different purposes. With theater taking so many forms, it is important in approaching the subject not to have a preconceived or rigidly fixed notion of what it is.

Chapters 1, 2, and 3 have dealt with the part the audience plays in the theater experience. We have looked at their vital role in the actor-audience equation, at the way the audience uses its imagination to participate in theater, and at the background knowledge and experience that affect the experience. In Chapter 4 we will look at the work of a specialized audience member—the critic. The critic observes the play just as ordinary spectators do, but brings to his or her observations background knowledge and powers of analysis which can be useful to regular audience members.

✳ SUMMARY ✳

1   All individuals attending a theater event bring to it a personal background of experience which becomes a vital ingredient in their response to the event.

2 Theater—like other arts—is closely linked to the society in which it is produced; it mirrors and reflects the attitudes, philosophy, and basic assumptions of its time.

3 Spectators attending a play written in their own day bring to it an awareness of the society's values and beliefs, and this background information forms an important part of the overall experience.

4 A play from the past can be understood better if the spectator is aware of the culture from which it came.

5 For any play which presents difficulties in language, style, or meaning, familiarity with the work itself can add immeasurably to a spectator's understanding and appreciation of the play in performance.

6 With an unfamiliar work, it is also helpful to learn about the playwright and his or her approach to theater.

7 In the past, theater experiences were relatively uniform within a given society, but in contemporary society the time, place, content, and purpose of theater experiences are far more varied. Expectations about the nature of the theater experience affect our reaction to it.

8 Theater events vary widely in terms of whether the play is a tragedy or comedy, and the circumstances in which it is presented. Spectators should attend the theater aware of this variety and expect different experiences depending on the type of play and the situation.

✳ TOPICS FOR DISCUSSION ✳

1 Have you ever become deeply involved with a play, a film, or a television show even though the characters and situation were far removed from your own experience? How would you explain this?

2 *A Raisin in the Sun* is set in the late 1950s—before the civil rights movement of the 1960s, led by Dr. Martin Luther King, Jr. Do the events and changes of the intervening years seem to lessen the impact of the play, or is it as powerful today as when it was first performed?

3 Women were barred from participation in Greek and Elizabethan theater, as we have seen in this chapter. Yet the plays of classical Greece and Elizabethan England are considered pinnacles not only of theater but of literature in general. How do you think the Greeks and Elizabethans managed to produce such magnificent art when, essentially, only half of society could be directly involved in it?

4   Today's theater is eclectic. This means, of course, that it gives us the opportunity to have many kinds of theatrical experiences. But it might be argued that eclecticism has a negative side. If producers, directors, performers, and so on are presenting plays from all times and in all styles, they may do many things passably but nothing superbly; to achieve excellence, it would be necessary to concentrate on one type of theater. Defend or attack this argument.

"A HIT!"
—PEOPLE MAGAZINE

ARTIFICIAL INTELLIGENCE in

Tony n' Tina's Wedding

"AUDACIOUSLY IMAGINATIVE."
— NY TIMES

"A DEVASTATINGLY FUNNY, THOROUGHLY COMIC EXPERIENCE. YOU'LL LAUGH, SING AND DANCE, PARTY LIKE CRAZY, LOVING EVERY MINUTE!"
—NY POST

FOR RESERVATIONS CALL: (212)279-4200
GROUP SALES: (212)889-4300
INFORMATION: (212)599-0070

4

THE CRITIC
AND THE AUDIENCE

The *critic*, loosely defined, is someone who observes theater and then analyzes and comments on it. In a sense the critic stands between the theater event and the audience, serving in ideal circumstances as a knowledgeable and highly sensitive audience member. At the same time, most theatergoers are amateur critics. When a person says about a performance he or she has seen, "It started off great, but it fizzled," or "The star was terrific, just like someone in real life," or "The woman was okay, but the man overacted," the person is making a critical judgment. The difference between a critic and an ordinary viewer is that the critic presumably is much better informed about the event and has developed a set of critical standards by which to judge it.

The reason audiences can learn from critics is not only that critics impart information and judgments but, as suggested above, that the critic shares with audience members the point of view of the spectator. Unlike those who create theater—writers, actors, designers—critics sit out front and watch a performance just as members of the audience do. By understanding how the critic goes about his or her task, audience members should be able to improve their own knowledge of how theater works and make individual theater experiences more meaningful.

✳ THEATRICAL CRITICISM ✳

What Is Criticism?

The popular image of the theater critic is a caustic writer who takes sharp, rapierlike thrusts at performers and playwrights. Some epithets of critics have become legendary. John Mason Brown described the actress Tallulah Bankhead in a production of Shakespeare's *Anthony and Cleopatra* by saying, "Tallulah Bankhead barged down the Nile last night as Cleopatra and sank." When Katharine Hepburn, who was a stage actress before she went into films, appeared in a play called *The Lake,* the critic Dorothy Parker wrote that Hepburn "ran the gamut of emotion from A to B." Before he was a playwright, George Bernard Shaw was a critic, and he had harsh things to say about a number of people, including Shakespeare. Shaw wrote that Shakespeare's *Cymbeline* was "for the most part stagey trash of the lowest melodramatic order." About Shakespeare himself Shaw said: "With the single exception of Homer, there is no eminent writer, not even Sir Walter Scott, whom I can despise so entirely as I despise Shakespeare when I measure my mind against his."

The word *criticize* has at least two meanings. One, perhaps the most familiar, is "to find fault," and that is what we see in the comments above. But *criticize* also means "to understand and appraise," and this meaning is much more important for a theater critic.

**GEORGE BERNARD SHAW:
CRITIC AS WELL AS PLAYWRIGHT.**
Most people know Shaw as an oustanding British playwright, but he was also one of the finest critics of modern times. Though opinionated and often caustic, Shaw, who began writing theater criticism in the 1890s, had many admirable attributes as a critic. In addition to a wide knowledge of theater, he understood the other arts as well as political and social affairs. He also had a clear set of criteria by which he judged plays and performances and a strong, lively writing style.

Preparation for Criticism

In order to make criticism more meaningful to audiences, the critic ideally should have a thorough theater background of the kind discussed in Chapter 3. It would consist of a full knowledge of theater history, as well as other aspects of theater, such as acting, directing, and design. The critic should be familiar with plays written in various styles and modes and should know the body of the work of individual writers. Also, the critic should be able to relate what is happening in theater to what is happening in the other arts and, beyond that, to events in society generally.

In addition, the critic should understand the production elements to be discussed later in the book—directing, acting, and design. The critic should have knowledge of what the director does and what constitutes good and bad direction. Has the director interpreted the play correctly? Has he or she given sound guidance to the performers and paced the flow of action so that the play unfolds smoothly? The critic should also understand acting and be able to judge whether a performer has the skills and the talent to be convincing in a role and whether the role has been interpreted properly. In addition, the critic should be familiar with the principles and practices of design—scenery, costume, and lighting. He or she should have some idea of what is called for in each area and be able to judge whether the design elements measure up in a given production.

67

(Ronald Searle, 1952)

Labels in drawing: Faith, Digestion, Adaptability to Weather, Bone, Hope, Love of crowds, Understanding, Notebook and pencil, Recollection, Charity, Knowledge of theatre, Deadlines, Bias, Anxiety to be read, Personality, Power, Command of telephone, Taste, Ambition, Sleep, Consideration for public, Memory, Lack of Thirst, Focus, Sight, Tolerance, Ability to read and write, Sight in dark, Hearing, Wit, Hunger, Ideality, Punctuality, Punctuation, Love of editors, Colour, Judgement, Turn of phrase, Modesty, Cut here, RS

THE IDEAL CRITIC.
In this drawing, the artist Ronald Searle humorously suggests the many qualities a person must have in order to be a good theater critic—everything from knowledge of the theater to adaptability to weather, from punctuality to punctuation.

Admittedly this is asking a great deal of a critic, and very few acquire the broad range of knowledge required, but it is an ideal to which all critics should aspire and which audiences have a right to expect of first-rate critics.

Critical Criteria

Along with a strong background, a good critic should develop criteria by which he or she judges a play and a production. The criteria should be a set of questions to ask each time the critic attends a performance.

One of the first questions is, *What is the play, and what is the production, attempting to do?* It is important to note that this question must be raised both about the script and about the production.

Regarding the script, the critic should make clear what the playwright is trying to accomplish in the play. Is it a tragedy meant to raise significant questions and stir deep emotions? Is it a light comedy intended to entertain and provide escape? Or is it a political drama arguing for a point of view? In order to answer these questions, the critic must be thoroughly steeped in the background material discussed above. Good critics include in their articles background information that can be of great value to audiences.

Turning from the script to the production, the critic must ascertain what the director, the performers, and the designers are attempting to accomplish. Are they trying faithfully to carry out the wishes of the playwright, or are they attempting to move in another direction? For example, are they representing the characters, the dialogue, and the situations in the play the way they were written, or are they altering these, as in the case of a director who wants to impose his or her own interpretation on a play? It is important for the critic to understand the

CRITICS PROVIDE BACKGROUND INFORMATION.

In addition to giving an opinion on the good and bad points of a theater production, the critic can provide important information to help audiences understand a theater event. For example, the production of Audience *by Vaclav Havel, shown here at the John Houseman Studio Theater with Lou Brockway and Kevin O'Connor, was far more meaningful to audiences who were aware of the background of the play and the playwright. Havel was a dissident Czechoslovakian dramatist who served time in prison and, after the change in government in Czechoslovakia in the fall of 1989, became president of the country. The play is set in a brewery where Havel was once forced to work when he was out of favor with the communist government.*

(*Suzanne Karp Krebs*)

69

CHAPTER 4 · THE CRITIC AND THE AUDIENCE

relationship between the production and the script and to see if they are integrated, and if they are not, why not.

A second question a critic must address is, *How well have the intentions of the playwright or the director been carried out?* In the case of a new script, if the play is intended to probe the deeper relationships in a family — of parents to children, or husbands to wives — how convincingly and how insightfully has the dramatist accomplished this? If the intention was to entertain, to make audiences laugh, the question must be asked, Just how funny is the play? Did it succeed in providing laughter and entertainment? Was it clever and witty and full of amusing situations, or did it fall flat?

In terms of production, a theater company may be producing an acknowledged masterpiece such as *Hamlet* or *Macbeth,* in which case the question becomes how well the play has been acted, directed, and designed. Have the performers brought Shakespeare's characters to life in a convincing and exciting way? Or has the director — perhaps by striving to be original or by updating the play and putting the characters into modern dress — distorted Shakespeare's intentions? In the latter case, the answer to the question, "Was the production well done?" would be a resounding "no."

A third question the critic might ask falls more in the realm of personal taste and evaluation. It can be stated as follows: *Is the play or production worth doing?* Many critics think that anything which succeeds at giving pleasure and providing entertainment is as worthwhile in its own way as a more serious undertaking. Others, however, do not. In cases like this, readers must make up their own minds. It is helpful, however, to have questions of value raised for spectators to consider when approaching a theater production.

If audience members are aware of these criteria, they can not only note whether critics — in print or on television — address these questions but can also ask the questions for themselves.

Descriptive and Prescriptive Criticism

In judging the worth of a play or theater event, critics frequently take one of two different approaches. One approach could be called *descriptive;* that is, it attempts to describe as clearly and accurately as possible what is happening in a play or a performance. The other could be termed *prescriptive* criticism, meaning that the critic not only describes what has been done but offers advice or comments about how it should be done.

Two theater critics from ancient times established these differing approaches to theater criticism. The Greek philosopher Aristotle (384–322 B.C.) undertook to analyze the tragedies of playwrights like Aeschylus (525–456 B.C.), Sophocles (ca. 496–406 B.C.), and Euripides (ca. 484–406

ARISTOTLE: THE FATHER OF THEATER CRITICISM.
The person who first undertook the analysis and definition of drama—especially of tragedy—was the Greek philosopher Aristotle. He described the elements of tragedy and discussed the effects of tragedy on spectators. All subsequent critics have built on his work.

B.C.). Aristotle was also a scientist, and his method was chiefly to describe tragedy: he attempted to break it down into its component parts and to note how it worked and what effect it had on spectators.

The Roman writer Horace (65–8 B.C.), on the other hand, attempted not just to describe but to *prescribe* what theater should be. In other words, Horace wished to establish rules for theater. He said, for example, that tragedy and comedy should never be mixed in the same play and that poetry should instruct as well as please the audience.

Since the time of Aristotle and Horace, critics have tended to fall into one category or the other: those who analyze and describe theater, and those who set down rules and say exactly what form plays and theater productions should follow. The second approach, it should be noted, can sometimes lead to a moralistic or overly rigid viewpoint about theater which restricts both the creativity of theater artists and the enjoyment of audiences.

The Reviewer and the Critic

One important distinction to be made on the subject of criticism is that between *reviewers* and *critics*.

A *reviewer*, who usually works for a television station, a newspaper, or a magazine, reports on what has occurred at the theater. He or she will tell briefly what the theater event is about, perhaps describing the plot and explaining whether it is a musical, a comedy, or a serious play.

The reviewer might also offer an opinion about whether the event is worth seeing or not. (Everyone has seen newspaper ads with quotations from reviewers saying such things as "A play not to be missed," and "A laugh riot; the whole family will enjoy it.") The reviewer is usually restricted by time, space, or both. The television reviewer, for instance, will have only a minute or two on the air to describe a play and offer a reaction. The newspaper reviewer, similarly, is restricted by the space available in the newspaper and by the newspaper's deadline.

Reviewers are frequently limited as well in terms of experience. A television or newspaper reviewer may have a strong background in theater studies or a good deal of practical experience, but that is the exception rather than the rule. Most often, reviewers have worked at other positions at a television station or on a newspaper and have simply been shifted to this beat. In such cases their work may lack depth and may not be based on knowledge of the critical criteria discussed above.

In contrast to the reviewer stands the *critic,* who attempts to go into greater detail in describing and analyzing a theater event. Critics generally work for magazines or scholarly journals. At times they write entire books about playwrights, groups of plays, and particular movements in the theater. The critic generally has more time to write his or her piece—perhaps several days or weeks rather than the few hours allotted to the reviewer. The critic also attempts to put the theater event into a larger context, relating the play to a category (nonrealism or realism, for instance). The critic will try to explain how the theater event fits into this framework or into the body of the work of the playwright. The critic might also put the theater event into a social, political, or cultural context. For example, plays by minority playwrights of the 1960s and 1970s could be looked at in terms of their relationship to the civil rights movement.

The critic attempts to analyze a theater event very closely, looking carefully at the purpose and point of view of the author, the dramatic structure, and the acting and directing, to determine how these elements fit together. Ideally, the critic has developed a personal point of view about various aspects of theater. He or she has arrived at an idea of how plays are put together, what constitutes good acting, what is expected of a realistic play as opposed to an experimental play, and so forth.

❊ THE AUDIENCE'S RELATIONSHIP TO CRITICISM: ❊ TWO ISSUES

As suggested earlier, when the audience combines an awareness of criticism with the theater event itself, the experience can be greatly enhanced, with background information and critical appraisals being

"Tell me, sir, is it good or bad?"

added to one's own firsthand reactions. There are cautionary notes, however, of which audience members should be aware.

The Audience's Independent Judgment

One word regarding critics: Quite often they state authoritatively that a certain play is extremely well written or badly written, beautifully performed or atrociously performed, and so on. Because critics often speak so confidently and because their opinions appear on television or in print, their words have the ring of authority. But theatergoers should not be intimidated by this. In New York City, where a number of critics and reviewers in various media comment on each Broadway production, there is a wide range of opinion. It is not unusual for half a dozen of them to find a certain play admirable, another half-dozen to find the same play highly objectionable, and still others to find a mixture of good and bad in it.

What this implies is that there is no absolute authority among critics, and that audience members should make up their own minds. If a critic, for example, dislikes a certain play because he or she finds it too sen-

73

timental and you happen to like that kind of sentiment, you should not be dissuaded from your own preferences.

In reading the works of critics, it is important to distinguish between *fact* and *opinion*. Opinion, as suggested above, should be carefully weighed. On the other hand, facts or insights presented by a critic can be extremely helpful. Critics can often make us aware of facts that we might not otherwise have known—for example, by explaining a point that was confusing to the audience or noting how a particular scene in a play relates to an earlier scene. The critic might also offer background information about the playwright, the subject matter of the play, or the style of the production. Such information can broaden the audience's understanding and appreciation of theater. The more we know about why a playwright arranges scenes in a given manner or about what a playwright is attempting to do, the better we will be able to judge the value of a theater event.

Analysis and Overanalysis

Is there a risk in trying to be very analytical and judgmental about a theater performance? There can be, of course. Some people are so preoccupied with trying to determine what is wrong with a play or performance that they lose all sense of immediacy. The spontaneity and joy of the experience are in danger of being sacrificed. Most critics, however, find that their alertness to what is happening during a performance helps rather than hinders their emotional response to the event. After all, human beings have an enormous capacity for receiving infomation on several levels simultaneously. We do it all the time in our daily lives. With a little practice the same thing can happen for audience members. We develop standards for theater events—a sense of what makes good theater—and we judge a performance by those standards; at the same time, however, we retain the capacity to lose ourselves in the overall experience.

In Chapters 1 through 4 we have examined the role of the audience and of a special audience member, the critic. Those who watch a theater performance are a necessary part of the theater equation. Earlier we said that the essence of the theater experience is the actor-audience relationship. In Part Two, we turn from the audience to the the other side of this theater equation: to the performers and the person who guides them, the director.

❋ SUMMARY ❋

1   Every person attending a theater event is an amateur critic, making judgments and drawing conclusions about what he or she sees.

2   The critic has several tasks: (*a*) to understand exactly what is being

presented, including the intentions of the playwright and the director; (*b*) to analyze the play, the acting, and the direction, as well as other elements such as scenery and lighting; (*c*) to evaluate the presentation—was this worth doing? does it serve a purpose? and so forth.

3   Criticism can be classified as *descriptive* and *prescriptive*. In descriptive criticism, the critic describes carefully and accurately what occurs. In prescriptive criticism, the critic undertakes to say not only what does happen but also what *should* happen in a theater production.

4   People commenting on theater can be divided into *reviewers,* who report briefly on a theater event in newspapers, magazines, or on television; and *critics,* who write longer articles analyzing in depth a performance or the work of a playwright.

5   Audience members must realize that critics, too, have their limitations and prejudices and that ultimately each individual spectator must arrive at his or her own judgment regarding a theater event.

✳ TOPICS FOR DISCUSSION ✳

1   Following are some hypothetical statements by critics. Are these types of statements by critics useful? Are they fair? Comment.

"I thought the humor was childish, but the audience seemed to love it." Is the critic implying that his or her standards are higher than those of the audience, and should the comment thus be dismissed as mere snobbery? Or does the critic have a responsibility to make it clear to readers that his or her reaction was not representative of the audience's?

"I left after the first act, because the play was so bad." Is a reviewer required to sit through an entire play, even if he or she considers it abysmal, in order to judge it fairly as a whole? Or is getting up and leaving a sensible, if extreme, comment in such a situation?

"The play was excellent, but the direction and the acting did not do it justice." Is it fair to separate elements in a production and find fault with one aspect while praising another? Or should a production be evaluated as a whole?

2   Would you add any criteria to the three outlined in this chapter? If so, explain them and defend them; if not, explain why you think these criteria are sufficient.

3   It was noted in the chapter that prescriptive criticism can tend to be moralistic or rigid and thus to restrict artists' creativity and audience enjoyment. Can you think of any drawbacks to the other school of criticism—descriptive criticism?

THE SPECIAL SKILLS OF ACTING

*In addition to talent and stage presence, acting requires a
number of special skills. In realistic drama, characters
must be made believable. Examples include Henrik
Ibsen's* A Doll's House *(preceding overleaf) and Anton
Chekhov's* Uncle Vanya *(opposite page, top).
American plays calling for realistic portrayals include
August Wilson's* The Piano Lesson *(opposite, bottom)
and, on this page, Eugene O'Neill's* Anna Christie
(top left) and Tennessee Williams's The Glass
Menagerie *(bottom left). Other types of drama require
special training in voice, body movement, and music.
Above is Cole Porter's musical* Kiss Me, Kate; *on the
following overleaf, Japanese kabuki (top left),* Electra
*by the Greek playwright Sophocles (top right), and
Shakespeare's* Much Ado about Nothing *(bottom).*

PART TWO

THE PERFORMERS
AND
THE DIRECTOR

THE MAGIC OF THEATER CREATED BY PERFORMERS AND THE DIRECTOR
In the drawing by Al Hirshfeld on the following pages, we see the director Jerome Robbins and a host of performers from Jerome Robbins' Broadway. *Acting in the theater—as well as singing and dancing—requires rigorous training on the part of performers in addition to dramatic talent. Performers must be completely believable in the characters they portray, but they must also train their voices and bodies to be able to perform the many special tasks called for in the theater. Guiding the work of performers is the director, shown here in the person of Mr. Robbins.*

5

ACTING:
OFFSTAGE AND ON

PLAYING A PART: IN THEATER AND IN LIFE.
*In life, people play many roles—as parents, teachers, students, lawyers, salesclerks, and so forth.
The theater often depicts these roles. For example, the play A Few Good Men, shown here with
Mark Nelson and Tom Hulce as military officers, is about a court-martial. Anyone who is in
the armed services (the navy or the marines, for instance) is playing a role as a military person,
in addition to his or her more personal roles with family and friends.*

P erformers, by their presence, set theater apart from films, television, and the visual arts; they serve as the direct, immediate contact which members of the audience have with theater. More than that, performers embody the heart and soul of theater. The words of the script, the characters created by the dramatist, and the scenery and costumes come to life only when an actor or actress steps on a stage.

In order to gain a preliminary understanding of the process of acting, it will be helpful to examine certain activities with which everyone is familiar—types of "acting" in everyday life. Though markedly different from stage acting, they demonstrate some of the resources on which performers draw.

✴ "ACTING" IN EVERYDAY LIFE ✴

Two forms of "acting" in daily life are *imitation* and *role playing*. After looking at these, we will explore some studies of everyday "acting."

Imitation

It may surprise some of us to realize to what degree "acting" is a part of our lives, beginning almost the day we are born. This offstage acting takes several forms, one of the most common being imitation, where one person mimics another's vocal patterns, gestures, facial expressions, posture, and the like. Children are among the best imitators in the world; and we are frequently amused at a child who imitates a parent or some other grown-up: a 5-year-old girl, for instance, who puts on a long dress, makeup, and high heels.

For children, imitation is more than just a matter of show; it is also a way of learning, a matter of education and even of survival. The child watches a parent open a door or walk up a flight of stairs and learns by imitation how to complete the same maneuver. Speech patterns, too, are imitated by children.

As we grow older, imitation continues to be a part of our experience: in every class in school, from elementary school through college, there is usually one person—a clever mimic—who imitates the teacher or the principal with great humor, and sometimes cruelty. A familiar type of imitation is the attempt to follow the lifestyle of a hero—a singer, a film actor, or some other well-known personality. In the 1950s it was Elvis Presley or James Dean; in the 1960s, the Beatles; in the 1970s, Mick Jagger, Carly Simon, or John Travolta; and in the 1980s, Michael Jackson, Cyndi Lauper, or Madonna. The imitator adopts the same wardrobe, the same stance, the same physical movements, and the same hairstyles as the hero or heroine.

(Giboux/Gamma-Liaison)

IMITATING ROLE MODELS.
Public figures like Madonna—the singer and film actress shown here—become models whose dress, mannerisms, etc., other people frequently imitate. Such imitation is a form of acting in everyday life.

Role Playing

A second type of "acting" prevalent in our daily lives is role playing, about which much has been written in recent years. A popular term in recent years is *role model,* referring to those people whose lives, or "roles," serve as models or guides for others. Broadly speaking, roles can be classified as *social* and *personal.*

SOCIAL ROLES   Social roles are general roles recognized by society: father, mother, child, police officer, store clerk, teacher, student, business executive, physician, and so on. Every culture expects definite types of behavior from people in these roles. For many years in western culture, for example, the roles of women as secretaries or housewives were considered subordinate to the roles of men. Even when women held similar positions to those of men in business and the professions, they frequently received smaller salaries for the same job. In recent years, the women's movement has challenged the notion of subservient roles of women. So entrenched was the idea, however, that it took an entire movement to call it into question. (*Consciousness-raising* was one aspect of the movement, making people aware of social attitudes toward women.) Before changes could begin to be made in the subordinate roles women played, everyone had to understand that they *were* roles.

CHAPTER 5 • ACTING: OFFSTAGE AND ON

In role playing, anyone occupying a given position is expected to adopt a predetermined attitude: a clerk in a store, for instance, or someone behind the counter in a fast-food chain is expected to take care of customers with patience and courtesy, and not bring individual frustrations to the job. It is important to remember, too, that each of us fills not one but many social roles. A young woman in college, working part time, might have the following roles: student, employee, daughter, sister, and friend, not to mention female, young person, and citizen.

PERSONAL ROLES Aside from social roles, we develop personal roles with our family and friends. For example, some of us become braggarts, boasting of our feats and accomplishments (some of them imaginary), and we embellish the truth to appear more impressive than we are. Others become martyrs, constantly sacrificing for others and letting the world know about it. A third type consists of conspirators, people who pull their friends aside to establish an air of secrecy whenever they talk. Frequently, two people fall into complementary roles, one dominant and the other submissive, one active and the other passive.

ROLE PLAYING ILLUSTRATED IN DRAMA Interestingly enough, drama contains many illustrations of the kind of acting we do in our everyday lives. A good example is a scene from *Death of a Salesman* by Arthur Miller, in which Happy, the salesman's son, tries to be a "big shot" in a restaurant where he is about to meet his father and his brother, Biff. Happy's father, the salesman, has just lost his job and is on the verge of losing his sanity as well. Happy should be thinking only of his father, but he cannot resist trying to impress a woman who enters the restaurant. (Biff, Happy's brother, enters in the middle of the scene. As the scene begins, Stanley, the waiter, speaks to Happy about the woman.)

STANLEY: I think that's for you, Mr. Loman.
HAPPY: Look at that mouth. Oh, God, and the binoculars.
STANLEY: Geez, you got a life, Mr. Loman.
HAPPY: Wait on her.
STANLEY: [Going to the Girl's table] Would you like a menu, ma'am?
GIRL: I'm expecting someone, but I'd like a—
HAPPY: Why don't you bring her—excuse me miss, do you mind? I sell champagne, and I'd like you to try my brand. Bring her a champagne, Stanley.
GIRL: That's awfully nice of you.
HAPPY: Don't mention it. It's all company money. [He laughs]
GIRL: That's a charming product to be selling, isn't it?
HAPPY: Oh, gets to be like everything else, selling is selling, y'know.
GIRL: I suppose.
HAPPY: You don't happen to sell, do you?

PLAYING THE BIG SHOT.

Shown here is a scene from the Hartman Theater Company's production of Arthur Miller's Death of a Salesman, *in which Happy (right) attempts to impress a woman with how important he is. In doing so, Happy overstates his accomplishments, just as people in life sometimes do.*

GIRL: No, I don't sell.

HAPPY: Would you object to a compliment from a stranger? You ought to be on a magazine cover.

GIRL: [Looking at him a little archly] I have been. [Stanley comes in with a glass of champagne]

HAPPY: What'd I say before, Stanley? You see? She's a cover girl.

STANLEY: Oh, I could see, I could see.

HAPPY: [To the Girl] What magazine?

GIRL: Oh, a lot of them. [She takes the drink] Thank you.

HAPPY: You know what they say in France don't you? "Champagne is the drink of the complexion"—Hiya, Biff! [Biff has entered and sits with Happy]

BIFF: Hello, kid. Sorry I'm late.

HAPPY: I just got here. Uh, Miss—?

GIRL: Forsythe.

HAPPY:	Miss Forsythe, this is my brother.
BIFF:	Is Dad here?
HAPPY:	His name is Biff. You might've heard of him. Great football player.
GIRL:	Really? What team?
HAPPY:	Are you familiar with football?
GIRL:	No, I'm afraid not.
HAPPY:	Biff is quarterback with the New York Giants.
GIRL:	Well, that is nice, isn't it? [She drinks]
HAPPY:	Good health.
GIRL:	I'm happy to meet you.
HAPPY:	That's my name. Hap. It's really Harold but at West Point they called me Happy.
GIRL:	[Now really impressed] Oh, I see. How do you do? [She turns her profile]
BIFF:	Isn't Dad coming?
HAPPY:	You want her?
BIFF:	Oh, I could never make that.
HAPPY:	I remember the time that idea would never come into your head. Where's the old confidence, Biff?
BIFF:	I just saw Oliver—
HAPPY:	Wait a minute. I've got to see that old confidence again. Do you want her? She's on call.
BIFF:	Oh, no. [He turns to look at the Girl]
HAPPY:	I'm telling you. Watch this. [Turning to the Girl] Honey? [She turns to him] Are you busy?
GIRL:	Well, I am . . . but I could make a phone call.
HAPPY:	Do that, will you, honey? And see if you can get a friend. We'll be here for a while. Biff is one of the greatest football players in the country.
GIRL:	[Standing up] Well, I'm certainly happy to meet you.
HAPPY:	Come back soon.
GIRL:	I'll try.
HAPPY:	Don't try, honey, try hard.[1]

In this scene, Happy is pretending to be something he is not. He is "playing the role" of the successful operator—the man with numerous accomplishments and abilities, which, of course, he does not actually possess. Like imitation and similar activities, this kind of "acting" is encountered frequently in daily life.

Studies of "Acting" in Daily Life

Erving Goffman states in his book *The Presentation of Self in Everyday Life,* "Life itself is a dramatically enacted thing. All the world is not, of course, a stage, but the crucial ways in which it isn't are not easy to specify."[2] Goffman is saying, in effect, that acting is so much a part of the real world that it is often difficult to identify it.

Studies by others—scholars and popular writers alike—attest to the importance of various kinds of "acting" in real life. Among studies on this subject are *Games People Play*, a successful book of some years ago concerned with role playing in interpersonal relationships; and *Body Language*, dealing with the gestures and movements we make to signal feelings, emotions, and responses to one another.

In a more scholarly vein, writers have argued that only in our various roles do we have any personality at all. Robert Ezra Park, in an important book, *Race and Culture*, noted a relationship between the words *person* and *mask*—the latter being closely associated with theater. He writes:

> It is probably no mere historical accident that the word person, in its first meaning, is a mask. It is rather a recognition of the fact that everyone is always, and everywhere, more or less consciously, playing a role. . . . It is in these roles that we know each other. It is in these roles that we know ourselves.[3]

✳ ACTING ONSTAGE ✳

Acting in Life and Acting Onstage: Similarities and Differences

The better we understand acting in daily life, the better we understand acting on the stage. There are similarities between the two: the processes and techniques which ordinary people employ to convey an image of themselves—words, gestures, "body language," tone of voice, subtle suggestions of intent—are the same tools actors use to create a stage character. Further, an actor or actress plays both a social and a personal role. An actress playing the part of a matronly woman dominating her household adopts the mannerisms and attitudes of a strong mother figure as understood in a given society.

For all the similarities between the two kinds of acting, however, the differences are crucial and reveal a great deal about the nature of stage acting. Some of the differences are obvious. For one thing, actors and actresses onstage are always being observed. In real life there may be observers, but their presence is not essential to the event. Bystanders on a street corner where an accident has occurred form a kind of audience, but their presence is incidental and unrelated to the accident itself. Onstage, however, the performer is always on display and always in the spotlight.

Acting onstage, too, requires a performer to play roles he or she does

87

PART TWO • THE PERFORMERS AND THE DIRECTOR

Opposite page: In the theater, more than in life, performers are called on to play widely diverse parts. Frequently, also, they portray people unlike themselves. Christopher Walken, for instance, is shown here in three quite different parts. At top, he is Vershinin, an unhappy military man in nineteenth-century Russia in Chekhov's The Three Sisters; *at bottom left, he is the headstrong Coriolanus in the play of that name by Shakespeare; and at bottom right, he is a documentary film maker in a modern play,* Cinders, *by the Polish playwright Janusz Glowacki.*

not play in life. A scene between a father and his son arguing about money or between a young husband and wife discussing whether or not to have children is one thing when it actually occurs, but something quite different onstage. Generally, the roles we play in life are genuine. A father who accepts his responsibilities toward his children does not just *play* a father; he *is* a father. A woman who writes for a magazine does not just *play* a magazine writer; she *is* one.

In real life, a lawyer knows the law; but onstage, an actor playing the role of a lawyer may not know the difference between jurisprudence and habeas corpus, and probably has never been inside a law school. Playing widely divergent parts or parts outside their personal experience requires actors and actresses to stretch their imagination and ability. For example, a young actress at one time or another might be called on to play parts as dissimilar as the fiery, independent Antigone in Sophocles's play, the vulnerable, love-struck Juliet in *Romeo and Juliet,* and the neurotic, obsessed heroine in Strindberg's *Miss Julie.*

At times performers even have to *double,* that is, play several parts in one play. In the Greek theater it was customary to have only three principal actors; each of them had to play several parts, putting on masks and different costumes to assume the various roles. Bertolt Brecht, a German dramatist, wrote many large-cast plays which call for doubling. His play *The Caucasian Chalk Circle* has forty-seven speaking parts, but it can be produced with only twenty-five performers. Another Brecht play, *The Good Woman of Setzuan,* has a fascinating situation written into the play calling for doubling. The actress playing the lead character, who gets pregnant during the course of the play, must also play the part of her cousin, who is a man. *The Screens,* by the French playwright Jean Genêt (1909–   ), has ninety-eight characters; but—as Genêt himself has written—"each actor will be required to play five or six roles."

Another important difference between acting onstage and in real life is that a theatrical performance is always *conscious.* There is an awareness by actors and audience that the presentation has been planned ahead of time. This consciousness of a performance sometimes leads to a more *truthful* reenactment than we encounter in real life. The facade, or false face, that people sometimes present in daily life can never occur

DOUBLING IN ONE PLAY.

At times performers play two or more parts in a single play. An example is Tom Irwin in The Grapes of Wrath. *At the top he is a narrator in the production; at the bottom he portrays a man in rags (right).*

in stage acting, because there is no attempt in the theater to deceive the audience about the imaginary nature of stage acting. As Theodore Shank explains it: "Acting is not pretense. An actor does not pretend to be Macbeth as an imposter pretends to be what he is not; instead he creates an appearance which is intended for perception as an illusion."[4]

Shank's statement that a performer "creates an appearance which is intended for perception as an illusion" underscores a significant difference between acting for the stage and "acting" in life: that dramatic characters are not real people. In discussing symbol and metaphor in Chapter 2, we said that an actress standing onstage in the role of Joan of Arc was a metaphor for Joan. Any stage character—Joan of Arc, Antigone, Oedipus, Hamlet—is a symbol or an image of a person. Stage characters are fictions created by dramatists and performers to represent people. They remind us of people—in many cases they seem to *be* the people—but they are not. They have no corporeal reality, as you and I do, but rather exist in our imaginations. (We will discuss this concept in more detail in Chapter 12 on dramatic characters.)

The Discipline of Acting

As noted above, unlike "acting" in daily life, performing on the stage is always observed; it requires performers to play roles not part of their own training and experience; and it is conscious and deliberate. Because of these factors, acting for the stage is hard work. Professional acting calls for a dedication of resources, a mental toughness, and a willingness to persist that are often camouflaged by the glamorous life and the financial rewards reported in the media. Successful performers are interviewed on television or written up in newspapers and magazines; books are written about them. The publicity is deceptive, however; it disguises the fact that acting for the stage is a difficult, disciplined profession. For all its glamor, it requires years of study and training— and weeks or months of preparation for a single role.

One objective of a performance is to make it look natural and easy— to suggest to the audience that playing the role is effortless, just as a juggler attempts to look as casual and carefree as possible. One reason for the attempt to make acting look effortless is to relax the audience and let it concentrate on believing in the character rather than focusing on the lengthy and arduous preparation required of the performer.

To achieve such ease and grace of performance calls for a dedication and discipline that few people outside competitive sports or the performing arts can understand. Rigorous training, long hours of dull repetition, bouncing back from discouragement: all this and more is called for if one is to make even a beginning in the profession. Just how one prepares for stage acting is the subject of Chapter 6.

✻ SUMMARY ✻

1   Acting is not as mysterious or removed from daily life as it is sometimes thought to be; all human beings engage in certain forms of acting.

2   Imitation and role playing are excellent examples of acting in everyday life.

3   Acting on the stage differs from acting in everyday life, in the first place, because the stage actor or actress is always being observed by an audience.

4   Acting for the stage involves playing roles for which the performer has no direct experience in life.

5   Stage performers must play roles which are symbolic and which make special demands on their skills and imagination.

6   Acting is a difficult, demanding profession. Despite its glamor, it calls for arduous training and preparation.

❋ TOPICS FOR DISCUSSION ❋

1 Role playing has become an important concept in psychology and sociology. Why would you suppose it is so useful in describing and explaining human personality and social interactions?

2 As the chapter notes, roles can be broadly classified as *social* and *personal*. Should these two types of roles complement one another? Explain. What happens if they do not complement each other?

3 In this chapter, Robert Ezra Park is quoted as saying that we know both ourselves and others in terms of roles. Defend or attack the following statement: "We may indeed know others primarily through roles, but we know ourselves in other, more immediate terms."

4 The chapter points out that there are similarities and differences between acting in life and acting onstage. Which do you think gives us more, or deeper, insights about stage acting—the similarities or the differences? Why?

5 In the chapter, it is noted that one reason for trying to make acting seem effortless is to relax the audience and let it concentrate on believing in a character. What other reasons might there be?

6

STAGE
ACTING

THE CHALLENGE OF STAGE ACTING.
To play a character convincingly, a performer must learn to develop both outer techniques and inner, emotional resources. Seen here are two actresses in an emotional scene from Chekhov's The Three Sisters, *in a production at the Hartman Theater Company.*

There are two main challenges involved in becoming a successful actress or actor: one is to learn how to make the characters portrayed believable, and the other is to acquire the many special skills—both physical and vocal—that stage performances demand. As if these two tasks were not enough, there is a third challenge, perhaps the most difficult of all, which is to combine the two: to integrate special skills with credibility of the character.

In order to understand these two aspects of acting, we will examine them separately, beginning with the believability of the character and then moving to special skills. We will then examine how they are combined. Finally, we will consider how this understanding enables us to judge performers.

❋ MAKING DRAMATIC CHARACTERS BELIEVABLE ❋

In order for the audience to believe the characters onstage, performers must be credible and convincing in their roles. One enemy of credibility is exaggeration. The stage is a showplace: a performer stands on a platform in the spotlight—the focus of the audience's attentions. The natural temptation under these circumstances is to "show off"—to use broad, grandiose gestures; speak in a loud, rhetorical voice; or otherwise call attention to oneself. Some exaggeration is necessary in stage acting, and certain roles call for eloquent speech and the grand gesture, particularly in classical theater, but never to the point of overacting or doing too much. When the audience focuses on the performer's behavior, the character is forgotten; in its most extreme form overacting becomes laughable.

Historical Precedents of Naturalistic Acting

In view of this, it is not surprising that throughout the history of theater we find commentators cautioning performers against excessive, unnatural acting. In Shakespeare, Hamlet's advice to the players is an example.

> Speak the speech, I pray you, as I pronounced it to you, trippingly on the tongue: but if you mouth it, as many of your players do, I had as lief the town-crier spoke my lines. Nor do not saw the air too much with your hand, thus, but use all gently; for in the very torrent, tempest, and, as I may say, the whirlwind of your passion, you must acquire and beget a temperance that may give it smoothness. Oh, it offends me to the soul to hear a robustious periwig-pated fellow tear a passion to tatters, to very rags. . . . Be not too tame neither, but let your discretion be your tutor: suit the action to the word, the word to the action; with this special observance, that you o'erstep not the modesty of nature: for anything so overdone is from the purpose of playing, whose end, both at the first and now, was and is, to hold, as't were, the mirror up to nature.

96

Shakespeare himself was an actor, and no doubt he had seen performers "saw the air" with their hands and "tear a passion to tatters."

In France, in the seventeenth century, Molière spoke out for honest acting in his short play *The Impromptu of Versailles*. He mocked actors in a rival company who ended each phrase with a flourish in order to get applause. (The term *claptrap*, incidentally, comes from a performance practice of that period: actors often concluded a speech with some final flourish of the hand or vocal inflection, thereby setting a "clap trap" and provoking applause.) Molière criticized actresses who preserved a silly smile even in a tragic scene; he pointed to the ridiculous practice of two performers in an intimate scene—two young lovers together or a king alone with his lieutenant—declaiming as if they were addressing the multitudes.

In England, throughout the eighteenth and nineteenth centuries, acting alternated between exaggerated and natural styles. Most performers tended toward the former approach; but every generation or so, someone came along who approached acting in a more down-to-earth manner. A good example is the eighteenth-century actor David Garrick (1717–1779), who gained fame for his reasonable approach to acting. A commentator described the contrast between Garrick and his predecessors playing the role of Shakespeare's Richard III:

> Instead of declaiming the verse in a thunderous, measured chant, this actor [Garrick] *spoke* it with swift and "natural" changes of tone and emphasis. Instead of patrolling the boards with solemn pomp, treading heavily from pose to traditional pose, he moved quickly and gracefully. Instead of standing on his dignity and marbling his face into a tragedian's mask, his mobile features illustrated Richard's whole range of turbulent feelings. He seemed, indeed, to identify himself with the part. It was all so *real*.[1]

From the mid-seventeenth century on, serious attempts were made to define the craft or technique of acting, the most noteworthy being those of Denis Diderot (1713–1784) in the eighteenth century and François Delsarte (1811–1871) in the nineteenth century. Diderot attempted to introduce more realism and believability into acting by endorsing the use of prose dialogue instead of poetry. In the next century, Delsarte devised a system of expression in which the performers' thoughts and emotions are reduced to a fixed set of poses and attitudes accomplished through a selective use of body and voice. In time, however, Delsarte's system became overly mechanistic and unworkable.

Realistic Acting Techniques in the Modern Theater: The Stanislavski System

A realistic approach to acting became more important than ever at the close of the nineteenth century, when the drama of that time began to depict characters and situations close to everyday life. Not only the spirit

97

REALISTIC ACTING.

In contrast to some of the classics, which often call for more declamatory acting, many modern plays require natural performances—closer to the behavior we see in daily life. An example is Burn This *by Lanford Wilson; shown here is a scene with John Malkovich (left) and Joan Allen (right).*

of the part but also the details had to conform to what people saw of life around them. This placed great demands on actors and actresses to avoid any hint of fakery or superficiality.

Before the late 1900s no one had successfully devised a method for achieving this kind of absolute believability. Individual actresses and actors through their talent and genius had achieved it, of course, in every age, but no one had developed a system whereby it could be taught to others and passed on to future generations. The person who was able to accomplish this was the Russian actor and director Constantin Stanislavski (1863–1938).

A cofounder of the Moscow Art Theater in Russia and the director of Chekhov's most important plays, Stanislavski was an actor as well as a director. He was involved in both classic theater—using nonrealistic techniques—and the emergence of the modern realistic approach. It is the latter aspect of his work that we will look at.

By closely observing the performances of great actors of his day, such as Tommaso Salvini (1829–1916), Eleonora Duse (1859–1924), and Feodor Chaliapin (1873–1938), and by drawing on his own acting experience, Stanislavski isolated and described what these gifted performers did naturally, intuitively. From his observations he compiled and then codified a series of principles and techniques which serve as the foundation of realistic actor training still practiced today.

At first glance, it would seem that the easiest thing in the world would be for actors to stand onstage and be themselves: to wear their own clothes and to speak normally. All we have to remember, however, is what it is like to stand up in front of a classroom to make a statement or give a report. Even if we only have to "say a few words," our mouth goes dry, our legs tremble, and the most difficult task in the world is to "be natural." You can multiply this feeling—*stage fright*, it is sometimes called—many times over for actors and actresses who stand onstage, bright lights in their eyes, trying to remember lines and movements, knowing that hundreds of eyes are focused on them. Fine actresses and actors learn to deal with the feeling—and even turn it to advantage—but many will admit that they never completely lose the terror any human being feels when being observed and judged by others.

Stanislavski, keenly aware of this problem, wrote:

> All of our acts, even the simplest, which are so familiar to us in everyday life, become strained when we appear behind the footlights before a public of a thousand people. That is why it is necessary to correct ourselves and learn again how to walk, sit, or lie down. It is essential to re-educate ourselves to look and see, on the stage, to listen and to hear.[2]

Stanislavski amplified his notions about the "reeducation" of performers to get rid of mechanical, external acting and to replace it with naturalness and truth. In his words: "The actor must first of all believe in everything that takes place onstage, and most of all, he must believe what he himself is doing. And one can only believe in the truth."[3]

To give substance to his ideas, Stanislavski studied how people acted in everyday life and how they communicated feelings and emotions. Then he found ways to accomplish the same things onstage by developing a series of exercises and techniques for performers.

The following are the major features of Stanislavski's technique.

RELAXATION   In his observation of the great actors and actresses of his day, Stanislavski noticed how fluid and lifelike their movements were. They seemed to be in a complete state of freedom and relaxation, allowing the behavior of characters to come through effortlessly. He concluded that unwanted tension has to be eliminated and that the performer must attain at all times a state of physical and vocal *relaxation*.

As long as you have this physical tenseness you cannot even think about delicate shadings of feeling or the spiritual life of your part. Consequently, before you attempt to create anything it is necessary for you to get your muscles in proper condition, so they do not impede your actions.[4]

CONCENTRATION AND OBSERVATION   Along with relaxation, Stanislavski discovered that the gifted performer always appeared fully concentrated on some object, person, or event while onstage. It is as if fully concentrated performers achieve "public solitude" because they appear oblivious of the audience. That is, while in the presence of the audience, their concentration separates them from the audience. Stanislavski referred to the actor's extent or range of concentration as a *circle of attention*. The circle of attention can be compared to a circle of light on a darkened stage. The performer should begin with the idea that this is a small, tight circle including only the performer and perhaps one other person, and a single piece of furniture such as a desk or chair. After focus is firmly fixed on this circle, the spotlight can be widened to include other people and a wider area on the stage. When the performer has established a strong circle of attention, he or she can enlarge concentration outward to include the entire stage area. In this way performers stop worrying about the audience and lose their self-consciousness.

To help actresses and actors develop powers of concentration onstage, Stanislavski encouraged them to observe and concentrate in real life. They had to learn to see, not superficially but with penetration and depth, storing images for eventual use onstage. They were to seek out beauty, especially in nature, as well as familiarize themselves with the "darker side of life"; they had to be knowledgeable about human relationships.

> After you have learned how to observe life around you and draw on it for your work you will turn to the study of the most necessary, important, and living emotional material on which your main creativeness is based. I mean intercourse with other human beings. This material is difficult to obtain because in large part it is intangible, indefinable, and only inwardly perceivable.[5]

IMPORTANCE OF SPECIFICS   One of Stanislavski's techniques was an emphasis on concrete details. A performer should never try to act *in general*, that is, try to convey the idea of a feeling such as fear or love in some vague, amorphous way. In life, Stanislavski said, we express emotions in terms of specifics: an anxious woman twists a handkerchief, an angry young boy throws a rock at a trash can, a nervous businessman jangles his keys. Performers must find the same *concrete* activities. Stanislavski points out how Shakespeare has Lady Macbeth in her sleepwalking scene—at the height of her guilt and emotional upheaval—try to rub blood off her hands.

THE IMPORTANCE OF SPECIFICS IN ACTING.
In keeping with Constantin Stanislavski's idea that performers should concentrate on specifics, the playwright Tennessee Williams has provided the character of Laura in his play
The Glass Menagerie *with a collection of glass animals with which she is preoccupied. Seen here is Tracy Sallows as Laura, holding a glass unicorn, in a production at the Guthrie Theater in Minneapolis.*

Many times playwrights provide such specifics for performers: King Lear asks to have his coat unbuttoned in his final moments; Laura, in *The Glass Menagerie* by Tennessee Williams, plays with glass animals. Bertolt Brecht in *Mother Courage* gives the characters many specific props to work with, such as a wagon which Mother Courage and her children pull throughout the play and a drum which her mute daughter Kattrin beats to warn a nearby town of a military attack. In *The Cherry Orchard* by Anton Chekhov, Varya, the daughter of Madame Lyubov, as manager of the household, keeps at her side a large bunch of keys.

When a script does not indicate such tangible actions, the performer must find them. Michael Chekhov, nephew of the playwright and a follower of Stanislavski, coined the term *psychological gesture* for a typical, characteristic movement or activity which would sum up a character's motives and preoccupations. A man who is confused or has trouble "seeing clearly," for example, might continually try to clean his glasses.

THE CHERRY ORCHARD (1904)

ANTON CHEKHOV (1860–1904)

CHIEF CHARACTERS:
Lyubov Andreyevna—owner of the estate
Anya—her daughter, 17 years old
Varya—her adopted daughter, 24 years old
Gaev—her brother
Lopahin—a merchant
Trofimov—a student
Charlotta—a governess
Firs—an old servant
Yasha—a young servant

ACT I: The scene is the nursery in the country estate of Lyubov Andreyevna. Lyubov has returned to Russia from a self-imposed exile in Paris to seek peace in her girlhood home. She is accompanied by her daughter, Anya, age 17, who had gone to Paris to make the return trip with her mother, and Lyubov's brother Gaev, an ineffectual aristocrat whose chief interests are playing billiards and eating caramels. Lyubov's estate, with its famous cherry orchard, is heavily mortgaged and is about to be foreclosed, leaving the family virtually penniless. Lyubov, absent since the death of her husband seven years before, laments her past. Among those who have come to greet her is Lopahin, a merchant who recalls Lyubov as a splendid, kindhearted woman who befriended him when he was a peasant child. Lopahin's father had been a serf on the estate.

Varya, Lyubov's adopted daughter, is the housekeeper of the estate. Anya tells Varya that her mother simply cannot understand the change in their fortunes. Although they had only enough money for the trip from Paris, Lyubov brought her young valet Yasha with her, as well as Anya's governess Charlotta. Along the way she also wasted money on expensive meals. The merchant, Lopahin, is supposed to marry Varya, but Varya tells Anya that Lopahin still has failed to propose to her, despite a neighborhood assumption that they are to marry.

ACT II: The scene is a meadow near an old chapel not far from the house. Lopahin tells Madame Lyubov that he will always be grateful to her for her kindness to him when his father and grandfather were serfs of her family. He tells her that she can avert the forced sale of the estate, set for August, if she will tear down the cherry orchard and develop the land for summer villas. He offers a loan to help, but Lyubov and Gaev cannot bear the thought of destroying the beautiful old orchard. Trofimov, a student, makes a speech about the lazy intelligentsia of Russia and says that they should work. He himself, however, does not work.

Later, Lopahin persists, but Lyubov chatters of a telegram from her lover, demanding that she return to Paris; she talks of summoning an orchestra for a dance some evening and laments the drabness of the peasants' lives. She promptly discourages Gaev's plan to work in a bank. In other words, she does nothing to save the estate. Although the servants and family have only soup to eat, she gives a beggar a gold piece and calls for another loan from Lopahin.

ACT III: It is an evening in August in the drawing room of the house. Lyubov has engaged an orchestra for a dance, although it is the evening of the sale of the estate. Her daughter Varya comforts her with the assurance that Gaev, who has attended the sale, probably has bought the estate with money to be sent by a wealthy great-aunt, but Lyubov knows that the sum is not enough. She tells Trofimov, the penniless student who has won the heart of Anya, that she cannot conceive of life without the house and orchard. Madame Lyubov also tells Trofimov that he should experience more of life, perhaps even have a mistress. He angrily stamps out of the room. Gaev and Lopahin, the latter giddy with joy, return. Lyubov demands to know at once if the home is lost. Lopahin cries: "I have bought it! . . . Now the cherry orchard's mine! Mine! . . . I have bought the estate where my father and grandfather were slaves." Lyubov sits down, crushed and weeping.

ACT IV: The scene is the same as Act I, the nursery. The nursery is now stripped bare, and the time for leave-taking has come. Lyubov, her face pale and quivering, has given her purse to the peasants. Gaev is to work in a bank; Lyubov is going to Paris to live as long as possible on the money sent by the great-aunt; Varya, still waiting in vain for Lopahin's proposal, is to be a housekeeper in a distant town; Anya is to remain in school while Trofimov, her betrothed, completes his studies in Moscow. Lopahin has brought a bottle of champagne, but only Yasha drinks. An ax is heard in the distance, and Anya pleads for the workers chopping down the cherry trees to wait until Madame Lyubov has gone. Lyubov, gallantly courageous now, says her farewells and speaks of only two cares: the health of the old butler Firs and the future of her daughter Varya. She is assured that Firs has been sent to the hospital and is promised by Lopahin that he will marry Varya; but Lopahin is left alone with

Varya, and again he fails to propose to the weeping girl.

Everyone leaves. Lyubov and Gaev, the last to go, wait until they are alone and fall into each other's arms in smothered sobs, afraid of being overheard. Lyubov weeps: "Oh, my orchard!—my sweet, beautiful orchard! My life, my youth, my happiness, good-bye!" They leave, and the ancient servant Firs, who has not been sent to a hospital and is deathly ill, totters in and lies down on a sofa; he has been left behind. Nearby is the sound of an ax cutting down the trees of the cherry orchard.

(Martha Swope/BAM)

INNER TRUTH   An innovative aspect of Stanislavski's work has to do with *inner truth*, which deals with the inner or subjective world of characters—that is, their thoughts and emotions. Inner truth is what we sense when a performer's conveying of an emotion or feeling—sorrow, anger, joy—is an accurate reflection of a character's feelings. Even when we are confronted with hypocrisy or insincerity, we can see beyond these to a truthful representation of the character's inner state.

Coincidental with Stanislavski's research was his work directing the major dramas of Chekhov. Plays like *The Cherry Orchard* have less to do with external action and what the characters say than with what the characters are feeling and thinking and often do not verbalize. It becomes apparent that the Stanislavski approach would be very beneficial in realizing the inner life—the values—of such characters.

We can better understand Stanislavski's achievements in the theater if we compare "inner truth" with the pioneering efforts of Sigmund Freud in psychology. Before Freud, little was understood about the function of the unconscious mind and its effects on emotional health. But Freud, by using such techniques as hypnosis and the analysis of dreams, was able to reach the unconscious mind. Similarly, Stanislavski discovered that the unconscious, creative energies of the performer (which are inaccessible to his or her conscious will) can be tapped through a deliberate, controllable technique.

Stanislavski had several ideas about how to achieve a sense of inner truth, one being the "magic if." *If* is a word which can transform our thoughts. Through it we can imagine ourselves in virtually any situation. "*If* I suddenly became rich . . . " "*If* I were in the Carribean . . . " "*If* I had great talent . . . " "*If* that person who insulted me comes near me again . . . " *If* is a powerful lever of the mind, which can lift us out of ourselves and give us a sense of absolute certainty about imaginary circumstances.

To take an example: if we spend a night alone in a strange room, in a cabin in the woods or a house far from home, and we hear a noise in the night—a floorboard creaking or a door opening—we become frightened, particularly if there have been stories of burglaries or break-ins in the area. If the noise comes again, our anxiety increases. We lie absolutely still, our breath shortens, and our heartbeat quickens. Finally, after a time, if nothing has happened, we find the courage to get out of bed and turn on a light. It turns out to be nothing—a rusty hinge on a door or a tree limb brushing the side of the house—but before we discovered the truth, the "magic if" worked its magic: we were convinced that we were in great danger.

Stanislavski urged actors and actresses to use this same power of fantasy and imagination as a tool to induce reality on the stage. A performer can never actually *be* a dramatic character, but the performer can use *if.* "If *I* were a frightened, crippled young woman, how would *I* feel about meeting a young man I once admired?'' This is the question an actress playing Laura in *The Glass Menagerie* can ask herself; through the power of imagination she can put herself in Laura's place.

EMOTIONAL RECALL   A useful tool in achieving a sense of emotional truth onstage is what Stanislavski referred to as *emotional recall,* which is the remembering of a past experience in the performer's life that is similar to the one in the play. By recalling sensory impressions of an experience in the past (such as what color a room was painted, what the temperature was, where the furniture was placed) emotions from that time are aroused and can be used as the basis of feelings called for in the play.

A good example would be a scene of farewell, such as Emily saying good-bye to her family in Thornton Wilder's *Our Town*. Though dead, Emily goes back to earth for one day, after which she leaves forever. The actress playing Emily might recall a time in her own life when she had to say good-bye and was reluctant to do so—the first time she left home, perhaps, or the time she said good-bye to a young man she loved. Again, Stanislavski emphasizes details; the important thing for the actress to remember is where she was, what she wore, who she was with—not how she felt. From these concrete facts and images the feeling will follow. In Stanislavski's words:

> On the stage there cannot be under any circumstances, action which is directed immediately at the arousing of a feeling for its own sake. . . . All such feelings are the result of something that has gone on before. Of the thing that goes before, you should think as hard as you can. As for the result, it will produce itself.[6]

ACTION ON THE STAGE: WHAT? WHY? HOW?   Another important principle of Stanislavski's system is that all action onstage must have a purpose. This means that the performer's attention must always be focused on the enactment of a series of physical actions that are linked together by the circumstances of the play. Stanislavski determined these actions by asking three essential questions: What? Why? How? An action (the *what*) is performed, such as opening a door. What prompts the opening of the door is that someone calls the character's name (the *why*). The door is opened slowly, hesitantly (the *how*) because it is two o'clock in the morning and no one is expected.

Operating along with physical actions and forming an indivisible bond is the psychological aspect of stage action. Concerning this, Stanislavski said:

> The bond between body and soul is indivisible. The life of the one gives life to the other. Every physical act . . . has an inner source of feeling. Consequently we have both an inner and outer plane in every role, inter-

105

laced. A common objective makes them akin to one another and strengthens their bonds.[7]

In other words, for every physical action there is an underlying reason that justifies and motivates it.

THROUGH LINE OF A ROLE   In order to develop continuity in a part, the actor or actress should find the *superobjective* of the character. What is it, above all else, that the character wants to attain or achieve during the course of the play? If a goal can be established toward which the character strives, it will give the performer an overall objective. From this objective can be developed a core, or *through line*, which can be grasped, as a skier on a ski lift grabs a towline and is carried upward.

Harold Clurman, a well-known critic and director, refers to the through line as the *spine;* and when directing a play, he assigns a spine, or superobjective, to characters as a group and to each character individually. For Chekhov's *Uncle Vanya,* Clurman says that all the characters are dissatisfied with their lives and grumble a great deal; their spine, therefore, is "to make life better, find a way to be happy."[8] The title character, Vanya, hopes to escape from his dull, frustrating existence, but he fails. Other characters follow equally futile courses in pursuit of happiness—in their spine, or superobjective, in the play.

To help develop the through line, Stanislavski urged performers to divide scenes into units (sometimes called *beats*). In each unit there is an objective, and the intermediate objectives running through a play lead ultimately to the overall objective.

ENSEMBLE PLAYING   Except in one-person shows, performers do not act alone; they interact with other people. Stanislavski was aware that the tendency for many performers is to "stop acting," or lose their concentration, when they are not the main characters in a scene or when someone else is talking. These performers make a great effort when they are speaking but not when they are listening. This tendency destroys a performer's through line and causes the person to move in and out of a role.

To overcome this problem, Stanislavski urged performers to include other people onstage in their "circle of attention"—to listen carefully to others and to maintain their sense of inner truth even when they are not speaking or are not the focus of attention in a scene. In short, he emphasized what he called *communication.*

Stanislavski stressed that the performer should respond to the unceasing flow of stimuli by listening and *hearing,* by looking and *seeing,* by using all five senses to respond believably—not mechanically—to the impact of external and internal stimuli. In time, when a group of performers work closely together—listening attentively to one another, re-

PLAYING TOGETHER.

Good actors are aware of the importance of ensemble playing. Performers coordinate their work by listening carefully to one another, sensing one another's actions and moods, and responding alertly. Here we see Dana Ivey and Morgan Freeman, from the original cast of Driving Miss Daisy.

sponding genuinely and spontaneously—they begin to work as an *ensemble,* that is, a close-knit unit that communicates a sense of truth as a group, not just as individual actresses and actors.

VOICE AND BODY   Stanislavski championed the development of a highly trained voice and body that could express the myriad thoughts and feelings of the performer's inner life. He emphasized that the inner life of performers is insufficient by itself to convey to the audience the many shadings of character; therefore, a sensitive body and vocal instrument are an indispensable part of the craft of acting. This view is borne out in Stanislavski's last two books to be translated into English, *Building a Character* and *Creating the Role,* in which he stressed the importance of an extremely well developed and responsive instrument.

A NOTE ON APPLYING THE STANISLAVSKI SYSTEM   Stanislavski's views have been the cause of some controversy since his books were translated into English, almost fifty years ago; mostly, this is because there have been some misconceptions and confusion about his contribution to theater, specifically his "system." In many cases these mis-

107

conceptions stem from followers of Stanislavski who mistakenly emphasize only the inner, or emotional, side of his technique.

Also, because of the emergence of realism as a significant theater movement, the Stanislavski system has been seen by many as having value *only* in realistic theater and acting. But his system is in fact the equivalent of scales and études for a musician or bar work and body exercises for a dancer. Therefore, it is *fundamental* to the craft of acting. Stanislavski's work, viewed as a whole, can be seen as *universal,* serving the performer not only in realism but in stylized and avant-garde acting.

❋ SPECIAL SKILLS OF ACTING ❋

It was noted at the beginning of this chapter that there are two aspects to actors' training and the art of stage performance. The first, making a character believable, we have just examined. The second is a wide range of special skills. They are the equivalent of the technical skills in the other arts—such as learning the movements of ballet and developing the physical agility to carry them out, or learning to play a musical instrument and mastering difficult pieces in order to be able to perform them successfully in public.

Classical dramas from the past make special demands on both the voice and the body. So, too, do the nonrealistic plays of the modern era. We can understand these skills more clearly if we look at them separately, beginning with the voice.

Vocal Projection

A primary requirement for actors or actresses is to make certain that the lines they speak are clearly heard by the audience. In modern, realistic plays this requirement is made more difficult by the necessity of maintaining believability. The words of a man and a woman in an intimate love scene in real life would be barely audible even to people a few feet away. In the theater, however, every word must be heard by the entire audience, and to be heard throughout a theater seating a thousand people, a performer must *project,* that is, throw the voice into the audience so that it penetrates to the uttermost reaches of the theater. The performers must strike a balance, therefore, between credibility—in the case of a love scene, this means confidential, quiet tones—and the need to project. In order to develop projection and to achieve the kind of balance just described, the performer must train and rehearse extensively.

In the classic theater of the past—the theater from the fifth century B.C. in Greece to the middle of the nineteenth century—vocal demands on actors and actresses were even greater. The language of the plays was most often poetry, which required intensive training in order for the performer to speak it distinctly. There were added problems of projection, too. Greek amphitheaters, while marvels of acoustics, seated as many as 15,000 spectators in the open air, and to throw the voice to every corner of the theater without strain was no small task.

In the Elizabethan period in England, Christopher Marlowe, a contemporary of Shakespeare, wrote superb blank verse which makes severe demands on a performer's vocal abilities. An example is a speech in Marlowe's *Doctor Faustus,* addressed by Faustus to Helen of Troy, who has been called back from the dead to be with Faustus. In the speech Faustus says to Helen:

> O' thou art fairer than the evening's air
> Clad in the beauty of a thousand stars;
> Brighter art thou than flaming Jupiter
> When he appear'd to hapless Semele;
> More lovely than the monarch of the sky
> In wanton Arethusa's azured arms;
> And none but thou shalt be my paramour!

These seven lines of verse are part of a single sentence and, when spoken properly, should be delivered as part of one overall unit with the meaning carried from one line to the next. How many of us could manage that? A fine classical actor can speak the entire section at one time, giving it the necessary resonance and inflection as well. Beyond that, he can stand on the stage for 2 or 3 hours delivering such lines.

With the use of microphones and sound amplification so widespread today, we have increasingly lost our appreciation of the power of the spoken word. In the past, public speakers from Cicero to Abraham Lincoln stirred men and women with their oratory. Throughout its history, the stage has provided a natural platform for stirring speeches. Beginning with the Greeks, and continuing through the Elizabethans, the French and Spanish theaters of the seventeenth century, and other European theaters at the close of the nineteenth century, playwrights wrote magnificent lines, lines which performers, having honed their vocal skills to a fine point, delivered with zest. Any performer today who intends to act in revivals of classical plays must learn to speak and project stage verse, and this requires a vocal power and breath control usually found only among opera singers.

Physical Movement Onstage

As with the voice, traditional theater makes strong demands on the performer's body. In Shakespeare, for instance, characters are always running up and down steps or ramps, acting out prolonged death scenes, or meeting other characters in sword fights. Anyone who has

THE PHYSICAL DEMANDS OF STAGE ACTING.
Performers must frequently perform difficult physical feats which require training, discipline, and expert timing. An example would be a duel or sword fight; another example is musical theater. Shown here are dancers in a scene from The King and I *which was included in the production* Jerome Robbins' Broadway.

seen a first-rate sword fight onstage knows how difficult and impressive it can be. A duel—in which the combatants strike quickly at one another, clashing swords frequently without hitting each other—resembles a ballet in its precision and grace.

Adeptness in physical movement is also required in realistic acting. For example, an equivalent activity in a modern play would be a fistfight or a headlong fall down a flight of stairs.

There are other cases requiring special discipline or training. Obviously musical theater requires talent in singing and dancing. Coordination is important too: the members of a musical chorus must sing, dance, or move together, frequently in unison. Pantomime provides another demanding category of performance: without words or props a performer must indicate everything by physical suggestion, lifting an imaginary box or walking against an imaginary wind in a convincing fashion.

Similar stylization and symbolism characterize the acting of the classical theaters of India, China, and Japan. To achieve the absolute con-

FINGER LANGUAGE: A PART OF INDIAN ACTING AND DANCING.

The precise gestures of this Indian art—the graceful, symbolic movements—require extensive training and discipline to perfect. In the finger language shown above, the numbers indicate the following states or emotions: (1) separation or death, (2) meditation, (3) determination, (4) joy, (5) concentration, (6) rejection, (7) veneration, (8) proposal, (9) vexation, and (10) love.

THE FORMAL GESTURES OF ASIAN THEATER.

Most Asian acting requires careful, precise, formal gestures. Years of training are necessary before actors can perform correctly in Japanese kabuki theater and the more classic noh theater. Shown here, with careful gestures of hand, head, and body, are two performers in a scene from a kabuki production.

111

trol, the concentration, and the mastery of the body and nerves necessary to carry out the movements, the performers of the various classical Asian theaters train for years under the supervision of master teachers. Every movement of the performers is prescribed and carefully controlled, combining elements of formal ballet, pantomime, and sign language. Each gesture tells a story and means something quite specific—a true symbolism of physical movement. Between the fourth and the ninth centuries, plays in Sanskrit became the classical drama of India. For these Sanskrit plays, the gestures of the performers were conventionalized and rigidly adhered to. These included thirteen movements of the head, thirty-six of the eyes, seven of the eyebrows, six of the nose, five of the chest, twenty-four of the hands, thirty-two of the feet, and so forth.

Acting Requirements for Avant-Garde Theater

As in the classical theaters of Asia and the west, various forms of modern avant-garde theater also require special techniques.

AN ACTOR TRANSFORMED INTO A BEETLE.
In a stage version of Kafka's Metamorphosis, *Mikhail Baryshnikov—with his gestures, his posture, and his body movements—changed himself into a creature strongly resembling a beetle. Such effects require skill and prolonged practice.*

(Martha Swope)

(Chris Bennion/Seattle Repertory Theater)

SPECIAL PROBLEMS IN ACTING.
Pantomime, improvisation, dance movements, acrobatics: these are among the types of performance requiring arduous training as well as skill and talent. A good example would be the postmodern vaudeville piece called Largely New York *which featured the mime artist Bill Irwin (left) and the dancer Margaret Eginton.*

A good example is Eugène Ionesco's play *Rhinoceros*. During the course of the play, one of the two chief characters turns into a rhinoceros. The actor playing this part does not actually put on horns or a leathery hide. Rather, he must physically transform himself by means of his posture, voice, and general demeanor. The critic Walter Kerr described how the actor Zero Mostel did this in the original Broadway production:

> Now the rhinoceros beneath the skin begins to bulge a little at the eyes. The Kaiser Wilhelm mustache that has earlier adorned the supposed Mr. Mostel loses its spiky endpoints, droops, disintegrates into a tangle that makes it second cousin to a walrus. The voice starts to change. "I hate people—and I'll r-r-run them down!" comes out of a larynx that has stiffened, gone hollow as a 1915 gramophone record, and is ready to produce a trumpet-sound that would empty all of Africa. The shoulders lift, the head juts forward, one foot begins to beat the earth with such native majesty that dust—real dust—begins to rise like the afterveil that seems to accompany a safari. The transformation is on, the secret is out, evolution has reversed itself before your horrified, but nevertheless delighted, eyes.[9]

In another avant-garde play, Samuel Beckett's *Happy Days,* an actress is buried onstage in a mound of earth up to her waist in the first act, and up to her neck in the second. She must carry on her performance through the entire play while virtually immobile.

In some types of avant-garde theater, the performers become acrobats, make human pyramids, or are used like pieces of furniture. In the play *Suitcase* by the Japanese playwright Kobo Abe (1924–   ), the suit-

(Richard Feldman)

THE UNIQUE DEMANDS OF AVANT-GARDE THEATER.
Experimental theater often demands special training and techniques. An example would be the theater productions of Robert Wilson; in this scene from his Knee Plays, *the performers must deal with unwieldy objects and move with the precision of dancers or acrobats.*

case of the title is played by an actor who must move about as if he is being carried like a piece of luggage. In another play by Abe, *The Man Who Turned into a Stick,* an actor must play the part of a stick.

The theater of Robert Wilson (1944–), and of Mabou Mines and similar groups, is sometimes referred to as *performance art.* In this type of theater, story, character, and text are minimized or even eliminated. The stress, rather than being on a narrative or on exploring recognizable characters, is on the visual and ritualistic aspects of theater. The overall effect is sometimes like a series of tableaux or a moving collage. As might be expected from this description, there is an affinity between this kind of theater and painting, because of the emphasis on the visual picture formed onstage. Stage movement in performance art is often closely related to dance, which means the performers must have the discipline, training, and control that dancers have.

In Robert Wilson's work, performers are frequently called on either to move constantly or to remain perfectly still. In pieces such as his *A Letter to Queen Victoria,* two performers turn continuously in circles like dervishes for long periods of time, perhaps 30 or 40 minutes. In other works by Wilson, performers are also called on to remain frozen like statues.

The demands made on performers by experimental and avant–garde theaters are only the most recent example of the rigorous, intensive training which acting generally requires. In every age, performers must develop the sensitivity and insight to penetrate the secrets of the human soul and, at the same time, must train their voices and bodies to express their feelings so that they are readily apparent to the audience.

✳ COMBINING THE TWO ASPECTS OF ACTING ✳

It was said earlier that the supreme challenge for a performer is to combine a realistic portrayal of a character with special vocal and physical skills. The two aspects of performing—the inner and the outer—must be integrated into a seamless whole and must reinforce and support each other.

In Chapter 2, on the imagination of the audience, we examined realistic and nonrealistic theater. It could be argued that realistic theater puts the primary emphasis on credibility and "inner truth" and that nonrealistic theater emphasizes vocal and physical techniques, but performing is almost never an either-or situation. Although the emphasis on making a character believable is paramount in a modern realistic play, control of the voice and body is still an essential part of the performer's training and technique. In a more classical piece—a Greek tragedy, or a farce from the Italian commedia dell'arte—vocal prowess and body movement come to the fore, but even in the most far-out farce, a measure of belief in the characters is called for. In short, although the emphasis in various forms of theater may be on the inner or outer aspect of performing, both are essential in successful acting.

✳ JUDGING PERFORMANCES ✳

As observers, we study the techniques and problems of acting so that we will be able to understand and judge the performances we see. If a performer is unconvincing in a part, we know that he or she has not mastered a technique for truthful acting, such as the one developed by Stanislavski. We become watchful for exaggeration, overacting, and bombast. We recognize that if a performer moves awkwardly or cannot be heard clearly, the performer has not been properly trained in body movement or vocal projection. We learn, too, to notice how well performers play together: whether they listen to one another and respond properly. We also observe how well they establish and maintain contact with the audience.

Earlier we saw the necessity for projection of the performer's voice into the audience. In fact, the performer must project his or her total personality, because (as has frequently been noted) it is the contact between actor and audience which forms the basic encounter of theater. In many types of theater the performers appear to act as if the audience were not there; what of the actor-audience relationship in this situation? From the audience's standpoint, it is very intense, because audience members focus exclusively on the stage. The involvement is so intense that a cough or whisper, unnoticed in an ordinary room, is magnified a thousandfold. But the performers are conscious of the relationship too. They may concentrate on an object onstage, or on one another, but a part of them continually senses the audience and monitors its reaction.

In short, although performers are concentrating on one another, there is still great variation in the intensity and honesty with which they perform. If they are absorbed in a life-and-death struggle onstage, the audience will be absorbed too, like bystanders at a street fight. If they are listless and uninvolved with the play or with one another, the audience will be turned off as well.

For the audience, the most immediate and powerful impact of a theater experience is the encounter with live performers: watching actors and actresses impersonate other human beings, admiring their imagination and skill, and, above all, feeling the strong link, the sense of communication, which develops between performers and spectators. The person who guides the performers in establishing this link is the director, whose work will be discussed in Chapter 7.

✳ SUMMARY ✳

1 Performers must make the characters they portray believable and convincing. One challenge facing the performer is the need to avoid exaggerated gestures or speech. The tendency to "show off" destroys credibility.

2 Beginning with the end of the nineteenth century and continuing to the present, many plays have been written in a very realistic, lifelike style. The characters in these plays resemble ordinary people in their dialogue, behavior, etc. The interpretation of the characters in these plays calls for truthful acting of a high order.

3 A Russian director, Constantin Stanislavski, developed a system or method of acting to enable performers to be truthful. His suggestions included applying relaxation and concentration techniques, dealing with specific objects (a handkerchief, a glass of water, etc.); using the power of fantasy or imagination (the "magic if") to achieve a sense of

inner truth in a role; developing a *spine,* or *through line,* which runs through a role from the beginning to the end of a play; playing together as an ensemble; and developing voice and body.

4   The stage makes demands aside from credibility in a role. Among these are the ability to project the voice, even in a quiet, intimate scene; the development of the voice in order to be able to speak verse and other declamatory speech; and the training of the body to perform many demanding tasks, such as fighting duels, falling down stairs, and managing physical transformations (as in the play *Rhinoceros*).

5   Avant-garde theater makes additional demands on the performer in terms of voice and body training. The voice is sometimes used to emit odd sounds—screams, grunts, and the like. The body must perform feats of acrobatics and gymnastics.

6   Audience members should familiarize themselves with the problems and techniques of acting in order to judge performances properly.

✳ TOPICS FOR DISCUSSION ✳

1   At the opening of this chapter it was noted that actors and actresses face two main challenges: making a character believable and acquiring the physical and vocal skills demanded on the stage. Which do you think would be easier: starting with a talent for portraying characters and then learning the physical and vocal skills; or starting with physical and vocal aptitude and then learning to portray characters? Why?

2   Naturalistic acting is, of course, admired today; but, as was pointed out in the chapter, exaggerated acting has from time to time prevailed. Can you think of any reasons—theoretical or practical—why "unnatural" acting might be accepted or even valued?

3   The Stanislavski system of acting involves a number of techniques. As you read the descriptions of these in the chapter, did any of them seem to you to be more basic than others? Would any of them be "prerequisites" for any of the others?

4   Examine the synopsis of *The Cherry Orchard* in this chapter and discuss the chief acting demands that would be made on performers appearing in a production of the play.

5   On Broadway, at least, many (if not most) productions today are "miked"—that is, the sound is electronically amplified. What, if anything, does this trend imply about vocal projection as a requirement of acting?

6   Consider a performance you saw recently which you did *not* like, and analyze it in terms of the aspects of acting discussed in this chapter. Can you pinpoint what was wrong with the acting?

7

THE DIRECTOR
AND
THE PRODUCER

THE DIRECTOR GUIDES THE PERFORMERS.
*The person who works most closely with actors and actresses is the director. He or she develops
the production concept, explains it to the performers, guides the performers in creating their
characters, and shapes ensemble playing. Shown here is the director Frank Galati (right), in a
rehearsal of* The Grapes of Wrath, *working with Lois Smith and Cheryl Lynn Bruce.*

A key element of a theater event is the work of the director—the person who rehearses the performers and coordinates their actions with those of others, such as the designers, to make certain that the script is performed in an intelligent, exciting, and appropriate way. In this chapter, we will look at the work of the director, and also at the role of the producer—the person who is responsible for the management and business aspects of theater.

✻ THE THEATER DIRECTOR ✻

The person who works most closely with performers in the theater is the *director*, who guides them in shaping their performances. When a new play is being presented, the director also works closely with the playwright and is responsible for coordinating other aspects of the production, such as the work of scenic, costume, and lighting designers.

It is worth noting that the director's work on a production is one of the last elements of which the audience becomes aware. Performers, scenery, and costumes are onstage and are immediately visible to spectators, and the words of the playwright are heard throughout the performance; but the director's work consists of interpreting and blending these elements and takes place largely behind the scenes. It is therefore much less readily apparent to the audience but no less crucial. Except for the playwright, the director is the first person to become involved in the creative process of a production, and the choices he or she makes at every stage along the way have a great deal to do with determining whether the ultimate experience will be satisfactory for the spectators.

In Chapter 13 we will learn that it is important for the playwright to incorporate in his or her script a clear point of view toward the material being dramatized. Is it a tragedy, for example, or a comedy? It is crucial for the director to understand this point of view and translate it into production terms, making it clear to the performers, designers, and other artists and technicians involved. Alhough they work together, these artists and technicians must of necessity work on segments of the production rather than the entire enterprise. The performers, for instance, are much too busy during rehearsals—working on their roles or their interactions with other performers—to worry much about scenery. Also, a performer who appears only in the first act of a three-act play has no control over what happens in the second and third acts. The one person who does have an overall perspective is the director.

Evolution of the Director

A HISTORICAL PERSPECTIVE   It has sometimes been argued that the director did not exist in the theater before 1874, when a German nobleman, George II (1826–1914), duke of Saxe-Meiningen, began supervising every element of his theatrical productions—rehearsals, scenic elements, and other aspects—coordinating them into an integrated whole. Beginning with Saxe-Meiningen, the director emerged as a full-fledged, indispensable member of the theatrical team, taking a place alongside the playwright, the performers, and the designers.

Although the title may have been new, however, the *function* of the director had always been present in one way or another. We know, for example, that the Greek playwright Aeschylus directed his own plays and that the chorus for Greek plays rehearsed for many weeks under the supervision of a leader before a performance. At various times in theater history, the leading performer or playwright of a company served as a director, though without the name. Molière, for instance, not only was the playwright and the chief actor of his company but functioned as the director also. We know from Molière's short play *The Impromptu of Versailles* that he had definite ideas about the way actors and actresses should perform; no doubt the same advice he offered in that play was frequently given to his performers in rehearsal.

When Hamlet gave instructions and advice to the players who were to perform the play-within-the-play in *Hamlet*, he was functioning as a director. After the time of Shakespeare in England—from the seventeenth through the nineteenth century—there was a long line of actor-managers who gave strong leadership to individual theater companies and performed many of the functions of directors, although they were not called by that name. Among the most famous were Thomas Betterton (1635?–1710), David Garrick, Charles Kemble (1775–1854), William Charles Macready (1793–1873), and Henry Irving (1838–1905).

It was toward the end of the nineteenth century that the term *director* came into common usage and the clearly defined role of the director was first recognized. It is significant, perhaps, that the emergence of the director as a separate creative person coincides with important changes which began to take place in society during the nineteenth century. First, there was a breakdown in established social, religious, and political concepts which came with Freud, Darwin, and Marx. Second, there was a marked increase in communication. With the advent of the telegraph, the telephone, photography, motion pictures, and finally television, various cultures which had remained remote or unknown to one another were suddenly quite aware of each other. The effect of these two changes was to alter the monolithic, ordered view of the world which individual societies had maintained before.

Before these developments, consistency of style in theater was easier to achieve. Within a given society there was common ground among writers, performers, and spectators. For example, the comedies of the English writers William Wycherley (1640–1716) and William Congreve (1670–1729), written at the end of the seventeenth century, were aimed at a specific audience—the elite upper class, which relished gossip, acidic remarks, and well-turned phrases. The code of behavior of the society was well understood by performers and audience alike; and questions of style in a production hardly arose, because a common approach to style was already present in the fabric of society. The way a man took a pinch of snuff, or a nobleman flirted with a maid, or a lady flung open her fan was so clearly delineated in daily behavior that performers had only to refine and perfect these actions for the stage. The director's task was not so much to impose a style on a production as to prevent the performers from overacting and to see that they spoke their lines properly and that the cast worked as a cohesive unit. Today, however, because style, unity, and a cohesive view of society are so elusive, the director's task is more important.

Modern directors get their training in various ways. Many begin as actors and actresses and find that they have a talent for working with other people and for coordinating the work of designers as well as performers. Others train in the many academic institutions that have specific programs for directors. These include universities with theater as part of a liberal arts focus and special conservatories and institutes.

THE AUTEUR DIRECTOR   *Auteur* is a French word meaning "author." Just after World War II, French critics began using the word in connection with certain film directors, who, they said, were really the authors of the films they made. The point of view and its implementation came almost entirely from the director, not from a writer. The term has since been used to apply to a type of stage director as well.

Once the director came to the forefront as a full-fledged member of the creative theatrical team, most directors operated with a script. Almost from the start, however, there was a breed of director who took a different approach. Interestingly enough, one of the first and most important of these began his work with Stanislavski and then went out on his own. He was Vsevolod Meyerhold (1874–1940), and he developed a type of theater in which he controlled all the elements. The script was only one of many aspects that he used for his own purposes. He would rewrite or eliminate text in order to present his own vision of the material. Performers, too, were subject to his overall ideas. Often they were called on to perform like circus acrobats or robots. The finished product was frequently exciting and almost always innovative, but it represented Meyerhold's point of view, strongly imposed on all the elements, not the point of view of a writer or anyone else.

Following in Meyerhold's footsteps, many avant-garde directors, such as Jerzi Grotowski (1933–) and Robert Wilson, can also be classified as auteur directors in that they demand that a text serve their purposes, not the other way around. In some cases, such as many of Wilson's pieces, the text is only fragmentary and one of the least important elements. In the Soviet Union and eastern Europe, before the recent political changes, certain directors, who had not been allowed to deal with material that questioned the government hierarchy, drastically reworked established texts in order to make a political comment. These people, too, imposed their own vision, rather than that of the playwright, on the material.

The Director's Work

Let us return now to the more traditional role of the director as the chief interpreter of an established script. For the most part, spectators see theater as a unified experience; but, as pointed out before, theater is a complex art involving not one or two elements but many simultaneously: script, performance, costumes, scenery, lighting, and point of view. These diverse elements—a mixture of the tangible and intangible—must be brought together into an organic whole, and that is the responsibility of the director.

THE DIRECTOR AND THE SCRIPT   Frequently the director chooses the script to be produced. Generally it is a play which the director is attracted to or feels a special affinity for. If the director does not actually choose the script but is asked to direct it by a playwright or a producer, he or she must still have an understanding and appreciation of the material. The director's attraction to the script and basic understanding are important in launching a production. Once the script is chosen, the actual work on the production begins.

If the play is new and has never been tested in production, the director may see problems in the script which must be corrected before rehearsals begin. The director will have a series of meetings with the playwright to iron out the difficulties ahead of time. The director may feel, for example, that the leading character is not clearly defined, or that a clash of personalities between two characters never reaches a climax. If the playwright agrees with the director's assessment, he or she will revise the manuscript. Generally there is considerable give-and-take between the director and playwright in these preliminary sessions, as well as during the rehearsal period. Ideally, there should be a spirit of cooperation, compromise, and mutual respect in this relationship.

THE "SPINE" OF THE PLAY   One of the first steps for a director in preparing a production is to discover the "spine" of the play. In his book *On Directing*, Harold Clurman explains how the director should begin this process: "To begin active direction a formulation in the simplest terms must be found to state what general action motivates the play, of what fundamental drama or conflict the script's plot and people are the instruments."[1]

124

THE DIRECTOR AT WORK.
No function of the director is more important than guiding cast members during the rehearsal process. Seen here are four directors in rehearsals with performers. Opposite page, top: Jerome Robbins preparing dancers for Jerome Robbins' Broadway. *Opposite, below: Peter Hall (right) working with the actor Brad Sullivan on the script of* Orpheus Descending *by Tennessee Williams. This page, top: George C. Wolfe (second from right) directing Reggie Montgomery, Ann Duquesnay, and K. Todd Freeman in* Spunk. *This page, below: Marshall Mason (in the background) guiding John Malkovich and Joan Allen in Lanford Wilson's* Burn This.

Clurman calls the formulation of the action or conflict the *spine* of the play. The spine could also be called the *main action*. Clurman says that the spine for the characters in Eugene O'Neill's *A Touch of the Poet* is "to make a place for themselves."[2] In one way or another, Clurman feels, every character in the play is seeking this same goal.

By finding a spine for the play, the director acquires a key to the action, or a springboard from which to develop it. Different directors may find different spines for the same play. With *Hamlet,* for instance, several spines are possible: much will depend on the period in which the play is produced and the point of view of the individual director. Clurman says that such varied interpretations are to be expected and are acceptable as long as the spine chosen remains true to the spirit and action of the play.

Clurman warns of the dangers of not finding a main action or spine: "Where a director has not determined on a spine for his production, it will tend to be formless. Each scene follows the next without necessarily adding up to a total dramatic 'statement.' "[3]

THE STYLE OF THE PRODUCTION   Once the spine has been found, the second task for a director, according to Clurman, "is to find the manner in which the spine is to be articulated."[4] Clurman is speaking here of the *style* of the production.

Style in a theatrical production is a difficult concept to explain. It means the *way* in which a play is presented. In clothes, when we speak of a "casual style" or a "1920s style," we mean in the first case that the clothes are loose and informal, and in the second that the clothes have the look and feel of those worn in the 1920s.

In the theater, one way to look at style is in terms of realistic or nonrealistic theater. In Chapter 2 the differences between these two types of theater were discussed, but they can be further subdivided.

Realism, for example, is of several types. At one extreme is *naturalism,* a kind of superrealism. (For a further discussion of naturalism and other forms, see Appendix 4.) The term *naturalism* was championed by several French writers in the nineteenth century. They wanted a theater that would show human beings—many of them in wretched circumstances—as products of heredity and environment. Aside from this special use, the term *naturalism* is used more broadly for attempts to put onstage as exact a copy of life as possible, down to the smallest detail. In a naturalistic stage set of a kitchen, for instance, a performer can actually cook a meal on the stove— the toaster makes toast, the water tap produces water, and the light in the refrigerator goes on when the door opens. Characters speak and act as if they had been caught unobserved by a camera and tape recorder. In this sense, naturalism is supposed to resemble an undoctored documentary film. Naturalism is sometimes called *slice-of-life* drama, as if a section has been taken from life and transferred to the stage.

At the other extreme of realism is *heightened realism,* sometimes referred to as *selective realism.* Here the characters and their activities are intended to resemble life, but a certain license is allowed. The scenery, for example, might be skeletal—that is, incomplete and in outline—although the words and actions of the characters are realistic. Or perhaps a character is allowed a modern version of a soliloquy in an otherwise realistic play. All art calls for selectivity, and heightened realism recognizes the necessity for the artist to make choices and to inject creativity into the process.

Realism itself occupies the middle ground between naturalism and heightened, or selective, realism but includes the extremes at each end.

Nonrealism can also be divided into types: two well-known types of nonrealism are *allegory* and *expressionism.*

Allegory is the representation of an abstract theme or subject through the symbolic use of characters, actions, or other elements of a production, such as scenery. Good examples are the medieval morality plays in which characters personify ideas in order to teach an intellectual or moral lesson. In *Everyman,* actors play the parts of Good Deeds, Fellowship, Worldly Goods, and so on. In less direct forms of allegory, a relatively realistic story serves as a parable or lesson. *The Crucible* by Arthur Miller (1915–) is about the witch-hunts in Salem, Massachusetts, in the late seventeenth century; but it can also be regarded as dealing with specific investigations by the United States Congress in the early 1950s which Miller and others felt treated ordinary citizens unfairly, becoming modern "witch-hunts."

Although *expressionism* was at its height in art, literature, and the theater during the first quarter of the twentieth century, traces of it are still found today, and contemporary plays using its techniques are termed *expressionistic.* In simple terms, expressionism gives outward expression to inward feelings. In Elmer Rice's *The Adding Machine,* the feelings of Mr. Zero when he is fired from his job are conveyed by having the room spin around in a circle amid a cacophony of shrill sounds, such as loud sirens and whistles.

Deciding on a directorial style for a production involves giving a signature and an imprint to an entire production: the look of the scenery and lights, the way performers handle their costumes and props, the manner in which performers speak. It also involves the rhythm and pace at which the play moves, a subject to be taken up shortly.

When a director arrives at a style for a production, two things are essential: first, the style should be appropriate for the play, and, second, it should be consistent throughout every aspect of the production.

THE DIRECTORIAL CONCEPT   One way for the director to embody the spine in a production and to implement style is to develop a *directorial concept.* Such a concept derives from a controlling idea, vision, or point of view which the director feels is appropriate to the play. The concept should also create a unified theatrical experience for the spectators.

Concept and period   To indicate what is involved for the director in developing a concept, let us begin with *period*. Shakespeare's *Troilus and Cressida* was written in the Elizabethan period but is set at the time of the Trojan War, when the ancient Greeks were fighting the Trojans. In presenting the play today, a director has several choices as to the period in which to set the production.

One director might choose to stick to the period indicated in the script and set the play in Troy, with both Trojans and Greeks wearing armor, tunics, and other appropriate garments. Another might set the play in the time when Shakespeare wrote it, and in this case the director and the designers would devise court and military costumes reflecting Shakespeare's day.

Another option for the director would be to modernize the play. There have been a number of modern productions of *Troilus and Cressida* in recent years. Shakespeare's words are retained, but since many of the play's antiwar sentiments and statements about the corruption of love in the face of war are quite relevant today, the play is transferred to the present by means of costumes, settings, and behavior. For example, in 1956 Tyrone Guthrie (1900–1971), a British director, presented a version which was set in the period just prior to 1914 in England, that is, just before World War I. The play was shifted to English drawing rooms and other localities conveying the clear impression of England in the early twentieth century. The uniforms were those of English soldiers of the period, and the women wore dresses typical of that era. The set had grand pianos, the men drank cocktails, and the women used cigarette holders—all intended to portray a sophisticated urban environment. A successful 1986 production of the same play, by the Royal Shakespeare Company, shifted the time of the play to the Crimean War in the middle of the nineteenth century.

This kind of transposition has been carried out frequently with Greek plays, Elizabethan plays, French plays of the seventeenth century, and other dramatic classics.

Concept and central image   Rather than place the play in a historical period, the director's concept might involve another approach. One other way to implement a directorial concept is to find a *central*, or *controlling*, *image* or *metaphor* for a theatrical production.

An example would be a production of *Hamlet* that envisioned the play in terms of a vast net or spider web in which Hamlet is caught. The motif of a net or spider web could be carried out on several levels: in the design, in the ways in which the performers relate to one another, and in a host of details relating to the central image. There might be a

DIRECTORIAL CONCEPTS.
A production of Shakespeare's The Merry Wives of Windsor *at the Repertory Theater of St. Louis was set in the American west to give it modern relevance; for the same reason, a production of* Much Ado about Nothing *at the Old Globe Theater in San Diego was set in the Raj period in India.*

huge rope net hanging over the entire stage, for instance, and certain characters could play string games with their fingers. In short, the metaphor of Hamlet's being caught in a net would be emphasized and reinforced on every level.

Concept and purpose The directorial concept should serve the play; the best concept is one that remains true to the spirit and meaning of the script. If the director can translate that spirit and meaning into stage terms in an inspired way, he or she will have created an exciting theater experience, but if a director is too intent on displaying his or her own originality, the integrity of the script may be distorted or violated. The metaphor of a net or spider web described above might appear to be theatrical and inventive, but it would be quite wrong for certain plays because it would distract the audience's attention from quieter moments

129

or deeper meanings at the heart of the script. This would be the case, for example, with most realistic plays. A directorial concept which is flashy on the surface may call too much attention to itself and rob the spectators of the full, honest experience to which they are entitled.

In arriving at a concept, the director must keep these factors in balance. In most instances the best directorial concept is a straightforward one deriving from the play itself and not a scheme superimposed from the outside.

CASTING   Having chosen a play and settled questions of concept and style, the director then casts the play.

Obviously derived from the phrase "casting a mold," the word *casting* in the theater means fitting performers into roles. Generally speaking, directors attempt to put performers into the roles for which they are best suited insofar as their personalities and physical characteristics are concerned. A young woman will play Juliet in *Romeo and Juliet,* an elderly actor with a deep voice will play King Lear, and so on. When a performer closely resembles in real life the character to be enacted, this is known as *type casting.* There are times when a director will deliberately put someone in a role who is obviously wrong for the part. This is frequently done for comic or satiric purposes and is called *casting against type.* For example, a sinister-looking actor might be called on to play an angelic part.

In the modern theater, performers frequently *audition* for parts in a play, and the director casts from those performers who audition. In an audition, actors and actresses read scenes from a play or perform portions of the script to give the director an indication of how they talk and move and how they would interpret a part. From this the director determines whether or not a performer is right for a given part.

Historically, casting was rarely done by audition, because theatrical companies were more permanent. In Shakespeare's time, and in Molière's, certain people always played certain parts in a theatrical troupe: one person would play heroic parts, for example, while another always played the clown. Under these conditions, when a play was selected, it was a matter of assigning roles to the performers who were on hand; auditioning might occur only when a new member was chosen for the company.

From the audience's standpoint it is important to be aware of casting and the difference it can make in the effectiveness of a production. Perhaps the actor or actress is just right for the part he or she is playing. On the other hand, sometimes the wrong performer is chosen for a part: the voice may not be right, or the gestures or facial expressions may be inappropriate for the character being played. One way to test the correctness of casting is to imagine a different kind of actor or actress in a part while watching a performance.

REHEARSALS   Once the play is cast, the director supervises all rehearsals. He or she listens to the performers as they go through their lines and begin to move about the stage. Different directors work in different ways in the early stages of rehearsal: some directors *block* the play in advance, giving precise instructions to the performers. (The term *blocking* means deciding where and when performers move and position themselves on the stage.) Other directors let the actors and actresses find their movements, their vocal interpretations, and their relationships on their own. And of course there are directors who do a bit of both. It is worth pointing out that in recent years directors have tended to move toward the less structured approach, directing far less in terms of specific instructions or commands than was the case throughout the whole of the nineteenth and the early part of the twentieth century. In former times it was customary for directors to give performers precise commands: "Move three paces to the right, and then turn to face the audience. Now speak the next line in a stage whisper." Today this approach is less common.

During the rehearsal period, the director must make certain that the actors and actresses are realizing the intention of the playwright—that they are making sense of the script and bringing out its meaning. Also, the director must ensure that the performers are working well together—that they are listening to one another and beginning to play as an ensemble. The director must be aware of performers' needs, knowing when to encourage them and when to challenge or criticize them. The director must understand their personal problems and help them overcome such obstacles as insecurity about a role or fear of failure.

THE PHYSICAL PRODUCTION   At the same time that rehearsals with the performers are going forward, the director is also working with the designers on the physical production. At the outset—once the director's concept is established—the director confers with the costume, scene, and lighting designers to give shape and substance to the concept in visual terms. It is the responsibility of designers to provide images and impressions which will carry out the style and ideas of the production. (See Chapters 17, 18, and 19.)

During the preproduction and rehearsal period, the director meets with the designers to make certain that their work is on schedule and keeping pace with the rehearsals. Obviously the preparation of these elements must begin long before the actual performance, just as rehearsals must, so that everything will be ready before the performance itself takes place. Any number of problems can arise with the physical elements of a production. For example, the appropriate props may not be available, a costume may not fit a performer properly, or scene changes may be too slow. Early planning will allow time to solve these problems.

USING STAGE AREAS PROPERLY.

One responsibility of the director is to make appropriate use of stage areas to create balance, emphasis, and striking visual effects. In this scene from Shakespeare's Coriolanus, *note the symmetrical arrangement of figures and the focus on the woman sitting in the center. The production at the Public Theater in New York City was directed by Steven Berkoff.*

THE DIRECTOR AS THE AUDIENCE'S EYE   One could say that there are two people in theater who stand in for the audience, serving as surrogate or substitute spectators. One, the critic (discussed in Chapter 4) does his or her work after the event; the other, the director, does his or her work before.

In the preparation of a theatrical production, the director acts as the eye of the audience. During rehearsals, the director is the only one who sees the production from the spectator's point of view. For this reason the director must assist the performers in showing the audience exactly what they intend to show. If one performer hides another at an important moment, if a crucial gesture is not visible, if an actor makes an awkward movement, if an actress cannot be heard when she delivers an emotional speech, the director points it out.

Also, the director underscores the meaning of specific scenes through *visual composition* and *stage pictures*, that is, through the physical arrangement of performers onstage. The spatial relationships of performers convey information about characters. As an example, important characters are frequently placed on a level above other characters—on a platform or step, for instance. Another spatial device is to place an important character alone in one area of the stage while grouping other

132

characters in another area. This causes the eye to give special attention to the character standing alone. If two characters are opposed to each other, they should be placed in positions of physical confrontation on the stage.

Certain areas on the stage assume special significance: a fireplace, with its sense of warmth, can become an area to which a character returns for comfort and reassurance. A door opening on a garden can serve as a place where characters go when they want to renew their spirits or to escape from a hemmed-in feeling. By guiding performers to make the best use of stage space, the director assists them in communicating important visual images to the audience—images consistent with the overall meaning of the play.

BALANCE, PROPORTION, AND PACE The director gives shape and structure to a play in two spheres or dimensions: in *space,* as was just described, and in *time.* Since a production occurs through time, it is important for the director to see that the *movement,* the *pace,* and the *rhythm* of the play are correct. If the play moves too quickly, if we miss words and do not understand what is going on, it is the director's fault. The director must determine whether there is too short or too long a time between speeches or whether a performer moves too slowly across the stage. The director must attempt to control the pace and rhythm within a scene—the dynamics and the manner in which the actors and actresses move from moment to moment—and the rhythm between scenes.

One of the most common faults of directors is not to establish a clear rhythm in a production. An audience at a performance is impatient, almost unconsciously so, to see what is coming next; and if expectations are frustrated too long, the audience will become unhappy. The director must see to it that the movement from moment to moment and scene to scene has a thrust and a drive that maintains our interest. Variety is important too. If the play moves ahead at only one pace, whether slow or fast, the audience will be fatigued simply by the monotony of that pace. The rhythm within scenes and between scenes works on audience members in an unconscious but very real way. It enters our psyche as we watch a performance and thus contributes to our overall response.

Of course, it must be borne in mind that the responsibility for pace, proportion, and overall effect, while initially the director's, ultimately rests with the performers. Once the performance begins, the actors and actresses are onstage and the director is not. Unlike the cinema, in which the pace and rhythm can be determined in the editing room, in theater there is great elasticity and variety; much depends on the mood of the performers. The director must instill and implant such a strong sense of inner rhythm in the performers that they have an internal clock which tells them how they should play. Then, too, audience reaction will vary from night to night and alter the pace as well. The director's work is done before the performance and behind the scenes. But if it is done well, the director will imbue the work with a rhythm that will carry through in the final performance.

TECHNICAL REHEARSAL Just before public performances begin, a *technical rehearsal* is held. The performers are onstage in their costumes with the scenery and lighting for the first time, and there is a *run-through* of the show from beginning to end, with all the props, costumes, and scene changes. The stagehands move scenery, the crew handles props, and the lighting technicians control the dimming and raising of lights. All of them must coordinate their work with that of the performers.

Let us say that one scene ends in a garden, and the next scene opens in a library. Once the performers leave the garden set, the lighting fades, the scenery is removed, and the garden furniture is taken off the stage. Following that, the scenery for the library must be brought onstage by stagehands and the books and other props put in place. Then the performers for the new scene in the library take their places as the lighting comes up. Extensive rehearsals are required to ensure that the lighting comes up at just the moment when the scenery is prepared and the performers are in place. Any mishap on the part of the stage crew, lighting crew, prop crew, or performers would affect the illusion and destroy the aesthetic effect of the scene change. The importance of the technical rehearsals is therefore considerable.

TRYOUTS Once the technical rehearsals are completed and the problems which occurred are solved, the next step arrives: a performance in front of an audience. I have stressed from the beginning the importance of actor-audience interaction and the fact that no play is complete until it is actually performed for an audience. It is crucial, therefore, for a production to be tried out before a group of spectators. What has gone before, in terms of rehearsals and other elements, must now meet the test of combining harmoniously in front of an audience. For this purpose there is a period of *tryouts*—also called *previews*—when the director and the performers discover which parts of the play are successful and which are not. Frequently, for example, the director and performers find that one part of the play is moving too slowly; they know this because the audience becomes restless and begins to cough or stir. Sometimes, in a comedy, there is a great deal of laughter where little was expected, and the performers and the director must adjust to this.

The audiences in this tryout period become genuine collaborators in the shaping of the play. (In the days when Broadway was the chief forum for new plays in the United States, tryouts were held in other cities—Philadelphia, New Haven, or Boston—before the play was exposed to critics in New York. When that opportunity was not available, a series of previews would be given.) After several performances in front

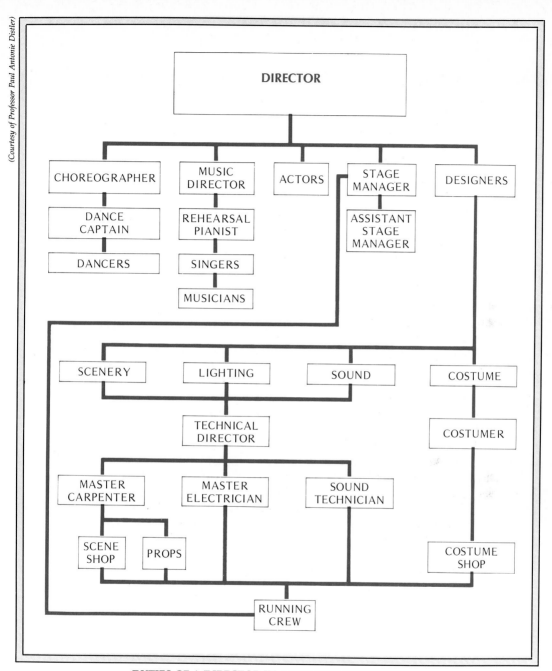

DUTIES OF A DIRECTOR IN A THEATER PRODUCTION.

Once a director has decided on a script (and worked with the playwright, if it is a new play), he or she must organize the entire artistic side of the production. This chart indicates the many people the director must work with and the many elements that must be coordinated.

135

of an audience, the director and the performers get the "feel" of the audience and sense whether the play is ready or not.

For an idea of the director's full range of responsibilities, see the chart on the preceding page.

The Director's Power and Responsibility

Clearly, the director has great power. Whether a director takes the traditional or the auteur approach, one of the great dangers is that he or she will use this power to overstress certain elements to the detriment or exclusion of other elements. A second danger lies in the possibility that the director will develop an inconsistent or incongruous scheme. As suggested previously, the director might go overboard with a production concept. For instance, a director might decide to make *Macbeth* into a cowboy play, with Duncan as a sheriff and Macbeth as a deputy who wishes to kill the sheriff in order to take the job himself. In this version, Lady Macbeth would be the deputy's wife, whom he had met in a western saloon. *Macbeth* could be done this way, but it might be ludicrous, carrying reinterpretation too far. It would be an attempt to rewrite the play and make the director's work more important than Shakespeare's.

Any artistic event must have a unity not encountered in real life. We expect the parts to be brought together so that the total effect will enlighten us, move us, or amuse us. All the parts must fit and be consistent with one another; there must be no jarring notes unless they are intentional. This is the director's responsibility. When the director has a strong point of view—one which is correct for the play—the experience for the audience is likely to be meaningful and exciting. By the same token, if the director gets too carried away with one idea or lets the scene designer create scenery which overpowers the performers and buries the production in a mountain of scenic effects, the experience will be neither satisfactory nor complete. The director must have a keen sense of proportion so that various elements work together rather than against one another. This juggling act—or, to put it another way, this weaving together of the tangible and the intangible, the spiritual and the physical, the symbolic and the literal—is the final responsibility of the director.

❊ THE PRODUCER OR MANAGER ❊

When attending the theater, the audience focuses on the event onstage, but no production would ever be performed for the public without a technical and business component. Here, too, the coordination of elements is crucial, and the person chiefly responsible is the behind-the-scenes counterpart of the director, known as the *producer* or *manager*.

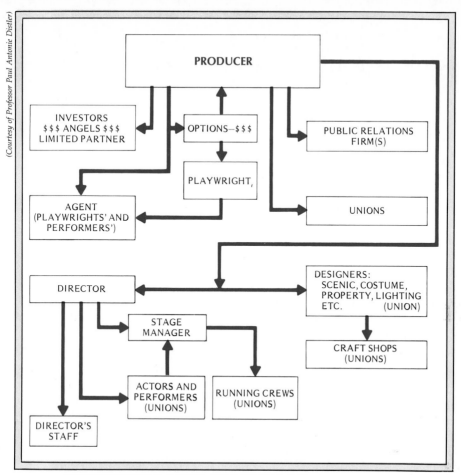

RESPONSIBILITIES OF THE COMMERCIAL THEATER PRODUCER.

When a commercial theater production is mounted, the person responsible for organizing the full range of nonartistic activities is the producer. This chart, which shows the producer at the top, indicates the people the producer must deal with and the numerous elements he or she must coordinate.

(Courtesy of Professor Paul Antonie Distler)

The Commercial Producer

In a commercial theater venture, the producer has many responsibilities. (See the chart above.) In general, he or she oversees the entire business and publicity side of the production and has the following duties:

1 Raising money to finance the production
2 Securing rights to the script
3 Dealing with the agents for the playwright, director, and performers
4 Hiring director, performers, designers, and stage crews

137

5   Dealing with all theatrical unions

6   Renting the theater space

7   Supervising the work of those running the theater: in the box office, the auditorium, the business office

8   Supervising the advertising

9   Overseeing the budget and the week-to-week financial management of the production

The producer must have the artistic sensibility to choose the right script and hire the right director if a production is to succeed. Aside from raising capital and having the final say in hiring and firing, the producer oversees all financial and business operations in a production. In a nonprofit theater the person having these same responsibilities is called the *manager*.

The Work of the Producer or Nonprofit Manager

Whether in a commercial production or in the running of a nonprofit theater organization, the tasks of the person in charge of administration are many and complex.

The producer or manager is responsible for the maintenance of the theater building, including the dressing rooms, the public facilities, and the lobby. The producer or manager is also responsible for the budget, making certain that the production stays within established limits. This includes salaries for the director, designers, performers, and stage crews, and expenditures for scenery, costumes, and music. Again, an artistic element enters the picture; important decisions as to whether a certain costume needs to be replaced or whether scenery needs to be altered affect costs. The producer or manager must find additional sources of money or determine that changes are important enough artistically to take sums from another item in the budget. In other words, the producer or manager must work very closely with the director and the designers in balancing artistic and financial needs.

The producer or manager is also responsible for publicity. The audience would never get to the theater if it did not know when and where a play was being presented. The producer or manager must advertise the production and decide whether such advertisements should be placed in daily newspapers, on radio, on television, in student newspapers, in magazines, or elsewhere.

A host of other problems come under the supervision of the producer or manager: tickets must be ordered, the box office maintained, and plans made ahead of time for the way in which tickets are sold. The securing of ushers, the printing of programs, the maintenance of the auditorium—usually called the *front* of the *house*—are also the responsibility of the producer or manager.

(Courtesy of Professor Paul Antonie Distler)

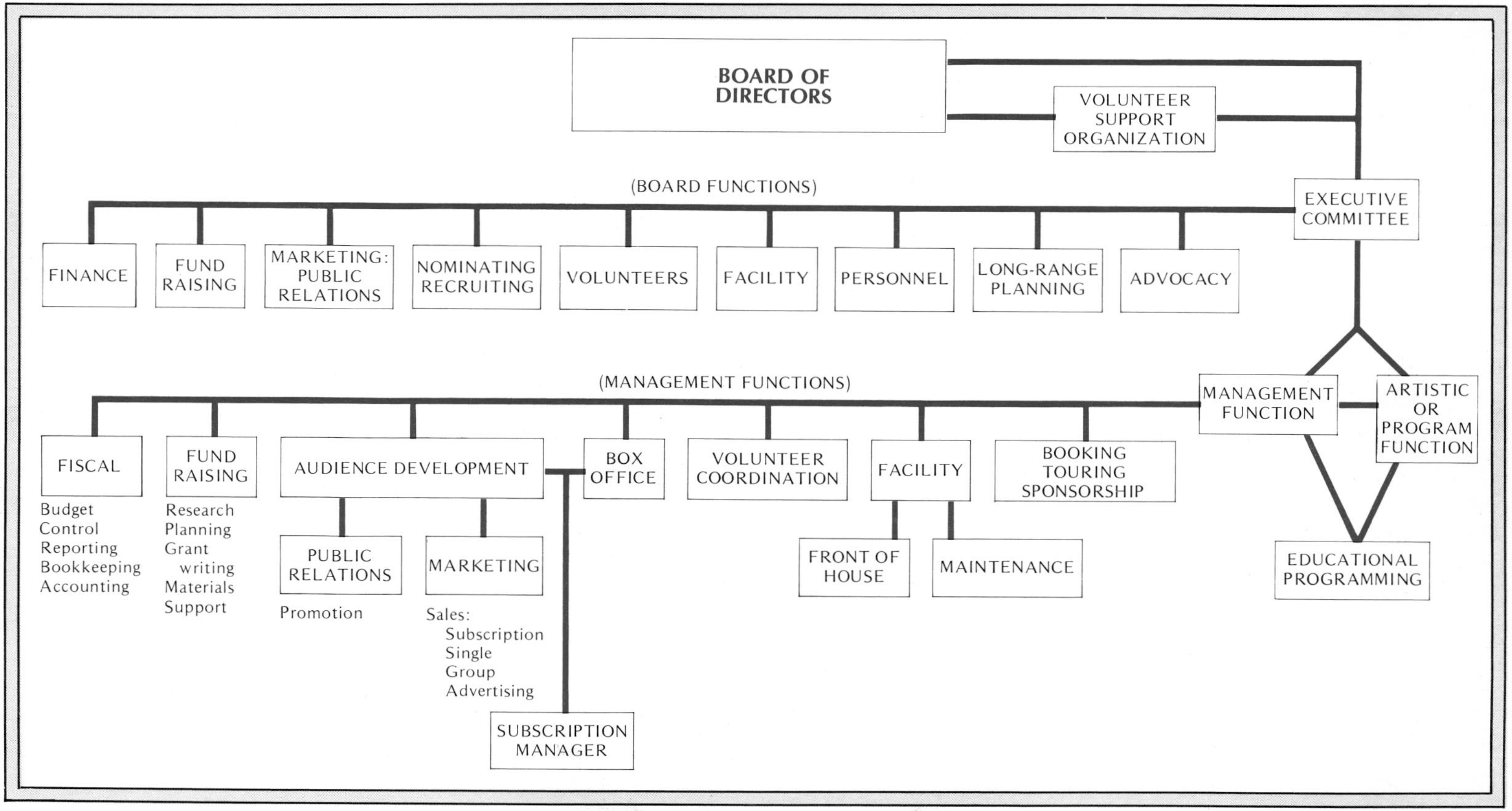
BOARD OF DIRECTORS
VOLUNTEER SUPPORT ORGANIZATION
EXECUTIVE COMMITTEE
(BOARD FUNCTIONS)
FINANCE
FUND RAISING
MARKETING: PUBLIC RELATIONS
NOMINATING RECRUITING
VOLUNTEERS
FACILITY
PERSONNEL
LONG-RANGE PLANNING
ADVOCACY
(MANAGEMENT FUNCTIONS)
MANAGEMENT FUNCTION
ARTISTIC OR PROGRAM FUNCTION
EDUCATIONAL PROGRAMMING
FISCAL
Budget
Control
Reporting
Bookkeeping
Accounting
FUND RAISING
Research
Planning
Grant writing
Materials
Support
AUDIENCE DEVELOPMENT
PUBLIC RELATIONS
Promotion
MARKETING
Sales:
Subscription
Single
Group
Advertising
SUBSCRIPTION MANAGER
BOX OFFICE
VOLUNTEER COORDINATION
FACILITY
FRONT OF HOUSE
MAINTENANCE
BOOKING TOURING SPONSORSHIP

A MODEL OF THE ORGANIZATIONAL STRUCTURE OF A NONPROFIT THEATER COMPANY.
A nonprofit theater is a complex institution with many facets. This chart shows the various activities that must be organized for the successful management of such a theater.

Once again, plans must be made well in advance. In the case of many theater organizations, an entire season—the plays to be produced, the personnel who will be in charge, and requirements in terms of supplies—is planned a year ahead of time. It should be clear that coordination and cooperation are as important in this area as they are for the production onstage. (For the organization of a nonprofit theater company, see the chart on the preceding page.)

✳ COMPLETING THE PICTURE: ✳
PLAYWRIGHT, DIRECTOR, AND PRODUCER

A theater presentation can be compared to a mosaic consisting of many brightly colored pieces of stone fitting together to form a complete picture. The playwright puts the words and ideas together, the director puts the artistic elements together. the producer or manager coordinates the business side of a production. The separate pieces in the mosaic must become parts of an artistic whole, thereby providing a complete theater experience.

An absolutely crucial piece in the mosaic is the script on which the production is based. The script is the work of the playwright, to whom we turn in Part Three.

✳ SUMMARY ✳

1　The term *director* did not come into general use until the end of the nineteenth century. Certain functions of the director, however—organizing the production, instilling discipline in the performers, setting a tone for the production—have been carried out since the beginning of theater by someone in authority.

2　The director's duties became more crucial in the twentieth century. Because of the fragmentation of society and the many styles and cultures existing side by side, it became necessary for someone to impose a point of view and a single vision on individual productions.

3　*Auteur* directors demand that texts serve their purposes, rather than shaping their own purposes to serve the texts.

4　The director has many responsibilities:

Selecting the script

Working with the writer on a new play

Finding the *spine*, or main action, of the play

Arriving at the style of the production

140

Evolving a *concept,* or an approach to the script

Holding auditions and casting roles

Conducting rehearsals

Ensuring that stage action communicates the meaning of the play

Working with the performers to develop their individual roles

Developing the visual side of the production with the designers

Supervising the technical and tryout rehearsals

Establishing proper pace and rhythm in the movement of the scenes

Establishing the dynamics of the production as a whole

5 Because the director has such wide-ranging power and responsibilities, he or she can distort a production and create an imbalance in elements or an improper emphasis. The director is responsible for a sense of proportion and order in the production.

6 The producer or manager of a production is responsible for the business aspects: maintaining the theater, arranging publicity, handling finances, and managing ticket sales, budgets, ushers, etc.

✳ TOPICS FOR DISCUSSION ✳

1 It is noted in the chapter that at various times in theater history a leading performer or the playwright has served as director of a production. What would be the advantages and disadvantages of having the leading actor or actress function as director? What would be the advantages and disadvantages of having the playwright serve as director?

2 In the section on the director and the script, it is noted that a director may ask a playwright to make revisions, and that there is likely to be considerable give and take between director and playwright. This, of course, describes an ideal situation; reading between the lines, you can probably imagine situations that are less than ideal. What kinds of conflicts might arise between a director and a playwright over a script? What kinds of considerations and arguments might each bring to bear in a disagreement? How might they resolve their differences of opinion?

3 Today there is considerable controversy about the auteur director. Some people argue that the practice is innovative and creative, bringing new life and vision to theater productions. Others argue that it is nothing more than an ego trip for the director: that it is presumptuous and sets the director above acknowledged masters of stagecraft like Shakespeare. Discuss the pros and cons of these two points of view. When is the auteur approach valid, and when is it not?

4 Do you think it would be more difficult to be a producer in commercial theater or in nonprofit theater? Why?

PART THREE

❋ ──────────────────────── ❋

THREE

THE PLAYWRIGHT: DRAMATIC STRUCTURE AND DRAMATIC CHARACTERS

LONG DAY'S JOURNEY INTO NIGHT— A POWERFUL PLAY IN THE CLIMACTIC FORM

The playwright is responsible for creating a dramatic structure and dramatic characters in his or her play. For Long Day's Journey, *the playwright Eugene O'Neill developed four characters from one family—based on the members of his own family—and fashioned an action that takes place during one day and evening in one place. Shown on the following pages is Al Hirschfeld's drawing of a production that featured Jason Robards (far right) as the father and Colleen Dewhurst (next to him) as the mother.*

8

THE PLAYWRIGHT
AND
CONVENTIONS OF
DRAMATIC STRUCTURE

CHARACTERS IN CONFLICT.
One way a dramatist develops action in a play is by setting up conflicts between characters. In Arthur Miller's The Crucible, *set at the time of the Salem witch hunts in Massachusetts, there are a number of such conflicts. Different religious leaders are set against each other; young women accuse older women of being witches; husbands are set against wives.*

Thus far we have looked at several types of people who play crucial roles in creating theater: audiences, critics, performers, directors. Among these, two groups—the audience and the performers—are essential; without them theater would not exist. A third person who is equally necessary is the *playwright*, sometimes referred to as the *dramatist*. The playwright creates the vision that guides the production and provides a blueprint for carrying it out.

There have been times in theater history when a group of actors created the script: one example is commedia dell'arte, the improvisatory theater of the Italian Renaissance; another example is found in some improvisatory experimental theater groups in the United States during the 1960s and 1970s. But in such cases, the actors are substituting for the playwright, not eliminating his or her work. The *function* of the playwright remains essential no matter who is providing it, and that function involves developing the subject of the play, the dramatic structure, the characters, and the purpose, or point of view.

Once these elements have been determined, the main task of the playwright then becomes to *dramatize* the story, to transform it into action and conversation (which is called *dialogue*), since ultimately everything onstage must be acted or spoken by a performer.

In this chapter, we will first consider the playwright's subject and then examine the fundamentals of dramatic structure: what is essential to structure, what conventions shape it, and how playwrights go about creating it. In Chapters 9, 10, and 11, we will take up specific kinds of dramatic structure; and in Chapter 12—the last chapter of Part Three—we will look at dramatic characters. Part Four will bring us to the playwright's purpose and its embodiment in theatrical genres.

✳ THE PLAYWRIGHT'S SUBJECT: HUMAN BEINGS ✳

The focus of the story in a drama is always the same: human beings and human concerns. Theater has always focused on human beings, even though different aspects of their concerns have been emphasized in different plays: the pretenses of men and women in society in *The Way of the World* by William Congreve; the conflict between high principle and expediency in *Antigone* by Sophocles; the terrible way in which members of one family can drive one another into desperation and despair in *Long Day's Journey into Night* by Eugene O'Neill; the alternating hope and futility of men waiting for salvation in *Waiting for Godot* by Samuel Beckett; the celebration of life in a small town in Thornton Wilder's *Our Town*.

HUMAN CONCERNS: THE FOCUS OF THEATER.
Unlike art forms that concentrate on colors and shapes (painting), movement (dance), or sound (music), theater focuses on encounters between human beings. Performers impersonate characters who engage in a series of personal exchanges. Even in a play dealing with moral ideas, like the medieval drama Everyman, *the emphasis is on the central character. Everyman faces a challenge that comes to each of us: the inevitable approach of death. Shown here, in an adaptation of* Everyman *by Hugo von Hofmannsthal, is Klaus Maria Brandauer in the title role.*

Drama concentrates on human concerns even when performers play animals, inanimate objects, or abstract ideas. The medieval morality play *Everyman* is a good example. Although some of the roles are abstract ideas such as Fellowship, Knowledge, Good Deeds, Beauty, and Strength, the central character is Everyman, a human character if there ever was one. And the problem of the play—death coming to human beings before they want it to come—is a universal human theme.

The way in which gods are depicted provides a further illustration of the person-centered quality of theater. In Greek drama, the gods sometimes appeared at the end of the play to intervene and tie up loose ends of the plot. The manner of their entrance is noteworthy: they were lowered to the orchestra level from the top of the stage house by a large

CHAPTER 8 · THE PLAYWRIGHT AND CONVENTIONS OF DRAMATIC STRUCTURE lever or crane, called a *machine*. The term *deus ex machina*, which means literally "god from the machine," has come to stand for any device, divine or otherwise, brought in to solve problems in a play arbitrarily. The gods were introduced, however, at the end, after the main characters—all human beings—had been through the anguish and struggle of the play. The emphasis was on the human problem, and the appearance of a god was almost an afterthought.

In the modern world, human beings have lost the central place they were once believed to occupy in the universe. In the Ptolemaic view of the universe, which prevailed until the sixteenth century—when Copernicus discovered that the earth revolved around the sun—it was assumed that the earth, ruled by human beings, was the center of everything. Of course, we have long since given up that notion, particularly in light of recent explorations in outer space. The human being has become seemingly less and less significant, and less and less at the center of things. But not in theater. Theater is one area where the preoccupations of men and women, for better or worse, are still the core; they are the center of gravity around which other elements orbit—the center, in other words, of the dramatic universe.

In films, too, the emphasis is generally on human affairs, and people are even shown in outsized close-ups. But films present only images, not live human beings; in addition, we often find that in a film the frame of reference moves far away from the human scale. An aerial shot from a helicopter, for example, will present a panorama of a whole countryside, with a scale sometimes so vast that the human being hardly figures in it at all. In theater this could never happen; the human being is always center stage, literally and figuratively.

The playwright's subject, then, is human beings. But clearly a play cannot simply be about "people" or even about "people's concerns," and the first task of the dramatist is therefore to decide what *aspect* of people and their concerns to write about.

Will the drama be based on history—for example, an episode or incident from the American Civil War, from World War II, or from the Vietnamese War? Perhaps it will be based on biography—on the life of Abraham Lincoln, Eleanor Roosevelt, or Martin Luther King, Jr. The dramatist may want to explore some aspect of his or her own life: the problems of growing up or facing a personal crisis as an adult. Still another possibility would be an imaginary story, such as a fantasy or a nightmare.

Once the playwright has developed a subject, a second decision will center on how to treat the subject. Treating the subject has to do with dramatic structure, characters, and point of view. We begin with the all-important question of dramatic structure.

BUILDING A PLAY:
* THE SIGNIFICANCE OF STRUCTURE *

Every work of art has some kind of *structure*. Whether it is loosely connected or tightly knit is not important; what is important is that a framework does exist. There is a loose analogy or parallel between the structure of a play and that of a building. An architect and an engineer work together like the playwright and the director. The architect and engineer plan a skeleton or substructure which will provide the inner strength for the building. They determine the depth of the foundation, the weight of the support beams, and the stress on the side walls. In a similar fashion the playwright and the director establish a premise for the play which serves as its foundation; they introduce various stresses and strains in the form of conflicts; they establish boundaries and outer limits to contain the play; they calculate the dynamics of the action. In short, they "construct" a play.

Buildings vary enormously in size and shape: they can be as diverse as a skyscraper, a cathedral, and a small cottage. Buildings can come in clusters, such as the homes in a suburban development or the buildings on a college campus. Engineering requirements will vary according to the needs of individual structures: a gymnasium roof must span a vast open area; this calls for a different construction from that of a sixty-story skyscraper, which in turn calls for something different from a ski lodge on the side of a mountain. Plays, too, vary; they can be tightly constructed or loosely arranged. The important point is that each play, like each piece of architecture, has its own internal laws and its own framework, which give it shape, strength, and meaning. Without structure, a theater event falls apart, just as a building collapses which has been put together improperly.

Naturally, structure manifests itself differently in theater from the way it manifests itself in architecture. A play is not a building. It unfolds through time rather than occupying space. It evolves and develops like a living organism, and we become aware of its structure as we sense the underlying pattern and rhythm of the production. The repeated impulses of two characters in conflict or the tension which mounts as the pace quickens—these insinuate themselves into our subconsciousness like a drumbeat. Moment by moment we see what is happening onstage; but below the surface we sense a substructure, giving the event meaning and purpose.

Underscoring the significance of structure are the problems that arise when it is not developed satisfactorily. Frequently we see a production in which most elements—the acting, the costumes, the scenery, the words, even the situation—appear correct. But somehow the play does not seem to progress; it becomes dull and repetitious. Or perhaps the play becomes confusing and diffuse, going off in several directions at once. When this happens, the chances are that the problems are struc-

151

tural. Either no clear structure existed to begin with, or the structure which did exist was violated along the way. This points up two principles of dramatic structure: (1) every theatrical event must have an underlying pattern or organization, and (2) once the pattern or organization is established, it must remain true to itself—it must be organic and have integrity. A rigid plot which suddenly becomes chaotic two-thirds of the way through the play will cause confusion. Conversely, a loosely organized play that suddenly takes on a tight structure appears artificial and contrived.

Although structure is sometimes less apparent than the performances of the actors and actresses or less obvious than the words and actions of the play, it is no less important. No matter how stimulating a performance onstage might be, it is not a complete theater experience if it has no form or shape.

❋ ESSENTIALS OF DRAMATIC STRUCTURE ❋

In the theater, structure usually takes the form of a *plot*, which is the arrangement of events or the selection and order of scenes in a play. Plot, in turn, is generally based on a story.

The Form of Drama: Plot versus Story

Stories—narrative accounts of what people do—are as old as the human race: they form the substance of daily conversation, of newspapers and television, of novels and films. But every medium presents a story in a different form.

In theater, the story must be presented by living actors and actresses on a stage in a limited period of time, and this requires selectivity. It is important to remember that the plot of a play differs from a story. A *story* is a full account of an event, or series of events, usually told in chronological order. *Plot,* as opposed to story, is a selection and arrangement of scenes taken from a story for presentation on the stage. It is what actually happens onstage, not what is talked about. The story of Abraham Lincoln begins with his being born in a log cabin and continues to the day he was shot at Ford's Theater in Washington. In a play about Abraham Lincoln, therefore, the playwright must make choices. Does the dramatist include scenes in Springfield, Illinois, where Lincoln served as a lawyer and held his famous debates with Stephen A. Douglas? Or does everything take place in Washington after Lincoln became president? Are there scenes with Lincoln's wife, Mary Todd, or only with government and military officials? The plot of a play about Lincoln and his wife would include scenes and characters related primarily to their lives. The plot of a play about the Lincoln-Douglas debates would include scenes relating chiefly to that subject.

152

Even when a play is based on a fictional story, the plot must be more restricted and structured than the story itself is. A good example is Henrik Ibsen's *Ghosts* (which will be discussed in Chapter 9). In such a story, invented by the playwright, the characters and scenes must still be selected and the sequence determined.

Creating the plot is the responsibility of the playwright, who decides at what point in the story the plot will begin, which characters will participate, what scenes will be included, and in what sequence they will occur. In developing a plot, two ingredients are essential: action and conflict.

The Subject and Verb of Drama: People and Action

As was pointed out above, the subject of theater is always people—their hopes, their joys, their foibles, their fears. In other words, if we were to construct a grammar of the theater, the *subject* would be people, the dramatic characters that represent human concerns. In grammar, every subject needs a verb; similarly, in theater, dramatic characters need a verb—some form of action—to define them.

The terms *to act* and *to perform* are used in theater to denote the impersonation of a character by an actor or an actress, but the words also mean "to do something," or "to be active." The word *drama* derives from a Greek root, the verb *dran,* meaning "to do" or "to act." At its heart, theater involves action.

The Crucible of Drama: Conflict

One theory of history maintains that the growth and well-being of a civilization lie in its ability to respond successfully to environmental and human challenges. Without speculating on the accuracy of this as a theory of history, we can say that *people* often define themselves by the way they handle challenge and response. If they cannot face up to a challenge, it tells us one thing; if they meet it with dignity, even though defeated, it tells us another; if they triumph, it tells us something else. It is the same in our own lives. We get to know the members of our family, our friends, and our enemies by seeing how they respond to us and to other people, and how they meet crises in their own lives and in ours.

In life this process can take years—in fact, it continues to unfold for as long as we know a person. But in the theater we have only a few hours, and the playwright, therefore, must devise means by which the characters will face challenges and be tested in a short space of time. The American dramatist Arthur Miller named one of his plays *The Crucible.* Literally, a *crucible* is a vessel in which metal is tested by being exposed to extreme heat. Figuratively, a crucible has come to stand for

CHAPTER 8 • THE PLAYWRIGHT AND CONVENTIONS OF DRAMATIC STRUCTURE

A PLAYWRIGHT GOES TO THE FOUNTAINHEAD.
*The American playwright Arthur Miller is shown at the Greek theater at Epidaurus, Greece.
The Theater Dionysus in Athens is where the first Greek playwrights began to develop
dramatic structure along with dramatic characters and dramatic poetry. Miller—as well as
thousands of other dramatists in the past 2,500 years—follows in their footsteps.*

any severe test of human worth and endurance—a trial by fire. In a
sense, every play provides a crucible: a test devised by the playwright
to show how the characters behave under conditions of stress. Through
this test the meaning of the play is brought out.

The crucible of a play can vary enormously: it might be a fight for a
kingdom, or in modern terms a fight for "turf," but it can just as easily
be a fight over a person. It can be an intellectual or moral confrontation.
There may be no overt clash at all, as in Samuel Beckett's *Waiting for
Godot,* in which two men wait on a barren plain for a creature named
Godot who never comes. But there must be tension of some sort. In
Waiting for Godot, for instance, there are several sources of tension or
conflict: the ever-present question whether the mysterious Godot will
come or not; the friction between the two main characters, who get on
one another's nerves but desperately need each other; the unfolding
revelation of men deluding themselves, over and over again; and on
top of these, a constant probing of religious and philosophical ideas in
a series of questions posed by the author.

154

Though the conflict or tension in drama may take a number of forms, its presence is essential. Every play must have "kinetic energy," a "magnetic field," a "flow of electrical current"—you may use whatever figure of speech you choose. This is the only way we come to know dramatic characters, to experience a play, and ultimately to absorb its meaning.

✳ STRUCTURAL CONVENTIONS: ✳ THE RULES OF THE GAME

In order to ensure that the events onstage will be dynamic and that the characters will face a meaningful test, a set of conventions or "ground rules" have evolved in dramatic structure. A good analogy would be the rules in games such as card games, board games, and sports. In each case rules are developed to ensure a lively contest. Let us consider, for example, the comparison with sports. Theater is more varied and complex than most sports events, and its rules are not so clearly defined or so consciously imposed. Nevertheless, there are similarities which point up the ways in which a play achieves maximum impact.

Limited Space

Most sports have a limited playing area. In some cases this consists of a confined space: a boxing ring, a basketball court, a baseball field. The playing area is clearly defined and invariably there is some kind of "out of bounds."

Theater is, of course, usually limited to a stage; but there is also a limit within the play itself. The action of a play is generally confined to a "world" of its own— that is, to a fictional universe which contains all the characters and events of the play—and none of the characters or actions moves outside the orbit of that world. Sometimes the world of a play is restricted to a single room. In his play *No Exit*, Jean-Paul Sartre (1905–1980), a French existentialist, confines three characters to one room, from which, as the title suggests, there is no escape. The room is supposed to be hell, and the three characters—a man, Garcin; and two women, Estelle and Inez— are confined there forever. Estelle loves Garcin, Garcin loves Inez, and Inez (a lesbian) loves Estelle. Each one, in short, loves the one who will not reciprocate; and by being confined to the one room, they face a form of permanent torture—in other words, a form of hell.

Writers like Ibsen and Strindberg frequently confined their plays to one room as well. Among modern plays, there are numerous instances in which the action takes place in a single room, a good example being *'Night, Mother* by Marsha Norman (1947–). Even plays that are not so closely contained usually occupy a restricted area. The action might take place in one castle and its environs, as in *Hamlet,* or in the general area of a battlefield, as in Bertolt Brecht's *Mother Courage.* But the sense of a private universe, with outer limits, is always there.

Limited Time

Sporting events put some limit on the duration of action. In football and basketball, there is a definite time limit. In golf, there is a given number of holes; and in baseball or tennis, there is a limited number of innings or games. Theoretically, sports which are open-ended, such as baseball and tennis, can go on forever; but fans get impatient with this arrangement, as is indicated by the move in tennis in recent years to establish a "sudden death" or tie-breaker playoff when a set reaches six-all. A time or score limit ensures that the spectators can see a complete event; they can live through a total experience in miniature, with a clear winner and loser and no loose ends.

The notion of a time limit in theater can be looked at in two ways: first, as the length of time it takes a performance to be completed; second, as the time limit placed on the characters within the framework of the play itself. Let us look at each of these.

Most theatrical performances last anywhere from 1 to 3 hours. The longest theatrical productions about which we have records are medieval cycle plays. A series usually lasted several days; and one, at Valenciennes, France, in 1547, went on for twenty-five days. Generally, however, these presentations comprised a group of separate plays—one on Adam, another on Noah, a third on Abraham and Isaac, etc.—each one complete in itself, with the series strung together like beads on a chain.

In the ancient Greek drama festivals, plays were presented for several days in a row. On a single day there might be a trilogy of three connecting plays followed by a short comic play. Even if we count a Greek trilogy as one play, it lasted only the better part of a day. These examples are exceptions, though; most performances are limited to 2 or 3 hours.

More important than the actual playing time of a performance is the time limit or deadline *within* the play. Frequently one finds in a play a fixed period within which the characters must complete an action. At the end of the second act of Ibsen's *A Doll's House,* the heroine, Nora, is trying desperately to get her husband to put off until the following evening the opening of a letter which she fears will establish her as a forger and will threaten their marriage. When he agrees, Nora says to herself, "Thirty-one hours to live."

Strongly Opposed Forces

Most sports, like many other types of games, involve two teams, or two individuals, opposing each other. This ensures clear lines of force: the

OPPOSING FORCES IN A PLAY.
Traditional plot structure calls for strongly opposing forces in a play: the antagonist opposes the protagonist; one group opposes another. In Garcia Lorca's The House of Barnarda Alba, *shown here, three daughters oppose their mother as well as each other.*

good guys and the bad guys, the home team and the visitors. The contest is straight and simple, like a shoot-out on Main Street at high noon between the sheriff and the outlaw. (A perfect example in a board game is chess.) The musical *West Side Story* (which is based on Shakespeare's *Romeo and Juliet*) features two opposing gangs, not unlike opposing teams in sports. In the simplest dramatic situations, one character directly opposes another—the *protagonist* against the *antagonist*.

In a manual on playwriting, the critic Kenneth MacGowan emphasized that characters in a play "must be so selected and developed that they include people who are bound to react upon each other, bound to clash."[1] In the vast majority of dramas, playwrights have followed this approach. A perfect example of characters bound to clash are the man and woman, Julie and Jean, in Strindberg's *Miss Julie*. Julie, an aristocrat, is the daughter of the owner of an estate. She has had an unhappy

FAMILY MEMBERS IN CONFLICT.
Drama frequently puts members of the same family in conflict with one another. In this scene from August Wilson's The Piano Lesson, *Charles S. Dutton (right) is arguing vehemently with his sister, played by S. Epatha Merkerson (left), about the fate of the family piano.*

engagement and is deeply suspicious of men but at the same time sexually attracted to them. Jean, an aggressive male, is a servant with dreams of escaping his life of servitude and becoming a hotel owner. These two, drawn together by strong forces of repulsion and attraction, meet on midsummer's eve in a climactic encounter.

A similar confrontation occurs in Tennessee Williams's *A Streetcar Named Desire* between Blanche DuBois and Stanley Kowalski. For Blanche, a faded southern belle trying desperately to hold onto her gentility, the crude aggressive Stanley is the chief threat to her stability and her survival. On his side, Stanley, who is insecure about his lack of education and refinement, is provoked by Blanche and her superior airs almost to the breaking point.

A device frequently used by dramatists to guarantee friction or tension between forces is the restriction of characters to members of one family. Relatives have built-in rivalries and affinities: parents versus children, sisters versus brothers. Being members of the same family, they have no avenue of escape. Mythology, on which so much drama is based, abounds with familial relationships.

Shakespeare frequently set members of one family against one another: Hamlet opposes his mother; Lear opposes his daughters; Jessica opposes her father, Shylock, in *The Merchant of Venice.* In modern drama, virtually every writer of note has dealt with close family situations: Ibsen, Strindberg, Chekhov, Williams, Miller, and Edward Albee (1928–   ), to mention a few. The American dramatist Eugene O'Neill—who used the Agamemnon myth in his *Mourning Becomes Electra*—wrote what many consider his finest play, *Long Day's Journey into Night,* about the four members of his own family.

A Balance of Forces

Rules ensuring that the contest will be as equal as possible without coming to a dead draw are a feature of most sports. We all want our team to win, but we would rather see a close, exciting contest than a runaway; nothing is duller to a sports fan than a lopsided game. The struggle, as much as the outcome, is the source of pleasure. And so rules are set up, with handicaps or other devices to equalize the forces. In basketball or football, the moment one team scores, the other team gets the ball so that it will have an opportunity to even the score.

In theater, a hard-fought and relatively equal contest is implicit in what has been said about opposing forces: Jean stands opposite Miss Julie, and Blanche opposite Stanley. Even in the somewhat muted, low-key plays of Anton Chekhov, there is a balance of forces among various groups. In *The Cherry Orchard,* those who own the orchard are pitted against the man who will acquire it; in *The Three Sisters,* the sisters of the title are opposed in the possession of their home by their acquisitive sister-in-law.

Incentive and Motivation

In sports, as in other kinds of games, a prize is offered to guarantee that the participants will give their best in an intense contest. In professional sports it is money; in amateur sports, a trophy such as a cup. In addition, there is the glory of winning, the accolades of television and the press, and the plaudits of family and friends.

For its part, good drama never lacks incentive or motivation for its characters: Macbeth wants desperately to be king; Saint Joan wishes to save France; and Blanche DuBois must find protection and preserve her dignity in order to survive.

Using the conventions discussed above, the playwrights sets out to develop his or her dramatic structure. It begins with the crucial opening scene of the play.

The Opening Scene

The first scene of a drama starts the action and sets the tone and style for everything that follows. It tells us whether we are going to see a serious play or a comic one and whether the play will deal with affairs of everyday life or some fantasy. The opening scene is a cue or signal as to what lies ahead; it also sets the wheels of action in motion, giving the characters a shove and hurtling them toward their destination.

The playwright provides this initial shove by posing a problem to the characters, establishing an imbalance of forces or a disturbance in their equilibrium which compels the characters to respond. Generally this imbalance occurs just before the play begins or arises immediately after it opens. In *King Oedipus,* for example, a plague has hit the city just before the opening of the play. In *Hamlet,* "something is rotten in the state of Denmark" before the play opens; and early in the play the ghost of Hamlet's father tells Hamlet to seek revenge. At the beginning of *Romeo and Juliet,* the Capulets and the Montagues are at one another's throats in a street fight. Strindberg's *Miss Julie* begins on midsummer's eve and opens with Miss Julie acting "wildly," obviously on the verge of some precipitous act.

As these examples suggest, the opening scene initiates the action. Characters are presented with a challenge and thrust into a situation which provides the starting point for the entire play.

Obstacles and Complications

Having met the initial challenge of the play, the characters then move through a series of steps alternating between achievement and defeat, between hope and despair. The moment they seem to accomplish one goal or reach a plateau of satisfaction, certain factors or events cut across the play to upset the balance and start the characters on another path. In theater these may be *obstacles*, which are impediments put in a character's way; or they may be *complications,* which consist of outside forces, or new twists in the plot, introduced at an inopportune moment.

Shakespeare's *Hamlet* provides numerous examples of obstacles and complications. Hamlet stages a play-within-the-play in order to confirm that his uncle Claudius has killed his father. When Claudius reacts to the play in a manner that makes his guilt obvious, Hamlet's path to achieving revenge seems clear. But when Hamlet goes to kill Claudius,

PLOT COMPLICATIONS IN HAMLET.

In traditional plot structure, a series of problems confronting the characters prolongs the action and increases tension. A good example is the twists and turns in the plot of Shakespeare's Hamlet, *shown here with Christopher Walken (right) in the title role.*

he discovers him at prayer. An obstacle has been thrown in Hamlet's path: if Claudius dies while praying, he may go to heaven rather than to hell. Since Hamlet does not want Claudius to go to heaven, he does not kill him. Later, Hamlet is in his mother's bedroom when he hears a noise behind a curtain. Surely Claudius is lurking there, and Hamlet can kill him instantly. But when Hamlet thrusts his sword through the curtain, he finds that he has killed Polonius instead. This complicates matters because it provides Claudius with an excuse to send Hamlet to England with Rosencrantz and Guildenstern, who carry with them a letter instructing the King of England to murder Hamlet. Hamlet gets out of that trap and returns to Denmark. Now, at last, he can carry out his revenge. But upon his return, he discovers that Ophelia has killed herself while he was away, and her brother, Laertes, is seeking revenge on Hamlet. This complicates the situation once again; Hamlet is prevented from meeting Claudius head-on because he must also deal with

Laertes. In the end Hamlet does carry out his mission, but only after many interruptions.

As stated above, dramatic characters have objectives or goals that they are strongly motivated to obtain. Macbeth wants to become king; Miss Julie wants to conquer the servant, Jean. But there are obstacles to achieving these goals, and other characters oppose the main characters' wishes and interfere with their plans. The result is inevitable tension and conflict.

Crisis and Climax

As a result of conflicts, obstacles, and complications in a play, characters become involved in a series of *crises*—some less complicated than those in *Hamlet*, some more complicated. A play in the traditional mode builds from one crisis to another. The first crisis will be resolved only to have the action lead to a subsequent crisis. The final and most significant crisis is referred to as the *climax*. Sometimes there is a minor climax earlier in the play and a major climax near the conclusion. In the final climax the issues of the play are resolved, either happily or, in the case of tragedies, unhappily, usually with the death of the hero or heroine.

In this chapter we have been looking at the subject and structure of theater, and particularly at the development of plot, which thrusts characters into action. So far, we have examined general principles; when we look at dramatic construction more closely, we discover that certain forms have recurred throughout theater history. In Chapters 9, 10, and 11, we will examine forms of dramatic structure.

✳ SUMMARY ✳

1   We learn about dramatic characters by what they do and say, just as we learn about people in everyday life.

2   The action of a play frequently consists of a test, or crucible, for the characters, in which their true nature is defined.

3   The usual test for a character involves being enmeshed in activities or events—a dramatic plot.

4   A dramatic plot is not the same as a story. A *story* is a complete account of an episode or a sequence of events, but a *plot* is what we see onstage. In a plot the events have been selected from a story and arranged in a certain sequence.

5   Dramatic conventions, ensuring a strong plot and continuation of tension, are analogous to rules in sports. In both sports and theater there are limited spaces or playing areas, time limits imposed on the

action, strongly opposing forces, evenly matched contestants, and prizes or goals for the participants.

6 A play generally begins with an imbalance of forces or a loss of equilibrium by one of the characters; this propels the characters to action.

7 As a play progresses, the characters meet a series of complications as they attempt to fulfill their objectives or realize their goals. These encounters produce the tension and conflict of drama.

8 In developing a plot, the playwright uses the conventions and tools of dramatic construction to emphasize specific characters or other elements.

✳ TOPICS FOR DISCUSSION ✳

1 The novelist E. M. Forster suggested that in novels a crucial difference between *story* and *plot* is that a plot emphasizes causality. "The king died and then the queen died" is a story, he said; "The king died, and then the queen died of grief" is a plot.[2] Would you agree that causality is equally important in the plot of a play? Why or why not?

2 Try to imagine a play without conflict, and then try to write a brief synopsis of such a play. Does this exercise convince you that conflict is essential to drama?

3 Imagine a play in which the opposing forces were very much *un*-balanced. What would be wrong with such a play?

4 Do the motivations of dramatic characters seem to differ in any way from those of people in real life?

CHAPTER 8 · THE PLAYWRIGHT AND CONVENTIONS OF DRAMATIC STRUCTURE

9

DRAMATIC STRUCTURE: CLIMACTIC AND EPISODIC FORMS

CLIMACTIC AND EPISODIC STRUCTURE.
One of the two major forms of plot structure in traditional drama is episodic structure. A good example is found in Ibsen's Peer Gynt, *which ranges widely over many countries and a long period of time. It also includes numerous characters. Shown here is Peer's long-suffering wife Solveig, played by Tara Hugo in a production at the Hartford Stage Company directed by Mark Lamos.*

Throughout theater history, we find basic dramatic forms reappearing. In western civilization, a form adopted in Greece in the fifth century B.C. emerges, somewhat altered, in France in the seventeenth century. The same form shows up once more in Norway in the late nineteenth century. This form, which will be discussed shortly, can be referred to as *climactic*. Another, contrasting form, best illustrated by the plays of Shakespeare, can be called *episodic*. One or the other of these forms—or some combination of the two—has been the predominant dramatic structure through most of the history of western theater. Another approach, in which dramatic episodes are strung together without any apparent connection, has emerged in a new guise in recent times. The absurdist approach is a more modern phenomenon. Finally, the structure based on a ritual or pattern is both old and new.

The characteristics of the basic types will be clearer when we look at each separately, and in its purest forms. This chapter begins with the climactic form and goes on to examine the episodic form; Chapter 10 takes up additional forms.

❊ CHARACTERISTICS OF CLIMACTIC STRUCTURE ❊

The Plot Begins Late in the Story

The first hallmark of climactic drama is that the plot begins quite late in the story. Ibsen's *Ghosts,* written in 1881, affords an example. Before the play begins, the following has occurred: Mrs. Alving has married a dissolute husband who fathers an illegitimate child by another woman and contracts a venereal disease. Discovering this early in her marriage, she visits the family minister, Pastor Manders, to try to get out of the marriage. Although she is attracted to Manders and he to her, and although he realizes that she is wronged and miserable, he sends her back to her husband. She stays with her husband out of a Victorian sense of duty, sending her own son away to escape the father's influence. When her husband dies, Mrs. Alving builds an orphanage in his honor to camouflage his true character.

As is typical with a climactic plot structure, the play still has not begun; it begins later, when the son returns home and the facts of the past are unearthed, precipitating the crisis of the play. Thus, in climactic structure the play begins when all the roads of the past converge at one crucial intersection of the present—at the climax, in other words.

The fact that the plot begins so late in climactic drama has at least two important consequences. First, it is frequently necessary to explain what has gone before by having one character report the information to another. The technical term for this revelation of background information is *exposition.* During the early parts of *Ghosts,* the information about the unhappy marriage of Captain and Mrs. Alving, with all its

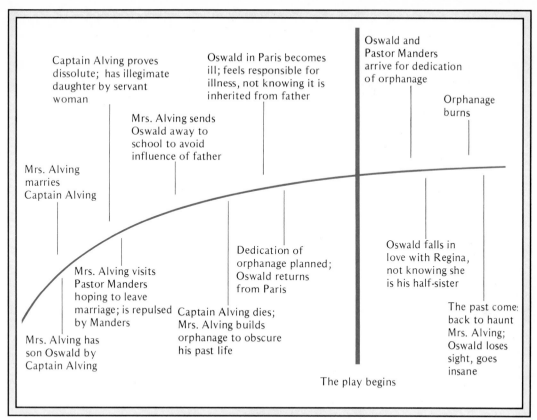

CLIMACTIC STRUCTURE IN GHOSTS.

Henrik Ibsen's play follows the climactic form, in which the play begins toward the very end—or climax—of the sequence of events. The parts of the story that occur before the play begins are to the left of the vertical line. Only the events to the right occur in the play; the ones before them must be described in exposition.

consequences for their own lives as well as the life of their son Oswald, must be conveyed by one character to another. Though the information may be presented in an interesting and suspenseful way, it nevertheless is material from the past, and thus is exposition. Another form of exposition is a description of something that happens offstage during the course of the play. An example in *Ghosts* would be an account of the fire that takes place in the new orphanage between Acts II and III.

A second consequence of the climactic form's beginning late in the story is that the time span covered by the play is usually brief, in many cases a matter of a few hours. At the most, events in a climactic play cover a few days. Some playwrights, attempting to push events as near the climax as possible, have stage time (the time we imagine is passing

167

GHOSTS (1881)

HENRIK IBSEN (1828—1906)

CHIEF CHARACTERS:
Mrs. Alving—a widow
Oswald Alving—her son, an artist
Manders—a pastor
Engstrand—a carpenter
Regina Engstrand—his daughter
Mrs. Alving's maid

SETTING: The sitting room of Mrs. Alving's house on a large fjord (inlet of the sea) in western Norway.

TIME: The late nineteenth century.

BACKGROUND: Mr. Alving, a prominent local businessman, was also a womanizer. Because of this, Mrs. Alving left him once and went to seek advice from Pastor Manders. She was attracted to Manders and he to her, but she was persuaded by Manders to return to her "duty." She returned to Mr. Alving. Although Mr. Alving did not change, Mrs. Alving covered up for him. Their son Oswald was sent away to school by Mrs. Alving so that he would not be under his father's influence. One of the women with whom Alving had a liaison was the family's maid Joanna, which resulted in Joanna's becoming pregnant. The Alvings married Joanna off to the carpenter Engstrand, and when the child was born, it was a daughter whom they named Regina. Now, many years later, Joanna has died, and Regina has become a maid in the Alving household.

ACT I: Engstrand arrives at the Alving house to try to persuade his "daughter" Regina to leave the Alvings and come live with him in the new sailors' home he plans to open in the nearby town. Regina, however, is ambitious and wants to stay with the Alvings, hoping to better herself. She becomes angry and tells Engstrand to leave. Pastor Manders arrives and tries to convince Regina to go with Engstrand as a "daughter's duty."

Mrs. Alving is building an orphanage to obliterate the memory of Mr. Alving's dissolute life. Manders has come for the dedication of the orphanage, but when Mrs. Alving asks him to stay at her home rather than in town, he refuses, fearing for his reputation. He also advises her not to take out insurance on the new orphanage because people would think he and Mrs. Alving had a lack of faith in God's power to protect the orphanage. She warns him of a small fire the day before, most likely caused by Engstrand, who is careless, but Manders insists that there be no insurance. Mrs. Alving also tells him she is against Regina's moving to the sailors' home Engstrand has planned. A weary Oswald, who had arrived from Paris the night before, enters. Manders regrets that Oswald never learned what a "well-regulated home means," but Oswald replies that he lived with couples who were not married but who were, nevertheless, hard-working and principled. Manders is scandalized, but Mrs. Alving thinks Oswald is right no matter what he does. After Oswald leaves the room, Manders reminds Mrs. Alving that when she left her husband, he made her "do her duty" and return home. She then tells Manders the truth about everything: that her husband died a profligate, that he had a child by her maid, Joanna, and that it was then that she sent Oswald away to escape his father's influence. She is building the orphanage not really to honor Alving but to silence all rumors about her dead husband. Meanwhile, Oswald makes advances to Regina in the dining room; when Mrs. Alving hears this, she is agitated because she envisions the "ghost" of her dead husband in Oswald's actions.

ACT II: After dinner, Mrs. Alving tells Manders that because Oswald is pursuing Regina, she must find another place for Regina. She also tells him that after Alving got Joanna pregnant, Engstrand married her and took responsibility for the child, Regina. Manders is shocked that Engstrand would marry a "fallen woman." Mrs. Alving points out that she was married to a "fallen man." When Engstrand comes to ask Manders to lead the workers at the orphanage in prayer, Manders questions him about his relationship with Regina and tells him that he knows the truth. The clever Engstrand says that he did it for the welfare of Joanna and the baby and convinces Manders that he is repentant.

After Manders leaves, Oswald tells his mother that he fears he is losing his mind; he has violent headaches which have been interfering with his work. A doctor has told him that he has inherited a venereal disease: "The sins of the fathers are visited on the children," he says. Oswald has assumed that he had contracted the disease himself because he did not think it could have come from his righteous father. Now Oswald looks upon Regina as his chance for happiness, and he wants to take her to Paris. Mrs. Alving is about to reveal the truth—that his father was dissolute and Regina is his half-sister—when Manders enters. A moment later they look out the window and discover that the orphanage is on fire.

ACT III: Manders is lamenting the ruined orphanage when Engstrand says that the fire was caused because Manders was careless with a candle. Engstrand plans to blackmail Manders with this untrue accusation, but he tells Manders that he will take the blame if Manders will give him financial help for his sailors' home. Manders is relieved and prom-

(Martha Swope)

ises to help him, but Oswald says that the sailors' home will be destroyed also, that nothing will be left in his father's memory. At this point, Mrs. Alving reveals to Regina and Oswald who Regina's true father is.

Mrs. Alving and Oswald talk about the bleak prospects for the future. Oswald is desperate with fear. He had thought that Regina could help him, but she has decided to leave. Mrs. Alving assures him that she will always be there. Oswald makes his mother promise that when he can no longer take care of himself, she will give him some pills so that he can die peacefully. When dawn comes, Oswald has gone blind; the disease has taken over. As the curtain falls, Mrs. Alving is trying to decide whether to help her son take his own life.

THE RESTRICTIONS OF CLIMACTIC DRAMA.

Climactic drama is limited to a few characters in a restricted locale, and the action takes place in a short period of time. A good example of a recent climactic drama is A. R. Gurney's The Cocktail Hour, *which has only four characters and takes place in the living room of the parents' home over a very short span of time. The characters shown here are (left to right): the father, played by Keene Curtis; the mother, Nancy Marchand; the son, Bruce Davidson; and the sister, Holland Taylor.*

when we are watching a play) coincide with real time (that is, clock time). An example is Tennessee Williams's *Cat on a Hot Tin Roof:* the events depicted in the story last the same 2½ hours as the play itself.

Scenes, Locales, and Characters Are Limited

A limited number of long segments, or acts, mark climactic drama. In Greek plays there are generally five episodes separated by choral interludes. The French neoclassicists invariably used five acts. For much of the nineteenth and twentieth centuries, three acts were standard. Today, the norm is two acts. The long one-act play performed without intermission is also used frequently in modern theater.

Limited scenes in a play usually entail a restricted locale as well. In the discussion of the "rules" of drama, we saw that the action can be confined to a single room, as in Sartre's *No Exit*. Such close confinement is a hallmark of climactic drama.

Along with restriction of locale, there is a restriction of characters. Aside from the chorus, Greek drama generally has four or five principal characters. Many modern plays have the same number.

170

Construction Is Tight

Because it is carefully constructed, a climactic play fits tightly together, with no loose ends. It is like a chain indissolubly linked in a cause-and-effect relationship. As in a detective story, A leads to B, B to C, which causes D, leading in turn to E, and so on. Just as the space and the time frame afford no exit, so the chain of events is locked in; once action begins, there is no stopping it.

To give an illustration: in *Phaedra* by Jean Racine (1639–1699), the heroine, Phaedra, is secretly in love with her stepson, Hippolytus. When she hears (A) that her husband, Theseus, is dead, she (B) confesses her love to Hippolytus, causing him (C) to react in horror and disgust. Theseus, unknown to Phaedra, is not dead, however; and when he returns home, Phaedra, fearing disclosure of her incestuous love, (D) allows her nurse to tell Theseus that Hippolytus has made advances toward her. Thereupon, Theseus (E) invokes a god to punish Hippolytus. Hippolytus (F) is slain, leading Phaedra (G) to poison herself, confessing the truth to Theseus before she dies.

Anouilh, in his *Antigone,* compares tragedy to the workings of a machine.

> The spring is wound up tight. It will uncoil of itself. That is what is so convenient in tragedy. The least little turn of the wrist will do the job. . . . The rest is automatic. You don't need to lift a finger. The machine is in perfect order; it has been oiled ever since time began and it runs without friction.[1]

Anouilh claims that this notion applies only to tragedy, but in fact it fits every play which is in the climactic form; the aim always is to make events so inevitable that there is no escape—at least not until the very last moment, when a *deus ex machina* may intervene to untangle the knot. Because a climactic drama is so carefully and so tightly constructed, in the modern period it has frequently been referred to as a *well-made play.*

Clearly, the method of climactic drama is one of compression. Every element—characters, locale, events—is severely restricted. As if by centripetal motion, everything is forced to the center, in a tighter and tighter nucleus, making the ultimate eruption that much more explosive. It is like the cylinder in an automobile engine: a mixture of gasoline and air is compressed by the piston in the cylinder to such extreme intensity that when a spark is introduced, the resulting detonation pushes the piston out, thereby providing power for the car. And so it is with climactic drama; since the story begins near its conclusion, people and events are forced together in a sort of compression chamber, making an explosive confrontation inevitable.

The climactic plot is a popular form of structure. The countries and periods (together with the names of a few well-known playwrights) in which it has been the dominant form include these:

Greece, fifth century B.C.—Aeschylus, Sophocles, Euripides

Rome, third to first centuries B.C.—Plautus (ca. 254–184 B.C.), Terence (ca. 185–ca. 159 B.C.)

France, seventeenth century—Pierre Corneille (1606–1684), Racine, Molière

France, nineteenth century—Augustin-Eugène Scribe (1791–1861), Victorien Sardou (1831–1908)

Europe and United States, late nineteenth and twentieth centuries—Ibsen, Strindberg, O'Neill, Williams, Miller

❋ CHARACTERISTICS OF EPISODIC STRUCTURE ❋

When we turn to examples of the episodic plot, we see a contrast in construction. Episodic drama begins relatively early in the story and does not compress the action but expands it.

People, Places, and Events Proliferate

The typical episodic play covers an extensive period of time, sometimes many years, and ranges over a number of locations. In one play we can go anywhere: to a small antechamber, a large banquet hall, the open countryside, and mountaintops. Short scenes, some only a half-page or so in length, alternate with longer ones. The following examples, giving the number of characters and scenes in each play, indicate the extended nature of episodic drama:

Antony and Cleopatra by Shakespeare has thirty-four characters and forty-plus scenes.

The Sheep Well by Lope de Vega (1562–1635) has twenty-six characters and seventeen scenes.

The Caucasian Chalk Circle by Brecht has fifty-plus characters and approximately seventeen scenes.

Unlike climactic drama, episodic plays do not necessarily follow a close cause-and-effect development. Both the methods and the effects of episodic drama are different from those of climactic. The forces are centrifugal rather than centripetal, moving out to embrace additional elements.

EPISODIC DRAMA: MANY CHARACTERS, PLACES, AND EVENTS.

Such plays as Shakespeare's Julius Caesar, *shown above with Al Pacino (center), and Georg Büchner's Woyzeck, shown at left, are episodic in construction, covering long periods of time and many locales, and also involving a number of characters.*

CHAPTER 9 • DRAMATIC STRUCTURE: CLIMACTIC AND EPISODIC FORMS

The possibilities of the episodic or extended approach are discussed by John Gassner in the following description of Bertolt Brecht's work:

> He favors a type of dramatic composition that grasps the various facets of man's life in society without limiting itself to unity of time, place, and action. Some of his plays . . . even have the extensiveness of an Elizabethan chronicle such as *Henry IV, Parts I* and *II* and as much variety of action and tone. One scene may convey a realistic situation while another may symbolize it; or the scene may take the form of a debate or narration; or there may be no scene at all, only a song or recitation, at points in the play. But the episodes, combined with narrative and lyrical passages, and augmented with pantomime, dance, signs or placards, slides and motion-picture sequences if necessary—all following one another in rapid succession or alternation—will form one rich tumultuous play.[2]

There May Be a Parallel Plot or Subplot

In place of compression, as Gassner suggests, episodic drama offers other techniques. One is the *parallel plot*, or *subplot*. In *King Lear*, by Shakespeare, Lear has three daughters, two evil and one good. The two evil daughters have convinced their father that they are good and that their sister is wicked. In the subplot—a counterpart of the main plot—the Earl of Gloucester has two sons, and one son has deceived his father into thinking he is the loyal son when the reverse is true. In both cases the old men have misunderstood their children's true worth, and in the end they are punished for their mistakes: Lear is bereft of his kingdom and his sanity, Gloucester loses his eyes. The Gloucester plot, with complications and developments of its own, is a parallel and reinforcement of the Lear plot.

Juxtaposition and Contrast Occur

Another technique of episodic drama is *juxtaposition* or *contrast*. Rather than moving in linear fashion, the action alternates between elements. We identify colors by relating one color to other colors, and in music we identify melody by relating one note to another. We determine size in the same way: a man 6 feet tall is of no particular significance unless he is surrounded by other men who are shorter by contrast—then he stands out.

To develop its theme and story and to provide contrast, episodic drama employs a number of alternations and juxtapositions:

Short scenes alternate with longer ones. King Lear begins with a short scene between Kent and Gloucester, goes to a long scene in which Lear divides his kingdom, then returns to a brief scene in which Edmund declares his intention to deceive his father.

Public scenes alternate with private ones. In Brecht's *The Caucasian Chalk Circle,* the first bustling scene of revolution in the town square contrasts with a quiet scene between the two lovers, Grusha and Simon, which follows immediately.

We move from one group to an opposing group. In Shakespeare's *Othello* we move back and forth from scenes with Iago developing his plot to arouse Othello's jealousy to scenes with Othello himself. We can view both sides in action as the tragedy unfolds.

Comic scenes alternate with serious scenes. In *Macbeth,* just after Macbeth has murdered King Duncan, there is a knock on the door of the castle. It is one of the most serious moments of the play, but the man who goes to open the door is a comical character, a drunken porter, whose speech is a humorous interlude in the grim business of the play. In *Hamlet,* the gravedigger and his assistant are preparing the grave for Ophelia when Hamlet comes on the scene. The gravediggers are joking about death; but for Hamlet, who soon learns that the grave is Ophelia's, it is a somber moment. This juxtaposition of the comic with the serious may seem incongruous; but properly handled, it can bring out the irony and poignancy of an event in a way rarely achieved by other means.

There are, of course, other forms of alternation in episodic drama, but the above illustrations give an indication of the ways in which this technique can be used to create dramatic effects.

The Overall Effect Is Cumulative

As for cause and effect in episodic drama, the impression created is of events piling up: a tidal wave of circumstances and emotions sweeping over the characters. Rarely does one letter, one telephone call, or one piece of information determine the fate of a character. Time and again, Hamlet has proof that Claudius has killed his father; but it is a rush of events which eventually leads him to kill Claudius, not a single piece of hard evidence. The corruption in the court of Denmark is pervasive, and it is the combined weight of events and the atmosphere, rather than a single precipitating incident, that makes the outcome inevitable.

Episodic drama, by developing a series of extensions, parallels, contrasts, juxtapositions—in fact, a whole web or network of characters and events—achieves a cumulative effect all its own, at its best creating what Gassner referred to as a "tumultuous play."

The countries and periods in which the episodic form has predominated include these:

England, late sixteenth and early seventeenth centuries—Shakespeare, Marlowe

KING LEAR by William Shakespeare

I-1 **Lear's Palace.** Kent and Gloucester discuss the division of the kingdom and Gloucester's sons. Lear comes. The division of the kingdom: first Goneril and then Regan praise Lear. Cordelia cannot. Kent intercedes and is banished. Gloucester enters with Burgundy and France. Burgundy will not have her without dowry. France takes her. Goneril and Regan begin plotting. (305 lines)

I-2 **Gloucester's Castle.** Edmund's soliloquy and scheme. Letter and plan against Edgar begins. Gloucester leaves, Edgar comes, scheme furthered. (173 lines)

I-3 **Albany's Palace.** Goneril and Oswald scheming. (26 lines)

I-4 **The same.** Kent enters disguised; Lear comes, then Oswald, Kent trips him. Fool enters and talks to Lear. Goneril comes, chides Lear. He curses her and leaves. Goneril, Albany and Oswald conspire further, then leave. (336 lines)

I-5 **In Front of Palace.** Lear, Kent, Fool. Lear sends letters to Gloucester, starts to Regan. (46 lines)

II-1 **A Court in Gloucester's Castle.** Edmund and Curan. Edgar comes, then leaves. Edmund stabs himself; Gloucester comes, Edmund blames Edgar, Gloucester finds letter. Cornwall and Regan enter. (The forces of evil join.) (129 lines)

II-2 **Before Gloucester's Castle.** Kent confronts Oswald, Cornwall comes; Kent put in stocks. (168 lines)

II-3 **The Open Country.** Edgar's soliloquy: he will disguise and abase himself. (21 lines)

II-4 **Before Gloucester's Castle.** Lear comes, sees Kent; confronts Regan. She is stubborn too. Goneril comes. He sees a league. Begs; leaves as storm begins. (306 lines)

III-1 **A Heath.** Kent with a Gentleman. (55 lines)

III-2 **Another Part of Heath.** Lear comes with Fool. Storm and insanity begin. Kent comes. (95 lines)

III-3 **Gloucester's Castle.** Gloucester tells Edmund of divisions between Dukes and of letter from France. (23 lines)

III-4 **The Heath Before a Hovel.** Lear, Kent, Fool – Storm. Lear's madness and beginning self-realization. Edgar joins them, then Gloucester with a torch. (172 lines)

III-5 **Gloucester's Castle.** Cornwall and Edmund scheming. (22 lines)

III-6 **A Farmhouse Near Glouster's Castle.** The mock trial for Lear. Kent, Gloucester, Fool, Edgar. All leave but Edgar. (112 lines)

III-7 **Gloucester's Castle.** Cornwall, Regan, Goneril, Edmund. They send for Gloucester (the "traitor"), prepare to blind him. Servant is killed, they pluck out Gloucester's eyes. (106 lines)

IV-1 **The Heath.** Edgar. Enter Gloucester, blind. Edgar prepares cliff scene. (79 lines)

IV-2 **Before Albany's Palace.** Goneril and Edmund. Enter Oswald. Intrigue of Goneril and Edmund. Albany comes, she chides him. Servant comes telling of Cornwall's death. (979 lines)

IV-3 **The French Camp Near Dover.** Kent and Gentleman reports Lear ashamed to see Cordelia. (55 lines)

IV-4 **The French Camp.** Cordelia and Doctor enter; plan to go to England. (29 lines)

IV-5 **Gloucester's Castle.** Regan and Oswald. She says Edmund is for her. (40 lines)

IV-6 **Country Near Dover.** Gloucester and Edgar - jumping scene. Lear comes, mad. The two wronged, mad men together. Gentleman comes, then Oswald attacks him. Edgar kills Oswald, finds letters to Edmund - Goneril is plotting Albany's death to marry Edmund. (283 lines)

IV-7 **Tent in French Camp.** Cordelia and Kent. Lear brought in. The awakening and reconciliation. (96 lines)

V-1 **British Camp Near Dover.** Edmund, Regan, etc. Goneril comes, also Albany. Edgar enters, leaves. (69 lines)

V-2 **A Field Between Camps.** Cordelia and Lear cross. Edgar and Gloucester come. (11 lines)

V-3 **British Camp.** Edmund comes, Lear and Cordelia are prisoners; are sent away. Edmund sends note with guard. Enter Albany, Goneril and Regan, who quarrel. Edgar comes; challenges Edmund and wounds him. Truth about Goneril's plan comes out; she leaves. Edgar talks. Goneril and Regan are brought in dead. Edmund dies. Lear enters with the dead Cordelia; then he dies. Kent and Albany pronounce the end. (326 lines)

EPISODIC STRUCTURE IN KING LEAR.

Shakespeare's play sets up a juxtaposition of scenes. Note how the scenes move from place to place and alternate from one group of characters to another. Note, too, that the scenes move back and forth from intimate scenes to those involving a number of characters (an alternation of public and private scenes) and that the length of the scenes varies, with short scenes followed by longer ones and so forth. This structure gives the play its dynamics, its rhythm, and its meaning.

Spain, late sixteenth and early seventeenth centuries—Lope de Vega, Calderón de la Barca (1600–1681)

Germany, late eighteenth and early nineteenth centuries—Johann Wolfgang von Goethe (1749–1832), Gotthold Lessing (1729–1781), Friedrich von Schiller (1759–1805), Georg Büchner (1813–1837)

Europe and the United States, late nineteenth and twentieth centuries—Ibsen, Brecht, Genet

It will be noted that in modern theater both climactic and episodic forms have been adopted, sometimes by one playwright. This is characteristic of the diversity of our age. Ibsen, for example, wrote a number of well-made plays—*Ghosts, Hedda Gabler,* and others—but also several episodic plays, such as *Peer Gynt.*

✴ COMPARING CLIMACTIC AND EPISODIC FORM ✴

The table on the opposite page outlines the chief characteristics of the two major forms and illustrates the differences between them. It is clear that the climactic and episodic forms differ from each other in their fundamental approaches. The one emphasizes constriction and compression on all fronts; the other takes a far broader view and aims at a cumulative effect, piling up people, places, and events.

✴ COMBINING CLIMACTIC AND EPISODIC FORM ✴

There is no law which says that a play must be exclusively episodic or climactic. These forms are not watertight compartments. It is true that during certain periods, one form or the other has been predominant. And it is not easy to mix the two, because as we have seen, each has its own laws and its own inner logic. In various periods, however, they have been successfully integrated.

For example, I have been referring to Greek drama as conforming to climactic structure. In the case of the main plot of the play, this is true. In *King Oedipus* by Sophocles, for instance, the plot begins late in the story, the action takes place in one location, and there are very few characters. There is an element in Greek drama, though, that gives it an added dimension, and this is the *chorus.* By the time of Sophocles, the chorus consisted of fifteen performers who sang, danced, chanted, and sometimes interacted with the principal characters. The Greek chorus stood outside the action, arguing with the main characters, making connections between present events and the past, warning the main characters of impending danger, and drawing conclusions from what

CLIMACTIC	EPISODIC
1 Plot begins late in the story, toward the very end or climax.	Plot begins relatively early in the story and moves through a series of episodes.
2 Covers a short space of time, perhaps a few hours, or at most a few days.	Covers a longer period of time: weeks, months, and sometimes many years.
3 Contains a few solid, extended scenes, such as three acts with each act comprising one long scene.	Many short, fragmented scenes; sometimes an alteration of short and long scenes.
4 Occurs in a restricted locale, one room or one house.	May range over an entire city or even several countries.
5 Number of characters severely limited, usually no more than six or eight.	Profusion of characters, sometimes several dozen.
6 Plot is linear and moves in a single line with few subplots or counterplots.	Frequently marked by several threads of action, such as two parallel plots, or scenes of comic relief in a serious play.
7 Line of action proceeds in a cause-and-effect chain. The characters and events are closely linked in a sequence of logical, almost inevitable development.	Scenes are juxtaposed to one another. An event may result from several causes, or no apparent cause, but arises in a network or web of circumstances.

had occurred. The choral sections, which alternated with the episodes of the main plot, make Greek drama less rigidly climactic than a play like *Ghosts* or classical French plays like those of Racine.

A group of plays that combine elements of the climactic and episodic forms are the comedies of the Restoration period in England (from 1660, when the English monarchy was restored, to 1700). These comedies usually had large casts, a subplot as well as a main plot, and several changes of scene. They did not, however, cover extended periods of time or move rapidly from place to place as the plays of Shakespeare did. For example, in *The Country Wife* by William Wycherley, there are thirteen characters plus several extras. In addition to the main plot concerning Horner, who has an affair with Margery, the country wife of Mr. Pinchwife, there is a subplot dealing with a fop named Sparkish, who allows his fiancée to be stolen from under his eyes by a friend of Horner's. The scene shifts back and forth from Horner's house to Pinchwife's house, and there are two scenes in other locations. At the same time, there is an organic quality about the play usually associated with climactic drama.

COMBINING THE CLIMACTIC AND THE EPISODIC.
The plays of Chekhov combine features of the climactic and episodic structures. They move from one location to another, cover an extended period of time, and involve a number of characters. But they do not range in time and place in the way that full-scale episodic drama does. A good example is The Three Sisters, *a scene from which is shown here in a production at the Williamstown Theater Festival in Massachusetts.*

The climactic and episodic forms have frequently been mixed successfully in the modern period. Chekhov, who generally wrote about one principal action and set his plays in one household, usually has more characters than is customary in climactic drama—fifteen in *The Cherry Orchard*, for instance. Frequently, too, Chekhov's plays cover a period of several months or years.

Arthur Miller, in *Death of a Salesman*, combined the two forms in still a different way. The main frame of the story is in climactic form and covers the last hours of Willie Loman's life. Events from the past, however, are not described in exposition, as is usually the case, but are presented as full-fledged scenes. Rather than merely being told about the past, we see it for ourselves, enacted in a series of flashback scenes. In this way Miller achieved the finality of the climactic play but opened his drama up in the fashion of an episodic drama.

✳ DRAMATIC DEVICES USED WITH ✳ CLIMACTIC AND EPISODIC FORM

Before leaving climactic and episodic plots, we should look at two devices often employed with these forms: a chorus or narrator, and intellectual or conceptual conflict.

A Chorus or Narrator

A technique used in many plays is a *dialectic* or *counterpoint* between a party outside the play and characters in the central action. (*Counterpoint* is a term from music denoting a second melody that accompanies or moves in contrast to the main melody.) Two good examples of this device are the chorus in Greek drama and the narrator in a modern play.

In *Our Town*, the author Thornton Wilder used the Stage Manager to comment on the action. Wilder set up a counterpoint between the episodes of the play—most of them simple, everyday events—and the more general, universal observations of the Stage Manager. By setting one element next to another, he gave broader meaning to specific epi-

THE CHORUS IN MEDEA.
Devices used with both climactic and episodic structures include a narrator, such as the one in Thornton Wilder's Our Town; *and the chorus of Greek drama, a group acting together to recall the past, to caution the main characters against rash actions, and to draw philosophical conclusions from the action. Shown here with masks is the chorus for a production of Euripides's* Medea *at the North Carolina School of the Arts.*

sodes and, at the same time, gave a concrete, down-to-earth reality to philosophical observations.

As an example, at the opening of the play, one of the characters, Joe Crowell, Jr., while delivering the morning paper, sees Doc Gibbs and talks to him about such things as the marriage of Joe's schoolteacher and Joe's trick knee—perfectly ordinary topics of conversation. But later in the play, the Stage Manager gives a broader perspective to Joe's life when he tells us that after graduating from high school with honors, Joe won a scholarship to MIT, only to die shortly thereafter in France fighting in World War I. As the Stage Manager observes, "All that education for nothing."

INTELLECTUAL OR CONCEPTUAL CONFLICT.
In certain plays the main conflict among characters is not emotional but, rather, intellectual. A good example is Pirandello's Six Characters in Search of an Author, *shown here in a production at the American Repertory Theater in Cambridge, Massachusetts. The philosophical issues in* Six Characters *include art versus life and appearance versus reality.*

(Richard Feldman)

Bertolt Brecht used a narrator, and sometimes singers, in more drastic fashion. He wanted to startle members of the audience by a sudden shift from the main story to the presentation of a moral or political argument. In *The Caucasian Chalk Circle*, Grusha, the innocent, peace-loving peasant woman, steps out of character at one point to sing a song extolling the virtues of a general who loves war. Grusha, in other words, is asked to sing a song with a point of view opposite to her own. This wrenching of characters and attitudes is deliberate on Brecht's part: to make us think about war and the ravages of war. The pieces are meant to fit together, not in the play itself but rather in the minds of the spectators.

Intellectual or Conceptual Conflict

A second device used in conjunction with traditional plot structure is intellectual debate. This occurs particularly in the type of drama called the *play of ideas,* whose main conflict or problem is intellectual. It is worth pointing out that the purely intellectual approach to theater can be dangerous. When carried to extremes, it concentrates entirely on abstruse arguments, leaving behind flesh-and-blood characters. It ignores the foundation of theater—the experience embodied in the actor-audience relationship. Occasionally, writers present a discourse or debate in play form, but this is really a subterfuge. Such a play is a treatise in disguise, and no more related to the experience of theater than a description of the valves of the heart would be to falling in love. Ideas, insight, and perception are essential to meaningful drama, but they must serve the play and not the other way around.

At times a playwright successfully gives theatrical form to an intellectual concept. A good example is *Six Characters in Search of an Author,* by the Italian playwright Luigi Pirandello (1867–1936). Pirandello establishes an opposition between actors rehearsing a play and a group of fictional characters who are not real people but creations like Hamlet or Hedda Gabler. The characters urge the actors to perform their story instead of the play they are rehearsing, and in the process of this confrontation Pirandello raises questions of appearance versus reality, and fiction versus fact.

In this chapter we have examined two basic forms of dramatic structure—climactic and episodic—together with combinations of the two. We have also looked at other elements used with these forms. In Chapter 10 we will look at other forms of dramatic structure—some new forms and variations of old forms.

✳ SUMMARY ✳

1   There are several basic types of dramatic structure. The form adopted by the Greeks and used frequently since then is the *climactic* form. Its characteristics are a plot beginning quite late in the story, a limited number of characters, a limited number of locations and scenes, little or no extraneous material, and tight construction, including a cause-and-effect chain of events.

2   The *episodic* form of dramatic structure involves a plot covering an extended span of time, numerous locations, a large cast of characters, diverse events (including the mixing of comic and serious episodes), and parallel plots or subplots. Shakespeare's plays are good examples of the episodic form.

3   The climactic and episodic forms can be combined, as they have been in the modern period in the works of Anton Chekhov, Arthur Miller, and others.

4   Devices sometimes used with traditional plot structures are a narrator or chorus and an intellectual debate.

1 What might *Ghosts* have been like if Ibsen had conceived of it and developed it as an episodic rather than a climactic play? Rewrite the synopsis to illustrate an "episodic" *Ghosts*. How would the chart on page 167 have to be altered to depict this version?

2 In climactic drama, as the chapter explains, the plot begins late in the story; and this means that it is often necessary to use an exposition to explain what has happened before the play begins. What devices might a playwright use to keep the exposition from being boring or from seeming mechanical, artificial, or contrived?

3 Suppose that Shakespeare had conceived and developed *King Lear* as a climactic rather than an episodic play. How might the chart on pages 176–177 look for a "climactic" *King Lear*?

4 In episodic drama, what devices might playwrights use to keep plays from becoming sprawling or confusing?

5 Did your attempts to recast *Ghosts* as an episodic play and *King Lear* as a climactic play seem to give you any insights on the relationship between form and content in art? That is, would you say that a playwright is more likely to modify content to suit a form, or to choose a form to suit content? Or do you think that form and content are inseparable—that each affects the other?

10

DRAMATIC STRUCTURE: OTHER FORMS

NONTRADITIONAL DRAMATIC STRUCTURE.

A number of modern plays do not fit into the mold of climactic or episodic drama. Good examples are the absurdist plays of Beckett, Ionesco, and Pinter. The Homecoming *by Harold Pinter, shown here, is conventional in that it takes place in one room and has a limited number of characters, but in other respects it departs from tradition. The characters' past lives, for instance, are shrouded in mystery, and many of the actions have no clear explanation.*

Although climactic or episodic structure—or some combination of the two—has frequently been dominant, other forms of dramatic structure have emerged in theater history. In this chapter we will look at several of these important types of structure.

❋ THEATER OF THE ABSURD ❋

Following World War II a new type of theater emerged in Europe and America, which the critic Martin Esslin called *theater of the absurd*. Although the dramatists whose work falls into this category do not write in identical styles and are not really a "school" of writers, they do share enough in common to be considered together. Esslin took the name for this form of theater from a quotation in *The Myth of Sisyphus* by the French writer, dramatist, and philosopher Albert Camus (1913–1960). Camus maintains that in the present age we have lost the comfort and security of being able to explain the world by reason and logic. As he puts it in *The Myth of Sisyphus:*

> A world that can be explained by reasoning, however faulty, is a familiar world. But in a universe that is suddenly deprived of illusions and light, man feels a stranger. His is an irremediable exile, because he is deprived of memories of a lost homeland as much as he lacks hope of a promised land to come. This divorce between man and his life, the actor and his setting, truly constitutes the feeling of Absurdity.[1]

Camus is saying that the modern world is absurd; it makes no sense. One cannot explain the injustices, the inconsistencies, and the malevolence of today's world in terms of the moral yardsticks of the past.

Plays falling into the absurdist category express the ideas articulated by Camus and others like him. In one way or another they convey humanity's sense of both alienation and loss of bearings in an illogical, unjust, and ridiculous world. Although serious, this viewpoint is generally depicted in plays with considerable humor; an ironic note runs through much of the theater of the absurd.

A prime example of theater of the absurd is Samuel Beckett's *Waiting for Godot*. In the play Beckett has given us one of the most telling expressions of loneliness and futility ever written. There is nothing bleaker or more desolate than two tramps on a barren plain waiting every day for a supreme being called "Godot," who they think will come but who never does. But they themselves are comic. They wear baggy pants like burlesque comedians, and engage in any number of vaudeville routines, including one in which they grab each other's hats in an exchange where the confusion becomes increasingly comical. Also, the characters frequently say one thing and do just the opposite. One says to the other, "Well, shall we go?" and the other says, "Yes, let's go." But having

(Richard Feldman)

THEATER OF THE ABSURD.
Non sequitur, nonsensical language, existential characters, ridiculous situations—these are the hallmarks of theater of the absurd. A good example is Ionesco's The Bald Soprano, *shown here in a production at the American Repertory Theater, in which even the title has an absurd quality.*

said this, they don't move; they sit still, and the contrast between their words and deeds is comic.

Absurdist plays suggest the idea of absurdity both in what they say, that is, their content; and in the way they say it, their form. Their structure, therefore, is a departure from dramatic structures of the past.

Absurdist Plots: Illogicality

Traditional plot arrangements in drama proceed in a logical way from a beginning through the development of the plot to a conclusion. This in turn suggests an ordered universe. Even violent or disordered events, such as Macbeth's murder of Duncan or King Lear's madness, are presented in a rational framework. The same was true of writers in the 1920s and 1930s; many of their plays *described* absurdity, but the structure of their plays did not *demonstrate* absurdity. Some dramatists of the theater of the absurd—though certainly not all—set about correcting this discrepancy: their plays not only proclaim absurdity, they embody it.

An example is *The Bald Soprano,* by Eugène Ionesco. The very title of the play turns out to be nonsense; a bald soprano is mentioned once in the play, but with no explanation, and it is clear that the bald soprano has nothing whatever to do with the play as a whole. The absurdity of the piece is manifest the moment the curtain goes up. A typical English couple is sitting in a living room when the clock on the mantle strikes

WAITING FOR GODOT (1954)

SAMUEL BECKETT (1906–)

CHIEF CHARACTERS:
Estragon
Vladimir
Lucky
Pozzo
A boy

SETTING: A country road with a tree.

TIME: The present.

BACKGROUND: Estragon and Vladimir have been coming to this same bleak spot every day for some time to wait for an unknown person called Godot. The place is a crossroads, and it is bare except for a small tree in the background that has no leaves. While the men wait, they pass the time discussing the nature of humankind, religion, what they did yesterday, or whatever else happens to be on their minds.

ACT I: Estragon is attempting to pull off his boot when Vladimir enters. The two men discuss where Estragon spent the night and the fact that he was beaten again. Vladimir relates the tale of the two thieves who were crucified with Christ and describes how current religious scholars cannot agree on what happened to the thieves. As Estragon paces, the scene is punctuated by pauses which enhance the feeling of waiting. Occasionally the men talk of leaving and then decide that they cannot because they are waiting for Godot. They consider leaving each other; they argue; they make up. They discuss hanging themselves from the tree but decide that they can't do it because the limbs are slender and might break.

At the point where they have decided not to do anything, two other men, Pozzo and Lucky, enter. Lucky is carrying heavy baggage and has a rope around his neck held by Pozzo. Pozzo jerks occasionally on the rope and barks commands to Lucky, who responds mechanically. Pozzo sits, eats, and smokes his pipe. Estragon asks why Lucky doesn't put down the bags, and Pozzo explains that Lucky wants to impress Pozzo so that Pozzo will keep him. Pozzo says that it would be best to kill Lucky, which makes Lucky cry.

Estragon tries to comfort Lucky, and Lucky kicks him. As the sky changes from day to night, Pozzo tells Lucky to dance, which he does. Pozzo tells Lucky to think, and Lucky, who has been silent until this moment, goes into a long incoherent tirade which agitates the others. When they take Lucky's "talking hat" off, he stops talking and collapses in a heap. The men say goodbye, but no one is able to leave. Pozzo finally gets up and exits with Lucky in the lead, with the rope around his neck as before.

A Boy enters to tell Vladimir and Estragon that Godot will not be coming today, but will surely come tomorrow. After he exits, the moon suddenly rises. Estragon says that he will bring some rope the next day so they can hang themselves. They talk about parting, but they don't, as the curtain falls.

ACT II: The next day at the same time, in the same place. The scene opens with Estragon's boots and Lucky's hat on stage. The small tree that was bare now has four or five leaves. Vladimir enters in an agitated state, paces back and forth, and begins to sing. Estragon enters and appears to be in a foul mood. They embrace and Estragon says that he was beaten again the night before. Also, Estragon can't remember what happened the day before. They talk about random things so that they will not have to think.

They notice the tree and are amazed that leaves could appear on the limbs overnight. They discover Estragon's boots which seem to be the wrong color: perhaps someone came along and exchanged boots. They discuss leaving but can't because they are waiting for Godot. Estragon takes a nap, and Vladimir sings a lullaby. Estragon wakes, as if from a nightmare; Vladimir comforts him. They discover Lucky's hat, and they do a comic hat-switching routine. They hear a noise and think that finally Godot is coming. Rather than being pleased, the men are frightened; they rush around in an excited state, but nothing happens; no one comes. Once more, they insult each other and then make up.

Pozzo and Lucky enter, and Pozzo is now blind. Lucky stops short, falls, and brings Pozzo down with him. Pozzo calls for help, but Vladimir and Estragon think that finally Godot has arrived. They then discover that it is Pozzo and Lucky. Vladimir and Estragon try to help Pozzo up, but they fall also. Finally, everyone gets up. Estragon goes to Lucky and kicks him, and in the process, hurts his foot. Lucky gets up, gathers his things together, and he and Pozzo exit as before.

Estragon tries in vain to take off his boots, and then falls asleep, as Vladimir philosophizes. The Boy enters and again tells Vladi-

mir that Godot will not be coming that night but that he will come the next night. The Boy exits. The sun sets and the moon rises quickly. Vladimir and Estragon discuss leaving, but they can't go far because they feel they have to be back the next day to wait for Godot. They talk again of hanging themselves on the tree, but don't have any rope. As a substitute, they test the strength of Estragon's belt, but it breaks and his pants fall to the ground. Vladimir tells Estragon to pull up his trousers, and he does. Vladimir says, "Well? Shall we go?" Estragon says, "Yes, let's go." But they do not move, and they remain on stage as the play ends.

(Brigitte Lacombe)

CHAPTER 10 • DRAMATIC STRUCTURE: OTHER FORMS

seventeen times; the wife's first words are, "There, it's nine o'clock." Other Ionesco plays have equally ridiculous plots; in *Amédée*, for instance, a long-dead corpse in an adjoining room continues to grow and finally crashes through the wall of the apartment onstage during the course of the play.

Edward Albee, an American playwright, has also written absurdist plays. *The American Dream,* a study of the banality and insensitivity of American family life, introduces a handsome young man of around 20 as the embodiment of the "American dream." The Mommy and Daddy of the play wish to adopt him because he seems perfect to them. We learn, however, that he is only half a person; he is all appearance, with no inner feelings. He is the other half of a child Mommy and Daddy mutilated and destroyed years before when it began to have feelings, wanting to touch things and expressing curiosity about the world. Obviously Mommy and Daddy care more for appearance than for true human emotions. To further underscore the absurdity of Mommy and Daddy's world, Albee has them return from a search of their house to report that an entire room has disappeared. Plot, as well as other elements, becomes illogical.

Absurdist Language: Nonsense and Non Sequitur

Events and characters are frequently illogical in theater of the absurd, and so too is language. *Non sequitur* is a Latin term meaning "it does not follow"; it implies that one thing does not follow from what went before, and it perfectly describes the method of theater of the absurd, including the use of language. Sentences do not follow in sequence, and words do not mean what we expect them to mean. As Martin Esslin says, there is a tendency "toward a radical devaluation of language."

A passage from Ionesco's *The Bald Soprano* in which two couples are talking will illustrate the point:

MRS. SMITH: The car goes very fast, but the cook beats batter better.
MR. SMITH: Don't be turkeys; rather kiss the conspirator.
MRS. SMITH: I'm waiting for the aqueduct to come see me at my windmill.
MR. MARTIN: One can prove that social progress is definitely better with sugar.
MR. SMITH: To hell with polishing![2]

Most of the dialogue in the play is equally irrelevant and based on just such *non sequiturs.*

Another example of the irrationality or debasement of language is found in Samuel Beckett's *Waiting for Godot.* The character Lucky does not speak for most of his time on stage, but at the end of the first act

(Chris Bennion)

EXISTENTIAL CHARACTERS.

Among the characteristics of absurdist and other types of modern drama is the presence of dramatic characters with no biography, no history, no background. They seem to exist just as we find them at the moment of the play. This is particularly true of the plays of Samuel Beckett, an example being Happy Days, *in which a woman is buried in a mound of earth, at first up to her waist and later up to her neck. In this scene we see the woman (played by Eve Roberts) and her husband (Kurt Beattie), in a production at the Seattle Repertory Theater.*

he delivers a long speech of incoherent religious and legalistic jargon. The opening lines offer a small sample.

> Given the existence as uttered forth in the public works of Puncher and Wattmann of a personal God quaquaquaqua with white beard quaquaquaqua outside time without extension who from the heights of divine apathia divine athambia divine aphasia loves us dearly with some exceptions for reasons unknown but time will tell. . . .[3]

Numerous examples of such language appear not only in the plays of Ionesco and Beckett but in those of many absurdist writers.

Existential Characters in Absurdist Drama

A significant feature of the structure of absurdist plays lies in the handling of characters. Not only is there an element of the ridiculous in their actions but they frequently exemplify an *existential* point of view toward human behavior. Most traditional philosophies hold that es-

193

sence precedes existence—that is, that there is a quality for everything which is present even before it exists. There is a quality for apples, for instance, before an individual apple appears on a tree and, in personal terms, a *self* for each person preceding his or her existence. *Existentialism,* on the other hand, holds that existence precedes essence; a person creates himself or herself in the process of living. Beginning with nothing, the person develops a self in taking action and making choices.

When applied to theater, existentialism suggests that characters have no personal history before the play begins, no background, and therefore no specific causes for their actions. This is contrary to the practice of most traditional drama. In *A Streetcar Named Desire* by Tennessee Williams, we learn that the character Blanche DuBois has come from an aristocratic southern background, has had several unfortunate experiences with men, and has lost both money and prestige at home. These facts explain why she is so desperate when she arrives in New Orleans to stay with her sister and brother-in-law.

By contrast, the two main characters in Beckett's *Waiting for Godot* are devoid of biography and personal motivation. We are told nothing of their backgrounds, family life, or occupations. They meet every day at a crossroads to wait for Godot, but how long they have been coming there, or what they do when they are not there, remains a mystery.

This lack of concern for background and motivation has an effect on structure—specifically, in the absence of exposition. In theater of the absurd we see characters for whom little or no explanation is offered. We catch them in midair, or midstream, and there is no preoccupation with the past, no solving of riddles, as in *King Oedipus*.

❋ RITUAL AND PATTERN AS DRAMATIC STRUCTURE ❋

So far, we have looked at two forms of traditional structure—climactic and episodic—and one contemporary form, absurdist theater. We turn now to two other forms of structure—ritual and pattern.

Rituals

Like acting, ritual is a part of everyday life of which we are generally unaware. Basically, *ritual* is the repetition or reenactment of a proceeding or transaction which has acquired special meaning. It may be a simple ritual like singing the national anthem before a sports contest, or a deeply religious one such as the mass in the Roman Catholic Church or the kaddish for the dead in the Jewish faith. Every one of us in our personal or family life develops rituals: a certain meal we eat with the family once a week, for example, or a routine we go through every time we take an examination in school.

RITUAL IN MODERN THEATER.
Many avant-garde playwrights and producing groups incorporate ceremonies and rituals in their plays and performances. One example is the French dramatist Jean Genet. Here we see a scene from Genet's The Balcony, *which takes place in a brothel where the prostitutes play roles, such as a horse ridden by a general, and the men who visit the brothel dress up in exaggerated costumes as bishops, generals, judges, and so forth. The two groups play out elaborate rituals as a part of the action.*

Occasions like Thanksgiving, Christmas, and Passover become family rituals, with the same order of events each year, the same menu, and perhaps even the same conversation. Rituals give continuity, security, and comfort to human beings. Often, as in the case of primitive tribes, those performing a ritual assume that by carrying out a ceremony faithfully, they will be blessed or their wishes will be granted. Conversely, they assume that a failure to follow the ritual to the letter will lead to punishment.

In the theater, ritual is an area where the old and new come together. Traditional plays are full of rituals: coronations, weddings, funerals, and other ceremonies. And in modern theater, ritual has been discovered and given new life. Martin Esslin states that the plays of the French dramatist Jean Genet can best be understood in terms of ritual. According to Esslin, "The concept of the ritual act, the magical repetition of an action deprived of reality, is the key to any understanding of Genet's theater."[4] Of Genet's play *The Balcony*, Esslin says, "Essentially the play is a series of rituals, followed by their equally ritual debunking."[5] Other

195

recent avant-garde theater groups have made a conscious attempt to develop new rituals or revive old ones.

Ritual has structure. Actions are repeated in a set fashion, and have a beginning, a middle, and an end, and there is a natural progression of events. Despite this, we might ask: Where are the dynamics and tension? Does ritual not deteriorate into dull routine or hollow repetition? It can, of course; but ritual, though sometimes known by heart, is not static. Remember, it is a reenactment, or reliving, of an episode or occasion, and as such is active, not passive. Beyond that, ritual has special powers; it carries the magic or mystery of a meaningful, almost holy act. This can be its source of energy in theater, as in life.

Patterns

Related to ritual is a pattern of events. In Samuel Beckett's *Waiting for Godot*, the characters have no personal history, and the play does not build to a climax in the ordinary way. But if Beckett has sacrificed traditional plot structure, he has replaced it with a repeated sequence of events containing its own order and logic. The play has two acts, and in each act a series of incidents is duplicated. Each act opens with the two chief characters coming together on a lonely crossroads after having been separated. Then in both acts a similar sequence of events occurs: they greet each other, they despair of Godot's ever coming, they attempt to entertain themselves. Two other men, Pozzo and Lucky, appear and, following a lengthy scene, disappear. The men are left alone once more. The two acts continue to follow the same sequence: a small Boy comes to tell them that Godot will not come that day, the Boy leaves, and the men remain together for another night. There are important differences between the two acts—differences which give the play meaning and resonance—but the identical sequence of events in each act achieves a pattern which takes on a ritualistic quality.

✳ EXPERIMENTAL AND AVANT-GARDE THEATER ✳

Special Structures

During the last few decades a number of theater groups in Europe and the United States have experimented with theatrical forms, including ritual. These included the Polish Laboratory Theater headed by Jerzy Grotowski, and the Living Theater, the Open Theater, and the Performance Group in the United States. These groups were questioning long-held beliefs about theater. They had two things in mind. On one hand, they felt that the theater of the past was no longer relevant to the problems of the present and that new forms must be found to match the challenges and aspirations unique to the latter part of the twentieth century. On the other hand, they wanted to look back past the traditions of the last 2,500 years to the beginning of theater, to scrape off the many layers of formality and convention that had accumulated through the centuries, and to rediscover the roots of theater.

In many cases these two impulses led to similar results; and from the experiments of this radical theater movement, several significant departures from traditional theater practice were developed. Among them were the following: (1) emphasis on *nonverbal theater,* that is, theater where gestures, body movements, and sounds without words are stressed rather than logical or intelligible language; (2) reliance on improvisation or a scenario developed by performers and a director to tell the story, rather than a written text; (3) interest in ritual and ceremony; and (4) stress on the importance of the physical environment of theater, including the spatial relationship of the performers to the audience.

The theater groups that developed these ideas are referred to as *avant-garde,* a French term that literally means the "advance guard in a military formation." The term has come to mean an intellectual or artistic movement in any age that breaks with tradition and therefore seems ahead of its time.

Segments and Tableaux as Structure

The experimental theater pieces of the directors Robert Wilson and Richard Foreman (who were noted in Chapter 6), like other types of avant-garde theater, often stress nonverbal elements. At times they include *non sequitur* as well. In spite of this, their work does have structure.

(Richard Feldman)

SEGMENTS AND TABLEAUX IN AVANT-GARDE THEATER. *Many modern experimental theater directors use separate segments, very much like pictorial tableaux, in place of a story with a beginning, middle, and end. The emphasis is on the visual images, and on sounds, music, and dancelike movements. A good example is the tableau seen here, from Robert Wilson's the CIVIL WarS, with the elongated figure of Abraham Lincoln at the right.*

Often the various elements are united by a theme, or at least a pronounced point of view on the part of the director. Also, the material is organized into units analogous to the frames of film and television, or to the still-life tableaux of painting or the moving tableaux of dance.

Robert Wilson, in productions such as *A Letter to Queen Victoria*, *Einstein on the Beach*, and *the CIVIL warS*, begins a segment with a visual picture, like a large three-dimensional painting. The performers move from this static image into the activities of the segment. When one segment has concluded, another picture or tableau will be formed to initiate the next segment.

Frequently directors like Foreman and Wilson will employ rapid movements—as in silent films—or slow-motion movements. At times several activities will occur simultaneously. All of these, however, relate both to an image and to a tableau or frame.

✳ SERIAL STRUCTURE ✳

A special kind of structure is a series of acts or episodes—individual theater events—offered as a single presentation. In this case, individual segments are strung together like beads on a necklace. Sometimes a central theme or common thread holds the parts together; sometimes there is little or no connection between the various parts.

The musical revue is a case in point. In the *revue*, short scenes, vignettes, skits, dance numbers, songs, and possibly even vaudeville routines are presented on a single program. There may be an overall theme, such as political satire or the celebration of a certain year from the past. Sometimes a master of ceremonies provides continuity for the various segments. In a revue in which there is no visible connection between the parts, the primary consideration is the pace and variety of the acts. A song is usually followed by a dramatic scene, a serious number by a comic one, and so forth. Another form of musical revue is one that contains only musical numbers. Productions such as *Ain't Misbehavin'* and *Black and Blue*, celebrating the music of famous black composers like Fats Waller and Eubie Blake, are examples of this form. (The musical theater, with emphasis on the full-length book musical, will be discussed in Chapter 11.)

In today's theater we frequently see a program of short plays. Sometimes there will be a bill of one-act plays by the same author, but at other times there will be two or three plays by different authors. Also, on some occasions an attempt is made to relate the separate plays to a central theme, but on others the plays are chosen simply to complete an evening's entertainment.

In Chapters 8, 9, and 10, we have been examining the development of the dramatic structure for straight drama, meaning plays without music.

In Chapter 11 we discuss the history and structure of a form which has come to full flower in the United States in this century: the musical play.

✳ SUMMARY ✳

1 Nonsense, or *non sequitur,* a feature of theater of the absurd, can be the basis of dramatic construction: events do not logically follow one another, suggesting the chaos and absurdity of the world in which we live.

2 Avant-garde theater sometimes arranges events in a random way to suggest the random or haphazard manner in which life unfolds in everyday situations.

3 Ritual or pattern is often used as the basis of dramatic structure. Words, gestures, and events are repeated; they have a symbolic meaning acquired both through repetition and through the significance invested in them from the past.

4 Some experimental groups of the 1960s and 1970s used radical forms, including nonverbal and improvisational structures.

5 Segments and tableaux have also been used as structure.

6 In certain cases theater events are strung together to make a program. This could include a group of unrelated, one-act plays and a group of skits and songs in a revue. In this case, structure is within the individual units themselves; among the units the only structure might be the separate elements unfolding; or there can be a common theme uniting them.

✳ TOPICS FOR DISCUSSION ✳

1 The chapter describes *Waiting for Godot* as "one of the most telling expressions of loneliness and futility ever written." In the synopsis, find specific words and actions of the characters that reflect loneliness and futility.

2 An "existential character" has no history before the play begins—no background. This seems to imply that an existential character could not be used in a play which has a traditional climactic or episodic structure. Do you think that this implication is correct, or can you imagine ways in which a playwright might manage to have an existential character in a play with a traditional structure?

3 What specific devices might a playwright use to prevent ritual from becoming merely "ritualistic," and to prevent pattern from becoming merely "repetitive"?

4 Of the nontraditional forms described in this chapter, which do you think might prove to be most enduring? Why?

11

MUSICAL THEATER

THE MODERN AMERICAN MUSICAL.
During the twentieth century, American artists have been important in developing musical theater as a distinct art form. Their contribution has been both in the songs composed and in the dramatic structure, which has integrated music with the story. A good example is Kiss Me, Kate, *a 1948 musical about a theater company presenting Shakespeare's* The Taming of the Shrew. *Cole Porter wrote the words and music, and Sam and Bella Spewak wrote the libretto. The scene here, with Victor A. Young as Petruchio and Jayne Lewis as Kate, is from a production at the Stratford Festival in Ontario, Canada.*

Throughout theater history, drama has been closely associated with music and dance. In ancient Greek tragedy, choral sections were performed to the accompaniment of music and dance movements. Opera, which began in Italy around 1600, was composed by men who thought that they were imitating Greek drama. Shakespeare, who wrote at about the same time opera began, included songs as an important part of his comedies. In the ninteenth century the term *melodrama* came from "song dramas" in which music accompanied the action onstage. In other forms of ninteenth-century theatrical entertainment, such as vaudeville and burlesque, singing and dancing played a key role.

It has been in the twentieth century, however, that the form of musical theater with which we are most familiar has reached its highest form of development, in musicals like *Oklahoma!*, *West Side Story*, *My Fair Lady*, and *A Chorus Line*. Moreover, these musicals represent a form that came to full flower in the United States. Every other type of drama at which American playwrights and performers have excelled—such as modern tragedy, domestic drama, and farce—traces its origins to another time and another country. Modern musical theater, however, is largely a product of American talent and creativity. Proof of its significance and universal appeal is the fact that it is imitated and performed throughout the western world and in numerous other countries, such as Japan.

✳ BACKGROUND ✳

Before we look more closely at musical theater, it will be helpful to consider the special appeal of music and dance as a part of theater, and to examine the development of the American musical.

The Appeal of Music and Dance

It is not difficult to understand why singing and dancing have frequently been combined with dramatic productions. To begin with, all three are performing arts, and so there is a natural affinity among them. In the second place, singing and dancing have wide popular appeal. People enjoy listening to music at home as well as in the theater. They respond to the rhythms and emotional pull of a memorable melody, especially when it is performed by a star or by a singer with a captivating voice and a winning personality. Dancing can also be immensely appealing. The grace and agility of a talented and expertly trained solo dancer or the precision of a group of dancers moving in unison provides entertainment of a high order.

Beyond their entertainment value, singing and dancing possess an unmatched ability to capture the beauty of sound and movement and to communicate a wide range of emotions. In language there are thoughts and feelings which cannot be adequately expressed in everyday prose, and for these we turn to poetry. In the same way, there are expressions of beauty, anguish, and spirituality which can best be conveyed in vocal and instrumental music and in dance movements.

A Brief History of the American Musical

ANTECEDENTS   The modern American musical had a number of antecedents in the theater of the nineteenth and early twentieth centuries. Two of these were *vaudeville* and *burlesque*. In its later stages, burlesque became synonymous with vulgar sketches and "girlie shows," including versions of the striptease; but for most of the nineteenth century, burlesque featured dramatic sketches and songs that satirized or made fun of other theatrical forms.

Vaudeville was a series of variety acts—music, sketches, juggling, animal acts—that made up an evening's entertainment. Another form of musical production that flourished in the nineteenth century was the *minstrel show,* a variety show that featured white performers wearing blackface.

A production that many historians consider a significant forerunner of the modern musical happened by accident. A farfetched melodrama called *The Black Crook* was scheduled to open in 1866 at about the same time that a French ballet troupe was to appear in New York. The theater in which the ballet was to perform, however, burned down. The producer of *The Black Crook* had so little faith in his melodrama that he hired the dispossessed ballet company to perform as part of the production. The combination proved wildly successful and the show toured the country and returned to New York over and over again.

Another milestone was passed in the early twentieth century with the musical shows of George M. Cohan (1878–1942). A performer as well as a writer and composer, Cohan in such productions as *Little Johnny Jones* (1904) and *Forty-Five Minutes to Broadway* (1906) gave his songs a decidedly American flavor. Rather than imitating European models, as most American composers did, Cohan—in songs like "The Yankee Doodle Dandy" and "Give My Regards to Broadway"—introduced a strong American strain. Also, Cohan made his dialogue more realistic and down to earth than was common in musicals of the time, and he moved his show more toward the *book musical. Book musical* is a term referring to a show that has a story, or "book," which traces the fortunes of the main characters through a series of adventures with a beginning, middle, and end. (The book of a musical is sometimes referred to as the *libretto,* and the person who writes it as the *librettist;* the person who writes the lyrics to a musical score is called a *lyricist.)*

By the early twentieth century, with burlesque and vaudeville, the

GEORGE M. COHAN: A MUSICAL THEATER INNOVATOR.
George M. Cohan, who wrote the book, music, and lyrics for his musical shows, also performed in them. He was one of the first writers to focus on American subjects and to make his songs relate to the story; also, his characters were more down-to-earth than those in most operettas. He is seen here with Sallie Fisher in his musical Forty-Five Minutes from Broadway.

Cohan musicals, and American imitations of European operettas, the seeds of American musical comedy had been sown.

THE 1920s AND 1930s: MUSICAL COMEDIES   Around the time of World War I (1914–1918), a truly native American musical began to emerge. It featured a story that was often frivolous and silly, but at least it was a story rather than a series of patched-together blackout sketches, as in earlier attempts at musical shows. More important than the book, however, was the music. A group of exceptional composers and lyricists wrote the songs for these shows. These songs from the 1920s and 1930s became known as *standards,* that is, they were so popular that they were played over and over again, and many of them continue to be played on radio and television and made available to the public through records, cassettes, and compact disks.

Among the composers were Irving Berlin (1888–1989), who wrote such numbers as "Alexander's Ragtime Band," "What'll I Do?" and "Easter Parade"; Jerome Kern (1885–1945), who composed "Who?" "Why Was I Born?" "All the Things You Are," and "Smoke Gets in Your Eyes"; George Gershwin (1898–1937), who was responsible for

"Fascinating Rhythm," "Oh, Lady, Be Good," "Someone to Watch Over Me," and "Embraceable You"; Cole Porter (1893–1964), who wrote "Night and Day," "I Get a Kick out of You," and "Begin the Beguine"; and Richard Rodgers (1902–1979), who composed "My Romance," "Where or When?" and "Falling in Love with Love."

The work of these men was fresh and innovative. Their melodies ranged from the sprightly to the haunting and featured surprising modulations and developments in the melodic line. Matching the inventiveness of the composers were the words of the lyricists. Ira Gershwin (1896–1983) wrote lyrics for many of his brother George's tunes, and Lorenz Hart (1895–1943) teamed up with Richard Rodgers. Irving Berlin and Cole Porter wrote their own lyrics.

The lyrics were generally witty and clever, and they reflected a high order of intelligence. The rhymes were resourceful and often unexpected. As an example, observe the ryhmes in this lyric from the song "You're the Top" by Cole Porter:

> You're the top! You're the Colosseum.
> You're the top! You're the Louvre Museum.
> You're a Bendel bonnet, a Shakespeare sonnet, you're Mickey Mouse.
> You're the Nile, you're the Tow'r of Pisa,
> You're the smile on the Mona Lisa.
> I'm a worthless check, a total wreck, a flop,
> But, if, baby, I'm the bottom, You're the top![1]

THE 1920s AND 1930s: ADVANCES IN MUSICALS While the composers and lyricists were perfecting the art of their songs, a few shows were taking steps forward in the musical form. Among the first were a group of productions known as the *Princess musicals,* because they were presented at the small Princess Theater on Thirty-Ninth Street in New York. Between 1915 and 1919, seven musicals were produced, of which several marked a genuine advance in the musical form. They had music by Jerome Kern and books and lyrics by Guy Bolton (1884–1979) and P. G. Wodehouse (1881–1975); and used modern, humorous, intimate stories that were far more cohesive than those in previous musicals. In addition, the songs related more directly to the story than had been the case before.

While native musicals were developing, other composers, lyricists, and librettists were adapting European operetta to American purposes. One of the most successful composers in this form was Sigmund Romberg (1887–1951) whose operettas, including *The Student Prince* and *The Desert Song,* were immensely popular.

Collaborating with Romberg on *The Desert Song* was Oscar Hammerstein II (1895–1960), who was able to combine some of the best features of operetta with native musical comedy in the landmark musical *Showboat,* which opened in 1927. Hammerstein wrote the book and lyrics for

SHOWBOAT: A LANDMARK MUSICAL.

When Showboat *opened in 1927, it began a new chapter in the history of the American musical. The chorus line was eliminated, miscegenation (a romance between a white man and a black woman) was treated onstage for the first time, and other problems facing African-Americans were touched on. It also had a glorious score by Jerome Kern and Oscar Hammerstein II. Shown here is the scene for the well-known song "Ol' Man River."*

Showboat, and Jerome Kern composed the musical score. It represented an advance over previous musicals in several respects. The story was based on a novel by Edna Ferber about life on a Mississippi riverboat. Thus the story itself was thoroughly American, not an exotic romantic fable that was generally found in operetta. But it was a serious story, which set it apart from lighthearted musical comedies.

The story concerns Magnolia Hawks and Gaylord Ravenal, who meet, fall in love, perform on the showboat, but later lose their money because of Gaylord's gambling debts, and soon separate. Meanwhile, a second romance, between the characters Julie and Steve, represented a first for the American musical in that it was the love story of a black woman and a white man. At the time, nothing like this had been shown onstage. There was further daring and realism in the depiction of the lives of black workers on the levees of the Mississippi, as exemplified in the song "Old Man River."

The remarkable score of *Showboat* included such songs as "Why Do I Love You?" "Make Believe," and "Bill." Moreover, the songs were more carefully integrated into the plot than had previously been the case in musicals. Another innovation in *Showboat* was the elimination of a line of chorus girls, which had always been considered an indispensable part of any musical.

Another milestone for the American musical was passed in 1931 when *Of Thee I Sing* was awarded the Pulitzer Prize, the first time that a musical had been so honored and a sign that the form was beginning to be taken more seriously. *Of Thee I Sing* was a satire on political and cultural institutions such as presidential elections and Miss America contests. The music and lyrics were by George and Ira Gershwin, and the book was by George S. Kaufman (1889–1961) and Morrie Ryskind (1895–1985).

In 1935, eight years after *Showboat*, another important musical opened. This was *Porgy and Bess* with music by George Gershwin, a book by DuBose Heyward (1885–1940), and lyrics by Heyward and Ira Gershwin. Once again, the story was powerful and realistic—even more so than in *Showboat*. And the score by George Gershwin, which included "Summertime," "It Ain't Necessarily So," and "Bess, You Is My Woman Now," contained some of the finest compositions written for the musical theater.

The story is set in the black community of Charleston, South Carolina, known as "Catfish Row," and deals with Porgy, a crippled man who falls in love with Bess, who has been the woman of a man named Crown. When Crown has to leave because he has killed a man, Bess joins Porgy; and when Crown returns, Porgy kills Crown while defending himself. Bess, fearful that Porgy will never get out of jail, is talked into going to New York with the high-living Sportin' Life, and the play ends as Porgy sets out for New York to find Bess.

So forceful and complete is the musicalization of the story that there is some debate over whether *Porgy and Bess* should be considered musical theater or opera. It has been performed in both theaters and opera houses, including the Metropolitan Opera in New York.

Meanwhile, other steps were being taken to advance the musical. A 1936 musical called *On Your Toes* was about a Russian ballet company being persuaded to present a modern ballet. The musical score was by Rodgers and Hart, and the coauthor of the book was George Abbott (1887–   ). In addition to writing a number of musicals of the period, Abbott was the best-known director of musicals, and he was recognized for the energy, ebullience, and fast pace of his productions.

The innovative aspect of *On Your Toes* was that it introduced serious dance into musical comedy. The climax of the musical is a ballet called "Slaughter on Tenth Avenue," performed by a desperate hero who is forced to keep dancing to avoid being murdered by gangsters. The choreographer was George Balanchine (1904–1989), who became the premier choreographer of the New York City Ballet. In the years to come, serious modern dance was to become more and more a part of the musical theater.

In another Rodgers and Hart musical, *Pal Joey*, presented in 1940, the hero is a heel: a nightclub singer who takes advantage of women to get ahead. The presentation of an antihero as the leading character was a further step in the development of American musical theater, which in the 1940s and 1950s emerged full-blown.

MUSICAL THEATER OF THE 1940s AND 1950s In 1943 a musical opened that was to herald the golden era of American book musicals. This was *Oklahoma!*—which brought together for the first time the team of Richard Rodgers and Oscar Hammerstein II. Both had been involved in musical theater since the 1920s, but they had never collaborated before.

Oklahoma! is sometimes hailed as a more revolutionary musical than it really was; many of the innovations it is credited with had actually appeared in musicals before. Set against the background of the founding of the state of Oklahoma, it tells the love story of Curley and Laurie, who are thwarted by a character named Jud. During the course of the action, Curley kills Jud onstage. This was considered extremely daring, but several years earlier, Porgy had killed Crown onstage in *Porgy and Bess. Oklahoma!* was also praised for integrating the songs with the story, but this too had happened previously.

Even so, *Oklahoma!* in many respects offers a prime example of how complete and effective a musical can be. An important achievement was the inclusion in a musical for the first time of ballet as a crucial element throughout the piece. Agnes de Mille (1905–   ), a choreographer with classical training, created several dances that carried forward the story and became an indispensable part of the fabric of the musical. What's more, the entire piece—story, music, lyrics, dances—fit together in tone, mood, and intention to present a seamless whole. From *Oklahoma!* on, American musicals could tackle any subject, serious as well as frivolous, and present it as an integrated art form with acting, dancing, and singing masterfully intertwined.

We should note that one feature of the musical score in *Oklahoma!* is the variety of songs. The score contains choral numbers, such as the title song; love songs, like "People Will Say We're in Love"; comic songs, such as "Everything's Up to Date in Kansas City"; and ballets, like "Out of My Dreams." This variety became a hallmark of the musicals that followed.

It should be added that the choreography which became such an integral part of musical theater in the decades to follow encompassed a

A GOLDEN AGE BEGINS WITH OKLAHOMA!

In 1943, Oklahoma! *inaugurated a quarter-century in which an outpouring of American musicals set the standard for similar shows throughout the world. Written by Rodgers and Hammerstein,* Oklahoma! *told the story of the founding of the state of Oklahoma and featured ballet as an important element; it also had songs that were fully integrated with the plot.*

number of dance forms, from the classical lifts and turns of Agnes de Mille's work, to the energetic athleticism favored by Jerome Robbins (1918–   ), to the sharp, angular, eccentric moves created by Bob Fosse (1927–1987). In order to execute the many kinds of dance steps required of them, dancers became highly trained and enormously versatile, and they were able to perform everything from classical pirouettes to muscular leaps and rapid-fire tap dancing.

Returning to *Oklahoma!*, for Rodgers and Hammerstein it represented the first in a long line of successful musicals that included *Carousel* (1945), *South Pacific* (1949), *The King and I* (1951), and *The Sound of Music* (1959). Some commentators have noted that several of their musicals are very close to latter-day versions of operetta. Although Hammerstein has at times been criticized as overly sentimental or moralistic, on the whole these musicals are marked by exceptional music, carefully wrought stories, and full integration of dance with other elements.

The outpouring of such first-rate musicals in the 1940s and 1950s remains unparalleled today. Several writers who had been involved in musicals in previous decades did their best work in this period. These include Irving Berlin with *Annie Get Your Gun* (1946), a musical version of the Annie Oakley story, and Cole Porter with *Kiss Me, Kate* (1948), a treatment of a theater company putting on Shakespeare's *Taming of the Shrew*.

MUSICALS WITH A SERIOUS SIDE. *Some of the musicals written in the 1940s and 1950s tackled serious subjects in addition to providing entertainment. A good example is* Gypsy, *with a book by Arthur Laurents and words and music by Jule Styne and Steven Sondheim. In this musical, Mama Rose tries to fashion her reluctant daughters into musical stars—something she herself could never be. Seen here as Mama Rose (left) is Tyne Daly in a recent Broadway revival.*

In addition, a number of new composers, lyricists, and writers appeared on the scene and produced memorable musicals: Frank Loesser (1910–1969), who wrote the words and music for *Guys and Dolls* (1950), a humorous and perceptive look at the hard-bitten characters from the stories of Damon Runyon; Alan Jay Lerner (1918–1986), who wrote the book and lyrics, and Frederick Loewe (1904–1988), who wrote the music for *My Fair Lady* (1956), a musical version of *Pygmalion* by George Bernard Shaw (1856–1950); the composer Leonard Bernstein (1918–1990), the lyricist Stephen Sondheim (1930–), and the book writer Arthur Laurents (1918–), who created *West Side Story* (1957), a modern version—set on New York's West Side—of the story of Romeo and Juliet; and the composer Jule Styne (1905–), who joined with Sondheim and Laurents to create *Gypsy* (1959), an adaptation of the autobiography of the stripper Gypsy Rose Lee.

The two decades of the 1940s and 1950s were remarkable not only for the number of outstanding musicals produced but for the range and depth of those musicals. A wide variety of subjects were covered, and the quality was impressive not only in the better-known shows but in many shows in the second rank. Not only composers and writers but performers, directors, designers, and choreographers were all working at the top of their form.

MUSICALS FROM THE 1960s THROUGH THE 1980s *Fiddler on the Roof,* which opened in 1964, is believed by many to mark the end of the golden era of book musicals. *Fiddler on the Roof,* with music by Jerry Bock (1928–), lyrics by Sheldon Harnick (1924–), and a book by Joseph Stein (1912–) tells of a Jewish family whose father tries to uphold the traditions of the past in a small village in Russia, where the Jewish community faces persecution and a pogrom. It was directed and choreographed by Jerome Robbins, who gave the piece an overall style and point of view that represented the best of the American musical.

Following *Fiddler*, a further indication of a change in the musical was the opening in 1967 of *Hair*, a celebration of the informal, antiestablishment lifestyle of young people in the 1960s. *Hair*, written by Galt MacDermot (1928–) and Gerome Ragni (1942–), had no real story line and represented a radical departure from the book musicals that had dominated the scene for the past twenty-five years.

After *Hair*, the musical scene became increasingly fragmented. In the 1970s and 1980s, fewer and fewer book musicals were written, though some successful ones continued to appear. In place of book musicals there were other approaches, one being the *concept musical*, in which a production is built around an idea rather than a story. Two examples, both composed by Stephen Sondheim and directed by Harold Prince (1928–), are *Company* (1970), which centers on the life of a New York bachelor, and *Follies* (1971), about former stars of the Ziegfeld Follies who look back at their lives.

Occasionally a musical came up with a variation on old formulas and appeared to break fresh ground. Such a musical was *A Chorus Line*, which presents a group of aspiring dancers auditioning for a Broadway

RECORD-BREAKING MUSICAL: A CHORUS LINE.

A Chorus Line concerns a group of aspiring dancers who audition for the chorus in a Broadway show. Directed by Michael Bennett, who was a choreographer before he became a director, it is symbolic of the importance of choreography and dance in modern musicals. A Chorus Line closed in the spring of 1990 after breaking all records for long-running Broadway musicals.

(Martha Swope)

BRITISH MUSICALS OF THE 1980s AND 1990s.
Beginning with such musicals as Evita *and* Cats, *both with music by Andrew Lloyd Webber, British composers and producers began to dominate the musical scene with shows that had continuous music and featured elaborate scenic effects. Other such shows included* The Phantom of the Opera, Miss Saigon, *and* Les Misérables, *a scene from which is shown here.*

show. *A Chorus Line,* which was directed by Michael Bennett (1943–1987), opened in 1975 and closed in 1990. It was, to date, the longest-running musical of all time.

There is something especially significant about the success of *A Chorus Line:* it symbolized the ascendancy of dancers and choreographers in the musical. Beginning with Jerome Robbins, the "vision" of musicals was furnished more and more by choreographers-turned-directors. In addition to Robbins and Bennett, these included Gower Champion (1920–1980), who was responsible for *Hello, Dolly* (1964) and *42nd Street* (1980); and Bob Fosse, who directed *Sweet Charity* (1966) and *Pippin* (1972).

In recent years these choreographer-directors have not worked with a solid book or with inspired scores, and as a result, they have emphasized the outward aspects of their productions, stressing the look and style of the production. The result in many cases has been a substitution of style for substance.

Still another trend of the 1970s and 1980s was the emergence of British composers and lyricists in the creation of musicals. The British had been creating musicals for many years, and in the late nineteenth century William S. Gilbert (1836–1911) and Arthur Sullivan (1842–1900) wrote comic operettas that are still models of their kind. In the 1920s and 1930s came musical comedies similar to their American counterparts. A good example of these is *Me and My Girl,* which opened in 1937 and was brought to the United States in a successful revival in 1986. More recently British composers and lyricists have moved to the forefront in creating new musicals. The composer Andrew Lloyd Webber (1948–   ) and the lyricist Tim Rice (1944–   ) wrote *Jesus Christ Superstar* (1971) and *Evita* (1979), the story of Argentina's Eva Peron; and Webber wrote the music for *Cats* (1982) and *Phantom of the Opera* (1987). Two other large-scale British musicals of recent years are *Les Misérables* (1986) and *Miss Saigon* (1989).

Along with British imports, there has also been a trend toward revivals of earlier musicals—still another indication that there is not the same output of new work today as in earlier years. At the same time, the trend toward revivals demonstrates that these shows form part of an important heritage and that they have lasting value. In other words, despite the fact that in the 1980s top-flight American musicals were not being produced in profusion, the genre remains full of vitality, and American performers and directors are still the premier interpreters of the form.

❋ FORM AND STRUCTURE IN THE MUSICAL ❋

Types of Musical Theater

To understand the modern musical, it is necessary to define certain terms—*opera, operetta, musical comedy,* and *revue.*

Opera is a drama set entirely to music. Every part of the performance, including transitional sections between arias known as *recitatives*, is sung. As a result, opera is usually considered a branch of music. It could just as easily be argued that opera is a blend of drama and music and should be counted as both; but for our purposes, we will treat it in the traditional manner and consider it a part of music.

Operetta contains scenes of spoken dialogue that alternate with songs. An operetta is not entirely set to music as opera is; certain portions are spoken by the performers, as in a regular drama. Operetta generally features a romantic story set in some far-off locale. An air of unreality and make-believe makes most operettas remote from everyday life. But they do have beautiful, soaring melodies and a plot that tells a complete story, however fanciful. Operetta features solos, duets, and trios as well as stirring choral numbers.

Musical comedy is a form of musical entertainment that emerged in the

THE MUSICAL REVUE.

A popular form of musical entertainment during the first half of the twentieth century was the revue: a series of sketches, dramatic vignettes, specialty acts, and musical numbers strung together to make an evening's entertainment. The musical numbers frequently featured a chorus of beautiful women dressed in spectacular costumes. One of the most famous was the Ziegfeld Follies; another was George White's Scandals, shown here in a 1920 production with George White in the center.

United States in the 1920s which features a light, comic story interspersed with popular music. Originally, the story was often silly or farfetched, but it did relate to contemporary people and events, and thus musical comedy was closer to everyday life than operetta—although its music was not as operatic and it featured more popular songs. Both operetta and musical comedy are important parts of the musical theater, which we are exploring in this chapter.

To round out the range of musical entertainment, we should also note the *revue* (referred to in Chapter 10), in which sketches and vignettes alternate with musical numbers. The important thing to remember about the revue is that there is no single story that carries through from beginning to end; the scenes and songs stand alone and may have very little relationship to each other, although at times they may have a common theme.

Principles of Structure in Musicals

Turning to the question of structure, the way a musical is put together has similarities to episodic structure in that there is a clear principle of alternation and juxtaposition at work: musical numbers alternate with spoken scenes; solos and duets alternate with choral numbers; singing alternates with dance numbers; and sometimes comic songs and scenes alternate with serious ones.

Although each musical has its own structure and must be judged separately, there are certain underlying principles that most musicals follow. A good example of these principles is found in *My Fair Lady*, with book and lyrics by Alan Jay Lerner and score by Frederick Loewe. The story is based on George Bernard Shaw's play *Pygmalion*.

My Fair Lady concerns a speech teacher, Henry Higgins, who claims that the English judge people by how they speak. He bets his friend Colonel Pickering that he can take an ordinary cockney flower girl, Eliza Doolittle, and by teaching her correct diction, pass her off as a duchess. It was characteristic of musicals of this era to have a comic subplot, and *My Fair Lady* is no exception. The subplot deals with Eliza's father, Alfred P. Doolittle, a ne'er-do-well who doesn't want to achieve middle-class respectability, because if he did he would have to marry the woman he lives with.

The first song in the show is sung by Higgins—"Why Can't the English Learn to Speak?" The next song shifts to Eliza and her dreams of luxury as she sings "Wouldn't It Be Lovely?" She is joined in this number by a chorus. The action now shifts to the subplot, and Alfred Doolittle is joined by two buddies to sing of how he hopes to avoid

THE DRAMATIC STRUCTURE OF MUSICALS: MY FAIR LADY.
Musicals, like other forms of theater, require a definite structure. My Fair Lady by Lerner and Loewe, based on Shaw's play Pygmalion, *is a good example. Scenes of dialogue alternate with musical and dance numbers; solos alternate with duets and choral numbers. In this scene Professor Henry Higgins kisses the hand of Eliza Doolittle, the woman he is going to change from a flower girl into a duchess by making her speak properly.*

working "With a Little Bit of Luck." We then move back to a scene with Higgins, who is pushing Eliza very hard to learn to speak properly. Higgins, who is anything but ordinary, nevertheless has a song called "I'm an Ordinary Man." Eliza vows revenge on the harsh Higgins in her next song: "Just You Wait." After this Eliza begins to improve her speech. She celebrates this in a song with Higgins and Pickering called "The Rain in Spain." The scene then shifts to the Ascot horse races, where Eliza is dressed as a lady. This is an ensemble number, "The Ascot Gavotte."

The musical proceeds in this manner, moving from one character to another, from a solo to a trio to a dance routine to an ensemble. There is variety in these numbers—some are serious, some are comic, some explain the characters' feelings, some describe a situation. It is in the alternation—from one kind of song to another, from one scene to another, from one set of characters to another—that musical theater structure is built. Always, too, it must be remembered, spoken scenes are interspersed with musical numbers. Also, ballet or modern dance routines are generally interspersed with other numbers. The aim, as with other forms of theater, is to build excitement as the musical progresses.

In Chapters 8 through 11 we have examined the way in which playwrights construct a play and, in collaboration with composers and others, a musical. Clearly, there is both art and craft involved in the construction of a theater piece, and it is necessary for everyone connected with theater—not just playwrights but directors, performers, and designers, not to mention critics—to understand the principles involved. It is also helpful to spectators because when theater is successful, usually the structure has contributed to that success, and often when it fails, the structure must share the blame. In Chapter 12 we look at another aspect of the playwright's work when we examine the creation of dramatic characters.

❋ SUMMARY ❋

1   At many points in theater history, music and dance have been combined with drama.

2   The modern musical is largely an American creation—the only theatrical form developed primarily in the United States.

3   There were many forerunners of the modern musical in the nineteeth and early twentieth centuries: vaudeville, burlesque, the minstrel show, operettas.

4   In the early twentieth century the American musical began to take shape in works such as those written by George M. Cohan.

5   During the 1920s and 1930s, musical comedy emerged: comic, some-

times silly stories that contained glorious music with intelligent, witty lyrics, written by people like Irving Berlin, Jerome Kern, Cole Porter, and Richard Rodgers, and Lorenz Hart.

6   The period from the early 1940s to the late 1960s was the golden age of the American musical, with a great profusion of successful shows being written, many of them modern classics. These musicals integrated dancing as well as singing to form an overall structure that had great variety as well as unity.

7   In the past two decades the musical theater has become fragmented: fewer book musicals are being produced, choreographer-directors rather than writers or directors have been responsible for the total vision of the show; experiments are being made with other forms, such as the concept musical; and more musicals are being imported from Britain.

8   Types of musical theater include *opera*, a drama set entirely to music; *operetta*, scenes of spoken dialogue alternating with songs; *musical comedy*, a light, comic story interspersed with popular music; and the *revue*, a series of individual, independent songs and comic sketches.

9   Structurally, musical theater consists of different elements put together in a sequence, in which solo musical numbers alternate with group numbers and dances and these musical elements alternate with dramatic scenes.

❊ TOPICS FOR DISCUSSION ❊

1   Composers and lyricists are often asked, "Which comes first, the words or the music?" Make a case for either *a* or *b: (a)* writing the words first and composing appropriate music next; *(b)* writing the music first and then writing the words.

2   The chapter notes that in the 1980s the musical theater is still full of vitality. But do you think that any of the recent trends described—the decline in the number of book musicals, the predominance of choreographers as directors, and the increase in imports and revivals—seem ominous?

3   When an opera company presents a musical—such as *Porgy and Bess* or *South Pacific*—it is seldom without some controversy. Should the opera company use its own singers or engage musical comedy stars? Does a musical go over well in an opera house, which is likely to be larger than a theater? Will the people who support an opera company feel that it has no business putting on musicals? Will people who would ordinarily attend a musical feel intimidated by the idea of going to an opera house? On the other hand, if musical theater is a significant art form, doesn't it deserve an occasional production in the forum of serious music? In deciding where you stand, consider both the practical issues and the principles involved.

12

DRAMATIC
CHARACTERS

DRAMATIC CHARACTERS: THE BEST AND THE WORST.
Though sometimes based on real people, dramatic characters are the creations of playwrights.
Often they are characters at the extremes of human behavior, either heroes and heroines who
carry out extraordinary deeds, or persons who are fanatical and obsessive. A good example of this
last type of character is Harpagon, the miser in Molière's play of that name. Seen here on the
right, Harpagon (John Wylie) is so extreme in his miserliness that he becomes totally paranoid
about the money that he has hidden. The production, which featured Mikel Lambert as Frosine
(left), was by the Shakespere Theater at the Folger Library in Washington, D.C.

Although they often seem like real people, dramatic characters are actually created in the mind of the playwright. By carefully emphasizing certain features of a character's personality while eliminating others, the dramatist can show us in 2 hours the entire history of a person whom it could take us a lifetime to know in real life. In Tennessee Williams's *A Streetcar Named Desire*, for example, we come to know the leading character, Blanche DuBois, in all her emotional complexity, better than we know people we see every day. The dramatist reveals to us not only Blanche's biography but her soul, and we become intimately acquainted with the inner workings of her mind.

Also, the playwright has wide latitude in what to emphasize and how to present the character. A stage character can be presented in different ways: (1) drawn with a few quick strokes, as a cartoonist sketches a political figure, (2) given the surface detail and reality of a photograph, or (3) fleshed out with the more interpretive and fully rounded quality of an oil portrait.

❋ TYPES OF CHARACTERS ❋

Traditionally, several major types of characters have proved effective in the theater.

Extraordinary Characters in Traditional Theater

The heroes and heroines of most important dramatic works of the past are extraordinary in some way. They are "larger than life." Historically, major characters have been kings, queens, bishops, members of the nobility, or other figures clearly marked as holding a special place in society. A queen, for instance, is accorded respect because of her authority, power, and grandeur. In the same way, we respect Supreme Court justices because of the high place they occupy.

Dramatists go one step further, however, in depicting extraordinary characters. In addition to filling prestigious roles, dramatic characters generally represent men and women at their worst or best, at some

EXTRAORDINARY CHARACTERS.
Opposite page: The leading characters in drama, especially dramas of the past, are likely to be exceptional in some way. Often they are people in high positions—kings, queens, generals—or people of outstanding achievements who have privileges, authority, and responsibility. Seen here are three examples: top, St. Joan (in a production of Shaw's play at the Huntington Theater), a remarkable young woman in fifteenth-century France; below left, the Roman general Mark Antony (Robert Foxworth, at the Old Globe Theater in San Diego), in Shakespeare's play Antony and Cleopatra; *and, below right, King Lear in Shakespeare's play—a self-centered, larger-than-life monarch (Anthony Hopkins at Britain's National Theater).*

(Gerry Goodstein)

(Will Gullette/Old Globe Theater)

(Donald Cooper/Photostage)

CHAPTER 12 • DRAMATIC CHARACTERS

extreme of human behavior. Lady Macbeth is not only a noblewoman; she is one of the most ambitious women ever depicted on the stage. In virtually every instance, with extraordinary characters we see men and women at the breaking point, at the outer limits of human capability and endurance.

Antigone and Saint Joan are the epitome of the independent, courageous female, willing to stand up to male authority and suffer whatever consequences they are forced to endure. Prometheus and Oedipus are men willing to face the worst the gods can throw at them, with strength and dignity, as is the biblical figure Abraham when God confronts him. Thomas à Becket, archbishop of Canterbury under King Henry II of England—the subject of *Becket* by Jean Anouilh, and *Murder in the Cathedral* by T. S. Eliot (1888–1965)—was martyred for his defiance of a king.

Among those qualifying as men and women at their worst are Medea, who murdered her own children; and the brothers of the heroine of *The Duchess of Malfi* by John Webster (1580?–?1625), who forbade their sister to get married so that they could have her estate, and when they discovered that she had married, had her cruelly tortured and strangled.

Comic characters can also be extremes. The chief character in *Volpone* by Ben Jonson (1572–1637) is an avaricious miser who gets people to present him with expensive gifts because they think he will remember them in his will.

Some characters combine qualities of extreme virtue and extreme vice. Faustus, treated by Christopher Marlowe in *Doctor Faustus* and by Johann Wolfgang von Goethe in *Faust*, was a great scholar but so bored with his existence and so ambitious that he made a compact with the devil, forfeiting his soul in return for unlimited power. Cleopatra, an exceedingly vain, selfish woman, also had "immortal longings." Queen Elizabeth I of England and Mary Queen of Scots, rivals in real life, have made admirable dramatic characters, being women of both strong virtues and telling weaknesses.

In short, the heroes and heroines of traditional theater have been exceptional not only by virtue of their station in life but because they possess traits common to us all—ambition, generosity, malevolence, fear, and achievement—in such great abundance.

Exceptional Characters in Modern Theater

Kings, queens, and other extraordinary people have continued to be treated in drama of the last hundred years. Two good examples are Joan of Arc in George Bernard Shaw's *Saint Joan,* and the martyred saint Sir Thomas More in *A Man for All Seasons* by Robert Bolt (1924-   ). Beginning in the eighteenth century, however, ordinary people took over more and more from royalty and the nobility as the heroes and heroines of drama—a reflection of what was occurring in real life. Even so, the leading figures of drama continued in many cases to be exceptional men and women at their best and worst.

The heroine of August Strindberg's *Miss Julie* is a neurotic, obsessive woman at the end of her rope. So, too, in her own way is Blanche DuBois in *A Streetcar Named Desire*. In *Mother Courage* by Bertolt Brecht, we see the portrait of a woman who will sacrifice almost anything to survive; she even loses a son by haggling over the price of his release. *The Emperor Jones*, by Eugene O'Neill, shows the downfall of a powerful black man who has made himself the ruler of a Caribbean island.

Among modern characters who stand for people at their worst is Regina of *The Little Foxes* by Lillian Hellman (1905–1984), a cunning, avaricious woman who stands by while her dying husband has a heart attack, refusing to get the medicine which can save his life.

"Prototypical" Characters in Modern Theater

When ordinary characters replaced kings and queens as the leading figures in drama, a new type of character emerged alongside the extraordinary character, a character who might be called *prototypical*. The "prototypical" character is not a stereotype but a fully rounded, three-

(Roger Mastroianni)

"PROTOTYPICAL" CHARACTERS. *Characters in modern plays are rarely kings, queens, or saints; instead they are ordinary people. Their problems reflect those of people in everyday life, although they often go to extremes. Frequently the leading characters in modern plays are "prototypical": they sum up the characteristics of a whole group who are like them. A good example is Nora in Ibsen's A Doll's House, who is typical of women who are treated by their husbands as dolls and are not given respect or responsibility. Shown here is Randy Danson as Nora (right) and Mark Metcalf as her husband (left) in a production at the Great Lakes Theater Festival in Cleveland.*

dimensional figure. Rather than being notable as "worst," "best," or some other extreme, these characters are notable in the way they *embody* the characteristics of an entire group: not as a caricature but as a complete picture of a person.

A good example of a "prototypical" character from modern drama is Nora Helmer, the heroine of Henrik Ibsen's *A Doll's House.* A spoiled, flighty woman, she secretly forged a signature to get money for her husband when he was very ill and needed medical attention. All her life, first by her father, then by her husband, she has been treated like a doll or a plaything, not as a mature, responsible woman. In the last act of the play, Nora rebels against this attitude; she makes a declaration of independence to her husband, slams the door on him, and walks out. It has been said that Nora's slamming of the door marked the beginning not only of modern drama but of the emancipation of modern women. Certainly Nora's defiance—her claim to be treated as an equal—has made her typical of all housewives who refuse to be regarded as house pets. In one sense, she is an ordinary wife and mother—far from an Antigone or a Lady Macbeth, but she is unusual in the way she sums up an entire group of women. *A Doll's House* was written in 1879; but today, well over 100 years later, Nora is still a symbol of modern woman. The play is revived year after year, and Nora's message does not lose its relevance.

In *Who's Afraid of Virginia Woolf?* by Edward Albee, the main characters are a husband and a wife, quite commonplace in a way. He is a somewhat ineffectual college professor; she is the college president's daughter. They argue and fight almost to the point of exhaustion. Another unhappily married couple? Yes. But again, they are quintessential; that is, they are the essence of a certain type of married couple. To Albee, they represent an American type: a bitter, alienated couple, bored with themselves and with each other. And to underline this point, he names them Martha and George, giving them the same first names as Martha and George Washington—America's "first couple."

Another example is Willy Loman, in Arthur Miller's *Death of a Salesman,* who sums up all salesmen, traveling in their territories on a "smile and a shoeshine." Willy has accepted a false dream: the idea that by putting up a good front and being "well liked," he will be a great success and achieve material wealth.

Nora Helmer, Martha and George, and Willy Loman: all are examples of characters who stand apart from the crowd, not by standing above it but by summing up in their personalities the essence of a certain type of person.

Stock Characters

Many characters in drama are not the complete, three-dimensional figures described above. Rather, they symbolize in bold relief some par-

STOCK CHARACTERS OF COMMEDIA DELL'ARTE.
Italian comedy of the Renaissance developed stereotyped characters who were always the same: each character was famous for a certain trait—greed, boastfulness, gullibility, or the like—and always wore the same kind of costume. The etchings here show two commedia characters: Crispin (left) and Le Sabotier (right).

ticular type of person or some outstanding characteristic of human behavior to the exclusion of virtually everything else. Referred to as *stock* characters, they appear particularly in comedy and melodrama, though they can be found in almost all kinds of drama.

TRADITIONAL EXAMPLES OF STOCK CHARACTERS   Among stock characters, some of the most famous examples are those in *commedia dell'arte*, a form of popular comedy which flourished in Italy during the sixteenth and seventeenth centuries. In commedia dell'arte, there were no scripts but rather scenarios which gave an outline of the story. The performers improvised or invented words and comic actions to fill out the play. The stock characters of commedia were either straight or exaggerated and were divided into servants and members of the ruling class. In every case, however, one particular feature or trait was stressed. Wherever they appeared, these characters had the same propensities and wore the same costumes. The bragging soldier, called the

A STREETCAR NAMED DESIRE (1947)

TENNESSEE WILLIAMS (1911–1983)

CHIEF CHARACTERS:
Blanche DuBois—30 years old
Stella Kowalski—her sister, 25 years old
Stanley Kowalski—Stella's husband, 28 years old
Harold Mitchell (Mitch)—Stanley's friend
Eunice Hubbell—upstairs neighbor

SETTING: A two-story apartment building on a street named Elysian Fields in New Orleans. The section is poor but has a raffish charm.

SCENE 1: Blanche DuBois arrives from Mississippi at the New Orleans apartment of her sister Stella and Stella's husband Stanley. Blanche, who has lost her home and is destitute, is in an anxious state. She expresses disapproval of Stella's "earthy" living conditions.

SCENE 2: The next evening. Stanley's friends are coming over for a poker game; Stella takes Blanche out for dinner because her "sensibilities" will be upset by the men's crudeness. Later, Stanley accuses Blanche of swindling them by selling Belle Reve, the family estate, without giving Stella her share.

SCENE 3: The poker night. The women come home late; Blanche flirts with Mitch, one of the men in the poker game, while Stella dances to music on the radio. Stanley, who is very drunk, gets angry and throws the radio out the window and attacks Stella. The men subdue him while Blanche takes Stella, who is pregnant, to Eunice's apartment upstairs. Stanley yells for Stella to come home, and she obeys; Mitch sits with the distraught Blanche on the front steps.

SCENE 4: The next morning. Blanche is upset and harried, but Stella is happy. Blanche tells Stella she should leave Stanley, whom she calls an "ape," but Stella tells her that she loves him. Stanley overhears Blanche saying that he is "common" and "bestial." He sneaks out and reenters loudly, pretending that he hasn't heard.

SCENE 5: Blanche, highly nervous, begins drinking. Stanley asks her if she ever knew a man from a disreputable hotel in Laurel, Mississippi. She denies it, but her reaction makes it obvious that she did know the man. She finds relief in the idea of her forthcoming date with Mitch and admits to Stella that she is attracted to him.

SCENE 6: 2 A.M. that night. Mitch and Blanche come home from their date, go inside, have a drink, and chat awkwardly. Mitch has spoken to his sick mother, whom he lives with, about a possible future with Blanche, who confides to him that her first husband was a homosexual who killed himself.

SCENE 7: A late afternoon in mid-September. While Stella is preparing for Blanche's birthday party, Stanley tells Stella he has heard bad stories about Blanche's former life. Stanley admits that Mitch won't be coming to the party because he now knows the stories. When Blanche comes out of the bathroom, she realizes that something is wrong.

SCENE 8: Forty-five minutes later. Mitch has not appeared at the dismal birthday party, and Blanche is miserable. Stanley belligerently presents Blanche with his "present"— a one-way bus ticket back to Laurel, Mississippi. Blanche gets hysterical and runs into the bathroom; Stella gets so agitated while confronting Stanley that she goes into labor and is rushed to the hospital.

SCENE 9: Later that evening. Blanche is home alone when Mitch arrives drunk. Mitch says he's never seen her in full light; he rips the paper lantern off the light bulb and turns it on. When he looks at her, she cries out and covers her face. He makes a play for Blanche, but she breaks away and he runs out.

SCENE 10: A few hours later. Blanche, who has been drinking, is alone. Stanley returns from the hospital; he has been drinking too. She tells him a millionaire has invited her to go away. She also makes up a story about Mitch coming to beg her forgiveness. Stanley knows it is a lie. He puts on silk pajamas that he "wore on his wedding night." The two of them struggle, and he brutally carries her to bed offstage, where he rapes her.

SCENE 11: Several weeks later. Stella is packing Blanche's things while the men play poker: they are sending Blanche to a mental hospital. Blanche told Stella what Stanley did to her, but Stella won't believe it. When the doctor and matron arrive, Blanche thinks it is her millionaire; when she sees it is not, she runs into the bedroom. The doctor comes in

and gently leads Blanche out. Eunice hands the baby to Stella, as she stands crying, and Stanley comforts her.

(Martha Swope)

227

Capitano, always boasted of his courage in a series of fictitious military victories. (A forebear of this character had appeared in Roman comedy centuries before.) The young lovers were fixtures as well. Older characters included *Pantalone*, an elderly merchant who spoke in clichés and chased young girls, and a pompous lawyer called *Dottore*, who spoke in Latin phrases and attempted to impress others with his learning. Among servants, *Harlequin* was the most popular; displaying both cunning and stupidity, he was at the heart of most plot complications. These are but a few of a full range of characters, each with his or her own peculiarities.

As for examples of stock characters in melodrama, we are all familiar with such figures as the innocent young heroine, "pure as the driven snow"; and the villain, lurking in the shadows, twirling his moustache.

MODERN EXAMPLES OF STOCK CHARACTERS   The familiar figures on weekly situation comedies on television are good examples of stock or stereotypical characters. The conceited high school boy, the prejudiced father, the harried mother, the dumb blond waitress, the efficient career woman, the tough private detective: these characters are stereotypes whom we see every day on television. As with all stereotypes, their attitudes and actions are always predictable.

CHARACTERS WITH A DOMINANT TRAIT   Closely related to stock characters are characters with a single trait or "humor." A theory that the body was governed by four humors, which must be kept in balance for a person to be healthy, was widely held during the Renaissance. In the sixteenth century it was extended to include psychological traits, and the playwright Ben Jonson followed this notion extensively in his plays. In *Every Man in His Humour* and *Every Man out of His Humour*, for instance, he portrayed characters in whom one humor came to dominate all others, making for an unbalanced, often comic, personality. Jonson often named his characters for their single trait or humor. His play *The Alchemist* includes characters with names like Subtle, Face, Dapper, Surly, Wholesome, and Dame Pliant.

During and after the English Restoration, playwrights continued to give characters names indicating their personalities. In *The Way of the World*, by William Congreve, one character is called Fainall, meaning that he feigns all, or pretends everything. Other characters are named Petulant, Sir Wilful Witwound, Waitwell, and Lady Wishfort, the last being a contraction of "wish for it." Another play from the English Restoration, *The Country Wife* by William Wycherley, includes Mr. Pinchwife (a man who hides his wife from other men), Sparkish (a man who thinks he sparkles with wit), Sir Jasper Fidget, and Mrs. Squeamish. The French playwright Molière, while generally giving his characters regular names, frequently emphasized the dominant trait of the main character in the title: *The Miser, The Misanthrope, The Would-Be Gentleman,* and *The Imaginary Invalid.*

Minor Characters

Stock characters or characters with a dominant trait are not to be confused with *minor characters.* Minor characters are those—in all types of plays—who play a small part in the overall action. Generally they appear briefly and serve chiefly to further the story or to support more important characters. Examples of minor characters are servants, soldiers, and so forth. Even doctors, lawyers, or close friends of leading characters are considered minor if they play only a small role in the action. Since we see so little of these characters, they usually can show only one facet of their personalities. This is a different case from that of a main character who is deliberately portrayed as one-sided.

Nonhuman Characters

In Greece in the fifth century B.C., and in many primitive cultures, actors portrayed birds and animals; and the practice has continued to the present. Aristophanes, the Greek comic dramatist, used a chorus of actors to play the title parts in his plays *The Birds* and *The Frogs.*

(Martha Swope)

PERFORMERS PLAY NONHUMAN PARTS.
Sometimes theatrical characters are nonhuman, although they usually have human characteristics. Good examples are the characters in the musical Into the Woods, *based on several fairy tales. Here, in the original Broadway cast, we see Little Red Riding Hood (Danielle Ferland) with the Big Bad Wolf (Robert Westenberg).*

In the modern period, Eugène Ionesco has men turn into animals in *Rhinoceros;* and Edmond Rostand, a French playwright, wrote a poetic fable about a rooster called *Chantecler.* Karel Čapek (1890–1938), a Czechoslovakian dramatist, collaborated with his brother, Josef, to write *The Insect Comedy,* a picture of insect life as seen in the delirium of a dying vagabond.

Occasionally performers are called on to play other nonhuman roles. Karel Čapek also wrote a play entitled *R.U.R.,* in which people play robots. (The initials in the title stand for "Rossum's Universal Robots," and it was from this play that the word *robot* derives.) In the medieval morality play *Everyman,* characters represent ideas or concepts, such as Fellowship, Good Deeds, Worldly Possession, Beauty.

Dramatic characters in the guise of animals or robots are the exception rather than the rule. When they do occur, more often than not it is the human quality of the animal or robot which is being emphasized, and sometimes the reverse: the animalistic or robotlike quality of the human being.

✳ THE PLAYWRIGHT AND THE CHARACTERS: ✳
USING DRAMATIC CHARACTERS EFFECTIVELY

Juxtaposition of Characters

Since characters are the creation of the playwright, he or she can use them in combination with other characters to bring out certain qualities.

PROTAGONIST AND ANTAGONIST   From the Greek theater we have the terms *protagonist* and *antagonist.* The *protagonist* is the main character in the play—Othello, for instance—and the *antagonist* is the main character's chief opponent. In the case of *Othello,* the antagonist is Iago. It is through the contest of the two characters that their individual qualities are developed.

CONTRASTING CHARACTERS   There is another way in which dramatists contrast characters: by setting them side by side rather than in opposition. Sophocles created two exceptionally strong-willed, independent female characters—Antigone and Electra—each one the title character in a play. Both are young women intent on defying an older person and willing to risk death to fight for a principle. But Sophocles was not content to present them on their own. Unlike other dramatists who had told the same story, Sophocles gave them sisters whose characters contrasted sharply with theirs. To Antigone he gave Ismene, a docile, compliant sister who argued with Antigone that she should obey the law and give in to authority. To Electra, Sophocles gave a sister, Chrisothemis, a meek, frightened creature who protested that as

230

women they were powerless to act. Sophocles strengthened and clarified both Antigone and Electra by providing them with contrasting characters to show off their determination and courage.

Frequently a dramatist will introduce secondary characters to act as foils or counterparts to the main characters. In *Hedda Gabler*, by Henrik Ibsen, the main character is a willful, destructive woman, bent on having her own way. Mrs. Elvsted, another character in the play, is her opposite in almost every way: a trusting, warm, sincere woman, able to give of herself to others. This technique of setting parallel or contrasting characters beside one another is like putting one color next to another. A single color is sometimes difficult to judge; but the moment we put others beside it, we become aware of its relative brightness. For instance, a dark green looks much darker when it is seen next to pale green.

MAJOR AND MINOR CHARACTERS   Earlier, minor characters were mentioned. The *major* characters in a play are the important figures, the ones about whom the play revolves. In *Hamlet* the major characters include Hamlet, Claudius, Gertrude, Polonius, Laertes, and Ophelia. The minor characters include Marcellus and Bernardo, who are standing watch when the ghost appears; and Reynaldo, a servant to Polonius. Sometimes characters fall halfway between major and minor; examples in *Hamlet* are Rosencrantz and Guildenstern, or the gravedigger. In these instances the characters, each of whom has a distinctive personality, play a small but quite important part in the play.

Orchestration of Characters

Anton Chekhov, the Russian dramatist, is said to have "orchestrated" his characters. The reference is to a musical composition in which the theme is played first by one section of the orchestra, such as the violins, and then by another, such as the brass or woodwinds. Not only is the theme taken up by various sections but it can be played in different ways, first in a major key and then in a minor. In his plays, Chekhov drew a series of characters with a common problem, and each of the characters represented some aspect of the central theme. In Chekhov's *Uncle Vanya,* for example, the theme of disillusionment and frustration with life is shared by virtually every character in the play, each of whom longs for a love that cannot be fulfilled.

The title character, Uncle Vanya, has been working on an estate to help support a professor who he discovers is a fraud. In the midst of his disillusionment, Vanya falls in love with the professor's young wife, but she does not return his love. A neighbor, Dr. Astrov, has made sacrifices to be a doctor in a small rural community and then has grown dissatisfied with his life. He too loves the professor's wife, but nothing

ORCHESTRATION OF CHARACTERS.

Characters in a play serve as contrasts, counterparts, or complements to each other. Some-
times one group of characters is set in opposition to another. Chekhov was a master at
combining, blending, and contrasting characters—a technique sometimes referred to as "or-
chestration of characters." An excellent example is his play Uncle Vanya, *shown here in*
a production at the American Repertory Theater.

can come of it. Vanya's niece, a plain woman who works hard for little
reward, is in love with Dr. Astrov, but he does not return her love.
And so it goes; practically everyone embodies the theme. But it is subtly
and carefully done. The theme is brought out through the overall effect
in which gradations and shadings of meaning are interwoven in the
characters like threads in a tapestry.

Chekhov was a master at orchestrating his characters (*The Cherry Or-*
chard is another example of this), but he was not the only dramatist to
employ the technique. In one way or another, most dramatists try to
arrange their characters so that they produce a cumulative effect. It is
not what one character does or says but what all the characters do
together that creates the effect.

THE AUDIENCE AND THE CHARACTERS: IMAGES OF OURSELVES

Dramatic characters sometimes have an impact that seems more "real than real." In fact, Luigi Pirandello, an Italian dramatist, wrote a play, *Six Characters in Search of an Author,* in which he argued that dramatic characters are more permanent and less of an illusion than human beings. Speaking through the character of the Father, he says, "He who has had the luck to be born a character can laugh even at death. He cannot die. The man, the writer, the instrument of the creation will die, but his creation does not die." Arguing with a theater manager in the play, the Father points out that whereas human beings are always changing and are different from one day to the next, characters remain the same. The Manager picks up the argument, with the character of the Father:

THE MANAGER: Then you'll be saying next that you . . . are truer and more real than I am.

THE FATHER: But of course; without doubt! . . .

THE MANAGER: More real than I?

THE FATHER: If your reality can change from one day to another . . .

THE MANAGER: But everyone knows it can change. It is always changing, the same as anyone else's.

THE FATHER: No, sir, not ours! Look here! That is the very difference! Our reality doesn't change; it can't change! It can't be other than what it is, because it is already fixed forever.[1]

Their permanence, however, is not the only feature of dramatic characters. When well drawn, they present us with a vivid, incisive picture of ourselves. We see individuals at their best and at their worst; we see them perform acts of heroic courage, acts we like to feel we ourselves are capable of; and we see deeds of cowardice and violence—actions we fear we might commit in moments of weakness or anger. We see outrageous cases of folly and pretension, which make us laugh uproariously. In short, we see ourselves in the revealing and illuminating mirror theater holds before us.

We have seen that the exchange between performer and spectator is the basic encounter of theater. But the dramatic characters impersonated by the performers are images of ourselves. In truth, therefore, the basic encounter of theater is with ourselves. Sometimes, watching a theater event, we see a part of ourselves on the stage and realize for the first

MODERN CHARACTERS REFLECT THE MODERN WORLD.

Just as a play's action and setting reflect society at the time the play is written, so do characters reflect the world the playwright knows. The characters in John Guare's Six Degrees of Separation *are modern, urban people, separated and alienated from each other: husbands are separated from wives, parents from children, the rich from the poor, and different races from one another.*

time some truth about our lives. This confrontation is at the heart of the theater experience.

At the beginning of Chapter 8, I noted that one task of the playwright is to decide the purpose for which his or her play is intended, and the point of view he or she adopts toward the subject. This will be the material we investigate in Part Four.

✳ SUMMARY ✳

1 Dramatic characters are symbols of people and fall into several categories; the chief characters of traditional theater are extraordinary characters, men and women at the outer limits of human behavior.

2 In modern serious theater we frequently find *prototypical* characters—complete, fully rounded portraits of people who embody a whole

group or type. An example is Willy Loman, the salesman in *Death of a Salesman.*

3   Some characters are stereotypes. Stock characters, for instance, are predictable, clearly defined types. Other characters feature one dominant trait which overshadows all other features.

4   Occasionally performers are asked to play nonhuman parts—animals, birds, etc.—but generally with a strong human flavor.

5   Characters are placed together by the playwright in certain combinations to obtain maximum effectiveness. A *protagonist* may be opposed by an *antagonist; minor* characters support *major* characters; and individual characters are orchestrated into a whole.

6   Dramatic characters are symbols of people; therefore, the basic confrontation in theater is with ourselves.

❊ TOPICS FOR DISCUSSION ❊

1   Is the difference between an "extraordinary" character in classic drama and an "exceptional" character in modern drama only, or primarily, their station in life?

2   Stock characters, it is noted, appear in almost all kinds of drama but are most common in comedy and melodrama. What qualities of stock characters would make them less useful to a dramatist, or less effective, in a tragedy or even a tragicomedy?

3   Defend or attack this statement: "A playwright who uses contrasting characters is stacking the deck—or loading the dice—in the sense that this device makes the outcome, the audience's response, a sure thing."

4   The chapter describes Chekhov's *Uncle Vanya* in terms of "orchestration of characters." Take another multicharacter play that you have recently read or seen and determine if this notion applies to it. If so, explain in what way; if not, explain why the idea of "orchestration of characters" does not apply.

5   Consider the characters in *A Streetcar Named Desire* by Tennessee Williams. Discuss their relative importance and the relationships among them. Who are the major characters and who the minor? Is Mitch a major or minor character? Is there a protagonist? Who? Is there an antagonist?

A VARIETY OF EXPERIENCES

Today's audiences can see tragedies, comedies, farces, and domestic dramas; plays in different styles; classic plays from the past and avant-garde plays from the present. Examples of this wide range include, on the preceding overleaf, Shakespeare's Macbeth; *on the opposite page, Feydeau's bedroom farce* A Flea in Her Ear *(top) and George Wolfe's* Spunk *(bottom); on this page, Anton Chekhov's* Uncle Vanya *(top left), Samuel Beckett's* Waiting for Godot *(top right), and the musical* The Phantom of the Opera *(left); on the following overleaf, Bertolt Brecht's* The Good Woman of Setzuan *(top) and Shakespeare's* Twelfth Night *(bottom).*

PART FOUR

THEATRICAL GENRES

THE PURPOSE AND POINT OF VIEW OF THEATER.
Every play and every production should serve some purpose—sometimes several purposes at once—and reflect a point of view. Waiting for Godot by Samuel Beckett is entertaining but also intellectually and philosophically provocative. It is a tragicomedy, combining both the comic and the tragic points of view in a way that many contemporary plays do. In the drawing by Al Hirschfeld on the following pages, we see (from left to right) the actors Robin Williams, Steve Martin, F. Murray Abraham, and Bill Irwin.

13

PURPOSE AND POINT OF VIEW

Theater is art, and as such it mirrors or reflects life. It does not try to encompass the whole of life at one time but rather selects and focuses on a part of the total picture. Selectivity, therefore, is a key principle of all art; it is through this means that art can achieve a clarity, an order, and a beauty rarely found in life.

The selection process of art occurs in several ways. To begin with, all art forms use certain elements while eliminating others. Music, for instance, focuses on the sounds produced by musical instruments and the human voice. Painting uses only visual elements: the colors, shapes, and designs that can be put on a canvas. Dance focuses on the movements of the human body made to the accompaniment of music. Part of the force and effectiveness of art is due to its selectivity: when we look at a painting, we concentrate our full attention on the visual—on the surface of the canvas—and are not distracted by other considerations.

The means by which an art form presents its material is often referred to as the *medium*. Thus, sound produced by instruments or human voices is the medium of music. For theater, the medium is a story enacted by performers: theater always involves actresses and actors on a stage playing characters. We saw previously that the basic encounter in theater is between the performers and the audience; but this is a special type of encounter: the performers are playing other people. Moreover,

ART IS SELECTIVE.
Each art form focuses on certain elements to the exclusion of others. Painting, for example, concentrates on color, line, and design. Among the performing arts, ballet deals exclusively with movement set to music; no words or dialogue are used. An example of ballet movement is seen here in a production of the American Ballet Theater.

the people are part of a human story that has been written by a dramatist. This combination sets theater apart from other art forms.

✳ THE PURPOSE OF A THEATER EVENT ✳

Art goes further in its selectivity than using one medium as opposed to
another. An artist can paint with a special intention; one painter, for
example, simply wishes to reproduce a landscape, while another wishes
to paint a picture that makes a political statement. In a similar fashion,
a theater event can be performed for a special *purpose* and can be viewed
from a unique angle of vision. Again, this results in the clarity and the
power that such selectivity can achieve.

Every theater event is intended to serve some purpose. It may be a
casual, unconscious purpose—much as someone says, "Let's go to the
movies tonight," or "Let's watch television." Even in these seemingly
casual decisions, however, there is a purpose; in this case, movies or
television are seen primarily as entertainment or "escape." In Chapter
3, it was noted that various types of contemporary theater are presented
for a specific purpose: feminist theater, Hispanic theater, black theater.
In theater of this kind, both those who create the event and members
of the audience have a definite purpose in mind.

Historically, the creators of theater—playwrights, directors, performers, and others—have intended it to serve different purposes. There
have been times, for example, when the purpose of a theater event was
religious. In the medieval period, when very few people could read and
write, theater performances were employed to teach people stories from
the Bible and to instruct them in religious precepts. At times theater
serves a civic function. A pageant will be arranged to present a play
telling the history of a community. This kind of play is frequently given
on the anniversary of a town. In 1976, when the United States celebrated
its bicentennial, many dramas were presented depicting events surrounding the founding of the nation.

In the seventeenth century, playwrights in England frequently wrote
plays for the purpose of entertaining royalty as a part of a celebration.
In France, Molière wrote several of his plays as part of an entertainment
at some château, or for presentation before King Louis XIV at Versailles.
The play would be only one of several activities—including perhaps a
banquet, a dance, a fireworks display—arranged for an evening, or for
a celebration of several days' duration.

Throughout history some playwrights have written primarily to entertain their audience while others have written with a serious purpose
in mind, such as to call attention to injustice, to make a statement
against war, or to raise moral and philosophical questions.

(T. Charles Erickson)

CREATING FOCUS IN THEATER.
The center of attention in theater is the human being, and within individual plays, certain key characters are singled out to provide a focal point for audiences. A good example is Ibsen's Peer Gynt, *a sprawling play covering many years and many locales, with a multitude of characters. At the center, however, is the character of Peer, shown here as portrayed by Richard Thomas in a production at the Hartford Stage Company.*

Establishing Emphasis

As a part of fulfilling the purpose of a theater event, the dramatist determines who and what to focus on in a play. For example, he or she can emphasize a particular character trait in one play and its opposite in another. This is what Henrik Ibsen often did. In his *Brand*, the leading character is a stark, uncompromising figure who will sacrifice everything—family, friends, love—for his principles. On the other hand, Ibsen's Peer Gynt, from the play of the same name, is always compromising, always running away.

In carrying out the purpose of a play, the playwright determines how to interpret the characters or story, and in doing so, he or she sometimes might even change the order of events. A good example is the way the three prominent tragic dramatists of Greece in the fifth century B.C. treated the Electra myth. The story, referred to above, concerns Electra's revenge on her mother, Clytemnestra, and her stepfather, Aegisthus, for having murdered her natural father, Agamemnon. In carrying out her revenge, Electra enlists the help of Orestes, her brother, who has just returned from exile. In the versions by Aeschylus and Euripides, the stepfather is murdered first, and the mother, Clytemnestra, murdered last. This puts emphasis on the terror of murdering one's own mother. But Sophocles saw the story differently. He wished to emphasize that Electra and her brother were acting honorably and to play down the mother's murder. And so he reversed the order of the murders and had the mother killed first, then he built up to the righteous murder of the stepfather as the final deed. The change made by Sophocles indicates the latitude writers have in altering events to suit their artistic purposes. The manner in which a play unfolds is up to the playwright and is controlled by his or her individual approach.

Making the Purpose Clear

Whatever the approach, it is up to the playwright and his or her collaborators to make clear the purpose of a theater event. Sometimes, in the present-day theater, a playwright may begin work on a play without knowing its exact purpose— which may emerge only as the script goes through several revisions. Before a play goes into production, however, the playwright should know where it is headed.

Once the purpose is clear, the director, the performers, and the designers join the playwright in working to achieve it. One of the tasks of those developing a production is to make certain that all those concerned are moving toward the same goal. If they are not, various elements will be in conflict. If, for instance, the playwright intends the work to be serious and the acting company makes fun of it, the two are at cross-purposes.

One of the tasks of an alert audience member is to understand what purpose the work is intended to serve. The writer and the performers should make this clear as early as possible in a performance so that the audience will know on what basis to judge the production.

✳ THE VIEWPOINT OF A THEATER EVENT ✳

Closely related to purpose is *point of view*, which expresses the way we look at things.

People and events can always be interpreted in widely different ways. How we perceive them depends on our point of view. There is a familiar story of two people looking at a bottle half-filled with wine; the optimist will say that the bottle is half-full, but the pessimist will note that the same bottle is half-empty.

Anyone familiar with the presentation of evidence in a court trial— one involving an automobile accident, for instance—knows that different witnesses, each of whom may be honest and straightforward, will describe the same incident differently. One will say that she saw a yellow car go through a stoplight and hit a blue car; another will say that he remembers clearly that the blue car pulled out before the light had changed and blocked the path of the yellow car. The same variation in viewpoint affects our assessment of politicians and other public figures. To some people, a certain politician will be a dedicated, sincere public servant, interested only in what is best for the people. But to others, the same politician will be a hypocrite and a charlatan—that is, a fake concerned exclusively with personal gain.

Point of view influences the way we perceive virtually everything in life, but it plays a particularly important role in the arts. Under ordinary circumstances, those who attempt to determine our point of view, such as advertisers and politicians, frequently disguise their motives, employing subtle and indirect techniques to convince us that they are not trying to impose their views on us; but those who understand the process know that that is exactly what the advertiser or politician is trying to do. In the arts, on the other hand, the imposition of a point of view is direct and deliberate. Rather than being disguised, it is emphasized. The artist makes it clear that he or she is looking at the world from a highly personal point of view, perhaps turning the world upside down or looking at it from an unusual angle.

A good example can be found in films, where we have become familiar with the various points of view, angles of vision, and perspectives which the camera selects for us. In a close-up we do not see an entire room or even an entire person; we see one small detail: a hand putting out a cigarette or a finger on the trigger of a gun. In a medium shot we see more—a couple embracing, perhaps—but still only part of their bodies. In an exterior scene we might view a panorama of the vast Russian steppes or a full military parade. The camera also predetermines the angle from which we see the action. In a scene emphasizing the strength of a figure, the camera will look up from below to show a person looming from the top of a flight of stairs. In another scene we might look down on the action. In still other instances the camera might be tilted so that a scene looks off balance; a scene might be shot out of focus so that it is hazy or blurred; or it might be filmed through a special filter.

As with the other arts, point of view is an important ingredient of theater. It tells us how to interpret the words and actions of the characters we see onstage; it provides a key to understanding the entire experience. In most cases a point of view originates with the script of the playwright and then is carried out in the work of the director, in the actions of the performers, and in the design of the costumes, scenery, and lighting. When this process is successful, we are taken inside the work and we see the subject through the artists' eyes. Their world becomes our world.

The Dramatist's Point of View

"There is nothing either good or bad, but thinking makes it so," Shakespeare wrote in *Hamlet*. To this could be added a parallel statement: "There is nothing either funny or sad, but thinking makes it so." One's point of view determines whether one takes a subject seriously or laughs at it, whether it is an object of pity or of ridicule.

Horace Walpole (1717–1797), an English author of the eighteenth century, wrote: "This world is a comedy to those that think, a tragedy to those that feel." There may or may not be truth in Walpole's epigram, but the chief point it underlines is that people see the world differently. Just why some people look at the world and weep, and others look at it and laugh, is difficult to say; but there is no question that they do.

Once adopted, a point of view is transmitted to others in innumerable ways. In everyday life, for instance, we telegraph to those around us the relative seriousness of a situation by the way we behave. Anyone coming onto a scene where a person has been hurt in an accident will immediately sense that the situation is no laughing matter. The people looking on will have concerned expressions on their faces, and their voices and actions will reflect tension and urgency. In contrast, a person coming into a group where a joke is being told will notice an air of pleasurable expectancy among the spectators and a teasing, conspiratorial tone on the part of the storyteller.

A similar thing happens in the theater. Point of view begins when a dramatist takes a strong personal view of a subject, deciding that it is grave, heroic, or humorous. In theater, as in other art forms, the opportunities for selectivity are greater than in everyday life; and hence the adoption of a point of view can be included in drama in a quite conscious and deliberate way. In a serious play, for instance, the playwright says: "I know the world is not always somber; there are pleasant moments. Life is not made up exclusively of violence, treachery, and alienation. But at times it seems that way, and so for the duration of this play I will deal only with the serious side of life and put everything else aside."

Having taken this point of view, the dramatist then incorporates it into the play itself, giving the characters words to speak and actions to perform which convey that attitude. In a serious work the writer will choose language and actions suggesting sobriety and sincerity.

Take the lines spoken by Othello:

Oh, Now for ever
Farewell the tranquil mind! Farewell content!
Farewell the plumed troop and the big wars
That make ambition virtue!

These words express Othello's profound sense of loss in unmistakable fashion.

Another writer might take what is ordinarily a serious subject and treat it humorously. A good example is Arthur Kopit (1937–   ), who, in his play *Oh, Dad. Poor Dad. Mama's Hung You in the Closet, and I'm Feelin' So Sad,* gave a comic twist to a dead body. The title itself, with its mocking tone and its unusual length, makes it clear from the beginning that Kopit wants us to laugh at his subject.

CHAPTER 13 • PURPOSE AND POINT OF VIEW

Once the playwright's intentions are known, the director and the performers must transmit them to the audience. The actor playing Othello, for example, must deliver his lines in a straightforward manner and move with dignity, that is, without the exaggerations or excesses of comedy. When a series of gestures, vocal inflections, and activities on the part of performers are combined with the words and ideas of the dramatist—and set in an appropriate visual environment established by the designers—a world is created in a theatrical production. It might be a sad world, a bittersweet world, a hopeful world, or a tragic world. If it is fully and properly created, however, the audience becomes aware of it instantly, enters it, and lives in it for the duration of the performance. Entering and inhabiting a world which reflects a particular point of view is an indispensable part of the theater experience.

Society's Point of View

In discussing this subject, we cannot overlook the role that society plays in the point of view adopted by an artist such as a playwright. We saw earlier that there is a close relationship between theater and society. This relationship manifests itself particularly in the point of view artists adopt toward their subject matter.

(Nobby Clark)

A CLIMATE FOR TRAGEDY.
The world view of a society is one factor determining whether that society will embrace and encourage the creation of tragedy. Some cultures, such as Greece in the fifth century B.C., have an atmosphere in which tragic drama can develop. It was in such a climate that the playwright Aeschylus wrote his trilogy of plays, The Oresteia, about the aftermath of the Trojan War. The scene here shows Orestes in the final play, being pursued by furies after he has murdered his mother. The production was at the National Theater in Great Britain.

Tragedy, for example, generally occurs in periods when society as a whole assumes a certain attitude toward people and the universe in which they live. Two periods conducive to the creation of tragedy were the golden age of Greece in the fifth century B.C. and the Renaissance in Europe. Both periods incorporated two ideas essential to tragic drama: on the one hand, the concept that human beings are capable of extraordinary accomplishments; and on the other, the notion that the world is potentially cruel and unjust. A closer look at these two periods will demonstrate how they reflect these two viewpoints.

In both the fifth century B.C., in Greece, and the Renaissance (the fourteenth through the sixteenth centuries) in Europe and England, human beings were exalted above everything else; the gods and nature were given a much less prominent place in the scheme of things. A look at the history of the two periods shows that men and women of the time considered the horizons for human achievement unlimited. In the fifth century B.C., Greece was enjoying its golden age in commerce, politics, science, and art; nothing seemed impossible in the way of architecture, mathematics, trade, or philosophy. The same was true in Europe and England during the Renaissance. Columbus had discovered the new world in 1492, and the possibilities for trade and exploration appeared infinite. Science and the arts were on the threshold of a new day as well.

In sculpture during the two periods, the human figure was glorified as it rarely had been before or has been since. Fifth-century Greece abounded in statues—on friezes, in temples, in public buildings—of heroes, athletes, and warriors. And during the Renaissance, Michelangelo was only one of many who gave inimitable grace and distinction to the human form.

The celebration of the individual was apparent in all the arts, including drama. The Greek dramatist Sophocles exclaimed:

> Numberless are the wonders of the world,
> But none
> More wonderful than man.

And in the Renaissance, Shakespeare has Hamlet say:

> What a piece of work is man! How noble in reason! How infinite in faculty!
> In form, in moving, how express and admirable! In action how like an
> angel! In apprehension how like a god!

The credo of both ages was expressed by Protagoras, a Greek philosopher of the fifth century B.C.:

> Man is the measure of all things.

But there is another side to the tragic coin. Along with this optimistic and highly humanistic view, there was a simultaneous awareness of what life can do to men and women: a faculty for admitting, unflinchingly, that life can be—and in fact frequently is—cruel, unjust, and even meaningless.

Shakespeare put it this way in *King Lear:*

As flies to wanton boys, are we to the gods;
They kill us for their sport.

In *Macbeth,* he expressed it in these words:

Out, out brief candle!
Life's but a walking shadow, a poor player
That struts and frets his hour upon the stage
And then is heard no more; it is a tale
Told by an idiot, full of sound and fury,
Signifying nothing.

(Donald Cooper/Photostage)

SHAKESPEAREAN TRAGEDY.
Like the classic Greek period, the Elizabethan era in England was conducive to the creation of tragedy. The best-known tragic dramatist of the era was Shakespeare, whose hero Othello, from the play of that name, is shown here depicted by Willard White in a production by the Royal Shakespeare Company.

These periods of history—the Greek golden age and the Renaissance—were expansive enough to encompass both strains: the greatness of human beings on the one hand, and the cruelty of life on the other. These two attitudes form two indispensable sides of the tragic equation; without them, the possibilities for traditional tragedy are virtually nonexistent.

To clarify the distinction between tragic and other points of view, we need only examine other periods in history when one or both of the attitudes forming the tragic equation were absent or expressed in a quite different way. In Europe and Great Britain, the eighteenth century was known as the *age of enlightenment,* and the nineteenth century as the *century of progress.* The French and American revolutions were under way, and the industrial revolution as well; the merchant class and the middle class were in the ascendancy. Individual men and women— alone and unafraid—were not glorified so much as the groups, or masses, that were beginning to stir and throw off the yokes of the past. Enlightenment and progress: together they express the philosophy that men and women can analyze any problem—poverty, violence, disease, injustice—and by applying their intelligence to it, solve it. In general, it was an age of unbounded optimism in which no problem was thought insurmountable and feelings of moral justice ran strong. This is not the soil in which tragedy can grow.

Such an age can have a profound effect on art. For example, in 1681 a man named Nahum Tate (1652–1715) rewrote the ending of Shakespeare's *King Lear* so that Lear's daughter Cordelia does not die as she does in Shakespeare's play, but remains alive, thus softening the tragic effect. This version of the play was performed in England throughout the eighteenth century and much of the nineteenth. The critic Dr. Samuel Johnson (1709–1784), a cold-eyed realist in many respects, preferred the Tate version and wrote in 1765 that he found the death of Cordelia in Shakespeare so painful that he had been unable to bring himself to read the original play for many years. In times such as the eighteenth and nineteenth centuries in Europe, it is difficult for any dramatist, no matter what his or her personal inclinations, to produce tragedy.

As important as it is, however, the outlook of society serves only as the background in creating theater. In the foreground stands the point of view of the individual artist: that highly personal outlook referred to above. Proof of this is the variation among playwrights within the same era. At the same time that Euripides was writing tragedies in ancient Greece, Aristophanes (ca. 450–ca. 388 B.C.) was writing satirical farces. In France in the seventeenth century, Molière was writing comedies when Jean Racine was writing tragedies. In the modern period particularly, we have a multiplicity of individual viewpoints expressed in drama.

251

THE INDIVIDUAL POINT OF VIEW.
In addition to the social and cultural climate of an age, the individual artist's outlook also determines whether a work is serious or comic. Two people writing in the same place at the same time may view the world differently. An excellent example is France in the seventeenth century, when Molière wrote comedies, such as The Imaginary Invalid, *shown above; and Racine wrote tragedies, like* Phaedra, *shown at left in a production starring Glenda Jackson (right) in the title role.*

Viewpoint and Genre: The Problem of Categories

By combining the two elements—the view of society and the individual outlook of the artist—a wide range of serious and comic points of view are incorporated in individual plays. For the sake of convenience, people often classify plays according to point of view: tragedy, comedy, and so forth. A group of plays which form a single type is called a *genre*, after a French word which means "category," or "type."

In Chapter 14, we will study tragedy and other serious drama; and in Chapter 15, comedy. Before we turn to these subjects, however, I should express a word of caution about the question of genre, or categories of drama. The attempt to separate and organize plays according to categories can be a hindrance in developing a free and open understanding of theater. Shakespeare made fun of this problem in *Hamlet* when he had Polonius announce that the players who had come to court could perform anything: "tragedy, comedy, history, pastoral, pastoral-comical, historical-pastoral, tragical-historical, tragical-comical-historical-pastoral." In spite of such absurdities, there are those who continue to try to pigeonhole or label every play that comes along.

In other words, the attempt to assign plays to given categories can be a dangerous pursuit. In the first place, more often than not, plays do not fit neatly into categories. As the quotation from Polonius suggests, different dramas intersect and overlap: a few plays are pure tragedy, but some are heroic drama with tragic elements, and others are serious drama with no elements of tragedy. Also, the serious and the comic are often combined.

Dramatists do not write categories or types of drama; they write individual plays. The dramatist, as well as everyone else concerned with producing a theater event, deals with a specific play—and so should members of the audience. A preoccupation with establishing categories diverts our attention from the main purpose of theater: to *experience the play in performance.*

Having noted this warning, however, we will find that it is still helpful to understand the various genres into which drama usually falls. We learn the different types of drama not to spend our time pinning labels on plays, but to understand that writers, as well as those responsible for the production of a play, take a definite point of view with regard to their material. Members of the audience must be aware of that point of view if they are to understand a performance properly. A play which aims at a purely melodramatic effect, for instance, should be looked at differently from one which aspires to tragedy. A lighthearted comedy should not be judged by the same standards as a philosophical play. It is to understand these differences, and to grasp the various ways in which playwrights have traditionally approached their material, that we study the categories into which groups of plays frequently fall.

The category we will examine in Chapter 14 is serious drama. In Chapter 15, we will consider comedy and tragicomedy.

✳ SUMMARY ✳

1 Drama is written and produced for different purposes: to move us, to involve us, to amuse us, to entertain us, to inform us, to shock us, to raise our awareness, to inspire us. Audiences, too, go to the theater for different purposes.

2 Point of view is the way we look at things: the perspective, or angle of vision, from which we view people, places, and events.

3 In the arts, the establishment of a point of view is direct and deliberate; it is an integral part of a performance or work of art, providing a clue to the audience as to how to interpret and understand what is being seen and heard.

4 Whether a theater piece is serious, comic, or some combination of the two depends on the point of view of the artists who create it.

5 The viewpoint of society also affects the outlook of individual artists in terms of tragedy, comedy, etc.

6 In studying various types of drama—tragedy, comedy, farce—an overemphasis on labels and categories must be avoided; otherwise, theater is robbed of its immediacy and spontaneity.

✳ TOPICS FOR DISCUSSION ✳

1 The chapter states that a writer and performers should make the purpose of a theater event clear as early as possible. What means might they use to do this? In what ways might they fail to do it? Under what circumstances might they inadvertently send an audience misleading signals about purpose?

2 Can you think of any situations in which a writer or performers, or both, would *deliberately* give an audience misleading signals about the purpose of a theater event?

3 The chapter notes that point of view is reflected in the script of a theater event, in the performers' actions, and in its design. Describe some specific ways that script, actions, and design might convey a point of view. How might script, actions, and design fail to convey a point of view?

14

TRAGEDY
AND OTHER
SERIOUS DRAMA

THE TRAGIC HERO.
Serious drama emphasizes the somber aspects of life, and the highest form of such drama is considered to be tragedy. The tragic hero is a person of great stature who gets caught in a web of circumstances from which there is no escape and who accepts his or her fate. A prime example is Macbeth in Shakespeare's play of that name. Shown here are Lady Macbeth (Goldie Semple) pleading with her husband Macbeth (Brian Bedford) in a production of the Stratford Festival in Stratford, Ontario.

A wide range of theater experiences fall under the heading of serious theater. These experiences include (1) the inspiration and lofty feelings of high tragedy, (2) the strong identification in many serious dramas with dramatic characters who have problems like our own, (3) the intellectual challenge of plays of ideas, and (4) the fright and horror induced by melodrama.

Serious drama takes a thoughtful, sober attitude toward its subject matter. It puts the audience in a frame of mind to think carefully about what it sees and to become involved with the characters onstage: to love what they love, fear what they fear, and suffer what they suffer. The best-known form of serious drama, to which we will turn first, is *tragedy*. (For a discussion of theories of tragedy, turn to Appendix 2.) Other forms of serious theater are *heroic drama, domestic drama,* and *melodrama.*

❋ TRAGEDY ❋

Tragedy asks the most basic questions about human existence. Why are people sometimes so cruel to one another? Why is the world so unjust? Why are men and women called on to endure such suffering in their lives? What are the limits of human suffering and endurance? In the midst of cruelty and despair, what are the possibilities of human achievement? To what heights of courage, strength, generosity, and integrity can human beings rise?

Tragedy assumes that the universe is indifferent to human concerns, and often cruel or malevolent. Sometimes the innocent appear to suffer while the evil prosper. In the face of this, some human beings are capable of despicable deeds, but others can confront and overcome adversity, attaining a nobility which places them "a little lower than the angels."

We can divide tragedy into two basic kinds: traditional and modern. *Modern tragedy* generally includes plays of the last hundred years. *Traditional tragedy* includes works from several significant periods of the past.

Traditional Tragedy

Three noteworthy periods of history in which tragic drama was produced are Greece in the fifth century B.C., England in the late sixteenth and early seventeenth centuries, and France in the seventeenth century. The tragedies which appear in these three ages have several characteristics in common, characteristics which help define traditional tragedy. They include the following.

(Will Gullette)

AN EXTRAORDINARY CHARACTER CAUGHT IN THE WEB OF TRAGEDY. *The heroes and heroines of traditional tragedy are generally exceptional people, owing to a combination of personality and position. When tragic heroes or heroines fall, it has special significance. An example is Queen Cleopatra in Shakespeare's* Antony and Cleopatra, *shown here as portrayed by JoBeth Williams in a production at the Old Globe Theater in San Diego.*

TRAGIC HEROES AND HEROINES   Generally the hero or heroine of the play is an extraordinary person: a king, a queen, a general, or a nobleman—in other words, a person of stature. In Greek drama, Antigone, Electra, Oedipus, Agamemnon, Creon, and Orestes are members of royal families. In the plays of Shakespeare, Hamlet, Claudius, Gertrude, Lear, and Cordelia are also royalty; Julius Caesar, Macbeth, and Othello are generals; and others—Ophelia, Romeo, and Juliet—are members of the nobility. Because the heroes and heroines are important, the plays in which they appear have added importance; the characters of tragedy stand not only as individuals, but as symbols for an entire culture or society. The idea is expressed in *Julius Caesar* as follows:

> Great Caesar fell
> Oh! what a fall was there, my countrymen.
> Then I, and you, and all of us fell down. . . .

TRAGIC CIRCUMSTANCES   The central figures of the play are caught in a series of tragic circumstances: Oedipus, without realizing it, murders his father and marries his mother; Phaedra falls hopelessly and fatally in love with her stepson, Hippolytus; Othello is completely duped by Iago; and Lear is cast out by the very daughters he benefited. In traditional tragedy, the universe seems determined to trap the hero or heroine in a fateful web.

TRAGIC IRRETRIEVABILITY   The situation becomes irretrievable: there is no turning back, no way out. The figures of tragedy find themselves in a situation from which there is no honorable avenue of escape; they face a tragic fate and must go forward to meet it.

ACCEPTANCE OF RESPONSIBILITY   The hero or heroine accepts responsibility for his or her actions and also shows a willingness to suffer and an immense capacity for suffering. This is true whether the characters are praiseworthy or villainous; they endure calamities and fight back. Heroic figures accept their fate: Oedipus puts out his own eyes; Antigone dies; Othello kills himself. One who suffers immensely, King Lear, lives through personal humiliation, a raging storm on a heath, temporary insanity, and the death of his daughter, and finally faces his own death. A statement by Edgar in *King Lear* applies to all tragic figures: "Men must endure their going hence even as their coming hither."

TRAGIC VERSE   The language of traditional tragedy is *verse*. Because it deals with lofty and profound ideas—with men and women at the outer limits of their lives—tragedy soars to the heights and descends to the depths of human experience; and many feel that such thoughts and emotions can best be expressed in poetry. Look at Cleopatra's lament upon the death of Mark Antony; the sense of admiration for Antony, and of desolation now that he is gone, could never be conveyed so tellingly in less poetic terms:

> Oh, wither'd is the garland of the war,
> The soldier's pole is fall'n! Young boys and girls
> Are level now with men. The odds is gone,
> And there is nothing left remarkable
> Beneath the visiting moon.

These words have even more effect when heard in the theater spoken by an eloquent actress.

THE EFFECT OF TRAGEDY   When the above elements of traditional tragedy are combined, they appear to produce two contradictory reactions simultaneously. One is pessimistic: the heroes or heroines are "damned if they do and damned if they don't," and the world is a cruel, uncompromising place, a world of despair. When one sees *Hamlet*, for instance, one can only conclude that people are avaricious and corrupt and that the world is unjust. Claudius, Gertrude, Polonius, Rosenkrantz, Guildenstern, and even Ophelia are part of a web of deception, in which Hamlet is inextricably caught. And yet, in the bleakest tragedy—whether *Hamlet, Medea, Macbeth,* or *King Lear*—there is affirmation: the other side of the tragic coin. One source of this positive feeling is the drama itself. It has been pointed out that Sophocles, Euripides, Shakespeare, and Racine, although telling us that the world is in chaos and utterly lost, at the same time affirmed just the opposite by creating such carefully shaped and brilliant works of art. Why bother, if all is hopeless, to create a work of art at all? The answer must be some residual hope in the midst of the gloom.

Another positive element resides in the persons of the tragic heroes and heroines. They meet their fates with such dignity and such determination that they defy the gods. They say: "Come and get me; throw your worst at me, and I will not only absorb it but fight back. Whatever happens, I will not surrender my individuality and my dignity." In Aeschylus's play *Prometheus,* the title character, one of the first tragic heroes, says: "On me the tempest falls. It does not make me tremble." In defeat, the men and women of tragedy triumph. They lose; but in losing, they win. This paradox gives traditional tragedy much of its resonance and meaning and explains why we are both devastated and exhilarated by it.

As for the deeper meanings of individual tragedies, there is a vast literature on the subject, and each play has to be looked at and experienced in detail to obtain the full measure of its meaning. Certain tragedies seem to hold so much meaning—so much in substance, echoes, and reverberations—that one can spend a lifetime studying them.

Modern Tragedy

Tragedies of the modern period—that is, of the late nineteenth century and the twentieth century—do not have queens or kings as central figures, and they are written in prose rather than poetry. For these reasons, as well as more philosophical ones, a debate has raged for some time over whether they are true tragedies. Small men and women, the argument runs, lack the stature of tragic figures. According to this point of view, a traveling salesman, such as Hickey in *The Iceman Cometh* by O'Neill or Willy Loman in *Death of a Salesman* by Miller; a nymphomaniac southern woman like Blanche DuBois in *A Streetcar Named Desire* by Williams; and a housewife who shoots herself, like Hedda Gabler in the play of that name by Ibsen, lack the grandeur of royal rulers.

Similarly, it is argued that the present worldview, in our industrialized, computerized age, looks on the individual human being as a helpless victim of society. How can a hero or heroine defy the gods when people are not free to act on their own but are controlled by social or mechanical forces?

KING OEDIPUS (ca. 430 B.C.)

SOPHOCLES (ca. 496–406 B.C.)

CHIEF CHARACTERS:
Oedipus—King of Thebes
Jocasta—wife of Oedipus
Creon—brother-in-law of Oedipus
Teiresias—a blind seer
A shepherd
A priest
Chorus

SETTING: The entire play takes place in front of the palace at Thebes in Greece.

BACKGROUND: When Oedipus was born, an oracle told his parents, the king and queen of Thebes, that their son would kill his father and marry his mother. Fearing this prophecy, the king and queen gave Oedipus to a shepherd to be killed. But the shepherd pitied the child and instead of killing him sent him to Corinth, where he was adopted by the king and queen. Oedipus grew up, learned of the oracle's prediction, and thinking that the king and queen of Corinth were his real parents, fled from Corinth. On the journey toward Thebes, at a place where three roads met, Oedipus argued with a man and killed him—not knowing that the man was his natural father, Laius. When Oedipus arrived in Thebes, the city was plagued by a Sphinx who killed anyone who could not answer her riddle. Oedipus answered the riddle correctly and the Sphinx died. Oedipus then became king and married Jocasta, not realizing she was his mother. Years later, the city was struck by another plague; this is the point at which the play begins.

PROLOGUE: The priest describes the plague, and the people beg Oedipus to help. Creon enters and reports that the oracle at Delphi has said that the plague will end when the murderer of former King Laius is discovered. Oedipus vows to find the murderer.

PARADOS: The chorus prays to the gods to end the plague.

SCENE 1: Oedipus swears to track down the murderer and puts a curse on him. The blind prophet Teiresias is brought in; he knows the truth—that Oedipus has unknowingly killed his father—but does not want to tell Oedipus, who rages at him. Finally goaded to speak, Teiresias says that Oedipus himself is the guilty party. Oedipus, angrier than ever, cannot accept this and accuses Teiresias of plotting with Creon to gain power, but Teiresias vehemently denies this and leaves.

ODE 1: The chorus confirms its belief in Oedipus and refuses to accept the idea that he murdered Laius.

SCENE 2: Creon answers the charges brought against him by Oedipus; the two men argue until Jocasta makes peace between them. Jocasta discredits the oracle that instructs the people to find the murderer of Laius. She says that long ago the oracle had proved false because it had said that Laius would be killed by his son, but he was not—he was killed by a stranger where three roads meet. Oedipus becomes fearful that perhaps he did kill Laius after all, and he sends for the only witness to the murder.

ODE 2: The chorus speaks of the evils of pride, recklessness, and vanity. Their faith in the oracle of the gods is shaken.

SCENE 3: A messenger from Corinth arrives and tells Jocasta that the king of Corinth is dead and that the people there want Oedipus to be their new king. Oedipus is informed, but he is still concerned because his "mother" yet lives. The messenger tries to allay his fears by telling him that Merope, in Corinth, is not his mother—Oedipus was brought from Thebes by a shepherd when he was very young. Jocasta sees the truth and tries unsuccessfully to dissuade Oedipus from continuing his search.

ODE 3: The chorus prays to the gods to help Oedipus find out about his true birth.

SCENE 4: A messenger brings the old shepherd to Oedipus who forces the hesitant man to speak. The shepherd finally admits that Jocasta told him to kill the baby because the child was destined to kill his own father but states that he pitied the child and took him

far away, to Corinth; Oedipus was that boy. In despair, Oedipus rushes into the palace.

ODE 4: The chorus repeats the tale of the fall of the great man, Oedipus, and expresses its sorrow about the tragedy.

EXODOS: The second messenger enters from the palace to say that the queen has killed herself. He describes how Oedipus burst into Jocasta's room, to find her hanging, dead. He pulled her down, took a brooch from her dress, and blinded himself with it. The doors to the palace open to reveal the blinded Oedipus. Oedipus blames the god Apollo for leading him to his fate. When Creon enters, Oedipus begs him to exile him, to give Jocasta a proper funeral, and to take care of his daughters, who say a last farewell to their father. The chorus warns that man should take nothing for granted, and then exits.

A MODERN TRAGIC FIGURE.
Commentators debate whether or not modern tragedy is possible. The playwright Arthur Miller insists that there can be a "tragedy of the common man." Certainly many figures in modern drama bear the marks of tragedy. Shown here is Jason Robards as Hickey, the central figure in Eugene O'Neill's The Iceman Cometh. *In a long monologue in a bar, Hickey reveals the tragic circumstances in which he murdered his wife under the illusion that he was saving her.*

In answer to these questions, the playwright Arthur Miller argues that it is not necessary to have people of noble birth as tragic heroes and furthermore that modern characters do have an element of choice in determining their lives. In an essay entitled "Tragedy and the Common Man," Miller states: "Insistence upon the rank of the tragic hero, or the so-called nobility of his character, is really but a clinging to the outward form of tragedy." He adds: "I believe that the common man is as apt a subject for tragedy in its highest sense as kings were." Regarding the tragic feeling experienced by the audience, Miller has this to say: "The tragic feeling is evoked in us when we are in the presence of a character who is ready to lay down his life, if need be, to secure one thing—his sense of personal dignity. . . . Tragedy, then, is the consequence of a man's total compulsion to evaluate himself justly."[1]

In support of Miller's ideas about noble figures in tragedy, it should be pointed out that today we have no kings or queens—neither in a mythology nor, except in a few places like Great Britain, in real life. Does this mean that no one can stand for other people, or symbolize a group or culture?

In the sense of mythical figures like Oedipus and Antigone in ancient Greece, or kings and queens in Renaissance England, the answer is probably not. At the same time, many would agree that we have characters today who can stand as symbolic figures for important segments of society.

Another argument against modern tragedy is that the lofty ideas of tragedy can never be adequately expressed in the language of ordinary conversation. There is no doubt that poetry can convey thoughts and feelings to which prose can never aspire. Some prose, however, approaches the level of poetry; and beyond that, there is nonverbal expression: the structure of the plot, the movements and gestures of performers, the elements of sound and light. These nonverbal elements have a way of communicating meanings below the surface of the words themselves.

Speaking of the importance of nonverbal elements in theater, Friedrich Nietzsche (1844–1900), in *The Birth of Tragedy*, wrote:

> The myth by no means finds its adequate objectification in the spoken word. The structure of the scenes and the visible imagery reveal a deeper wisdom than the poet himself is able to put into words and concepts.[2]

The director Constantin Stanislavski, discussed in Chapter 6, stressed what he called the *subtext* of a play, by which he meant emotions, tensions, and thoughts not expressed directly in the text. These often appear much stronger than the surface expressions and when properly presented are abundantly clear to the audience.

Some modern dramatists have attempted to re-create Greek or Elizabethan tragedy in works featuring royal figures and written in blank verse. But the results are often archaic. They tend to be imitations, rather than fresh creations. These attempts provide a strong argument against imitation of the classics as a means of achieving modern tragedy, but this method is not the only way to go about it.

In attempting to create modern tragedy, the question is not whether we view the human condition in the same way as the French in the seventeenth century or the Greeks in the fifth century B.C.—the truth is that those two societies did not view life in the same way either—but whether our age allows for a tragic view on its own terms. The answer seems to be yes. Compared with either the eighteenth or the nineteenth century—the ages of enlightenment, progress, and unbounded optimism—our age has its own tragic vision. Despite a supposedly mechanistic approach to life, our dramatic heroes and heroines fight to the end. If there is sometimes less exaltation or exhilaration at the end of a modern tragedy than at the end of some classic tragedies, this does not negate the total effect.

Modern tragic dramatists probe the same depths and ask the same questions as their predecessors: Why do men and women suffer? Why is there violence and injustice in the world? And perhaps most fundamental of all: What is the meaning of our lives? Naturally they do it on

A MODERN TRAGIC FAMILY.
The family members in Sam Shepard's The Curse of the Starving Class *lack the scale and grandeur of figures from the past, but their problems have meaning for us today and speak more directly to us. The play therefore becomes a form of modern serious drama akin to tragedy. This scene is from a production at the Seattle Repertory Theater.*

their own terms; but many dramatists of the recent past have looked at life with the same level gaze, and the same sense of awe, as those who came before.

It is on this basis that many commentators would argue that writers like Ibsen, Strindberg, García Lorca, O'Neill, Williams, and Miller can lay claim to writing legitimate modern tragedy. The ultimate test of a play is not whether it meets someone's definition of tragedy but what kind of effect it produces in the theater and how successful it is subsequently in standing up to continued scrutiny. Eugene O'Neill's *Long Day's Journey into Night* takes as bleak a look at the human condition, with, at the same time, as compassionate a view of human striving and dignity, as it seems possible to take in our day.

❋ HEROIC DRAMA ❋

The term *heroic drama* is not used as commonly as *tragedy* or *comedy*, but there is a wide range of plays with common characteristics which are not tragedies and for which *heroic drama* seems an appropriate name. I use the term specifically to indicate serious drama of any period which features heroic or noble figures and includes other traits of traditional tragedy—dialogue in verse or elevated language, extreme situations, etc.—but differs from tragedy in important respects. Such serious drama may differ on the one hand in having a happy ending and on the other in assuming a basically optimistic worldview, even when the ending is sad. If there is a happy ending, the chief characters go through many trials and tribulations but emerge victorious at the end. The threatening events of the play turn out to have been narrow escapes, but escapes nevertheless. We agonize with the hero or heroine, knowing all the time that the play will end well.

Several Greek plays, ordinarily classified as tragedies, are actually closer to what we are calling *heroic drama.* In Sophocles's *Electra,* for instance, Electra suffers grievously, but at the end of the play she and her brother Orestes triumph. *The Cid,* written by Pierre Corneille in France in the seventeenth century, has a hero who leads his men to victory in battle and in the end, rather than being killed, wins a duel over his rival, Don Sanchez. (In the late seventeenth century in England, a form of drama called *heroic drama,* or *heroic tragedy,* was precisely the type about which I am speaking—the serious play with a happy ending for the hero or heroine.)

Many plays in Asian drama—from India, China, and Japan—although resisting the usual classifications and involving a great deal of dance and music as part of the presentation, bear a close resemblance to heroic drama. Frequently, for example, a hero goes through a series of dangerous adventures, emerging victorious at the end. The vast majority of Asian dramas end happily.

A second type of heroic drama involves the death of the hero or heroine, but neither the events along the way nor the final conclusion could be thought of as tragic. Several of Goethe's plays follow this pattern. *Egmont* depicts a much-loved count who fights for freedom and justice. He is imprisoned and dies, but not before he sees a vision of a better world to which he is going, where he will be a free man. (Many of Goethe's plays, along with those of his contemporaries in the late eighteenth and early nineteenth centuries, form a subdivision of heroic drama referred to as *romantic drama. Romanticism,* a literary movement which took hold in Germany at the time, and spread to France and throughout much of Europe, celebrated the spirit of hope, personal freedom, and natural instincts.)

A number of plays in the modern period fall into the category of heroic drama. *Cyrano de Bergerac,* written in 1897 by Edmond Rostand (1868–1918), is a good example. The title character of the play dies at the end, but only after the truth of his love for Roxanne, hidden for 15 years, is revealed. He dies a happy man, declaring his opposition to oppression and secure in the knowledge that he did not love in vain. *Saint Joan,* by George Bernard Shaw, is another example: Joan's death when she is burned at the stake is actually a form of triumph; and as if that were not enough, Shaw provides an epilogue to the play in which Joan appears alive after her death.

In the history of theater, the group of plays I am calling *heroic drama* occupy a large and important niche, cutting, as it does, across Asia and western civilization, and across periods from the Greek golden age to the present.

❋ BOURGEOIS OR DOMESTIC DRAMA ❋

With the changes in society that resulted from the rise in the middle class and the shift from kings and queens to more democratic governments, we moved from classic tragedy to modern tragedy. In the same way, during the past 150 years heroic drama has largely been replaced by *bourgeois* or *domestic* drama. *Bourgeois* refers to people of the middle or lower-middle class rather than the aristocracy, and *domestic* means that the plays often deal with the problems of the family or the home rather than great affairs of state. In the Greek, Roman, and Renaissance periods, ordinary people served as the main characters only in comedies; they rarely appeared as the heroes or heroines of serious plays. Beginning in the eighteenth century, however, as society changed, there was a call for serious drama about men and women with whom members of the audience could identify and who were like themselves.

In England in 1731, George Lillo (1693–1739) wrote *The London Merchant,* a story of a merchant's apprentice who was led astray by a prostitute and who betrayed his good-hearted employer. This play, like others that came after it, overstated the case for simple working-class virtues; but it dealt with recognizable people from the daily life of Britain, and audiences welcomed it.

From these beginnings, bourgeois or domestic drama developed through the balance of the eighteenth century and the whole of the nineteenth, until it achieved a place of prominence in the works of Ibsen, Strindberg, and more recent writers such as Arthur Miller, Tennessee Williams, and Lorraine Hansberry, whose *A Raisin in the Sun*

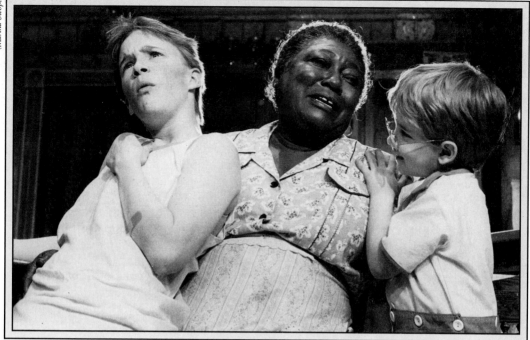

A MODERN DOMESTIC DRAMA.

A scene from Carson McCullers's play The Member of the Wedding, *as produced by the Roundabout Theater in New York City. In this play a young girl suffers the pains of growing up. She is jealous of her older brother and the woman he is marrying, and she feels left out by people her own age. She is comforted by the black woman who works for the family and a small boy who lives next door. Problems like these—problems of ordinary people—are the material of domestic drama. In the scene here are (left to right) Amelia Campbell, Esther Rolle, and Calvin Lennon Armitage.*

was discussed in Chapter 3. Problems with society, struggles within a family, dashed hopes, and renewed determination are frequent characteristics of domestic drama. When sufficiently penetrating or profound, domestic drama achieves the level of modern tragedy discussed earlier.

Included in the general category of bourgeois dramas are plays in which the hero is not one person but an entire group, such as people in a village or people forming their own small society. Examples include *The Sheep Well* by the Spanish playwright Lope de Vega; and, in the modern period, *The Weavers,* by the German writer Gerhart Hauptmann (1862–1946), and *The Lower Depths,* by the Russian dramatist Maxim Gorki (1868–1936). In one form or another, bourgeois or domestic drama has become the predominant form of serious drama throughout Europe and America during the last hundred years.

✳ MELODRAMA ✳

During the seventeenth and eighteenth centuries, one of the most popular forms of theater was *melodrama*. The word *melodrama* means "music drama" or "song drama." It comes from the Greek, but its modern form was introduced by the French in the late eighteenth century and applied to plays which employed background music of the kind we hear in movies: ominous chords underscoring a scene of suspense and lyrical music underscoring a love scene.

Melodrama is exaggerated theater, and we have come to use the term *melodramatic* as an expression of disdain or disapproval. When taken to extremes, melodrama is laughable; we have all seen silent movies where a heroine with curly blond hair, pure as the driven snow, is being pursued by a heartless villain, a man with a sinister moustache and penetrating eyes who will foreclose the mortgage on the home of the girl and her mother unless she will let him have his way with her. This is a caricature, however, for melodrama is an ancient and honorable form of serious drama. It does have a measure of exaggeration, but so does most theater. Actually, melodrama has much in common with all forms of serious drama, and in many cases the difference lies more in degree and emphasis than anything else.

Among the effects for which melodrama generally strives is fright or horror. It has been said that melodrama speaks to the paranoia in all of us: the fear that someone is pursuing us or that disaster is about to

(Martha Swope)

MELODRAMA.
In melodrama, the emphasis is on suspense and excitement; the good characters and the bad characters are clearly delineated. Shown here is a scene from Sweeney Todd, *a modern musical based on a famous nineteenth-century melodrama which tells the story of a London barber who kills people by slitting their throats and whose friend, Mrs. Lovett, uses the corpses to make meat pies. The gruesome quality of the story is a common characteristic of melodrama.*

overtake us. How often do we have the sense that others are ganging up on us or the premonition that we have a deadly disease? Melodrama brings these fears to life; we see people stalked or terrorized, or innocent victims tortured. Murder mysteries and detective stories almost invariably are melodramas because they stress suspense and a close brush with danger. This type of melodrama usually ends in one of two ways: either the victims are maimed or murdered (in which case our worst paranoid fears are confirmed); or, after a series of dangerous episodes, they are finally rescued (in which case the play is like a nightmare or a bad dream from which we awaken the following morning to realize that we are safe in bed and everything is all right).

Probably the easiest way to understand melodrama is to look at films and television. In the twentieth century these two forms have taken melodrama away from the stage; before that the only place audiences could see a cracking-good melodrama was in the theater. Melodrama puts a premium on effects. Will the heroine escape? Will the bad guys be caught and punished? Movies utilize many forms of melodrama— each with the characteristics of the form:

1   The audience is drawn into the action.

2   The issues are clear-cut, and there is a strong delineation of right and wrong.

3   The characters are clearly recognizable as being good or bad.

4   The action is exaggerated, with the main characters always living on the edge of danger.

5   There is a strong emphasis on suspense.

Melodrama is dedicated to results and will sacrifice reality and logic in order to achieve them. In this, it differs from modern tragedy and domestic drama. In those forms the characters and their problems are real; thus when something devastating happens—a family disaster, a serious illness, a confrontation between a parent and a child—we are meant to take it seriously. The problems in these plays have substance. In melodrama we identify strongly with the characters, but we do not take their difficulties completely to heart. We know that in the end everything will be all right.

Among the kinds of melodrama we find in movies and television are the *western* with the heroes and villains and a shootout on Main Street for the finale as in *High Noon*. We also find television *soap operas*, with their perpetual crises, complicated love interests, adulterous affairs, wicked, insincere villains, and sudden turns of fortune; *science fiction* epics like the *Star Trek* films, *Star Wars*, and *The Empire Strikes Back*, in which once again the good characters oppose the bad and which feature a series of spectacular narrow escapes; *horror films* like *Halloween*, *Night-*

**DIDACTIC MELODRAMA:
THE LITTLE FOXES.**

Some melodramas are intended to educate an audience and to persuade them to adopt a certain point of view. Lillian Hellman's The Little Foxes *is a condemnation of the ruthless behavior of the members of a southern family determined to seize control of a small business empire. By extension, the play condemns all such predators. The scene here is from a production by the Repertory Theater of St. Louis.*

mare on Elm Street, and *Friday the 13th* where an attempt is made to frighten the audience as much as possible; and *detective stories*, or *spy mysteries* like the 1940s classic *The Maltese Falcon* or the James Bond films that feature a series of sensational, dangerous adventures.

Still another form of melodrama argues a political or moral issue. One of the hallmarks of melodrama is that the characters tend to be simple and whole rather than complex and divided, as they are in tragedy. Melodrama invariably shows us the good guys against the bad guys. When a playwright, therefore, wishes to make a case, he or she will often write a melodrama in which the good characters represent the author's point of view.

Lillian Hellman, in order to depict the predatory nature of greedy southern materialists, wrote a forceful melodrama called *The Little Foxes*. The play takes place at the close of the Civil War, when the leading character, Regina Giddens, wishes to take control of the family cotton mills so that she can have wealth and move to Chicago. She will do anything to obtain her objectives: flirt with a prospective buyer, blackmail her own brothers, and even allow her husband to die. In a horrifying scene, she stands by while her husband has a heart attack, refusing to get the medicine which would save his life.

As with horror or suspense, melodramas arguing strongly for a point of view employ striking dramatic devices like the scene noted above. Hellman exaggerated the good qualities of the good people and the bad qualities of the bad. This technique is characteristic of all melodrama. To put it in gambling terms, those who write melodrama "load the dice" or "stack the deck."

A list of significant melodramas would range over most of theatrical history and would include writers from Euripides through Shakespeare and his contemporaries to dramatists throughout Europe and America in the modern period. Other types of serious drama, tragic and nontragic, frequently have strong melodramatic elements as well.

In this chapter we have seen that within the realm of serious drama, many different theater experiences are open to us. We observe people very much like ourselves and people far removed from our own lives; we see characters to admire and characters to abhor; we become deeply involved emotionally with the action onstage, or we probe the philosophical depths of what we see. As always, the direction the experience takes will depend on the point of view established in the theater event itself by the playwright and by those who implement the script onstage.

In Chapter 15, when we turn to the points of view reflected in comedy and tragicomedy, we will find a variety of experiences as well.

✳ SUMMARY ✳

1   Tragedy attempts to ask the most basic questions about human existence: Why do men and women suffer? Is there justice in the world? What are the limits of human endurance and achievement? Tragedy presupposes an indifferent and sometimes malevolent universe in which the innocent suffer and there is inexplicable cruelty. It also assumes that certain men and women will confront and defy fate, even if they are overcome in the process.

2   Tragedy can be classified as traditional or modern. In traditional tragedy the chief characters are persons of stature—kings, queens, and the nobility. The central figure is caught in a series of tragic circumstances which are irretrievable. The hero or heroine is willing to fight and die for a cause. The language of the play is verse.

3 Modern tragedy involves ordinary people rather than the nobility, and it is generally written in prose rather than verse. The deeper meanings of tragedy are explored in its modern form by nonverbal elements and by the cumulative or overall effect of events as well as by verbal means.

4 There are several kinds of nontragic serious plays, the most notable being heroic drama, melodrama, and bourgeois or domestic drama.

5 Heroic drama has many of the same elements as traditional tragedy—frequently dealing with highborn characters and being expressed in verse. In contrast to tragedy, it is marked by a happy ending or by an ending in which the deaths of the main characters are considered a triumph and not a defeat.

6 Bourgeois or domestic drama deals with ordinary people in a serious but nontragic manner. It stresses the problems of the middle and lower classes and has become a particularly prominent form in the past century.

7 Melodrama features exaggerated characters and events arranged to create horror or suspense or to present a didactic argument for some political, moral, or social point of view.

❋ TOPICS FOR DISCUSSION ❋

1 Traditional tragedy, as described in this chapter, produces two simultaneous but contradictory reactions: pessimism and affirmation. This, indeed, seems to be one reason why it is esteemed so highly. Why should we value something that sets up contradictory emotions? Defend one of the following explanations, or state and defend your own explanation. *(a)* "To be esteemed, and to endure, art must have a considerable degree of complexity. We value the great tragedies because the response they elicit is so complex." *(b)* "To be esteemed and endure, art must reflect life. We value the great tragedies because the contradictory response they elicit is like our response to life itself."

2 *King Oedipus* has probably had as strong an impact on human consciousness as any work of art ever created. It is not always easy to gain from a synopsis a true sense of the artistic qualities or emotional atmosphere of a play; but consider the synopsis given here to see if you can identify the elements of *King Oedipus* that have caused it to reverberate through so many centuries of human life.

3 In the debate on modern tragedy, which side would you take? Is true modern tragedy possible? Defend your position. If you believe that modern tragedy can and does exist, what arguments can you use other than those advanced in this chapter?

Melodrama is often caricatured in our minds as black-hearted villains menacing pure maidens, though it is a great deal more than that. The other forms of serious drama described in this chapter, however, do not seem to have been stereotyped in analogous ways. What reasons would you suggest to explain why melodrama seems to have taken on such a simplistic image?

15

COMEDY AND TRAGICOMEDY

COMEDY: MOSTLY FOR FUN

In pure comedy, no one gets hurt too seriously, but human foibles are exposed. An example is Feydeau's farce A Flea in Her Ear, *a French comedy of the late nineteenth century. Shown here is a scene featuring Nancy Mette (left) and Donal Donnelly (right) in a production at the Long Wharf Theater in New Haven, Connecticut. In farce, natural laws are suspended and both characters and situations are exaggerated.*

Aside from a basically serious point of view, there are two other fundamental approaches to dramatic material. One is *comedy*, with its many forms and variations; the other is a mixture of the serious and the comic, called *tragicomedy*. (For a discussion of theories of comedy, see Appendix 2.)

❋ COMEDY ❋

People who create comedy are not necessarily more frivolous or less concerned with important matters than those who create serious works; they may be extremely serious in their own way. Writers of comedy like Aristophanes, Molière, and George Bernard Shaw cared passionately about human affairs and the problems of men and women. But those with a comic view look at the world differently: with a smile or a deep laugh or an arched eyebrow. They perceive the follies and excesses of human behavior and develop a keen sense of the ridiculous, with the result that they show us things which make us laugh.

Laughter is one of the most elusive of human activities. Commentators from philosophers like Henri Bergson and Susanne Langer to the father of psychoanalysis, Sigmund Freud, have attempted to analyze laughter, and everyone agrees that no one person has provided an explanation of how it works. One thing most people do agree on is that it is a quintessentially human activity. Whereas other creatures express pain or sorrow—emotions we associate with tragedy—laughter appears to be exclusively human.

It should also be noted that there are many kinds of laughter. They range all the way from mild amusement at a witty saying or humorous situation, to a belly laugh at some wild physical comedy, to cruel, derisive laughter at someone who is different. An example of this last kind would be a group of children who mock a newcomer to the neighborhood who is different or who has some handicap such as a speech impediment. Theater, being reflective of society (as we have observed in previous chapters), incorporates comedies that display a similar range, from light comedies to outrageous farces.

Characteristics of Comedy

If we cannot fully explain comedy, we can at least understand some of the principles that make it possible. In the following pages we will look at the characteristics and assumptions that produce laughter in dramatic comedy.

SUSPENSION OF NATURAL LAWS   A characteristic of most comedy is the temporary suspension of the natural laws of probability and logic: Actions do not have the consequences they do in real life. In comedy,

278

A 1930s FARCE.
A number of farce comedies were written in the United States in the 1920s and 1930s. A good example is Arsenic and Old Lace, *in which two "little old ladies" poison several elderly men as an act of charity. Because the subject is treated humorously, the play is comic rather than serious. In the scene shown here, Jean Stapleton (left) is one of the ladies and Polly Holliday (right) is the other, with one of their victims (in the middle).*

when a haughty man walking down the street steps on a child's roller skate and goes sprawling on the sidewalk, we do not fear for his safety or wonder if he has any bruises. The focus in comedy is on the man's being tripped up and getting his comeuppance, not on any serious injury, because we have suspended disbelief.

In burlesque, a comic character can be hit on the backside with a fierce thwack, and we laugh, because we know that it does not hurt anything but his or her pride. At one point in stage history a special stick made of two thin slats of wood held close together was developed to make the sound of hitting even more fearsome. When this stick hits someone, the two pieces of wood slap together, making the whack sound twice as loud as normal. The stick is known as a *slapstick,* a name which came to describe all kinds of raucous, knockabout comedy.

Prime examples of the suspension of natural laws in comedy are silent movies and film cartoons. In animated cartoons, characters are sent through the air like missiles, are shot full of holes, and are flattened on the sidewalk when they fall from buildings. But they always get up, with little more than a shake of the head. There are no thoughts in the audience of real injury, of cuts or bruises, because the cause-and-effect chain of everyday life is not in effect.

Under these conditions, murder itself can be viewed as comic. In *Arsenic and Old Lace,* by Joseph Kesselring (1902–1967), two sweet old women, thinking they are being helpful, give elderberry wine containing arsenic to lonely old men, resulting, of course, in the men's deaths. The two sisters let their brother, who thinks he is Teddy Roosevelt, bury the bodies in the cellar, where the brother is digging his own version of the Panama Canal. Altogether, these innocent-seeming ladies murder twelve men before their scheme is uncovered. But we watch these proceedings with amusement; we do not really think of it as murder, and we have none of the feelings one usually has for victims. The idea of suffering and harm has been suspended, and we are free to enjoy the irony and incongruity of the situation.

CONTRAST BETWEEN THE SOCIAL ORDER AND THE INDIVIDUAL Generally, the comic viewpoint stems from a basic assumption about society against which the writer places other factors, such as the characters' behavior or the unusual events of the play. Comedy develops when these two elements—the basic assumption about society and the events of the play—cut against each other like the blades in a pair of scissors. Most traditional comic writers accept the notion of a clear social and moral order in their society—it is not the laws of society which are at fault when something goes wrong but the defiance of those laws by individuals. The excesses, the frauds, the hypocrisies, and the follies of men and women are laughed at against a background of normality and moderation. The comic writer (or the comic performer) is saying, in effect, "These characters I show you are amusing because they are eccentric; they go beyond the bounds of common sense and turn ordinary moral values upside down." This view, we should note, is in contrast to the view of many serious plays, particularly tragedies, which assume that society itself is upside down, or that "the time is out of joint."

In Molière's comedy *Tartuffe,* the chief character is a charlatan and hypocrite who pretends to be pious and holy, going so far as to wear clerical garb. He lives in the house of Orgon, a foolish man who trusts him implicitly. The truth is that Tartuffe is trying to possess Orgon's wife as well as his money; but Orgon, blind to Tartuffe's true nature, is completely taken in by him. The audience and the other members of Orgon's family are aware of what is going on; they can see how ludicrous these two characters are, and in the end both Tartuffe's hypocrisy and Orgon's gullibility are exposed. But it is the individual who is held up to ridicule; neither religion nor marriage is assailed by Molière. Rather, it is the abuse of these two basic institutions which is criticized.

Many modern comedies reverse the positions of the scissor blades: the basic assumption is that the world is not orderly but absurd or ridiculous. Society, rather than providing a moral or social framework, offers only chaos. Against this background, ordinary people are set at odds with the world around them, and the comedy in this case results from normal people being thrust into an abnormal world. (This is especially true of tragicomedy, which will be discussed later in this chapter; and of theater of the absurd, which was covered in Chapter 10.)

THE COMIC PREMISE The suspension of natural laws in comedy— together with the scissors effect of setting a ridiculous person in a nor-

COMIC TECHNIQUES.
Plot complications, mistaken identities, physical jokes, clever lines—these cascade on top of one another to provide the humor in comedy. Seen here are characters in Lend Me a Tenor, *about a missing opera star in Cleveland. The performers (left to right) are* Philip Bosco, Jane Connell, *and* Tovah Feldshuh.

mal world or a normal person in a ridiculous world—makes possible the development of a *comic premise*. The comic premise is an idea or concept which turns the accepted notion of things upside down and makes this notion the basis of a play. A writer of comedy uses the comic premise as the foundation on which to build the entire play. The premise can provide thematic and structural unity and can serve as the springboard from which comic dialogue, comic characters, and comic situations develop.

Aristophanes, the Greek satiric dramatist, was a master at developing a comic premise on which to build a play. There are times when it seems that he knew no bounds in creating ridiculous situations. In *The Clouds*, Aristophanes pictures Socrates as a man who can think only when perched in a basket suspended in the air. In *The Birds*, two ordinary men persuade a chorus of birds to build a city between heaven and earth. The birds comply, calling the place Cloudcuckoo Land, and the two men sprout wings to join them. In another play, *Lysistrata*, Aristophanes has the women of Greece agree to go on a sex strike: they will not make love to their husbands until the husbands stop fighting and sign a peace treaty with their opponents.

Techniques of Comedy

The suspension of natural laws and the establishment of a comic premise in comedy involve exaggeration and incongruity. In a way uniquely its own, comedy emphasizes the discrepancy between a norm and some aberration or excess.

TARTUFFE (1664)

MOLIÈRE (JEAN-BAPTISTE POQUELIN; 1622–1673)

CHIEF CHARACTERS:
Tartuffe—a hypocrite
Mme. Pernelle—Orgon's mother
Orgon—Elmire's husband
Elmire—Orgon's wife
Damis—Orgon's son; Elmire's stepson
Mariane—Orgon's daughter, in love with
Valère—in love with Mariane
Cléante—Orgon's brother-in-law
Dorine—Mariane's lady's maid

SETTING: Orgon's house in Paris in the 1600s.

BACKGROUND: Tartuffe, a hypocrite who pretends to be a holy man and dresses in religious clothes, is staying at Orgon's home. He has completely fooled Orgon by feigning a virtuous lifestyle.

ACT 1: When Orgon's mother, Mme. Pernelle, tells the family that they should be virtuous like Tartuffe, they try to persuade her that he is a fraud. The maid, Dorine, enters and tells Orgon's brother-in-law Cléante that Tartuffe has bewitched Orgon, who shows more affection toward Tartuffe than toward his own family. We learn that Orgon opposes the wedding of his daughter Mariane to Valère, the young man she loves. This is distressing to her brother Damis because he wants to marry Valère's sister. When the maid Dorine tells Orgon that his wife was sick while he was away, Orgon, instead of pitying his wife, inquires only about Tartuffe, who is perfectly healthy. Cleante tells Orgon that he is being deceived by Tartuffe, but Orgon continues to believe in Tartuffe's virtuousness.

ACT 2: Orgon tells his daughter Mariane that she should marry Tartuffe. Mariane is outraged. When Dorine tries to persuade Orgon that Tartuffe and Mariane are ill-suited, Orgon defends the hypocrite despite Dorine's insults. After Orgon leaves, Dorine tries to persuade Mariane to stand up to her father, but Mariane is weak-willed. Her fiancé Valère confronts Mariane with the rumor that Mariane doesn't love him and is planning to marry Tartuffe instead. The two quarrel until Dorine gets them to make up.

ACT 3: Dorine tells Damis that his stepmother Elmire, who is Orgon's present wife, might persuade Tartuffe not to marry Mariane. As Damis hides in a closet, Dorine tells Tartuffe that Elmire wants a word with him. When she is alone with Tartuffe, Elmire raises questions about her husband's plan to have Tartuffe marry Mariane. Tartuffe replies that he is not interested in the daughter but rather in Elmire herself, whereupon he tries to seduce her. Elmire says that she will not tell Orgon of Tartuffe's advances if he agrees not to marry Mariane. The stepson, Damis, who has overheard the conversation, tells Tartuffe that he will reveal all. When Damis tells Orgon of Tartuffe's adulterous offer to his wife, Tartuffe very cleverly admits the truth and begs Orgon to drive him out. Orgon, however, disbelieves Damis, thinking that he is merely trying to slander Tartuffe. When Tartuffe says that he should leave because he is upsetting the household, Orgon insists that he stay and, furthermore, disinherits his children and makes Tartuffe his sole heir.

ACT 4: Damis has left his father's house, and Cléante asks Tartuffe to help Damis regain his father's love. But Tartuffe says that if Damis comes back, he will go. Cléante then accuses Tartuffe of exerting influence on Orgon in order to get Damis' inheritance. The maid Dorine tries to enlist Cléante's aid in helping Mariane get out of marrying Tartuffe, but Orgon enters with a marriage contract. After the family vainly begs Orgon not to insist on the marriage, Elmire develops a plan to expose Tartuffe. She decides that Orgon should hide in the room while she is alone with Tartuffe. As Orgon hides under the table, she warns him that he should not be shocked by her attempts to trap Tartuffe. When Tartuffe enters, Elmire expresses her passion for him. Tartuffe says he will not believe her until he receives a "palpable assurance" of her favor, meaning that she must let him make love to her. Elmire expresses concern that her husband might be around, but Tartuffe says, "Why worry about the man? Each day he grows more gullible; one can lead him by the nose." On hearing this,

Orgon jumps out from under the table and confronts Tartuffe, who boldly replies that he now owns everything in the house and that Orgon will have to leave. In desperation Orgon goes to find his strongbox.

ACT 5: Orgon tells Cléante that, among other things, he had a friend's libelous papers in the strongbox and he fears they are now in Tartuffe's possession. Orgon laments that he was taken in by Tartuffe, but his mother still defends the hypocrite. M. Loyal, a bailiff, enters with an eviction notice ordering the family to leave the house, because everything now belongs to Tartuffe. At this point, the mother is finally convinced of Tartuffe's hypocrisy. Orgon expects to be arrested because of the libelous papers, but when Tartuffe and an officer enter, the officer arrests Tartuffe instead. The prince of the realm has realized the sham, invalidated the deed, and pardoned Orgon. Orgon thanks the prince, and all ends happily as Orgon gives his blessing to the marriage of Valère and Mariane.

The contradictions of comedy arising from exaggeration and incongruity show up in several areas—in verbal humor, in characterization, and in comic situations.

VERBAL HUMOR Verbal humor can be anything from a pun to the most sophisticated verbal discourse. A *pun*—usually considered the simplest form of wit—is a humorous use of words with the same sound but different meanings. A man who says he is going to start a bakery if he can "raise the dough" is making a pun. Close to the pun is the *malaprop*—a word which sounds like the right word but actually means something quite different. The term comes from Mrs. Malaprop, a character in *The Rivals* by the English playwright Richard Brinsley Sheridan (1751–1816). Mrs. Malaprop wants to impress everyone with her education and erudition but ends up doing just the opposite because she constantly misuses long words. For example, she uses "supercilious" when she means "superficial," and she insists that her daughter is not "illegible" for marriage, meaning that her daughter is not "ineligible" for marriage.

Frequently a character who wishes to appear to be more learned than he or she really is uses a malaprop. In *Juno and the Paycock*, by Sean O'Casey (1880–1964), the chief character is Captain Boyle, a man always pronouncing the last word on any subject. Throughout the play he complains that the world is "in a state of chassis," when he means "a state of chaos." The more pompous the speaker who uses a wrong word in this way, the more humorous the effect.

A man devoted to verbal humor, Oscar Wilde (1854–1900) often turned accepted values upside down in his epigrams. "I can resist anything except temptation," says one of his characters; and "A man cannot be too careful in the choice of his enemies," says another.

COMEDY OF CHARACTER In comedy of character the discrepancy or incongruity lies in the way characters see themselves or pretend to be, as opposed to the way they actually are. A good example is a person who pretends to be a doctor—using obscure medicines, hypodermic needles, and Latin jargon—but who is actually a fake; such a person is the chief character in Molière's *The Doctor in Spite of Himself.* Another example of incongruity of character is Molière's *The Would-Be Gentleman,* in which the title character, Monsieur Jourdain, a man of wealth, but without refinement, is determined to learn courtly behavior. He hires a fencing master, a dancing master, and a teacher of literature (the last tells him, to his great delight, that he has been speaking prose all his life). In every case Jourdain is made a fool of: he dances and fences awkwardly and even gets involved in a ridiculous courtship with a noblewoman. All along he is blind to what a ridiculous figure he makes, until the end, when his follies and pretenses are exposed. Comedy of

(Robert C. Ragsdale)

character is a basic ingredient of Italian commedia dell'arte and all forms of comedy where stock characters, stereotypes, and characters with dominant traits are emphasized.

PLOT COMPLICATIONS   Still another way in which the contradictory or the ludicrous manifests itself in comedy is in plot complications, including coincidences and mistaken identity. A time-honored comic plot is Shakespeare's *The Comedy of Errors*, based on *The Menaechmi*, a play of the late third century B.C. by the Roman writer Titus Maccius Plautus. *The Comedy of Errors* in turn was the basis of a successful American musical comedy, *The Boys from Syracuse*, with songs by Richard Rodgers and Lorenz Hart.

In *The Comedy of Errors*, identical twins and their identical twin servants were separated when young, with one master and servant growing up in Syracuse and the other growing up in Ephesus. As the play opens, however, both sets of masters and servants—unknown to one another—are in Ephesus. The wife and mistress of one master, as well as a host of others, mistake the second master and his servant for their counterparts in a series of comic encounters (with people making romantic advances to the wrong person, etc.) leading to ever-increasing confusion, until all four principals appear onstage at one time to clear up the situation.

A classic scene of plot complication occurs in Sheridan's *The School for Scandal*, written in 1777. Surface, the main character in the play, is thought to be an upstanding man but is really a charlatan, whereas Charles, his brother, is mistakenly considered a reprobate. In the scene called the "screen scene," the truth comes out and the popular images are reversed. As the scene opens, Lady Teazle, a married woman, is visiting Surface secretly. When her husband, Sir Peter Teazle, unexpectedly appears, she quickly hides behind a floor screen, but shortly after Sir Peter's arrival, Surface's brother Charles turns up as well, and in order not to be seen by Charles, Sir Peter starts for the screen. Sir Peter notices a woman's skirts behind the screen, but before he can discover it is his wife, Surface sends him into a closet. Once Charles enters the room, he learns that Sir Peter is in the closet and flings it open. As if this discovery were not enough, he also throws down the screen and in one climactic moment reveals both the infidelity of Lady Teazle and the treachery of Surface. The double, even triple, comic effect is due to the coincidence of the wrong people being in the wrong place at the wrong time.

A master of the device of characters hiding in closets and under beds was Georges Feydeau (1862–1921), a French dramatist who wrote over sixty farces in his lifetime. Variations of this form—complications and revelations arising from coincidences and mistaken identity—are found in plays from Roman times to the present; and this device, along with verbal wit and exaggerated characters, has been used as a major weapon of the comic dramatist.

Forms of Comedy

Comedy takes various forms, depending on the dramatist's intent and on the comic techniques emphasized.

FARCE   Most plays discussed in the section on plot complications are *farces*. Farce thrives on exaggeration—of broad physical humor, of plot complications, of stereotyped characters. It has no intellectual pretensions but aims rather at entertainment and provoking laughter. In addition to excessive plot complications, its humor results from ridiculous situations as well as pratfalls and horseplay. It relies less on verbal wit than the more intellectual forms of comedy do. Mock violence, rapid movement, and accelerating pace are hallmarks of farce. Marriage and sex are the objects of fun in *bedroom farce;* but medicine, law, and business can also be the subject matter.

BURLESQUE   Burlesque also relies on knockabout, physical humor, as well as gross exaggerations and occasionally vulgarity. Historically, burlesque was a ludicrous imitation of other forms of drama or of an individual play. A modern musical like *The Boy Friend* is a burlesque of the boy-meets-girl musicals popular earlier in the twentieth century. In the United States, the term *burlesque* came to describe a type of variety show featuring low-comedy skits and attractive women.

THE EXAGGERATION OF FARCE.

In farce everything is exaggerated: plot developments, physical mishaps, characters' obsessions, the travails characters suffer. Though it is painful for the people caught in the trap of farce, the action provides wild amusement for the audience. Seen here are three characters in the midst of a comic crisis in the farce Noises Off, *produced by the Seattle Repertory Theater.*

SATIRE A form related to traditional burlesque, but with more intellectual and moral content, is *satire*. Satire employs wit, irony, and exaggeration to attack or expose evil and foolishness. Satire can attack one figure, as *Rap Master Ronnie,* by the cartoonist Gary Trudeau, attacked Ronald Reagan; or it can be more inclusive, as in the case of Molière's *Tartuffe,* which ridicules religious hypocrisy generally, or the 1989 satire *Mastergate* which attacked a pattern of corruption in government. Satire that attacks an entire society is an exception to the notion (discussed above) that comedy usually exposes individuals who are foolish and excessive rather than criticizes society.

SATIRICAL COMEDY.
In satire, wit, irony, and exaggeration are used to expose foolishness and wrongdoing. A satire that attacked the evils of government corruption—in such episodes as the Watergate scandal and the Iran-Contra affair—was Mastergate *by the comic writer Larry Gelbart. Shown here in a scene from the production at the American Repertory Theater in Cambridge, Massachusetts, are Cherry Jones as a television reporter, Daniel Von Bargen as Major Manley Battle, and Bari Hochwald as the major's wife.*

DOMESTIC COMEDY   The comic equivalent of domestic or bourgeois drama is domestic comedy. Usually dealing with family situations, it is found most frequently today in television situation comedies—often called *sitcoms*—which feature members of a family or a neighborhood caught in a series of complicated but amusing situations. Television shows starring Bill Cosby, Bob Newhart, and Mary Tyler Moore are good examples. This type of comedy was once a staple of the theater and can still be found onstage in plays by writers like Neil Simon (1927–   ).

COMEDY OF MANNERS   Comedy of manners is concerned with pointing up the foibles and peculiarities of the upper classes. Against a cultivated, sophisticated background, it uses verbal wit to depict the charm and expose the social pretensions of its characters. Rather than horseplay, it stresses witty phrases. Clever barbs are at a premium in comedy of manners. In England a line of comedies of manners runs from William Wycherley, William Congreve, and Oliver Goldsmith (1730–1774) in the seventeenth and eighteenth centuries to Oscar Wilde in the nineteenth century and Noël Coward (1899–1973) in the twentieth.

COMEDY OF IDEAS Many plays of George Bernard Shaw could be put under a special heading, *comedy of ideas,* for Shaw used comic techniques to debate intellectual propositions and to further his own moral and social point of view.

In all its forms, comedy remains a way of looking at the world in which basic values are asserted but natural laws are suspended in order to underline the follies and foolishness of men and women—sometimes with a rueful look, sometimes with a wry smile, and sometimes with an uproarious laugh.

✳ TRAGICOMEDY ✳

In the twentieth century a new genre has come to the forefront in theater—tragicomedy, a form of drama we will examine in this section.

What Is Tragicomedy?

In the past, comedy has usually been set in opposition to tragedy or serious drama: serious drama is sad, comedy is funny; serious drama makes people cry, comedy makes them laugh; serious drama arouses anger, comedy causes a smile. True, the comic view of life differs from the serious, but the two are not always as clearly separated as this polarity suggests. As we saw earlier, many comic dramatists are serious people; "I laugh to keep from crying" applies to many comic writers as well as to certain clowns and comedians. A great deal of serious drama has comic elements in it. Shakespeare, for instance, employed comic characters in several of his serious plays. The drunken porter in *Macbeth,* the gravedigger in *Hamlet,* and Falstaff in *Henry IV, Part 1* are examples.

In medieval plays, comic scenes are interpolated in the basically religious subject matter. In a play about Noah and the ark, Noah and his wife argue, like a bickering couple on television, with Mrs. Noah refusing to go aboard the ark with all those animals. Finally, when the flood comes, she relents, but only after she has firmly established herself as a shrewish, independent wife. One of the best-known of all medieval plays, *The Second Shepherds' Play,* concerns the visit of the shepherds to the manger of the newborn Christ child. While they stop in a field to spend the night, Mak, a comic character, steals a sheep and takes it to his house, where he and his wife put it in a crib, pretending that it is their baby (a parody of Christ lying in the manger). When the shepherds discover what Mak has done, they toss him in a blanket, and after this horseplay the serious part of the story resumes.

The alternation of serious and comic elements is a practice of long standing, particularly in episodic plays; but *tragicomedy* does not refer to plays which shift from serious to comic and back again. In such cases the plays are predominantly one or the other—comic or serious—and the change from one point of view to the other is clearly delineated. In tragicomedy the point of view is itself mixed—the *overview*, or prevailing attitude, is a synthesis or fusion of the serious and the comic. It is a view in which one eye looks with a comic lens and the other with a serious lens; and the two points of view are so intermingled as to be one, like foods which taste sweet and sour at the same time.

In addition to his basically serious plays and his basically comic plays, Shakespeare wrote others which seem to be a combination of tragedy and comedy, such as *Measure for Measure* and *All's Well That Ends Well.* Because they do not fit neatly into one category or the other, these plays have proved troublesome to critics—so troublesome that they have been officially dubbed *problem plays.* The "problem," however, arises largely because of the difficulty in accepting the tragicomic point of view, for these plays have many of the attributes of the fusion of the tragic and the comic. In these plays, there is a sense of comedy pervading the play, the idea that all will end well and that much of what happens is ludicrous or ridiculous; at the same time, the serious effects of a character's actions are not dismissed. Unlike true comedy, in which the fall on the sidewalk or the temporary threat of danger has no serious consequences, the actions in these plays appear quite serious. And so we have tragicomedy. In *Measure for Measure,* for instance, a man named Angelo—a puritanical, austere creature—condemns young Claudio to death for having made his fiancée pregnant. When Claudio's sister, Isabella, comes to plead for her brother, Angelo is overcome by passion and tries to make the lady his mistress. Angelo's sentencing of Claudio is deadly serious, but the bitter irony, which arises when he proves to be guilty of even worse "sins of the flesh" than Claudio, is comic. The result is that we have tragic and comic situations simultaneously.

Modern Tragicomedy

It is in the modern period—during the last hundred years or so—that tragicomedy has become a predominant form, the primary approach, in fact, of many of the best playwrights of our day. As suggested before, these writers are not creating in a vacuum; they are part of the world in which they live, and ours is an age which has adopted a tragicomic viewpoint more extensively than most previous ages. As if to keynote this attitude and set the tone, the Danish philosopher Søren Kierkegaard made the following statement in 1842: "Existence itself, the act of existence, is a striving and is both pathetic and comic in the same degree." The plays of Anton Chekhov, written at the end of the nineteenth century, reflect the spirit described by Kierkegaard. Chekhov called two of his major plays *comedies;* but Stanislavski, who directed them, called

TRAGICOMEDY IN UNCLE VANYA.
In Chekhov's play about life in Russia at the turn of the century, a frustrated Uncle Vanya attempts to shoot a professor whom he despises. But the gun misfires, and rather than being tragic, the scene is comic. This scene is from a production at the Hartman Theater Company, Stanford, Connecticut.

them *tragedies*, which is an indication of the confusion arising from Chekhov's mixture of the serious and the comic.

As an illustration of Chekhov's approach, there is a scene in the third act of *The Cherry Orchard*, written in 1904, in which Madame Renevsky, the owner of the orchard, talks to an intense young graduate student about love and truth. She tells him that people should be charitable and understanding of those in love; no one is perfect and truth is not absolute, she argues. The student, however, insists that reason is all and that feelings must be put aside. She retorts that he is motivated not by purity but by "simple prudery." He is not above love, as he claims, but is actually avoiding it, and she insists that he should have a mistress at his age. He is incensed. Declaring that he cannot listen to such talk, he runs offstage. The stage directions say that a moment later he is heard falling down a flight of stairs. A crash is heard, women scream, and then, after a pause, they laugh. The women scream because they fear he is hurt—not the spirit of comedy—but once they learn he is all right, they laugh, realizing that the fall of this pompous lad is extremely comic. Here we have the perfect blend: a part of the scene is deadly serious; another part, genuinely comic.

A comparable, and even more significant, scene occurs at the end of the third act of Chekhov's *Uncle Vanya*, first produced in 1899. Vanya and his niece, Sonya, have worked and sacrificed for years to keep an estate going to support her father, a professor. At the worst possible moment, just when Vanya and Sonya have both been rebuffed by people they love, the professor announces that he wants to sell the estate, leaving Vanya and Sonya with nothing. Sonya explains how cruel and thoughtless this is, and a few moments later Vanya comes in to shoot

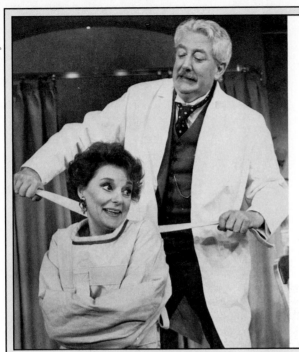

TRAGICOMEDY: FUNNY AND SAD AT THE SAME TIME.
In What the Butler Saw *by Joe Orton, a number of strange events occur, and the audience does not always know whether they are serious or comic. Witty, ironic, bitter, and amusing, all at the same time—this mixture is typical of the plays of Orton and of tragicomedy in general. This scene shows Carole Shelley and Joseph Maher in the Manhattan Theater Club production.*

the professor. He waves his gun in the air like a madman and shoots twice, but misses both times, and then collapses on the floor. In this scene, Vanya and Sonya are condemned to a lifetime of drudgery and despair—a serious fate—but Vanya's behavior with the gun (there is doubt that he honestly means to kill the professor) is wildly comic. Again, the serious and comic elements are inextricably joined.

Sean O'Casey, an Irish playwright, wrote plays with a similar outlook. In his *Juno and the Paycock,* mentioned above, Captain Boyle and his friend Joxer are complete comic figures, bragging about imaginary exploits, pretending bravery where none exists, and promising to go to work with no real intention of doing so. During the play, Boyle thinks he has received an inheritance and begins spending money with abandon, only to find that the supposed inheritance is a hoax. Other misfortunes strike: his daughter is abandoned by her fiancé, his son is dragged away to be shot as a traitor to the Irish cause, and the family is destitute. But since Boyle has never made provisions for his family or taken the problems of life seriously, he is of no help in this crisis. Instead, he comes in at the end of the play with his buddy, Joxer, drinking and carrying on just as they did earlier in the play—but it is not funny now. Their jokes ring hollow and serve only to underline the sadness of what has occurred.

Many of the plays in the category of theater of the absurd, discussed in Chapter 10, fall under the heading *tragicomedy.* They probe deeply into human problems and cast a dark eye on the world, and yet they are also imbued with a comic spirit, containing juggling, acrobatics, clowning, and verbal nonsense, among other traditional manifestations of humor. The plays of Harold Pinter (1930–   ), another writer associated with theater of the absurd, have been called *comedies of menace,* a phrase suggesting the idea of a theater simultaneously terrifying and entertaining. (For a closer look at theater of the absurd, see Chapter 10.)

In addition to the plays of the absurdists, other modern plays also incorporate the tragicomic spirit. A good example is *The Visit,* by Friedrich Duerrenmatt (1921–1990), a Swiss dramatist. In the play a wealthy woman returns to her birthplace, a small village which is poverty-stricken. She offers money—a billion marks—to the town on the condition that the citizens murder a storekeeper in the village who wronged her when she was young. The townspeople express horror at the idea, but at the same time they begin buying expensive objects on credit, some buying from the man's own store. There is a comic quality to these scenes: the man's wife, for instance, shows up in a flashy fur coat. The conclusion, however, is not funny, for the man is eventually murdered by his greedy neighbors.

In tragicomedy, a smile is frequently cynical, chuckles may be tinged with a threat, and laughter is sometimes bitter. Whereas in the past the attitude which produced these combinations was the exception and not the rule, in our day it seems far more prevalent, not to say relevant. As a result, tragicomedy has taken its place as a major form alongside the more traditional approaches.

❋ THE SIGNIFICANCE OF GENRE ❋

The combination of forms in tragicomedy reminds us that individual plays rarely fall completely into one category. Some plays are pure examples of their form, but many have characteristics of two genres, and some include more than two. Frequently melodrama overlaps with tragedy or heroic drama. In tragicomedies, the serious and the humorous intersect; and with comedy, burlesque crosses into farce, and farce into satire.

In considering the major forms of theater, we end where we began, with the notion that we should never rush to pigeonhole or label a play. Genre can be an aid or guide telling us how to interpret and understand a play, but it should never be an end in itself. The struggle should be less to discover what genre a play belongs to than to understand it. The important lesson of genre is that in a worthwhile production, a world is created which reflects a definite point of view. For spectators, entering and living in the world is central to the theater experience.

Unlike certain arts in which point of view is established largely by a single device—the brushstrokes of the artist in painting, or the use of the camera in films—in theater, point of view results from a collaborative effort of many artists. The creation of a viewpoint in theater is the responsibility not only of the dramatist, who establishes it and incorporates it into the script, but of the director, designers, and performers who must add to, reinforce, and underline the dramatist's point of view. As an example, in a production of Molière's comedy *Tartuffe,* the designers must strike just the right note of exaggeration and comment in the costumes and the scenery. There should be wit as well as elegance in the lines of the costumes and in the shapes and forms of the scenery. The color of the lighting, as well as the colors of the costumes and scenery, should be warm and bright—except, of course, for Tartuffe's black clerical costume, which stands in somber contrast to everything else and emphasizes his hypocrisy. The performances, too, must capture the dead seriousness of Molière's words, but with an awareness of the underlying humor and comment the words imply. The actions of the performers should be exaggerated without being excessive, comic without being ludicrous. The total effect of script, performances, and visual effects will be a comic world, with undertones of seriousness.

If any segment of a production fails to maintain a consistent viewpoint, the result will be confusion on the part of the audience. If the scene design suggests comedy when the play is serious, or if a performer is too realistic in a nonrealistic play, the spectators will lose their sense of direction. It is the responsibility of every artist working on a production to understand and follow through on the intentions and perspective of the playwright and director.

Point of view is not visible to the audience in the way that a piece of scenery is, but it is an essential element of theater. Without a point of view which permeates and informs a production, members of the audience have no compass to tell them where they are headed and no key to let them unlock the play's meaning. Whatever world we are introduced to in a theatrical production—a real world or a make-believe world, a despondent world or a carefree world—the point of view which produces it must color and illuminate everything onstage. It must cut across the production like a giant spotlight cutting across the stage, throwing on every object the same light and shadow.

In Part Four we have looked at the purpose a theater experience is intended to serve: to provide an escape from daily cares, to make us laugh, to make us think, to make us feel deeply. We have also examined the point of view—tragic, comic, tragicomic—that informs the experience. The person who initially gives a theater experience a point of view is the playwright. He or she incorporates into the script the language, the attitudes of the characters, and the chain of events that determine the nature of the play.

In Part Five we turn to another key group of theater artists and another crucial aspect of the theater experience. The physical environment in which a theater event takes place—the theater space itself—and the design elements of scenery, costume, lighting, and sound significantly affect the creation and the experience of theater.

✳ SUMMARY ✳

1 Comedy takes a different approach from serious forms of drama. It sees the humor and incongruity in people and situations. Comic dramatists accept a social and moral order and suspend natural laws (the man who falls flat on his face but does not really hurt himself).

2 Comedy is developed by means of several techniques. *Verbal humor* turns words upside down and creates puns, malapropisms, and inversions of meaning. *Comedy of character* creates men and women who take extreme positions, make fools of themselves, or contradict themselves. *Plot complications* create mistaken identity, coincidences, and people who turn up unexpectedly in the wrong house or the wrong bedroom. There are also physical aspects to comedy: slapstick and horseplay.

3 From the foregoing, the dramatist fashions various kinds of comedy. Depending on the degree of exaggeration, a comedy can be *farce* or *comedy of manners;* the former, for instance, features strong physical humor, while the latter relies more on verbal wit. Depending on its intent, comedy can be designed to entertain, as with *farce* or *burlesque,* or to correct vices, in which case it becomes *satire.* Many of Shaw's plays represent *comedy of ideas.*

4 Serious and comic elements can be mixed in theater. Many tragedies have comic relief: humorous scenes and characters interspersed in serious material.

5 Authentic tragicomedy fuses, or synthesizes, two elements—one serious, the other comic. We laugh and cry at the same time. Plays by Chekhov, Beckett, Duerrenmatt, and writers of theater of absurd employ tragicomedy. Some commentators feel that it is the form most truly characteristic of our time.

6 Many plays have elements of more than one genre; therefore, genre should not be overstressed. It is a guide or an aid to understanding a theater experience.

7   Ideally, a clear point of view should inform and permeate every aspect of a theatrical production. It should create in each play a world which the spectators can enter and inhabit. Point of view tells the audience how to approach what they are seeing and how to assess its meaning.

❋ TOPICS FOR DISCUSSION ❋

1   The comic premise frequently turns an accepted idea upside down. Why can we find this so enjoyable?

2   Suppose that you saw a play in which the comic premise upended an idea which you did *not* enjoy having reversed. Would that destroy the comedy as far as you were concerned?

3   *Tartuffe* was written over three centuries ago, but the characters it holds up for our amusement—the religious hypocrite and the gullible fool—are still with us today. Would you say, on the basis of the synopsis, that the persistence of these types in human society is probably the main reason why *Tartuffe* is still popular, or do other aspects of the play seem to be equally important?

4   Aestheticians—people who study the characteristics that define art and the qualities that make it "good"—often consider *unity* a criterion of good art. Tragicomedy might seem to violate this standard, but it is one of the most predominant theatrical forms today. Does this suggest that unity is not a valid criterion for art? Or does it suggest that tragicomedy, despite the fact that its viewpoint is mixed, can achieve unity?

PART FIVE

THE DESIGNERS:
ENVIRONMENT AND
VISUAL ELEMENTS

THE SPECTACLE OF SCENERY AND COSTUMES.
Visual elements play an important role in every theater production, but in certain productions—such as the musical The Phantom of the Opera—*they are a key factor.* Phantom, *shown in a drawing by Al Hirschfeld on the following pages, features elaborate scenery; glorious period costumes; sophisticated lighting; and special effects, including a chandelier that falls from the ceiling.*

16

STAGE
SPACES

THE IMPORTANCE OF THE PHYSICAL SETTING.
The physical environment of a theater production is an important part of the experience. Whether the theater space is indoors or outdoors, whether it is large or small, the shape of the stage and its relationship to the audience help determine the nature of the theater experience. Shown here, at the New York Public Theater, is one of the configurations that have been prominent through much of theater history—the thrust stage with audience seating surrounding it on three sides.

For those who create theater, the experience begins long before the actual event. The dramatist spends weeks, months, or perhaps years writing the play; the director and designers plan the production well ahead of time; and the performers rehearse intensively for several weeks before the first public performance.

For the spectator, too, the experience begins ahead of time. Members of the audience read or hear reports of the play; they anticipate seeing a particular actress or actor perform; they purchase tickets and make plans with friends to attend; and before the performance, they gather outside the theater with other members of the audience.

❋ CREATING THE ENVIRONMENT ❋

Once spectators arrive at the theater for a performance, they immediately take in the environment in which the event will occur. The atmosphere of the theater building has a great deal to do with the audience's mood in approaching a performance, not only creating expectations about the event to come but conditioning the experience once it gets under way.

Spectators have one feeling if they come into a formal setting, such as a picture-frame stage surrounded by carved gold figures, with crystal chandeliers and red plush seats in the auditorium. They have quite a different feeling if they come into an old warehouse converted into a theater, with bare brick walls, and a stage in the middle of the floor surrounded by folding chairs.

For many years people took the physical arrangement of a theater for granted. This was particularly true in the period when all houses were facsimiles of the Broadway theater, with its *proscenium* or picture-frame stage. In the recent past, though, not only have people been exposed to other types of theaters, they have become more aware of the importance of environment. Many experimental groups have deliberately made awareness of the environment a part of the experience.

An avant-garde production of Euripides's *The Bacchae*, called *Dionysus in 69*, by the Performance Group in New York, introduced the audience to the performance in a controlled manner. Spectators were not allowed in the theater when they arrived, but were made to line up on the street outside. The procedure is outlined in a book describing the production.

> The audience begins to assemble at around 7:45 P.M. They line up on Wooster Street below Greenwich Village. Sometimes the line goes up the block almost to the corner of Broome. On rainy nights, or during the coldest parts of the winter, the audience waits upstairs over the theater. The theater is a large space, some 50 by 40 and 20 feet high. At 8:15 the performance begins for the audience when the stage manager, Vickie May Strang, makes

the following announcement. Inside the performers begin warming up their voices and bodies at 7:45.

VICKIE: Ladies and gentlemen! May I have your attention, please. We are going to start letting you in now. You will be admitted to the theater one at a time, and if you're with someone you may be split up. But you can find each other again once you're inside. Take your time to explore the environment. It's a very interesting space, and there are all different kinds of places you can sit. We recommend going up high on the towers and platforms, or down underneath them. The password is "Go high or take cover." There is no smoking inside and no cameras. Thank you.

In an interview in the book, Strang gave her own view of this procedure.

We let the public in one at a time. People on the queue outside the theater ask me why. I explain that this is a rite of initiation, a chance for each person to confront the environment alone, without comparing notes with friends. People are skeptical. Some few are angry. Many think it's a put-on. I must confess to a perverse pleasure in teasing people on a line. Many will come up and ask anxiously, "Has it already begun?" "Well," I say, "it begins before we let anybody in, but it begins when everybody is in, and really it begins when you go in." True.[1]

By making spectators enter the theater in an unconventional way, and by rearranging the theater space itself, certain contemporary groups deliberately make the spectators conscious of the theater environment. But the feeling we have about the atmosphere of a theater building as we enter it has always been an important element in the experience. In the past, spectators may not have been conscious of it, but they were affected by it nevertheless. Today, with the many varieties of theater experience available to us, the first thing we should become aware of is the environment in which the event takes place. Whether it is large or small, indoors or outdoors, formal or informal, familiar or unfamiliar, it will inevitably play a part in our response to the performance.

✳ STAGE SPACES ✳

A consideration of environment leads directly to an examination of the various forms and styles of theater buildings, including the basic arrangements of audience seating. Throughout theater history, there have been four basic types of stages, each with its own advantages and disadvantages, each suited to certain types of plays and certain types of productions, and each providing the audience with a somewhat different viewing experience. The four are (1) the *proscenium,* or picture-frame, stage, (2) the *arena,* or circle, stage, (3) the *thrust* stage with three-quarter seating, and (4) the *created* and *found* stage space.[2]

Proscenium Stage

Perhaps the most familiar type of stage is the proscenium, or picture-frame, stage. Broadway theaters, which (as has been noted) were models for theaters throughout the country, have proscenium stages. The name *proscenium* comes from the *proscenium arch,* the frame which separates the stage from the auditorium and which was first introduced in Italy during the Renaissance. Although it was an arch in the past, today this frame is usually a rectangle which forms an outline for the stage itself. As the term *picture-frame stage* suggests, it resembles a large picture frame through which the audience looks at the stage. Before the 1950s there was usually a curtain just behind the proscenium opening; when the curtain rose, it revealed the picture. Another term for this type of stage is *fourth wall,* from the idea of the proscenium opening as

PROSCENIUM THEATER.
The audience faces in one direction, toward an enclosed stage encased by a picture-frame opening. Scene changes and performers' entrances and exits are made behind the proscenium opening, out of sight of the audience.

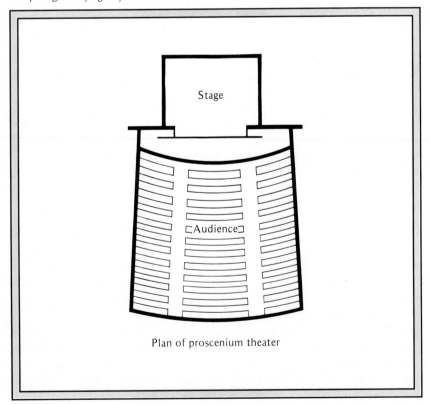

Plan of proscenium theater

PART FIVE · THE DESIGNERS: ENVIRONMENT AND VISUAL ELEMENTS

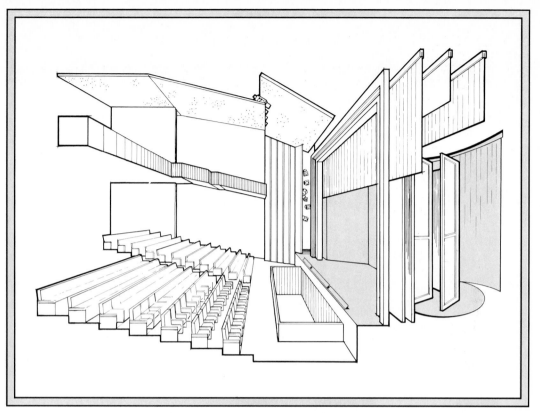

A MODERN PROSCENIUM-STAGE THEATER.

In this cutaway drawing we see the audience at the left, all facing in the one direction toward the stage. Behind the orchestra pit in the center is the apron on the stage, and then the proscenium frame behind which are the flats and other scenic elements, and at the far right, a cyclorama. Overhead, scenery can be raised into the fly loft above the stage area.

a transparent glass wall through which the audience looks at the other three walls of a room.

Because the action takes place largely behind the proscenium opening, or frame, the seats in the auditorium all face in the same direction—toward the stage, just as seats in a movie theater face the screen. The auditorium itself is slanted downward from the back of the auditorium—or *house,* as it is called—to the stage. (In theater usage, the slant of an auditorium or stage floor is called a *rake.*) The stage itself is raised several feet above the auditorium floor to aid visibility. There is usually a balcony (sometimes there are two balconies) protruding about halfway over the main floor. The main floor, incidentally, is called the *orchestra.* (In the ancient Greek theater, the orchestra was the circular acting area at the base of the hillside amphitheater, but in modern usage it is the

CHAPTER 16 • STAGE SPACES

(Bengt Wanselius)

A FORMAL PROSCENIUM THEATER.

The standard theater throughout Europe and the United States in the nineteenth and early twentieth century was a formal proscenium theater. The basic configuration features audience seating in the downstairs orchestra, in balconies, and in side boxes facing a picture-frame stage. One advantage of this type of stage is that it allows impressive scene changes and other visual effects, which can be set up behind the curtain that covers the proscenium opening. Shown here is the theater at Drottningholm, Sweden, first built in 1766 and closed in the 1790s. An excellent example of the proscenium stage, it was reopened in the early twentieth century, and productions have been presented there ever since.

main floor of the theater where the audience sits.) In certain theaters, as well as concert halls and opera houses which have the proscenium arrangement, there are horseshoe-shaped tiers or *boxes,* which ring the auditorium for several floors above the orchestra floor.

The popularity of the proscenium stage on Broadway and throughout the United States in the nineteenth and early twentieth centuries was partly due to its wide acceptance throughout Europe. Beginning in the late seventeenth century, the proscenium theater was adopted in every European country. Examples of theaters in this style in the eighteenth century included Drury Lane and Covent Garden in London; the Royal Theater in Turin, Italy; Hôtel de Bourgogne in Paris; the Bolshoi in St.

Petersburg, Russia; and the Drottningholm near Stockholm, Sweden. (This last is a theater still preserved in its original state.) In the nineteenth century, proscenium theaters included the Teatro Español in Madrid; the Haymarket in London; the Park Theater and Burton's Chambers Street in New York; the Burgtheater in Vienna, Austria; and the Teatro alla Scala in Milan, Italy.

The stage area of these theaters was usually deep, allowing for elaborate scenery, including scene shifts, with a tall *fly loft* above the stage to hold scenery. The loft had to be more than twice as high as the proscenium opening so that scenery could be concealed when it was raised, or "flown." (When pieces of scenery are raised out of sight, they are said to *fly* into the loft.) Scenery was usually hung by rope or cable on a series of parallel pipes running from side to side across the stage. Hanging the pieces straight across, one behind the other, allowed many pieces of scenery to be stored and then raised and lowered when necessary.

Several mechanisms for raising and lowering scenery were developed during the period when the proscenium stage itself was being adopted. An Italian, Giacomo Torelli (1608–1678), created a counterweight system in which weights hung on a series of ropes and pulleys balanced the scenery, allowing heavy scenery to be moved easily by a few stagehands. Torelli's system also allowed side pieces, known as *wings,* to move in and out of the stage picture. By attaching both the hanging pieces and the side pieces to a central drum below the stage, Torelli made it possible for everything to move simultaneously, and in this way a complete stage set could be changed at one time. Audiences seeing this effect when it was first developed must have thought it was magic; and indeed, Torelli was called *il gran stregone,* "the great wizard."

Shortly after Torelli, a dynasty of scenic artists emerged who carried scene painting to a degree of perfection rarely equaled before or since. Their family name was Bibiena, and for over a century, beginning with Ferdinando (1657–1743) and continuing through several generations to Carlo (1728–1787), they dominated the art of scene painting. Their sets usually consisted of vast halls, palaces, or gardens. Towering columns and arches framed spacious corridors or hallways which disappeared into an endless series of vistas as far as the eye could see.

Throughout this period, audiences, as well as scene designers and technicians, became so carried away with spectacle that it began to be emphasized to the exclusion of everything else, including the script and the acting. In Paris, the very name of the theater called *Salle des Machines*—"Hall of the Machines"—indicated that visual effects were the chief attraction. At times there was nothing on stage but visual display: cloud machines brought angels or deities from on high; rocks opened to reveal wood nymphs; the stage rotated on a turntable to change from

ELABORATE DESIGN FOR A PROSCENIUM STAGE.
In the eighteenth century, the Bibiena family from Italy created scene designs on a grand scale for theaters throughout Europe. They painted backdrops with vistas that seemed to continue into the infinite distance. This scene is by Giuseppe di Bibiena (1696–1757).

a banquet hall to a forest; smoke, fire, twinkling lights, and every imaginable effect appeared as if by magic.

Although there have been many changes in theater production, and today we have a wide variety of production approaches, audiences are still attracted to ingenious displays of visual effects in proscenium theaters. This is especially true of large musicals of recent years such as *Les Misérables* and *The Phantom of the Opera*. Because the machinery and the workings of the scene changes can be concealed behind the proscenium opening, this type of stage offers the perfect arrangement for spectacle.

In addition to providing the opportunity for spectacle, there are other advantages to the proscenium stage. Realistic scenery as well—a living room, an office, or a kitchen—looks good behind the proscenium frame. The scene designer can create the illusion of a genuine, complete room more easily with the proscenium stage than with any other. Also, the strong central focus provided by the frame rivets the attention of the audience. There are times, too, when members of the audience want the detachment, the distancing, which a proscenium provides.

Arena Stage

To some people, proscenium theaters, decorated in gold and red plush, look more like temples of art than theaters. They desire a more informal, intimate theater environment. A movement in this direction took root in the United States just after World War II when a number of theater practitioners decided to break away from the formality which proscenium theaters tend to create. This was part of an overall desire to bring theater closer to everyday life in many aspects of theater: in acting styles, in the subject matter of the plays, in the manner of presentation, and in the shape of the theater space. This last had to do both with the

PLAN OF AN ARENA STAGE.
The audience sits on four sides or in a circle surrounding the stage. Entrances and exits are made through the aisles or through tunnels underneath the aisles. A feeling of intimacy is achieved because the audience is close to the action and encloses it.

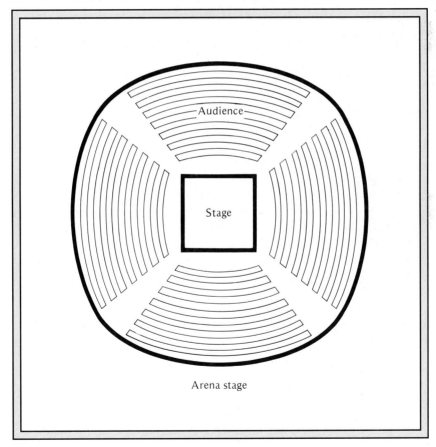

Arena stage

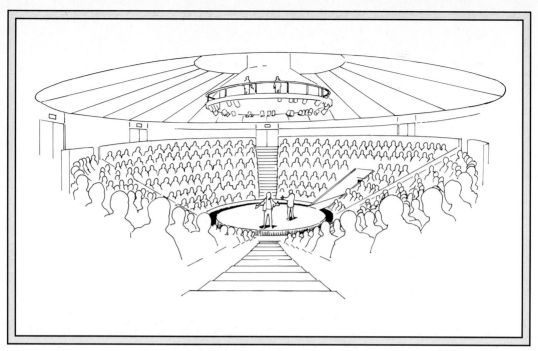

A CONTEMPORARY ARENA THEATER.

The arena theater attempts to capture the intimacy and immediacy of primitive theater. It uses the barest essentials of stage scenery and the full resources of contemporary stage lighting.

atmosphere of the building and with the audience-actor relationship. One result of this reaction was to return to the *arena stage*. As we shall see, this new movement was also a return to one of the most ancient forms of stage arrangement.

The arena stage (also called *circle theater* or *theater-in-the-round*) has a playing space in the center of a square or circle, with seats for spectators all around it. The arrangement is similar to that in sports arenas which feature boxing or basketball. The stage may be a raised area a few feet off the main floor, with seats rising from the floor level; or it may be on the floor itself, with seats raised on levels around it. When seating is close to the stage, there is usually some kind of demarcation indicating the boundaries of the playing area.

One advantage of the arena theater is that it offers more intimacy than the ordinary proscenium. With the performers in the center, even in a larger theater, the audience can be closer to them. As an example, if the same number of people attend an arena and a proscenium event, at least half of those at the arena will be nearer the action: someone who would have been in the twelfth row in a proscenium theater will be in the sixth row in an arena theater. Besides this proximity to the stage, the arena theater has another advantage: there is no frame or barrier to separate the performers from the audience.

Beyond these considerations, in the arena arrangement there is an unconscious communion which comes when people form a circle. This seems basic to human behavior—from the embrace of two people, to a circle for children's games, to a larger gathering where people form an enclosure around a fire or an altar. It is no accident that virtually all primitive forms of theater were "in the round."

There is also a practical advantage to the arena theater, and that is economy. All you need for this kind of theater is a large room. You designate a playing space, arrange rows of seats around the sides, and hang lights on pipes above, and you have a theater. Elaborate scenery is impossible because it would block the view of large parts of the audience. A few pieces of furniture, with perhaps a lamp or sign hung from the ceiling, are all you need to indicate where a scene takes place. Many low-budget groups have found that they can build a workable

THE ARENA STAGE OR THEATER-IN-THE-ROUND.
At the Arena Stage in Washington, D.C., the audience surrounds the action. Lighting instruments are visible above, and scenery is minimal; but a strong sense of place is suggested, and spectators are close to the action. The type of stage arrangement is one of the most ancient as well as one of the most modern.

(Arena Stage)

and even attractive theater-in-the-round when a proscenium theater would be out of the question.

These two factors—intimacy and economy—no doubt explain why arena theater is one of the oldest stage forms. From as far back as we have records, we know that tribal ceremonies and rituals, in all parts of the world, have been held in some form of circle theater. Many scholars believe that the ancient Greek theater evolved from an arena form. According to this theory, Greek tribes beat down a circle in a field of threshed grain; an altar was placed in the center, and ceremonies were performed around the altar while members of the tribe stood on the edge of the circle. This arrangement was later made more permanent, when the ceremonies and festivals and Dionysian revels—forerunners of the Greek theater—were held in such theaters.

The arena form has emerged at other times in history. Several of the cycle plays of the medieval period were performed in the round: in Lincolnshire and Cornwall in England, and in Touraine in France, for example. In the United States in the 1940s and 1950s there was a proliferation of arena stages across the country, such as a theater started by Margo Jones in Dallas, Texas, and the Penthouse Theater at the University of Washington in Seattle.

In spite of its long history and its resurgence in recent years, the arena stage has often been eclipsed by other forms. One reason is that its design, while allowing for intimacy, dictates a certain austerity. As I said before, it is impossible to have elaborate scenery because that would block the view of many spectators. Also, the performers must make all their entrances and exits along aisles that run through the audience, and they can sometimes be seen before and after they are supposed to appear onstage. The arena's lack of adaptability in this respect may explain why some of the circle theaters which opened 30 or 40 years ago have since closed. A number survive, however, and continue to do well. One of the best known is the Arena Stage in Washington, D.C. In addition, throughout this country there are a number of *tent theaters* in the arena form where musical revivals and concerts are given.

Thrust Stage

Falling between the proscenium and the arena is a third type of theater: the *thrust stage* with three-quarters seating. In one form or another it has been the most widely used of all stage spaces. The basic arrangement for this type of theater has the audience sitting on three sides, or in a semicircle, enclosing a stage which protrudes into the center. At the back of the playing area is some form of stage house providing for the entrances and exits of the actors as well as for scene changes. The thrust stage combines some of the best features of the other two: the

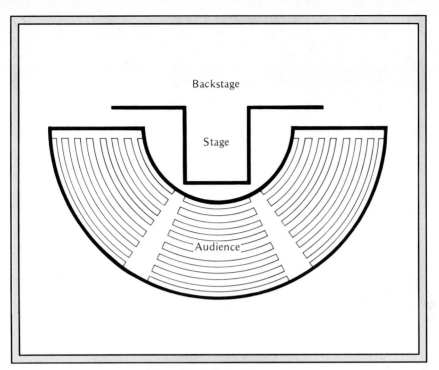

THRUST STAGE WITH THREE-QUARTERS SEATING.
*The stage is surrounded on three sides by the audience. Sometimes seating is a semicircle.
Entrances and exits are made from the sides and backstage. Spectators surround the action,
but there is still the possibility of scene changes and other stage effects.*

sense of intimacy and the "wraparound" feeling of the arena, and the
focused stage set against a single background found in the proscenium.

The thrust stage was developed by the Greeks for their great tragedies
and comedies. They took the circle, called the *orchestra*, used for tribal
rituals and other ceremonies, and placed it at the base of a curving
hillside. The slope of the hill formed a natural amphitheater for the
spectators, and the level circle at the foot formed the stage. At the back
of the circle, opposite the hillside, they placed a stage house, or *skene*.
The skene had formal doors through which characters made their entrances and exits and which formed a background for the action. It also
provided a place for the actors to change their costumes.

During the time of the Greek playwright Aeschylus, in the first half
of the fifth century B.C., the skene may have been a temporary wooden
structure, erected each year for the festivals. In the next two or three
centuries, however, the skene was refined to the point where it became
a permanent stone building, two or three stories in height, with a platform stage in front. At the same time, the wooden benches on the

THE GREEK STAGE AT EPIDAURUS.
One of the best preserved of the ancient Greek theaters is at Epidaurus. Theaters like this were carved into a hillside, with seating on three sides. At the bottom was a circular orchestra for the chorus, and at the back was a stage house in front of which the scenes with the major characters were staged. In the distance was an impressive natural landscape. Shown here is a rehearsal for The Trojan Women *by Euripides.*

hillsides for the spectators were replaced by stone seats. The largest Greek theaters seated 15,000 or more spectators, and their design was duplicated all over Greece, particularly in the years following the conquests of Alexander the Great (356–323 B.C.). Remnants of these theaters remain today throughout that part of the world, in such places as Epidaurus, Priene, Ephesus, Delphi, and Corinth, to name a few.

The Romans, who took the Greek form and built it as a complete structure, had a theater that was not strictly a thrust but a forerunner of the proscenium. Instead of using the natural amphitheater of a hillside, they constructed a freestanding stone building, joining the stage house to the seating area and making the orchestra a semicircle. In front of the stage house, which was decorated with arches and statues, they erected a long platform stage where most of the action occurred.

Another example of the thrust stage emerged in the medieval period when short religious plays began to be presented in churches and cathedrals in England and parts of Europe. Around A.D. 1200, performances of these religious plays were moved outdoors. One popular arrangement for these outdoor performances was the *platform stage*. A simple platform was set on trestles (it was sometimes called a *trestle stage*), with a curtain at the back which the actors used for entrances and costume changes. The area underneath the stage was closed off and provided, among other things, a space from which devils and other characters could appear, sometimes in a cloud of smoke. In some places the platform was on wheels (a *wagon stage*) and was moved from place to place through a town. The audience stood on three sides of the platform, making it an improvised thrust stage. This type of stage was widely used between the thirteenth and fifteenth centuries in England and various parts of Europe.

The next step was a thrust stage which appeared in England in the sixteenth century, just before Shakespeare began writing for the theater. A platform stage would be set up at one end of the open courtyard of an inn. The inns of this period were three or four stories high, and the rooms facing the inner courtyard served as boxes from which spectators could watch the performance. On ground level, spectators stood on three sides of the stage, while the fourth side of the courtyard, behind the platform, served as the stage house.

Interestingly enough, an almost identical theater took shape in Spain at the same time. The inns in Spain were called *corrales*, the same name given to the theaters which developed there. In addition to the similarity of theaters in England and Spain, a further coincidence lies in the fact that a very talented and prolific dramatist, Lope de Vega (1562–1635), was born within 2 years of Shakespeare and emerged as his Spanish counterpart.

In England, the formal theaters of Shakespeare's day, such as the Globe and the Fortune, were similar to the inn theaters: the audience stood in an open area around a platform stage, and three levels of spectators sat in closed galleries at the back and sides. A roof covered part of the stage, and at the back, some form of raised area served for balcony scenes (as in *Romeo and Juliet*). At the rear of the stage, also, scenes could be concealed and then "discovered." On each side at the rear was a door used for entrances and exits.

These theaters were fascinating combinations of diverse elements: they were both indoors and outdoors; some spectators stood while others sat; and the audience was composed of almost all levels of society. The physical environment must have been a stimulating one: performers standing at the front of the thrust stage were in the center of a hemisphere of spectators, on three sides around them as well as above and below. While these theaters held 2,000 to 3,000 spectators, no one in the audience was more than 60 feet or so from the stage, and most people were much closer. Being in the midst of so many people, enclosed on all sides but with an open sky above, must have instilled a feeling of great communion among the members of the audience and the performers.

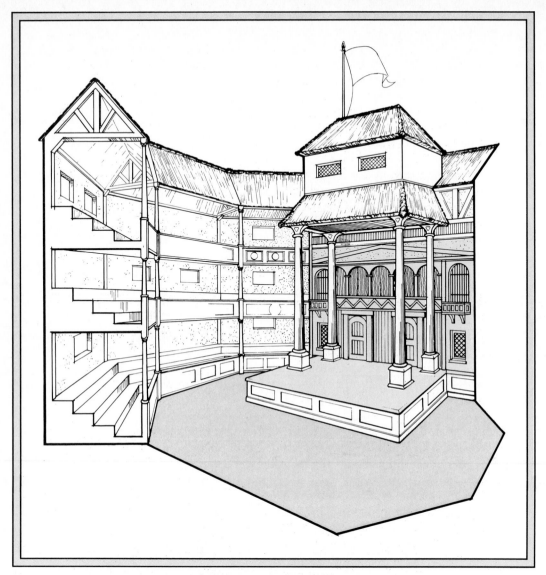

AN ELIZABETHAN PLAYHOUSE.

This drawing shows the kind of stage on which the plays of Shakespeare and his contemporaries were first presented. A platform stage juts into an open courtyard, with spectators standing on three sides. Three levels of enclosed seats rise above the courtyard. There are doors at the rear of the stage for entrances and exits and an upper level for balcony scenes.

Shortly after Shakespeare's day, in the latter part of the seventeenth century, two things occurred in England and Spain, as well as throughout Europe: (1) the theater moved completely indoors, and (2) the stage began a slow but steady retreat behind the proscenium opening, partly because performances were indoors, but more because the style of theater changed. For over two centuries the thrust stage was in eclipse, not to reappear until about 1900, when a few theaters in England began using a version of the thrust stage to produce Shakespeare.

The return to the thrust stage resulted from a growing realization that Elizabethan plays could be done best on a stage similar to the one for which they had been written. In the United States and Canada, it was not until after World War II that the thrust stage came to the fore again. Since then a number of fine theaters of this type have been built, including the Tyrone Guthrie in Minneapolis; the Shakespeare Theater in Stratford, Ontario; the Mark Taper Forum in Los Angeles; and the Long Wharf in New Haven.

A MODERN THRUST-STAGE THEATER.
This cutaway drawing of a thrust stage shows how the playing area juts into the audience, which surrounds the stage on three sides. This configuration affords intimacy, but at the back (shown here at the right) is an area that furnishes a natural backdrop for the action.

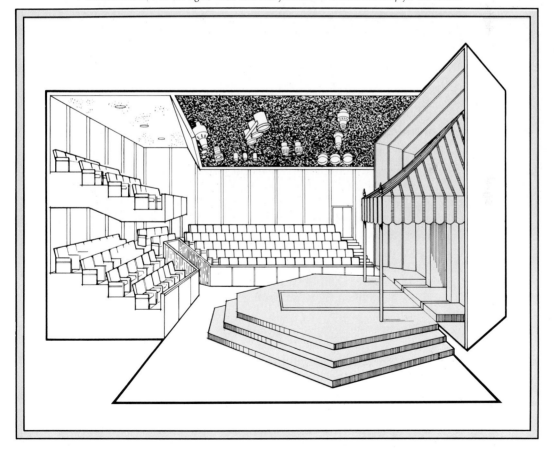

THE THRUST STAGE PROVIDES INTIMACY.
After being in eclipse for many years, the thrust stage has returned in the modern era, to become one of the most popular forms of stages, especially with regional, not-for-profit theaters. Shown here is the ACT in Seattle, Washington. As with all thrust theaters, it features both focus on the action in the stage area, and intimacy resulting from the "wrap-around" seating.

The basic stage of traditional Chinese and Japanese drama (including the noh theater of Japan) is a form of thrust stage: a raised, open platform, frequently covered by a roof, with the audience sitting on two or three sides around the platform stage. Entrances and exits are made from doors or ramps at the rear of the stage.

The obvious advantages of the thrust stage—the intimacy of the three-quarters seating and the close audience-actor relationship, together with the fact that so many of the world's great dramatic works were written for it—give it a significant place alongside the other major forms.

Created and Found Spaces

After World War II a number of avant-garde theater artists, such as the Polish director Jerzy Grotowski, undertook the task of reforming theater at every level. Since the various elements of theater are inextricably bound together, their search for a more basic kind of theater included a close look at the physical arrangement of the playing area and its relationship to the audience.

The Performance Group, which led spectators one at a time into the production of *Dionysus in 69* (as described earlier in this chapter), is typical in this regard. It presented its productions in a large garage converted into an open theater space. At various places in the garage, scaffolding and ledges were built for audience seating.

The Performance Group, like other modern avant-garde companies, owed a great debt to a Frenchman, Antonin Artaud (1896–1948), one of the first theater people to examine in depth the questions raised by the avant-garde. An actor and director who wrote a series of articles and essays about the theater, Artaud was inconsistent but brilliant. Although he spent several periods of his life in mental institutions, many of his ideas were to prove prophetic. Notions he put forward in the 1920s and 1930s, considered mad or impossible at the time, have since become common practice among experimental theater groups. Among his proposals was one on the physical theater.

> We abolish the stage and auditorium and replace them by a single site, without partition or barrier of any kind, which will become the theater of the action. A direct communication will be reestablished between the spectator and the spectacle, between the actor and the spectator, from the fact that the spectator, placed in the middle of the action, is engulfed and physically affected by it. This envelopment results, in part, from the very configuration of the room itself.
>
> Thus, abandoning the architecture of present-day theaters, we shall take some hangar or barn which we shall have reconstructed according to processes which have culminated in the architecture of certain churches or holy places, and of certain temples in Tibet.[3]

Some of Artaud's ideas were put into practice later, when the movement to explore new concepts became widespread. In the generation that came after Artaud, Jerzy Grotowski included the physical arrangements of stage space in his experiments. Not only Grotowski but others in the avant-garde movement have developed theater space in a variety of ways.

NONTHEATER BUILDINGS   Artaud mentioned a barn or hangar for performances. In recent years virtually every kind of structure has been used: lofts, warehouses, fire stations, basements, churches, breweries, and gymnasiums. This practice should not be confused with the conversion of unusual spaces to full-scale theaters, which has numerous precedents in the past. Historically, indoor tennis courts, palace ballrooms, and monastery dining halls have been converted into theaters. I am speaking here of using unusual structures as they are, with their original architectural elements intact. Special areas are carved out for acting and viewing, as with the garage of the Performance Group, but they are not to be mistaken for traditional theater buildings.

ADAPTED SPACES   One practice frequently adopted was the use of space to fit the play, rather than making the play fit the space, as is normally the case. Grotowski, in particular, pursued the notion of a different configuration for each production, one which seemed appropriate to the play being done. In Grotowski's production of the Doctor Faustus story, Faustus gives a banquet. For this, the theater was filled with two long tables at which spectators sat as if they were guests at a dinner party. The action took place at the heads of the tables and even on the tabletops. For Grotowski's production of *The Constant Prince,* a fence was built around the playing area, and the audience sat behind it, looking over the fence like spectators at a bullfight. In recent decades there have been similar attempts to deal with theater space in many parts of Europe and the United States.

STREET THEATER   One development—which was actually a return to the practices in medieval Europe—is theater held out-of-doors in non-traditional settings. A good example is *street theater*. Generally, street theater is of three types: (1) plays from the standard repertoire presented in the streets, (2) *neighborhood theater*, in which an original play deals with the problems and aspirations of a specific population of a city—such as Puerto Ricans, African Americans, or Italians; and (3) *guerrilla theater*, aggressive, politically oriented theater produced by an activist group in the streets in an attempt to persuade audiences to become more politically involved. Whatever the form, the important point for our purposes is that these productions take place not in a theater building but in places like parks, hospitals, jails, and bus stations.

In these productions theater is brought to people who might not see it otherwise. Also, those watching theater in such unusual settings are challenged to rethink what theater is all about. On the other hand, there are inherent disadvantages to impromptu productions in the streets or other "found space": the audience must be caught on the run, and there is rarely time for more than a sketch or vignette. Nor are there facilities to present a fully developed work—but then, that is often not the purpose of these undertakings in the first place.

MULTIFOCUS ENVIRONMENTS   An approach that sometimes accompanies these unusual arrangements is *multifocus theater*. In simple terms, this means not only that there is more than one playing area, such as the four corners of the room suggested by Artaud, but also that something is going on in several of them simultaneously. This is somewhat like a three-ring circus, where the spectator sees an activity in each ring and must concentrate on one.

There are several theories behind the idea of multifocus theater, most of them debatable. One is that a multifocus event is more like everyday life; if you stand on a street corner, there is activity all around you—in the four directions of the streets, in the buildings above—not just in one spot. You select which area you will observe, or perhaps you watch several at one time. The argument is that you should have the same choice in the theater.

In multifocus productions no single space or activity is supposed to be more important than any other. The spectator either takes in several impressions at once and synthesizes them in his or her own mind or selects one item as most arresting and concentrates on that. There is no such thing as the "best seat in the house"; all seats are equally good because the activity in all parts of the theater is equally important. Sometimes multifocus theater is joined with *multimedia theater*—presentations in which some combination of acting, films, dance, music, slides, and light shows is offered.

One problem with multifocus theater is that we seek in art precisely the selectivity and focus we do not find in everyday life. Besides, even those presentations which claim to be multifocus ultimately have a central point of interest—a three-ring circus, after all, has a center ring. It is difficult for a spectator to maintain interest in a multifocus event for very long. For some types of theater, a multifocus event is interesting, as well as appropriate; but by and large, members of the audience want to concentrate their attention on one space and one group of characters at a time.

Taken all in all, whether single-focus or multifocus, indoors or outdoors, the recent innovations in theater milieu have added a further alternative, rich in possibilities, to the settings for theatrical productions. They have also called attention to the importance of environment in the total theater experience.

✳ VARIETY IN THEATER ENVIRONMENTS ✳

Simply assigning a theater to a category does not adequately describe the environment. We must take into account a number of other variables in theater architecture as well. Two theaters may be of the same type and still be quite different in size, atmosphere, and setting. The small Sullivan Street Theater in New York, where the off-Broadway musical *The Fantasticks* has set records for its long run, seats fewer than 200 people. The theater experience in the Sullivan Street will be far different from that in a thrust theater several times larger, such as the Tyrone Guthrie in Minneapolis. Also, one theater may be indoors and another outdoors. Rather than having one type of theater building with only one form of stage, theater audiences today are fortunate in having a full range of environments in which to experience theater.

We have examined environmental factors influencing our experience at a theatrical event, including the location of the theater building, its size, its setting, its atmosphere, and its layout. In addition to a general environment in a theater building, there is a specific environment for the performer. Within the limits of the stage, or whatever has been designated as a playing area, a visual world is created for the actors and actresses to inhabit. Once a performance begins, the audience is always aware, even if unconsciously, of the scenery and lighting effects onstage. In Chapter 17 we will turn to a study of scenery.

✳ SUMMARY ✳

1   The atmosphere and environment of a theater space play a large part in setting the tone of the event.

2   Experimental theater groups in recent years have deliberately made spectators aware of the environment.

3   Throughout theater history there have been four basic stage and auditorium arrangements: proscenium, arena, thrust, and created or found space.

4   The proscenium theater features the picture-frame stage, in which the audience faces directly toward the stage and looks through the proscenium opening at the "picture." The proscenium stage aids illusion: placing the room of a house behind the proscenium allows the scene designer to create an extremely realistic-looking set. This type of stage also has the potential for elaborate scene shifts and visual displays because it generally has a large backstage area and a fly loft. It also creates a distancing effect which works to the advantage of certain types of drama. At the same time the proscenium frame sets up a barrier between the performers and the audience.

5   The arena or circle stage places the playing area in the center with the audience ranged in a circle or square around the outside. It offers an economical way to produce theater and an opportunity for great intimacy between performers and spectators. It cannot offer full visual displays in terms of scenery and scene changes.

6   The thrust stage with three-quarters seating has a platform stage with seating on three sides. Entrances and exits are made at the rear, and there is an opportunity for a certain amount of scenery. It combines some of the scenic features of the proscenium theater with the intimacy of the arena stage.

7   Created or found space takes several forms: use of nontheater buildings, adaptation of a given space to fit individual productions, use of outdoor settings, street theater, and multifocus environments.

8   The size and the location (indoors or outdoors, etc.), along with the shape and character of the theater building, affect the environment.

❋ TOPICS FOR DISCUSSION ❋

1   Consider *one* of the plays read or discussed so far and describe how it would be staged *(a)* on a proscenium stage, *(b)* on an arena stage, *(c)* on a thrust stage, and *(d)* in found space, such as a church or warehouse. Which space seems to be best for the play? Why?

2   Consider *each* of the plays read or discussed so far, and explain which type of space you think would be best for it.

3   Suppose that your community has a theater company which produces plays on a small arena stage or theater-in-the-round. Each time a play opens in this theater, at least one of the reviewers asserts that the play being produced would have been better on another kind of stage. Defend one of the following statements: *(a)* "The reviewers should not continue to comment on this; after dozens of productions in this theater, they should accept its limitations and concentrate on other aspects of the plays presented there." *(b)* "If the reviewers are always struck anew by the limitations of the arena stage in this theater, it means that the theater company is simply not dealing properly with the stage space; a well-directed, well-produced, and well-acted production would rise above those limitations." *(c)* "If the reviewers are always struck anew by the limitations of the arena stage, production after production, it probably implies that those limitations are insurmountable."

4   Which of the created or "found" spaces described in the chapter seems most practical to you? Which seems best in terms of artistic considerations? Do your choices seem to imply anything about the relationship between practicality and aesthetics in the theater?

17

SCENERY

SCENE DESIGN SETS THE TONE.

Good scene design creates a workable environment for performers; it sets the style and tone of the production, letting the audience know where and when the action takes place and whether the play is a tragedy, comedy, or some other type of drama; and it harmonizes with other elements of the production. The design shown here is for a production of Shakespeare's Pericles *at the Hartford Stage Company. Designed by John Conklin, it establishes the classic tone of the play and provides a haunting environment in which the action takes place.*

The theater experience does not occur in a visual vacuum. Spectators sit in the theater, their eyes open, watching what unfolds before them. Naturally, they focus most keenly on the performers as they speak and move about the stage; but always present are the visual images of scenery, costumes, and lighting—transformations of color and shape which add a significant ingredient to the total mixture of theater. The creation of these effects is the responsibility of *designers*. A *designer* is a person who creates and organizes one of the visual aspects or aural effects in a theater production.

The *scene designer* is responsible for the stage set, which can run the gamut from a bare stage with stools or orange crates to the most elaborate, large-scale production. No matter how simple, however, every set has a design. Even the absence of scenery constitutes a stage set and can benefit from the ideas of a designer: in the way the furniture is arranged, for example.

The *costume designer* is responsible for selecting, and in many cases creating, the outfits and accessories worn by the performers.

Stage lighting, quite simply, includes all forms of illumination on the stage. The *lighting designer* makes decisions in every area of lighting: the color of the lights, the mixture of colors, the number of lights, the intensity and brightness of the lights, the angles at which the lights strike performers, and the length of time required for the lights to come up or fade out.

A fourth designer might be referred to as the *aural,* or *sound, designer:* the person who arranges the sound system. The sound designer is responsible for all sound effects, recorded music, and the placement and synchronization of all microphones. He or she must not only plan all the sound but place microphones properly on and around the stage, and on the performers. For the performance itself, the sounds from both tape machines and microphones must be blended properly.

Designers must deal with practical as well as aesthetic considerations. A scene designer must know in which direction a door should open onstage and how high each tread should be on a flight of stairs. A lighting designer must know exactly how many feet above a performer's head a particular light should be placed and whether it requires a 500- or a 750-watt bulb. A costume designer must know how much material it takes to make a certain kind of dress and how to "build" clothes so that performers can wear them with confidence and have freedom of movement. A sound designer must know about acoustics and be familiar with echoes and electronic sound systems.

As in other elements of theater, symbols play a large role in design. A single item onstage can suggest an entire room: a bookcase, for instance, suggests a professor's office or a library; a stained-glass window suspended in midair suggests a church or synagogue. A stage filled with a bright yellow-orange glow suggests a cheerful sunny day,

326

whereas a single shaft of pale blue light suggests moonlight or an eerie graveyard at night. The ways in which designers deal with the aesthetic and practical requirements of the stage will be clearer when we examine the subject in detail, beginning with scene design in this chapter and going on to costumes (in Chapter 18) and lighting and sound (in Chapter 19).

❋ "STAGE SETS" IN EVERYDAY LIFE ❋

As with other areas of theater, there is an analogue, or a parallel, between scene design and our experiences in everyday life. Every building and room we go into can be regarded as a form of stage set. Interior decorating—the creation of a special atmosphere in a home or a public building—is scene designing for everyday life. A good example is the trend in recent years for restaurants to have a foreign motif—French, Italian, Spanish, Olde English. These restaurants have a form of setting, or "scenery," to give the feeling that you are in a different world when, in fact, you have just stepped off the street. A church decorated for a wedding is a form of stage set; so is the posh lobby of a hotel, or an apartment with flowers, candlelight, and soft music.

In every case the "designer," the person who has arranged the setting, has selected elements which signal an impression to the viewer. The combination of colors, fabrics, furniture, and styles tells the person entering the space exactly where he or she is. These things are often calculated with great care, and a premium is set on an appropriate environment and atmosphere. When we see a library with leather-bound books, attractive wood paneling, comfortable leather chairs, and a beautiful carved wooden desk, we get a sense of stability, tradition, and comfort. A totally different kind of feeling would come from a modern room with everything "hi-tech," with glass-top tables, furniture of chrome and stainless steel, and indirect lighting. From this spare, functional look, we get a "modern" feeling. Interior decorators know that appearance is important, that the visual elements of a room can communicate an overall impression to which an observer responds with a series of feelings, attitudes, and assumptions.

❋ SCENERY FOR THE STAGE ❋

We are accustomed to "stage settings" in everyday life; but, as with other elements in theater, there is an important difference between interior decorations in real life and set designs for the stage. Robert Edmond Jones (1887–1954), who is considered by many to be the most outstanding American scene designer of the first half of this century, put it in these terms:

A good scene should be, not a picture, but an image. Scene-designing is not what most people imagine it is—a branch of interior decorating. There is no more reason for a room on a stage to be a reproduction of an actual room than for an actor who plays the part of Napoleon to be Napoleon or for an actor who plays Death in the old morality play to be dead. Everything that is actual must undergo a strange metamorphosis, a kind of sea-change, before it can become truth in the theater.[1]

While a stage set signals an atmosphere to the viewer, in the same way as rooms in real life, the scene designer must go a step further. As has been pointed out many times, the theater is not life: it resembles life. It has both the opportunity and the obligation to be more than mere reproduction, as Jones suggests.

The special nature of scenery for the theater will be clearer when we examine the objectives and functions of scene design.

❈ OBJECTIVES OF SCENE DESIGN ❈

The scene designer has the following objectives:

1 Creating an environment for the performers
2 Helping to set the tone and style of the production
3 Helping to distinguish realistic from nonrealistic theater
4 Establishing the locale and period in which the play takes place
5 Developing a design concept
6 Where appropriate, providing a central image or metaphor for the production
7 Ensuring that the scenery is coordinated with other production elements
8 Solving practical design problems

Objectives 1 through 7 encompass the aesthetic aspects of stage design. Objective 8 encompasses several practical aspects.

❈ AESTHETIC ASPECTS OF STAGE DESIGN ❈

The Scenic Environment

There have been times in the history of theater when scene design was looked on as the painting of a large picture. In the discussion of the proscenium stage, I noted the temptation to use the proscenium arch as a frame and put behind it a gigantic picture. The tradition of fine scene painting, begun in Italy in the late seventeenth century, continued

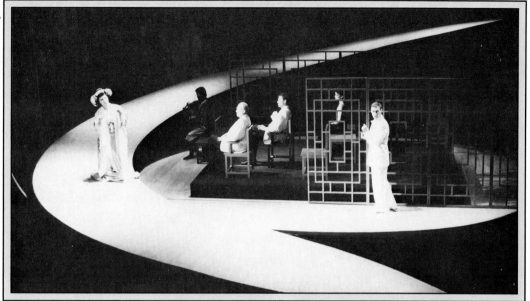

AN ENVIRONMENT FOR PERFORMERS.

For the Broadway production of M. Butterfly, *the designer Eiko Ishioka created a setting that established the east-west atmosphere of the play. The play tells of the affair and marriage between a French diplomat and a Chinese opera singer who turns out to be a man, not a woman, and also a spy. The designer incorporated many Asian elements in the design, the most striking being a large curved ramp that came from a top level to the stage floor. Colored bright red, it also encompassed a playing area where many scenes took place. The boldness and the appropriateness of the design were ideal for David Henry Hwang's drama.*

throughout Europe in the eighteenth and nineteenth centuries. It was still flourishing in Europe and the United States in the early part of this century, when many famous painters—including Pablo Picasso, Salvador Dalí, and Marc Chagall—undertook to design scenery.

Scene painting as an end in itself has not been the only case where the visual side of stage spectacle took precedence over other elements and was featured for its own sake. In Chapter 16, I mentioned the "Hall of the Machines" in Paris, where elaborate displays of stage effects—clouds descending, rocks opening, turntables rotating—were the main attraction. Throughout the nineteenth century, spectacular effects, such as chariot races onstage and houses burning down, were extremely popular.

Turning to the present day, we can find an example in "performance art," which is allied to painting and dance and which puts heavy emphasis on visual effects—much more so than on language, character, or story. Also, many modern musicals, such as *Cats, Starlight Express, The*

(Arena Stage)

A BEAUTIFUL STAGE PICTURE.

The scenic designer must deal with both aesthetic and practical considerations. Where appropriate, the design should have a visual appeal and a beauty all its own, as well as balance, symmetry, and other good design elements. A good example is this setting for The Importance of Being Earnest, *designed by Tony Straiges.*

Phantom of the Opera, and *Miss Saigon,* have tended to rely on the visual side of the production fully as much as on other elements such as the book or score.

The person responsible for these visual extravaganzas is the scene designer. He or she is always an important member of the creative team in a theater production, but in the case of an elaborate musical such as *Phantom of the Opera* or an avant-garde visual piece, the work of the scene designer becomes a major ingredient. To have a stage picture that constantly engages the attention of the audience and makes a comment all by itself requires inventiveness and imagination of a high order, not to mention a firm grasp of stage effects.

Although there is every reason for spectators to enjoy stage machinery and beautiful stage pictures, one element that must never be forgotten in scene design—just as it must never be forgotten when we read a play in book form—is the presence of the performer. Scene design creates an environment—a place for actors and actresses to move and have their being. Robert Edmond Jones spoke forcefully on this point when he said: "Players act in a setting, not against it."[2]

Jones went on to explain:

A stage setting holds a curious kind of suspense. Go, for instance, into an ordinary empty drawing-room as it exists normally. There is no particular suspense about this room. It is just—empty. Now imagine the same drawing room arranged and decorated for a particular function—a Christmas party for children, let us say. It is not completed as a room, not until the children are in it. And if we wish to visualize for ourselves how important a part the sense of expectancy plays in such a room, let us imagine that there is a storm and the children cannot come. A scene on the stage is filled with the same expectancy. It is like a mixture of chemical elements held in solution. The actor adds the one element that releases the hidden energy of the whole. Meanwhile, wanting the actor, the various elements which go to make up the setting remain suspended, as it were, in an indefinable tension. To create this suspense, this tension, is the essence of the problem of stage designing.[3]

Jones is saying that a stage set, rather than being a complete picture in and of itself, is an environment with one element missing—the performer. Empty, it has a sense of incompleteness. A stage set is like a giant piece of mobile sculpture, motionless until set in motion by the performers. This, of course, fits with our notion that theater is an experience, an unfolding encounter which moves through time. If the stage picture were complete when we first entered the theater or when the curtain went up, where would the experience lie? Scene design is at its best, therefore, when it underlines and emphasizes the primary values of the play—not competing with the play or overpowering it, but enhancing and supporting it.

Tone and Style

A stage setting can help establish the mood, style, and meaning of the play. A Roman farce, for example, calls for comic, exaggerated scenery, in the manner of a cartoon, perhaps with outrageous colors. A satire calls for a comment in the design, like the twist in the lines of a caricature in a political cartoon. A serious play calls for sober, straightforward scenery, even in a nonrealistic piece.

As examples of what is called for in scene design, let us consider two plays by the Spanish playwright Federico García Lorca. His *Blood Wedding* is the story of a young bride-to-be who runs away with a former lover on the day she is to be married. The two flee to a forest; and in the forest the play becomes expressionistic: allegorical figures of the Moon and a Beggar Woman, representing Death, appear in the forest and seem to echo the fierce emotional struggle taking place within the characters. It would be quite inappropriate to design a realistic, earthbound set for *Blood Wedding*, particularly for the forest scenes. The set-

SCENERY AS A COMMENT ON THE PLAY.

At times scenery runs counter to the style of a play, or is a comment on it. In Ionesco's
The Bald Soprano, *the playwright calls for a very plain, ordinary living room set that will
stand in contrast to the bizarre, absurd actions and conversation in the play—exactly what
the designer Anita Stewart provided in a production, shown above, at the American Repertory Theater.*

ting must have the same sense of mystery, of the unreal, which rules
the passions of the characters. We must see this visually in the images
of the forest as well as in the figures of the Moon and the Beggar
Woman.

Another play of García Lorca's, *The House of Bernarda Alba*, tells of a
woman and her five daughters. The woman has grown to hate and
distrust men, and so she locks up her house, like a convent, preventing
her daughters from going out. The action takes place in various rooms
of the house and an enclosed patio. From a design point of view it is
important to convey the closed-in, cloistered feeling of the house in
which the women are held as virtual prisoners. The sense of entrapment
must be omnipresent.

Occasionally, scenery runs deliberately counter to the play—as a comment on it. Ionesco's *The Bald Soprano*, a zany absurdist play (described
in Chapter 10), might be set in a realistic family living room as an ironic
contrast to the content of the play. This, however, is the exception rather
than the rule.

SCENERY, LIGHTING, AND COSTUMES

Designers add important elements to the theater experience. On the preceding overleaf we see the masks and headpieces for an imaginative production of Shakespeare's A Midsummer Night's Dream; *on this page, an outdoor setting of Shakespeare's* Twelfth Night *(above) and a spare design for Samuel Beckett's* Happy Days *(left); on the opposite page, Robert Wilson's haunting vision for Euripides's* Alcestis *(top) and the musical spectacular* Miss Saigon *(bottom); on the following two pages, a tableau from* The Serpent Woman *(left page, top), the elegant costumes from a production of Sheridan's* The School for Scandal *(left page, bottom), and the costumes, lighting, and settings for Büchner's* Woyzeck *(right page).*

THE DESIGNERS AT WORK

Visual elements of theater include a number of aspects, illustrated here. On the opposite page, an actress applying the elaborate makeup for Chinese theater (top), and fanciful costumes for Shakespeare's A Midsummer Night's Dream *(bottom); on this page, fairy-tale costumes for the musical* Into the Woods *(above left), elegant costumes for Calderón's* Life Is a Dream *(above right), and a costume for Molière's* The School for Wives *(bottom left); on the following overleaf, Tony Walton's sketch for a costume in the musical* Grand Hotel *(top left), the costume itself (top right), and Tony Walton's model of the stage set for John Guare's* Six Degrees of Separation *(bottom).*

GRAND HOTEL

LILIANE MONTEVECCHI - GRUSHINSKAYA -

#128

BUCKLE - SHOULD NOT LOOK
LIKE A HEART CANDY
ERTE - CHINESE EMPRESS

LORENZETTI 89

Realistic and Nonrealistic Scenery

The stage designer's role is of special importance in distinguishing between realism and nonrealism. In *realistic theater,* a setting is called for which looks very much like its counterpart in real life. A kitchen resembles a kitchen, a dining room resembles a dining room, and so on. One exponent of realism, David Belasco (1854–1931), a producer-director of the early twentieth century, sometimes reproduced an actual kitchen or another room from a house, including wallpaper and light fixtures, onstage.

A complete reproduction is an extreme, however, for even in realistic theater the stage designer selects items to go onstage, and his or her talent and imagination play an important role. The point is to make the room *resemble,* but not duplicate, its counterpart in real life. In the same way that a playwright does not simply take a tape recorder into the streets and record conversations, the scene designer does not reproduce each detail of a room. A set calls for selectivity and editing. In a realistic setting, it is up to the designer to pick and choose those items, or symbols, that will give the proper feeling and impression. At times the designer may provide only partial settings for realistic plays. We will see a portion of a room—a cutout with only door frames and windows, but no walls, or walls suggested by an outline. Whether a complete set or a partial one, the result should convey to us not only the lifestyle but the individual characteristics of the persons in the play.

In *nonrealistic theater,* the designer can give full reign to imagination, and the use of symbol is of special importance. Chinese theater affords a graphic example of the possibilities of symbol in stage design. Chinese theater, during its long history, has developed an elaborate set of conventions in which a single prop or item represents a complete locale or action. An embroidered curtain on a pole stands for a general's tent, an official seal signifies an office, and an incense tripod stands for a palace. A plain table may represent a judge's bench; but when two chairs are placed at each end of the table, it can become a bridge. When performers climb onto the table, it can be a mountain; when they jump over it, a wall. A banner with fish on it represents the sea, a man with a riding whip is riding a horse, and two banners with wheels are a chariot. Interestingly enough, such symbols are thoroughly convincing, even to westerners.

Productions in the United States also provide examples of imaginative nonrealistic scenery. Previously, the expressionistic play *The Adding Machine* was mentioned. In designing the original production of this play, Lee Simonson (1888–1967) used abstract settings, with vertical lines set at odd angles. Like the angle of vision in the play itself, the set was tilted, creating a sense of imbalance and unreality. For the revival of Sophocles's *Electra,* Ming Cho Lee (1930–) suspended large stone for-

(Martha Swope)

(Richard Feldman/American Repertory Theater)

REALISTIC AND NONREALISTIC SCENERY.

Generally realism and nonrealism call for different design elements, underscoring the difference in style between the two types of drama. Here we see a realistic design, by Steven Rubin, for the living room in A. R. Gurney's The Cocktail Hour *(top); and a nonrealistic set by Anita Stewart for Ionesco's* The Chairs *(bottom).*

mations on three sides of the stage. This design suggested the three doors of the ancient Greek theater; but more important, it conveyed the solidity, dignity, and rough-hewn quality of the play. In contrast, Boris Aronson (1900–1980), for the musical *Company,* designed a sharp, sleek set constructed partly of chrome and Lucite, with straight lines. Actors and actresses moved from one area to another in modern, open elevators which were symbolic of the chic, antiseptic world of the characters. The set was the epitome of sophisticated urban living.

Locale and Period

Whether realistic or nonrealistic, the stage set should tell the audience where and when the play takes place. Is the locale a saloon? A bedroom? A courtroom? A palace? A forest? The set should also indicate the time period. A kitchen with old-fashioned utensils and no electric appliances sets the play in the past. An old radio and an icebox might tell us that the time is the 1920s. A spaceship or the landscape of a faraway planet would suggest a futuristic period.

In addition to indicating time and place, the setting can also tell us what kinds of characters the play is about. For example, the characters may be neat and formal, or lazy and sloppy. They may be kings and queens, or an ordinary suburban family. The scene design should tell us these things immediately.

The Design Concept

In order to convey information, the scene designer frequently develops a *design concept* similar to the directorial concept discussed in Chapter 7. It is a unifying idea carried out visually. Examples of such a concept would be the claustrophobic setting for Lorca's *The House of Bernarda Alba* and Ming Cho Lee's Greek-influenced setting for *Electra,* described above.

A strong design concept is particularly important when the time and place of a play are shifted. Modern stage designs for Shakespeare's *A Midsummer Night's Dream* illustrate the point. In most productions it is performed in palace rooms and a forest, as suggested by the script. But for a production by Peter Brook (1925–) in the early 1970s, the designer Sally Jacobs (1932–) fashioned three white, bare walls—like the sides of a gymnasium. Trapezes were lowered onto the stage at various times, and in some scenes the performers actually played their parts suspended in midair. The clean, spare look of Jacobs's setting was nontraditional, to say the least.

The concept developed by a scene designer for a stage setting is closely related to the idea of a central image or metaphor, discussed next.

335

A DESIGN CONCEPT.

For a production of Chekhov's The Cherry Orchard *at Washington's Arena Stage, the designer Radu Boruzescu created the concept of a field of grain which sprouted onstage in the final act. The field was symbolic of the lovely past in which the main characters were lost, and which they could not find their way out of. It provided a visual image, as well as a physical environment, that summed up the situation in which they found themselves. The performers shown here are Shirley Knight, Tana Hicken, and Rebecca Ellens.*

The Central Image or Metaphor

Stage design not only must be consistent with the play; it should have its own integrity. The elements of the design—the lines, the shapes, the colors—should add up to a whole. In many cases, a designer tries to develop a central image or metaphor.

For the original production of *The Royal Hunt of the Sun*, a play about Pizarro and the conquest of Peru, Michael Annals (1938–) set a huge sunburst, resembling a gold medallion, in midair at the back of the stage. Twelve feet in diameter and symbolizing both gold and the sun, the sunburst dominated the stage, providing a vivid focal point for the production.

In *Mother Courage* by Bertolt Brecht, the playwright provided a central image for the designer to work with. This is the wagon which Mother Courage pulls throughout the play and from which she sells wares in order to support her family. The play takes place during the Thirty Years' War in Europe during the seventeenth century, and Mother Courage is a survivor. She sells goods to all sides in order to keep herself going. The wagon which she has with her at all times is a symbol of

A CENTRAL IMAGE OR METAPHOR.

At times designers conceive of a visual image or metaphor around which the entire design concept of a production can be created. Such an image was the broken-down truck employed by the designer Kevin Rigdon in the production of The Grapes of Wrath *developed by the Steppenwolf Company of Chicago. The truck took the Joad family from the dust bowl of Oklahoma to California in search of a better life, but— like their vehicle—the family had a terrible struggle.*

her transitory life—she is always on the move—and of the necessity she has to peddle merchandise. The wagon signifies the whole notion of commerce and its relationship to war. A designer, therefore, must create a wagon which will work onstage and which will embody all the characteristics called for in the script and the character of Mother Courage. It becomes a sort of mobile central image or metaphor around which the scene designer develops his or her entire visual concept.

Coordination of the Whole

Because scenic elements have such strong symbolic values and are so important to the overall effect of a production, the designer has an obligation to provide scenery consistent with the intent of the play and the director's concept. If the script and acting are highly stylized, the setting should not be mundane and drab. If the script and acting are realistic, the setting should not overpower the other elements in the production. It is a question, once again, of how the various parts of a production should contribute to an overall effect.

MOTHER COURAGE AND HER CHILDREN (1939)

BERTOLT BRECHT (1898–1956)

CHIEF CHARACTERS:
Mother Courage
Kattrin—her mute daughter
Eilif—her elder son
Swiss Cheese—her younger son
Cook
Chaplain
Yvette Pottier—a prostitute

SETTING: Various army camps in Sweden, Poland, Bavaria, and Germany.

TIME: 1624–1636.

BACKGROUND: Mother Courage is a canteen woman, Anna Fierling, who follows army camps with her wagon and sells her wares to soldiers. She has two sons and a daughter—all from different fathers—who help pull the wagon.

SCENE 1: Spring 1624, on a highway. A Swedish recruiting officer complains to a sergeant how difficult it is to get recruits. Mother Courage and her children enter, pulling the wagon from which Courage sells her goods. The sergeant distracts Courage while the recruiting officer persuades her son Eilif to join the army.

SCENE 2: The years 1625 and 1626; the setting is the kitchen of the Swedish commander, where the Cook is arguing with Mother Courage. The Swedish commander enters and praises Eilif for his bravery. Courage has not seen Eilif since he was taken away to the army. When she hears Eilif singing "The Song of the Wise Woman and the Soldier," she recognizes his voice and joins in.

SCENE 3: Three years later. Mother Courage, her two children, and parts of a Finnish regiment are prisoners. Courage's friend, Yvette Pottier, a prostitute who feels sorry for herself because her first husband left her, sings "The Fraternization Song" about loving a soldier. When cannon noises herald a surprise attack by the Catholics, Courage lends the Chaplain a cloak to disguise the fact that he is a Protestant. Swiss Cheese hides the cash box in the wagon, while Courage rubs ashes onto Kattrin's face to make her less attractive to the soldiers. Three days later, while Courage and the Chaplain are gone, Swiss Cheese leaves the scene to hide the cash box, but two soldiers, who have been watching, capture him. The soldiers return with Swiss Cheese, but Courage who has come back also, denies knowing him, even though he is her own son. While the Chaplain sings "The Song of the Hours," about Christ's death, Courage finds that she can free her son if she bribes the sergeant—but she haggles too long and Swiss Cheese is executed.

SCENE 4: Outside an officer's tent. A young soldier enters, raging against the captain who took his reward money. Mother Courage sings "The Song of the Great Capitulation," which persuades them both that there is no use complaining.

SCENE 5: Two years later. The Chaplain tells

Courage that he needs some linen to help the peasants wrap up their wounds, and when she refuses, he takes the linen by force. After Kattrin rescues a child, Courage tells her to give it back to the mother.

SCENE 6: Bavaria, 1632—the funeral of the fallen commander. The men are getting drunk instead of going to the funeral. When Kattrin gets wounded, Courage thinks it is lucky because it will make Kattrin less appealing to the soldiers.

SCENE 7: A highway, with the Chaplain, Mother Courage, and Kattrin pulling the supply wagon. Courage sings a song about war being a business proposition.

SCENE 8: A camp, 1632. Voices announce that peace is at hand. Courage is distraught because she has just purchased a lot of supplies and will be ruined because no one will buy them. Yvette goes with Courage to try to sell the goods. Eilif is arrested for killing some peasants—now that peace has come, such killing is a crime. Courage rushes back in with the news that the war is on again. The Cook and Kattrin pull the wagon while Courage sings.

SCENE 9: In front of a half-ruined parsonage; 1634. The Cook tells Courage that his mother has left him an inn that he wants to run with her, but without Kattrin. Kattrin overhears them and is about to leave when Courage stops her; Courage turns the Cook down, and she and Kattrin harness the wagon and march off.

SCENE 10: 1635. Courage and Kattrin pull the wagon up to a prosperous farmhouse and hear someone singing about warmth and comfort and safety, conditions that stand in sharp contrast to their own bleak situation.

SCENE 11: January 1636, and the wagon, in disrepair, stands outside a farmhouse. Soldiers gather up the peasants and pull Kattrin out of the wagon; they ask the way to the town. An old man climbs on the roof and sees the soldiers getting ready to launch a surprise attack on the sleeping town. Kattrin gets a drum out of the wagon, climbs up on the roof and beats a warning to save the people in the town. When the lieutenant tries to stop the noise, Kattrin goes on drumming, and the soldiers kill her. Cannon noises and alarm bells announce that Kattrin's warning was successful—the town is saved.

SCENE 12: Courage sits in front of the wagon by Kattrin's body, singing a lullaby. The peasants tell Courage that she must leave and that they will bury Kattrin. Courage harnesses up and, this time all alone, pulls the wagon behind a passing regiment.

(Michael Cooper/Stratford Festival)

339

❋ PRACTICAL ASPECTS OF SCENE DESIGN ❋

We have been examining aesthetic considerations of scenery and the process of design; but, as with everything in theater, there is a practical side to scenery as well.

The Physical Layout

The playing area must fit into a certain stage space; and, more important, it must accommodate the performers. In terms of space, a designer cannot plan a gigantic stage setting for a theater where the proscenium opening is only 20 feet wide and the depth of the stage is no more than 15 feet. By the same token, to design a small room in the midst of a 40-foot stage would be ludicrous. In dealing with the requirements of the play, the designer must take into account the physical layout of the stage space. If a performer must leave by a door on the right side of the stage and a few moments later return by a door on the left, the designer must obviously make allowance for crossing behind the scenery. If performers need to change costumes quickly offstage, the scene designer must make certain that there is room offstage for changing. If there is to be a sword fight, the actors must have space in which to make their turns, to advance and retreat.

Any type of physical movement requires a certain amount of space, and the scene designer must allow for this in his or her *ground plan.* The *ground plan* is the blueprint, or floor plan, outlining the various

GROUND PLAN.

In order to aid the director, performers, and stage technicians, the designer draws a ground plan, or blueprint, of the stage, showing the exact locations of furniture, walls, windows, doors, and other scenic elements.

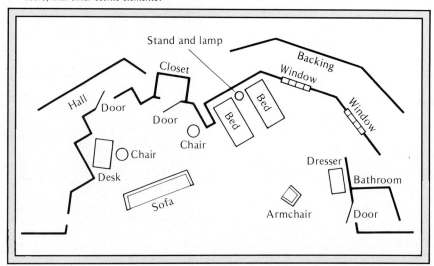

PART FIVE · THE DESIGNERS: ENVIRONMENT AND VISUAL ELEMENTS

```
                              ─Backstage─

        ┌──────────────┬──────────────┬──────────────┐
        │     Up       │     Up       │     Up       │
        │   right      │   center     │    left      │
        │              │              │              │
        ├──────────────┼──────────────┼──────────────┤
 Offstage│    Right     │              │    Left      │  Offstage
  right  │   center     │   Center     │   center     │    left
        │              │              │              │
        ├──────────────┼──────────────┼──────────────┤
        │    Down      │    Down      │    Down      │
        │    right     │   center     │    left      │
        │              │              │              │
        └──────────────┴──────────────┴──────────────┘
 Curtain                    Apron
  line

                           Audience
```

STAGE AREAS.

Various parts of the stage are given specific designations. Near the audience is downstage; *away from the audience is* upstage. Right *and* left *are from the performers' point of view, not the audience's. Everything out of sight of the audience is* offstage. *Using this scheme, everyone working in the theater can carefully pinpoint stage areas.*

levels on the stage and indicating the placement of all scenery, furniture, doors, windows, and so on. Working in conjunction with the director, the designer is chiefly responsible for developing a practical ground plan.

The way doors open and close, the way a sofa is set, the angle at which steps lead to a second floor—all are the responsibility of the designer and are important to both the cast and the play. Actresses and actors must be able to execute steps easily and to sit in such a way that the audience can see them clearly, and they must have the space to interact with other performers naturally and convincingly. If a performer opens a door onstage and is immediately blocked from the view of the audience, this is obviously an error on the part of the scene designer.

CHAPTER 17 • SCENERY

To designate areas of the stage, the scene designer uses terminology peculiar to the theater. *Stage right* and *stage left* mean the right and left sides of the stage, respectively, as seen from the performer's position facing the audience. In other words, when the audience looks at the stage, the side to *its* left is stage right, and the side to *its* right is stage left. The area of the stage nearest the audience is known as *downstage*, and the area farthest away from the audience is *upstage*. These designations, downstage and upstage, come from the time in the eighteenth and nineteenth centuries when the stage was raked (that is, the stage sloped downward from back to front). As a result of this downward slope, the performer farthest away from the audience was higher, or "up," and could be seen better. This is the origin of the expression *to upstage someone.* The term has come to mean that one performer grabs the spotlight from everyone else and calls attention to himself or herself by any means whatever. At first, however, it meant that one performer was in a better position than the others because he or she was standing farther back on the raked stage and hence was higher.

Materials of Scene Design

In creating a stage set, the designer begins with the stage floor itself. Sometimes the stage floor is a turntable; that is, a circle is set into the floor which can turn mechanically to bring one set into view as another disappears. At times trapdoors are set in the floor through which performers can enter or leave the stage. For some productions, tracks or slots are set in the stage floor and set pieces or *wagons* are brought onstage in the tracks and stopped at the proper point. A wagon in this case is a low platform set on wheels. Wagon stages are brought onstage mechanically or by stagehands hidden behind them. This type of scene change is frequently used in musical comedy.

Instead of scenery coming from the sides, it can be dropped from the fly loft—*to fly,* it will be recalled, is the term used when scenery is raised into the fly loft out of the view of the audience.

From floor level, ramps and platforms can be built to any height desired. To create walls or divisions of other kinds, the most common element is the *flat,* so named because it is a single flat unit. It consists of canvas stretched on wood, and the side facing the audience can be painted to look like a solid wall. Used in conjunction with other flats, it can be made to look like a complete room. The scene designer's art comes into play at this point, creating the illusion—with flats and other units—of virtually any type of room or architecture required. Other vertical units are *cutouts*—small pieces made like canvas flats or cut out of plywood. Again, they can be painted to create the illusion of a solid piece of architecture.

THE DESIGNER PREPARES A PRODUCTION.

After conferring with the director and deciding on a design concept, the scenic designer prepares the set. A ground plan is drawn, elevations—both front and side—are prepared, painting elevations are created, and a model of the set is made. Shown above are the model made by the designer Tony Walton for the Broadway musical Grand Hotel *(top) and a picture of the actual set (bottom) after it was constructed and painted by the scene designer's collaborators.*

343

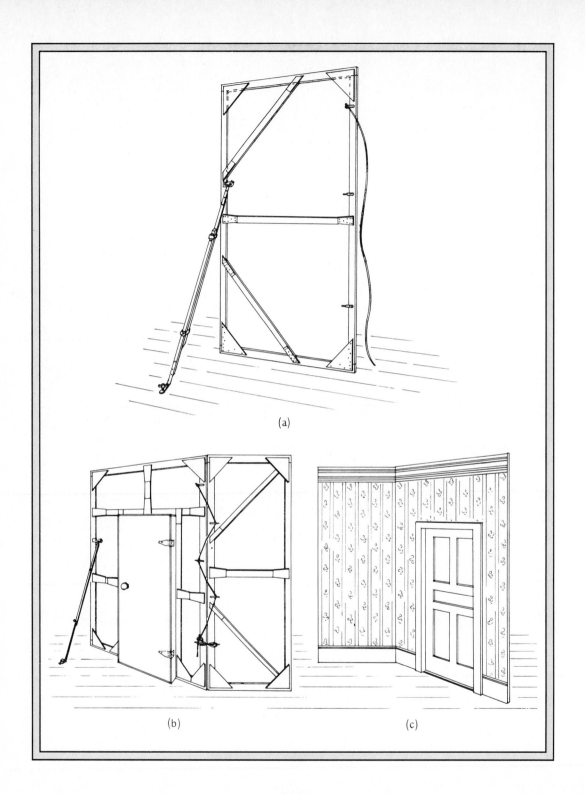

(a)

(b)

(c)

Opposite page: The designer Harry Lines has drawn these illustrations to show how the stage flat is built and used. In (a), we see the back side of a flat. It is made of a wooden frame with cross pieces and corner braces. On the reverse side of the flat a piece of canvas is stretched on which the walls of a room or other scenic effects can be painted. The flat is held upright on the stage floor by a stage brace (shown at the left) and is lashed to other flats by the rope at the right. In (b), we see the back view of two flats lashed together. Windows, doors, and other architectural features can be placed in flats; here, a door is placed in one of the flats. In (c), the two flats shown in (b) are reversed. This is how they will look from the audience's point of view. With wallpaper painted on the flats and molding on the walls and door, they form the corner of a room.

A very special type of scenery is the *scrim*. A *scrim* is a gauze or cloth screen which can be painted like a regular flat. The wide mesh of the cloth, however, allows light to pass through. When light shines on a scrim from in front—that is, from the audience's point of view—it is reflected off the painted surface, and the scrim appears to be a solid wall. When light comes from behind, however, the scrim becomes transparent and the spectators can see performers and scenery behind it.

The scrim is particularly effective in scenes where ghosts are called for or when an eerie effect is desired. Scrims are likewise useful in memory plays or plays with flashbacks: the spectators see the scene in the present in front of the scrim, and then, as lights in the front fade and those behind come up, they see through this gauzelike scrim a scene with a cloudy, translucent quality, indicating a memory or a scene in the past.

A development which has taken hold with great force in recent years is *screen projection*. A picture or drawing is projected on a screen either from in front—as in an ordinary movie house—or from behind the screen. The advantage of the latter is that because the performers will not be in the beam of the light, there will be no shadows or silhouettes. Obviously there are many advantages to projections: pictures can change with the rapidity of the cinema, and there is an opportunity to present vast scenes onstage in a way which would hardly be possible otherwise, except with tremendously elaborate scene painting.

Special Effects

The discussion of scrims and projections introduces the subject of *special effects*. These are effects of scenery, lighting, sound, and props that seem miraculous or unusual. (The term *prop* comes from the word *property*. It is the name given to any object in the theater that is not a permanent part of the scenery or costumes. Props include such things as lamps, ashtrays, glasses, typewriters, walking sticks, umbrellas, and fans.)

Special effects include fog, knives or swords that appear to stab victims, ghosts, walls that fall apart, and so on. In the modern era, films and television—because of their technical possibilities—have brought

SPECIAL EFFECTS.

An important challenge for both scenic and lighting designers is the creation of special effects. Such things as storms, lightning, smoke, and ghostly apparitions are the province of the designers, who use elaborate machinery, rear screen projections, and other devices to produce these effects. Seen here is the effect of smoke, clouds, and other eerie apparitions created by the designer George Psypin in a scene for a production of Shakespeare's Cymbeline *at New York's Public Theater.*

extreme realism to special effects. Examples include buildings on fire and blown-up cars. Special effects onstage, however, are almost as old as the theater itself. From the Greeks on, theater has tried to suspend natural laws and create the illusion of miraculous or extraordinary effects.

The see-through scrim and projections (mentioned above) are used to create a number of effects, such as dream sequences. Special fog machines create a cloudy vapor that can be blown across the stage by fans, giving the impression of clouds or fog. In *The Phantom of the Opera,* a gigantic chandelier falls from the top of the auditorium onto the stage; and in *Miss Saigon,* a helicopter lands on top of the American Embassy in Saigon to rescue fleeing soldiers and civilians.

In the area of lighting, there are several special effects that can be used to create interesting visual pictures. A simple one is positioning the source of light near the stage floor and shining the light on the performers from below. This creates shadows under their eyes and chins and gives them a ghostly or horrifying quality.

Another common special effect is the use of ultraviolet light. This is a very dark blue light that causes phosphorus to glow. When the stage is very dark, even black, costumes or scenery that have been painted with a special phosphorus paint will "light up."

The effect of slow motion or silent movies, where actors seem to be moving in jerks, is created by the use of a strobe light. A *strobe light* is a very powerful and bright gas discharge light which flashes at rapid intervals to create the effect.

In the area of sound there are also a number of special effects. Sometimes speakers are placed completely around the audience, and the sound can move around from side to side. Computerized noises and electronic music can be used to create special sounds for various situations, and tape loops can repeat the same sound over and over for a long period of time. Echoes can be created by means of a machine that causes reverberations in the sound waves.

✳ THE PROCESS OF SCENE DESIGN ✳

Steps in the Design Process

In meeting the objectives described above, how does the scene designer proceed? Although every designer has his or her own method, usually a general pattern is followed. The director reads the script and develops ideas about the scenery. Depending on the director, ideas about the scenery may vary considerably. The ideas may be few and vague, or they may include an exact picture of what the scenery should look like. Frequently they are somewhere between these two extremes. Meanwhile, the designer has developed his or her ideas.

The director and the designer meet at a preliminary conference. Both have read the script, and they exchange ideas about the design. During these discussions the director and designer will develop and discuss questions of style, a visual concept for the production, the needs of the performers, and so on. Following this, the designer develops rough sketches, called *thumbnail sketches,* and rough plans to provide the basis for further discussions.

As the designer proceeds, he or she attempts to fill out the visual concept with sketches, drawings, models and the like. In this work the designer makes use of the following elements:

1 *Line,* the outline or silhouette of elements onstage: for example, predominantly curved lines versus sharply angular ones

2 *Mass and composition,* the balance and arrangement of elements: for example, a series of high, heavy platforms or fortress walls versus a bare stage or a stage with one tree on it

3 *Texture,* the "feel" projected by surfaces and fabrics: for example, the slickness of chrome or glass versus the roughness of brick or burlap

4 *Color,* the shadings and contrasts of color combinations

The designer will use these four elements to produce effects on the audience in conjunction with the action and other aspects of the production.

Sometimes the designer will bring the director rough sketches showing several possible ideas, each emphasizing different elements to achieve different results.

When the director and the designer have decided on an idea and a rough design they like, the designer will make a more complete sketch, usually in color, called a *rendering.* If the director approves of this, the designer will make a three-dimensional, small-scale *model* which the director can use to help stage the show. There are two types of models. One shows only the location of the platform and walls, with perhaps some light detail drawn in, and it is usually white in color. The other is a complete finished model: everything is duplicated as fully as possible, including color and perhaps moldings and texture. An example is the model by Tony Walton (1934–   ) on page 343. In developing his or her designs, the scene designer is attempting to fulfill the objectives discussed previously, both aesthetic and practical.

Once a rendering or model is complete and has been approved, it is turned over to the technical director of the production. The technical director is also given the necessary ground plans and blueprints. Together with the building and paint crews, the technical director then sees that the scenery is built, painted, and installed onstage.

The Scene Designer's Collaborators

As in every element of theater, there is a collaborative aspect to scene design. It requires a number of important people in addition to the scene designer to create the scenic effects of any theater production.

First, there may be people who help the scene designer draw the architectural plans for platforms, ramps, flats, and other scenery. These require exact measurements that conform to the stage space and the proscenium opening if it is a proscenium stage. They must be drawn precisely to scale in the manner of a blueprint used by an architect and engineer in constructing a building.

Next, scenic construction requires a staff of stage carpenters, people who understand materials and methods of construction, in order to build the platforms, set pieces, flats, and other elements of scenery.

After the scenery is built, the scene artists must paint it. This requires both talent and technique: to create, for instance, the feeling of rare old wood in a library, or of bricks, or of a glossy, elegant surface in an expensive living room. Along with the painters, there are people who

THE TOTAL ENVIRONMENT.
In creating a setting for Shakespeare's Romeo and Juliet *at the Old Globe Theater in San Diego, the designer Steven Rubin provided a series of levels, platforms, arches, steps, and a bridge. In this atmosphere, which sets the tone for the play, the entire production can unfold and be embraced.*

must find fabric for draperies, slipcovers for furniture, and other items that "dress" the stage set.

When the time comes for technical rehearsals, dress rehearsals, and the actual performances after the official opening, a production requires stagehands and a stage manager to coordinate scene changes, to actually remove and replace both scenery and furniture, and to see that each setting is proper and has been put in place quickly.

Designing a Total Environment

Sometimes the designer goes beyond designing the scenery and special effects and designs the entire theater space, rearranging the seating for spectators and determining the relationship of the stage area to the audience. For instance, in an open space such as a gymnasium or warehouse, a designer will build an entire theater, including the seats or stands for the audience and the designated acting areas. In this case, the designer considers the size and shape of the space, the texture and nature of the building materials, the atmosphere of the space, and the needs of the play itself. These conditions apply in the case of multifocus theater as well. A recent version of an overall environmental design is the set for the musical *Cats,* in which the entire theater was transformed into a junkyard with objects such as automobile tires and toothpaste tubes constructed three or four times life-size to approximate the way they would appear to a cat.

In this chapter we have examined the work of the scene designer. Next, in Chapter 18, we turn to someone whose work is closely related: the costume designer.

✳ SUMMARY ✳

1 We encounter forms of scene design in everyday life: in the carefully planned decor of a restaurant or hotel lobby, for instance.

2 Scene design for the stage differs from interior decorating in that it creates an environment and an atmosphere which are not filled until occupied by performers.

3 In addition to creating an environment, the scene designer has the following objectives: set tone and style, distinguish realism from non-realism, establish time and place, develop a design concept, provide a central design metaphor, coordinate with other elements, and deal with practical considerations.

4 In practical terms the scene designer must deal with the limits of the stage space and the offstage area. For example, ramps must not be inclined too steeply, and platforms must provide an adequate playing area for the performers. In short, the stage designer must know the practical considerations of stage usage and stage carpentry, as well as the materials available, in order to achieve desired effects.

5 In theatrical productions that stress visual elements over the play or the acting, the scene design must constantly engage and entrance the spectator.

6 Special effects are those elements of scenery, lighting, costumes, props, or sound that appear miraculous or highly unusual. They require technical expertise to develop properly.

7 The scene designer works closely with the director and other designers and creates a series of drawings (sketches and renderings) and models of what the final stage picture will look like.

8 In dealing with created, or found, space, the designer must plan the entire environment: the audience area as well as the stage area.

✳ TOPICS FOR DISCUSSION ✳

1 At the end of Chapter 16, you were asked to assess created or "found" stage spaces in terms of artistic and practical considerations and to consider the implications for practicality versus aesthetics in theater. In what ways does the discussion of practical and aesthetic aspects of stage design in the present chapter deepen your understanding of this issue?

2 If practical and aesthetic demands for stage design are in conflict, would it seem best to *(a)* give practical considerations priority, *(b)* give artistic considerations priority, or *(c)* compromise? What would be the advantages and disadvantages of each option? Are any other options possible?

3 As noted in the chapter, a stage set requires selectivity and editing: a room onstage will resemble, but not duplicate, its real-life counterpart. Suppose that a college course in theater, like the one you are now taking, became the subject of a play and that the set represented a classroom or lecture room like the one you are now in. How might the stage set differ from the actual room? What might be omitted? What might be retained? What might be retained, but in altered form?

4 Robert Edmond Jones suggests that an empty stage set has a sense of tension because the performer is lacking—and that creating this suspense is at the heart of stage designing. Defend or attack the following comment on Jones's view: "If Jones were correct, the tension would be resolved as soon as an actor or actress entered the set, and we would have to say that at this point the function of stage design has been fulfilled. Obviously, this is not the case, since a stage design functions throughout a performance. Therefore, Jones's analysis must be incomplete."

5 *Mother Courage* is a play that covers many years and takes place in numerous locations. How would you design the scenery and utilize the stage space so that the action could move quickly through time and from place to place? Suggest several approaches to solving this problem.

18

STAGE
COSTUMES

STAGE COSTUMES: AESTHETIC, SYMBOLIC, AND ALSO PRACTICAL.
Costumes, in addition to being stylish and beautiful, can also convey a wealth of information about a character. This costume, designed by Susan Hirschfeld, shows the effete prince of Arragon in a production of The Merchant of Venice *by the Shakespeare Theater at the Folger Library in Washington, D.C. The costume is elaborate and filled with a wealth of detail; it also suggests that this is a character overly fond of himself who puts great store in the way he dresses and looks. The actor is Philip Goodwin.*

Of the various visual elements in theater, the most personal are costumes, because they are actually worn by the performers themselves. Closely related to costumes are other elements or accessories worn by performers such as makeup, hairstyles, masks, and personal items like bracelets and necklaces. Visually, the performer and the costume are perceived as one; they merge into a single image onstage. At the same time, costumes have a value of their own, adding color, shape, texture, and symbolism to the overall effect that is created onstage.

✳ COSTUMES IN EVERYDAY LIFE ✳

Aside from theater, most people think of costumes in terms of the outfits people wear in a holiday parade or at a masquerade ball, or in a pageant with historical figures, such as Queen Elizabeth, Dolly Madison, or George Washington. As with other aspects of theater, however, costumes play a significant role in daily life. People wear clothes not only for comfort but for the information they want to give others about themselves. If we look around us, we are surrounded by the costumes of daily life: the formal, subdued uniform of a police officer; the sparkling outfits of a marching band at a football game; sports gear such as hockey and baseball uniforms; the cap and gown for graduation; a priest's cassock; the dresses worn by bridesmaids at a formal wedding; and brightly colored bathing suits at a swimming pool.

In Chapter 2, we examined the power of symbols. Nowhere is this power more manifest than in clothes and personal adornments. Primitive people put on animal skins to give themselves the characteristics of an animal—ferocity or courage, for instance. Feathers and elaborate headdresses were worn to accentuate height; bracelets and belts with charms were worn as sources of power.

Today we still wear clothes to symbolize different qualities in society. A young person might wear informal clothes as a statement of independence from his or her parents. Adults, on the other hand, might wear conventional clothes in order not to stand out in a crowd or be criticized by friends. How one appears to one's peers or to those in an outside group is a paramount issue with many people, and this is especially noticeable in styles of dress.

Frequently we judge others by their appearance, particularly when we first meet them. If we see a man in a dark-blue pinstripe suit with a tie and vest, we assume that he is middle-class or upper-middle-class; we judge him to be conservative, and probably a banker or a lawyer. Beyond that, we will very probably make assumptions about his politics, his family life, his social attitudes, and in fact his whole psychological profile.

A good example of a symbolic outfit is a judge's robe. The black color of the robe suggests seriousness and dignity; also, the robe is draped from the shoulders straight to the ground, covering the whole person, thereby wrapping the person in the importance and presumed impartiality of the office. In our minds, the robe of a judge invests the wearer with authority and wisdom; and when we see someone in the judicial robe, we automatically accept that image. Although individual judges may be foolish or corrupt, it is considered important in our society for the *institution* of the judiciary to be just and incorrupt, and a judge's robe is an important factor in reinforcing that concept.

Clothes have always signaled a number of things regarding the wearer, including the following:

Position and status

Sex

Occupation

Relative flamboyance or modesty

Degree of independence or regimentation

Whether one is dressed for work or leisure, for a routine event or a special occasion

The moment we see the clothing people are wearing, we receive a great many messages and impressions about them; we instantaneously relate those messages to past experience and to our preconceptions; and we form judgments, including value judgments. Even if we have never before laid eyes on someone, we feel we know a great deal when we first see the clothes that he or she wears.

✳ COSTUMES FOR THE STAGE ✳

In the theater, clothes send us signals similar to those in everyday life; but, as with other elements of theater, there are significant differences between the costumes of everyday life and those in the theater. Stage costumes communicate the same information as ordinary clothes with regard to sex, position, and occupation; but onstage this information is magnified because every element in theater is in the spotlight. Also, on the stage, costumes must meet other requirements not normally expected in everyday life. These requirements will be clearer after we look at the objectives of costume design.

Objectives of Costume Design

Stage costumes should meet the following seven requirements:

1   Help establish the tone and style of a production
2   Indicate the historical period of a play and the locale in which it occurs
3   Indicate the nature of individual characters or groups in a play: their stations in life; their occupations; their personalities
4   Show the relationships among characters: separating major characters from minor ones; contrasting one group with another
5   Where appropriate, symbolically convey the significance of individual characters or the theme of the play
6   Meet the needs of individual performers, making it possible for an actor or actress to move freely in a costume, perhaps to dance or engage in a sword fight, and when required, to change quickly from one costume to another
7   Be consistent with the production as a whole, especially other visual elements

Let's now consider each of these objectives in turn.

INDICATING TONE AND STYLE   Along with scenery and lighting, costumes should inform the audience about the style of a play. For a production taking place in outer space, for instance, the costumes would be futuristic. For a Restoration comedy, the costumes would be quite elegant, with lace at the men's collars and cuffs and elaborate gowns for the women. For a tragedy, the clothes would be somber and dignified; seeing them, the audience would know immediately that the play itself was somber and its tone likely to be serious.

For the musical *Cats*, a fantasy in which performers impersonate a variety of cats, the costume designer John Napier created outfits made of fur and other materials that simulate the coat of a cat. He also put whiskers and other ornamentation on the faces and heads of the performers to give them a feline appearance. For another musical, *The Phantom of the Opera*, which is set in Paris in 1911, the designer Maria Bjornson fashioned romantic period outfits: the men in top hats with canes and capes, the women in long dresses with full skirts and elaborate hats and outer coats. For a straight play, *The Heidi Chronicles* by Wendy Wasserstein (1950–), which takes place in the United States in the 20 years between 1968 and 1988 and is concerned with what happens to its heroine and to feminism during that period, the designer Jennifer Von Mayrhauser created clothes that reflect the lifestyles of men and women in that era—street clothes, informal clothes, modern clothes.

COSTUMES INDICATE TONE AND STYLE.
Jennifer von Mayrhauser's costumes for The Heidi Chronicles *convey the modern, realistic, informal style and tone of the production called for by Wendy Wasserstein's play. Costumes, along with other elements, can tell us whether a play is realistic or nonrealistic, historical or modern, formal or informal.*

INDICATING PERIOD AND LOCALE Costumes indicate the period and location of a play: whether it is historical or modern, set in a foreign country or the United States, and so on. A play might take place in ancient Egypt, in Spain in the seventeenth century, or in modern Africa. Costumes should tell us when and where the action occurs.

Sometimes—as we have already seen—the costume designer and the director decide to shift the period of a play. For example, *Hamlet* might be performed in modern dress; there have been productions in which Hamlet was in a tuxedo and Gertrude in a long evening dress. Obviously such a shift comes as a shock to the audience, and it is up to the costume designer to assist the audience in adjusting to it.

For most historical plays, the director and the costume designer have a range of choices, depending on the directorial concept. For Shakespeare's *Julius Caesar*, the costumes could indicate the ancient Roman period when Caesar actually lived; they would then include togas and Roman soldiers' helmets. Or the costumes could feature Elizabethan dress; in Shakespeare's day costumes were heightened versions of the English clothes of the time, regardless of the period in which the play was set. Or the designer could create costumes for an entirely different period, including the modern. In any case, the historical period should be clearly indicated in the costumes.

COSTUMES IDENTIFY PERIOD AND STATION IN LIFE.
The Three Musketeers, *a drama based on the Dumas novel, is set in France in the period of Louis XIII. The costumes in this production at the Stratford Festival in Ontario, Canada, indicate very clearly the historical period and also show that the characters in the play are members of royalty, the clergy, the nobility, and so forth. The designer of the production was Christina Poddubiuk.*

IDENTIFYING STATUS AND PERSONALITY   As clothes do in everyday life, costumes can tell us whether people are from the aristocracy or the working class, whether they are blue-collar workers or professionals. But in the theater, these signals must be clear and unmistakable. For example, a woman in a long white coat could be a doctor, a laboratory technician, or a hairdresser. The costume onstage must indicate the exact occupation—by giving the doctor a stethoscope, for instance.

Costumes also tell us about the personalities of characters: a flamboyant person will be dressed in flashy colors; a shy, retiring person will wear subdued clothes. Costumes also indicate age. This is particularly helpful when an older actor is playing a young person, or vice versa. The young person can wear padding or a beard, for example.

SHOWING RELATIONSHIPS AMONG CHARACTERS   Individuals and characters can be set apart by the way they are costumed. Major characters, for example, will be dressed differently from minor characters. Frequently the costume designer will point to the major characters in a play by dressing them in distinctive colors—in sharp contrast to other characters. Consider, for example, Shaw's *Saint Joan,* a play about Joan of Arc. Obviously, Joan should stand out from the soldiers surrounding her. Therefore, her costume might be bright blue while theirs are steel-gray. Her costume signals her importance. In another play of Shaw's, *Caesar and Cleopatra,* Cleopatra should stand out from her servants and soldiers. Although dressed like them in an Egyptian costume, she should be clothed in brighter colors and wear a more elegant outfit.

Costumes underline important group divisions. In *Romeo and Juliet*, the Montagues wear costumes of one color, and the Capulets, another. In a modern counterpart of *Romeo and Juliet*, the musical *West Side Story*, the two gangs of young men are dressed in contrasting colors: the Jets might be in various shades of pink, purple, and lavender, and the Sharks in shades of green, yellow, and lemon.

CREATING SYMBOLIC AND NONHUMAN CHARACTERS   In many plays, special costumes, denoting abstract ideas or giving shape to fantastic creatures, are called for. Here the costume designer must develop an outfit which carries with it the imaginative and symbolic qualities required. How does one clothe the witches in *Macbeth* or the ghost of Banquo, for instance? A way must be found to symbolize the qualities they represent. To illustrate how costumes can suggest ideas or characteristics, a costume of animal skins can symbolize bestiality, and a costume of feathers can indicate a birdlike quality, while a costume made of a metallic material can suggest a hard and mechanical quality.

COSTUMES IDENTIFY SOCIAL AND FINANCIAL STATUS.
Among other functions, costumes should tell us the time period in which a play occurs and the social and occupational status of the characters. In this production of Churchill's Serious Money *at the Berkeley Repertory Theater, the characters are dressed in the business attire that signifies their high-pressure lives in the financial world. The costumes, designed by Dunya Ramicova, also tell us that it is today's world, and not that of fifty or a hundred years ago.*

(Ken Friedman)

THE TRANSFORMING POWER OF COSTUMES.

By means of costumes, performers can become birds, animals, and other exotic creatures. Many tribal ceremonies and rituals include masks and costumes that transform people into animals. A modern counterpart is found in the musical Cats. *By means of whiskers, fur, feathers, and makeup, human performers become feline creatures.*

A good example of a costume representing an animal is the outfit worn by the actors playing the part of horses in the play *Equus* by Peter Shaffer (1926–   ). They wore headpieces that looked like wire shaped in the outlines of a horse's head and thick footgear suggesting horses' hooves.

In *Peer Gynt* by Ibsen, the main character, Peer, meets a supernatural being in the mountains. It is called "the Boyg" and is a symbolic presence urging Peer to compromise in life and go "roundabout." A costume designer might fashion for the Boyg a soft, round outfit with no sharp outlines or edges—a large blob, like a sack of potatoes—to indicate its indecisive, amorphous quality.

A modern play which calls for exaggerated as well as symbolic costumes is *The Balcony*, by the French playwright Jean Genet. The play is set in a house of prostitution where ordinary men act out their fantasies: one pretends to be a general, another a bishop, and a third a judge. They dress in exaggerated costumes, looking almost like caricatures of the originals, with platform shoes, shoulder pads wider than their own shoulders, and high headpieces.

The women who serve them also dress fantastically. The woman serving the general is dressed as a horse, and the costume designer has the task of making a costume for her which will bring out her attractiveness as a person but still give her a horse's tail and mane.

MEETING PERFORMERS' NEEDS   Virtually every aspect of theater has practical as well as aesthetic requirements, and costume design is no exception. No matter how attractive or how symbolic, stage costumes must work for the performers. A long, flowing gown may look beautiful; but if it is too long and the actress wearing it trips every time she walks down a flight of steps, the designer has overlooked an important practical consideration. If actors are required to duel or engage in hand-to-hand combat, their costumes must stand up to this wear and tear, and their arms and legs must have freedom of movement and not be bound by the costume. If performers are to dance, they must be able to turn, leap, and move freely.

Quick costume changes are frequently called for in the theater. In the musical *Gypsy*, when at the end an emerging young star sings "Let Me Entertain You," she is required to go offstage between choruses and reappear a few seconds later in another costume. The actress goes through three or four dazzling costume changes in seconds, to the astonishment of the audience. The costumes must be made so that the actress, with the help of dressers offstage, can rapidly shed one outfit and get into another. Tearaway seams and special fasteners are used so that one costume can be ripped off and another quickly put on.

Unlike scenery, which stays in place until it is moved, a costume is constantly in motion; it moves as the performer moves. This provides an opportunity for the designer to develop grace and rhythm in the way a costume looks as it moves across the stage, but with that goes a great responsibility to make the costume workable for the performer.

(Martha Swope)

EXAGGERATED COSTUMES.
For the musical revue Black and Blue, *the designers Claudio Segovia and Hector Orezzoli fashioned a shimmering white gown with a voluminous skirt for the singer Carrie Smith. When she was lifted into the air on a swing, the skirt billowed out many feet in all directions, making for an arresting visual image.*

At times it is important for the costume designer to work closely with individual performers. Actresses and actors must know how to use the accessories and costumes provided for them. As an example, the character of Sparkish in the Restoration comedy *The Country Wife* by Wycherley is an outrageous fop. Sparkish wears a fancy wig, a hat, and petticoat breeches. He uses a handkerchief, a snuffbox, and other hand accessories. In creating a costume for Sparkish, the designer must provide an outfit that not only is correct for the style of the production but suits the physique and appearance of the individual actor. If the actor has never worn a wig or breeches of this kind and has never worked with a handkerchief—which he keeps in the cuff of his jacket—or with a snuffbox, he must learn to use these items, working closely with both the director and the costume designer.

MAINTAINING CONSISTENCY   Finally, costumes must be consistent with the entire production—especially with the various other visual elements. A realistic production set in the home of everyday people calls for down-to-earth costumes. A highly stylized production requires costumes designed with flair and imagination.

The Costume Designer

THE COSTUME DESIGNER'S RESPONSIBILITIES   The person putting into effect the ideas just discussed is the costume designer. Every production requires someone who takes responsibility for the costumes. This is true whether the costumes are *pulled* or *built*. *Pulling* is a term used when costumes are rented and the costume designer goes to a costume house and selects the costumes that are appropriate for the production. The designer must already know about period, style, and the other matters discussed above. He or she must also have the measurements of all the performers for whom costumes are to be pulled.

When costumes are *built*, they are created in a costume shop under the supervision of the designer. They must be sewn, fitted, and completed with all kinds of accessories such as spangles, brocade, piping, or whatever is appropriate.

Whether costumes are pulled from a rental house or cut and sewn from scratch, the costume designer determines how they will look. Obviously, this requires both training and talent.

The costume designer should begin with a thorough knowledge of the play: its subject matter, period, style, and point of view. The costume designer must also have an intimate knowledge of the individual characters in the play. The designer must know each character's personality, idiosyncrasies, relative importance to the play, relationship to other characters, and symbolic value. The designer must be aware, too, of the physical demands of each role: what is called for in terms of

362

sitting, moving from level to level, dancing, falling down, fighting, and so on. Finally, the designer must become thoroughly acquainted with the characteristics of the performers themselves in order to create costumes accommodating their physiques and movement patterns.

THE COSTUME DESIGNER'S RESOURCES   Among the elements a costume designer works with are: (1) line, shape, and silhouette; (2) color; (3) fabric; and (4) accessories.

Line   Of prime importance is the cut or *line* of the clothes. Do the lines of an outfit flow, or are they sharp and jagged? Do the clothes follow the lines of the body, or is there some element of exaggeration, such as shoulder pads for men or a bustle at the back of a woman's dress? The outline or silhouette of a costume has always been significant. There is a strong visual contrast, for instance, between the line of an Egyptian woman's garment, flowing smoothly from shoulder to the floor, and that of an empire gown of the early nineteenth century in France, which featured a horizontal line high above the waist, just below the breasts, with a line flowing from below the bosom to the feet. The silhouettes of these two styles would stand in marked contrast to a third design: a woman's dress in the United States of the early 1930s, a short outfit with a prominent belt or sash cutting horizontally across the hips.

Undergarments are an aspect of costume design often overlooked by

THE IMPORTANCE OF LINE IN COSTUME.
These three outfits suggest the variety of effects achieved by altering the outline or silhouette of a costume. The Egyptian dress has no horizontal lines but falls straight from the shoulders to the floor. The Empire style— popular in Europe in the early nineteenth century—is broken by a strong horizontal line just below the bosom, and the flapper dress from the 1920s has a much lower horizontal line across the hips. Not only various outlines but different fabrics and colors determine the appearance of costumes.

363

THE COSTUME DESIGNER AT WORK.

For the Broadway musical Grand Hotel, *the costume designer Santo Loquasto prepared sketches for each costume, such as the ones shown above left for the character Raffaela, played by Karen Akers. The costume designer also indicates the type of fabric used and any accessories—hats, capes, and so forth. After sketches are made, the designer's collaborators sew and alter the costumes to fit the performers. In some cases, costumes are purchased or rented and then altered. For a Broadway production like* Grand Hotel, *the costumes will be created especially for that show. Above right is Ms. Akers in a finished costume, based on one of those shown in the sketch by Mr. Loquasto.*

audience members. For women's costumes these may consist of hoop skirts that make ball gowns stand out from the body, bustles that exaggerate the lines in the rear, and corsets. Corsets can make a tremendous difference in the posture and appearance of women. For example, in some cases they cause women to stand very straight. But in the first decade of the twentieth century, women in society often bent forward because they wore a curved corset that forced them to thrust their shoulders and upper body forward. A costume designer will be aware of the importance of undergarments and will use them to create the proper silhouette, not only in the costume itself but in the bearing and movement of performers.

Color A second important resource for costume designers is *color.* Earlier we saw that the leading characters can be dressed in a color which contrasts with the colors worn by other characters and that the characters from one family can be dressed in a different color from those in a rival family. Color also suggests mood: bright, warm colors for a happy mood, and dark, somber colors for a more serious mood. Beyond these applications, however, color can indicate changes in character and changes in mood. Near the beginning of Eugene O'Neill's *Mourning Becomes Electra,* General Manon, who has recently returned from the Civil War, dies, and his wife and daughter wear dark mourning clothes. Lavinia, the daughter, knows that her mother had something to do with her father's death, and she and her brother conspire to murder the mother. Once they have done so, Lavinia feels a great sense of release. She adopts characteristics of her mother, and as an important symbol of this transformation, she puts on brightly colored clothes in the same colors her mother had worn before.

Fabric Fabric is a third tool of the costume designer. In one sense, it is the medium of the costume designer, for it is in the fabric that the silhouette and color are displayed. And just as important as those qualities is the texture and bulk of the fabric. What is its reflective quality? Does it have a smoothness or sheen that reflects light? Or is it rough so that it absorbs light? How does it drape on people? Does it fall lightly to the floor and outline physical features, or does it hide them? Does it wrinkle naturally, or is it smooth? Beyond its inherent qualities, fabric has symbolic values. Burlap, for example, or other roughly textured cloth suggests people of the earth or of modest means. Silks and satins suggest elegance, refinement, and perhaps even royalty.

Accessories Ornamentation and accessories can be utilized, too. Fringe, lace, ruffles, feathers, belts, beads, bracelets, earrings—all these add to the attractiveness and individuality of a costume. Also, walking sticks, parasols, purses, and other items carried or worn by people can give distinction and definition to an outfit.

Using the combined resources of line, color, fabric, and accessories, the costume designer arrives at individual outfits which tell us a great deal about the characters who wear them and convey important visual signals about the style and meaning of the play as a whole.

THE COSTUME DESIGNER'S COLLABORATORS   Once again, it is important to recognize that a number of collaborators aid in the process. As in other areas, the costume designer works closely with the people who sew and make the costumes, with those who fit them, and with those who care for them and maintain them throughout the run of a show. When people maintain a collection of period and other costumes, people must make certain that they are kept in first-class condition and that they are arranged so that they can be easily located.

❊ RELATED ELEMENTS ❊

Makeup

Related to costume is *makeup*—the application of cosmetics (paints, powders, and rouges) to the face and body. In terms of age and the special facial features associated with ethnic origins, a key function of makeup is to help the performer personify and embody the character he or she is playing. Makeup used to be more popular in the theater than it is today. In a modern small theater, performers playing realistic parts will often go without makeup of any consequence. But makeup has a long and important history in the theater. Sometimes it is a necessity, a good example being makeup to highlight facial features which would not otherwise be visible in a large theater. Even in a smaller theater, bright lights tend to wash out cheekbones, eyebrows, and so on.

Use of makeup is often essential because the age of a character differs from that of the performer. Suppose that a 19-year-old performer is playing the part of a 60-year-old character. Through the use of makeup—by putting a little gray in the hair or simulating wrinkles on the face—the appropriate age can be suggested. Another situation calling for makeup to indicate age is a play in which the characters grow older during the course of the action. In the musical *I Do, I Do,* based on the play *The Fourposter,* a husband and wife are shown in scenes covering many years in their married life, from the time when they are first married until they are quite old. In order to convey the passing years and their advancing ages, the actress and actor playing the wife and husband must use makeup extensively. For fantastic or other nonrealistic creatures makeup is a necessity too.

Asian theater frequently relies on heavy makeup. For instance, the Japanese kabuki, a highly stylized type of theater, employs completely nonrealistic makeup. The main characters must apply a base of white

(Tadishi Kimura/Japan Foundation)

MAKEUP: CREATING A NEW FACE.
Makeup is frequently used to highlight facial features that would be washed out by bright stage lights, or to change the appearance of a performer—to make a young person look older, for instance. At other times, makeup is used to create a kind of mask of the face. This is true in the kabuki theater of Japan, where the colors and lines on the face have symbolic significance. In this picture, we see a kabuki actor applying his elaborate makeup.

covering the entire face, over which bold patterns of red, blue, black, and brown are painted. The colors and patterns are symbolic of the character. In Chinese theater, too, the colors of makeup are symbolic: all white suggests treachery; black means fierce integrity; red means loyalty; green indicates demons; yellow stands for hidden cunning; and so forth.

Douglas Turner Ward (1930–   ), a black playwright, wrote *Day of Absence* to be performed by black actors playing in whiteface. The implications of this effect are many, not the least being the reversal of the old minstrel performances in which white actors wore blackface. Ward was not the first to put black actors in whiteface; Genet had part of the cast of his play *The Blacks* wear white masks.

When makeup is used, the face becomes almost like a canvas for a painting. The features of the face may be heightened or exaggerated; or symbolic aspects of the human face may be emphasized. In either case, makeup serves as an additional tool for the performer in creating an image of the character.

Hairstyles and Wigs

Closely related to makeup are *hairstyles.* In certain periods men have worn wigs: the time of the American Revolution is a good example. In England, judges wear wigs to this day.

For women, hairstyles can denote period and social class. In the middle of the nineteenth century, for example, women often wore ringlets like Scarlett O'Hara's in the film *Gone with the Wind*. A few decades later, in the late 1800s, women wore their hair piled on top of their

(Ohio State University)

WIGS AND HAIRSTYLES.
The way hair is worn indicates to the audience the social status and other facts about a character. Hairstyles also provide information about the time and period when a play takes place. Here we see Helen Murray as Celimene and Robert Moore as Clitandre in an Ohio State University production of Molière's The Misanthrope. *The play is set in seventeenth-century France, when men wore such wigs.*

heads in a pompadour. This was referred to as the *Gibson girl look.* In the 1920s, women wore their hair marcelled in waves, sometimes slicked down close to the head. In the modern period, women wear their hair in more natural styles; but again there is a tremendous variety. Some women wear short, curly hair; others wear long hair, perhaps even down to the waist.

Masks

Masks seem to be as old as theater, having been used in ancient Greek theater and in the drama developed by primitive tribes. In one sense, the mask is an extension of the performer—a face on top of a face. There are several ways to look at masks: they remind us, first of all, that we are in the theater, that the act going on before our eyes is not real in a literal sense but is rather a symbolic or an artistic presentation. For another thing, masks allow the face to be frozen in one expression: a look of horror, perhaps, which we see throughout a production. Masks can also make the face larger than life, and they can create stereotypes, similar to stock characters (see Chapter 12) in which one particular feature—for example, cunning or haughtiness—is emphasized to the exclusion of everything else.

There are other symbolic possibilities with the use of masks. In his play *The Great God Brown*, Eugene O'Neill calls for the actors to hold masks in front of their faces. When the masks are in place, the characters

MASKS: AN ANCIENT
THEATRICAL DEVICE.

Masks have been used in theater almost from its beginning. They can change the appearance of a performer, make the face and head larger than life, freeze the face into a fixed expression, and take on symbolic value. Here we see masks employed in three productions: (above left) Robert Sicular used a mask while playing a character in an adaptation of Dickens's Hard Times *at the South Coast Repertory Theater in Costa Mesa, California; (above right) Picasso-like masks were worn by characters in a play about Picasso and Gertrude Stein called* She Always Said, Pablo *at the Goodman Theater in Chicago; and (left) in O'Neill's* The Great God Brown, *the playwright called for masks which the characters took off when they expressed their inner thoughts, but wore when they adopted a public persona.*

CHAPTER 18 • STAGE COSTUMES

present a facade to the public, withholding their true characters. When the masks are down, the characters reveal how they feel inside. In *Motel*, a short play and part of a trilogy called *America Hurrah!* by Jean-Claude van Itallie, the actors—a man, a woman, and a woman motel keeper—wear enlarged papier-mâché heads and arms, giving the appearance of huge, somewhat grotesque dolls. The play deals with violence and loss of humanity in American life; and these impersonal, masklike figures underline the theme.

✳ COORDINATION OF THE WHOLE ✳

Costumes, makeup, hairstyles, and masks must be integrated with other aspects of a production. First, they have a close relationship with the performers and the parts they play. Each is highly personal in nature, being literally attached to a performer and moving when the performer moves. They are so much a part of the performers that we sometimes lose sight of them as separate entities. Actors and actresses, however, would have great difficulty in creating a part without the proper costume, and in some cases without makeup and a mask as well. They help the performer define his or her role.

On another level, costumes, makeup, and masks are essential in carrying out a point of view in a production. Masks, for instance, are clearly nonrealistic and signal to the audience that the character wearing the mask and the play itself are likely to be nonrealistic too. Costumes suggest whether a play is a comedy or a serious play, a wild farce or a stark tragedy.

To be effective in this respect, costumes must be coordinated with scenery and lighting. The wrong kind of lighting can wash out or discolor costumes and makeup. It would be self-defeating, too, if scenery were in one mood or style and the costumes in a different one. Ideally, these elements should support and reinforce one another, and spectators should be aware of how essential it is for them to work together. Visually, if something looks out of place in a production, lack of coordination among these elements might be the reason.

In Chapter 18 we have looked at costume design, and in Chapter 17, at scene design. Before turning to light and sound design, it is in order to mention that the designers do not work in isolation. We have suggested previously that the director confers with designers, but it is important to note too that the designers themselves consult frequently with one another. In the production process there are regular meetings between two or more designers to coordinate their efforts—not only on such matters as colors and style but also regarding cues and the way various design elements work together. In Chapter 19 we turn to a third visual element, lighting, and to the use of sound in the theater.

✳ SUMMARY ✳

1   The clothes we wear in daily life are a form of costume. They indicate station in life, occupation, and a sense of formality or informality.

2   On the stage, costumes similarly convey information about the people wearing them; more than that, they are consciously chosen and designed to provide the audience with important information.

3   The objectives of costume design are to set tone and style, indicate time and place, characterize individuals and groups, underline personal relationships, create symbolic outfits when appropriate, meet the practical needs of performers, and coordinate with the total production.

4   The designer works with the following elements: line and shape, color, fabric, and accessories.

5   Makeup and hairstyles are also important to the appearance of the performers and are part of the designer's concern.

6   Where called for, masks, too, are under the direction of the costume designer.

✳ TOPICS FOR DISCUSSION ✳

1   When a period play is performed in modern dress, it is presumably for artistic reasons—that is, to serve the directorial concept. But it is also true that modern dress is easier, and cheaper, to provide than, say, doublets and hose, suits of armor, or crinolines, brocades, lace, and powdered wigs. What specific qualities would a modern-dress production need to have to convince you that it was based on aesthetic considerations rather than expediency?

2   In the chapter, four resources of the costume designer are described—line, color, fabric, and accessories. Some people would argue that line is the most important of these. Do you agree that it is? If not, which element would you say is most important?

3   The chapter notes that makeup used to be more popular in the theater than it is now. What factors do you think might have contributed to this decline?

4   It is noted in the chapter that costumes help actors and actresses define their roles. Should costumes serve this function? Defend one of the following answers: (a) "Yes; performers should define their roles with the help of costumes, because they should use all the resources the theater offers." (b) "No; performers should be able to define their roles using only their own skill, training, talent, background, and so on."

19

LIGHTING AND SOUND

THE POWERFUL EFFECTS OF STAGE LIGHTING.
Lighting is one of the most versatile and potent visual resources in the theater. It can create a wide range of effects, including the one shown here from a production of Shakespeare's Pericles *at the Stratford Festival in Ontario, Canada. In the lighting design of Harry Frehner, Geraint Wyn Davies as Pericles is surrounded by light which forms a billowing, evanescent background for the character.*

Like scenery, costumes, and other elements of theater, stage lighting and sound have counterparts in everyday life. For example, the basic function of lighting is illumination—to allow people to see at night and indoors. But there are many theatrical uses of light in daily life. Advertising signs feature neon lights or brightly colored bulbs. Restaurants feature soft lights and candles. In homes, people put spotlights on special parts of the room, such as a dining room table. Also, in homes people frequently use a rheostat so that they can dim the lights to create a mood.

✴ STAGE LIGHTING ✴

Lighting, the last design element incorporated in theater production from a historical point of view, is the most advanced in terms of equipment and technique. Most of these advances have occurred in the past hundred years, and before looking at theater lighting today, it will be helpful to take a short historical view of its development.

A Brief History of Stage Lighting

For the first 2,000 years of its recorded history, theater was held mostly outdoors during the day—a primary reason being the need for illumination. Sunlight, after all, is an excellent source of illumination.

Since sophisticated lighting was unavailable, playwrights used imagination—the handiest tool available—to suggest nighttime or shifts in lighting. Performers brought on torches, or a candle, as Lady Macbeth does, to indicate night. Playwrights also used language. When Shakespeare has Lorenzo in *The Merchant of Venice* say, "How sweet the moonlight sleeps upon this bank," it is not just a pretty line of poetry: it also serves to remind us that it is nighttime. The same is true of the eloquent passage when Romeo tells Juliet that he must leave because dawn is breaking.

> Look, love, what envious streaks
> Do lace the severing clouds in yonder East:
> Night's candles are burnt out, and jocund day
> Stands tiptoe on the misty mountain tops.

Around A.D. 1600, theater began to move indoors. Candles and oil lamps were used for illumination until 1803, when a theater in London installed gaslights. With gas, lighting became more manageable during the eighteenth and nineteenth centuries, but it remained extremely limited in its effectiveness. In addition, the open flames of gas and other lighting systems posed a constant threat of fire. Through the years there were several tragic and costly fires in theaters, both in Europe and in the United States.

In 1879 Thomas Edison invented the incandescent lamp (the electric light bulb), and the era of imaginative lighting for the theater began. Not only are incandescent lamps safe, but they can be controlled. The brightness or intensity can be increased or decreased: the same lighting instrument will produce the bright light of noonday or the dim light of dusk. Also, by putting a colored film over the light or by other means, color can be controlled.

Beyond the power and versatility of the electric light, there have been numerous other advances in controls and equipment over the past 50 years. Lighting instruments have been constantly refined to become more powerful, as well as more subtle, and to throw a more concentrated, sharply defined beam. Moreover, lighting has leant itself more successfully to miniaturization and computerization than other theater elements. After all, costumes must still be sewn individually, and scenes on canvas flats must be painted by hand. Lighting, however, has proved to be a perfect tool for advances in electronics, because it is controlled by electricity. First came resistance systems, then thyratron vacuum tubes, and after that a series of technical innovations known by such names as *magnetic amplifiers* and *silicon-controlled rectifiers.*

When applied to lighting, these inventions allowed for increasingly complex and sophisticated controls. For a large college theater production there may be upward of 100 lighting instruments hung around and above the stage; for a large Broadway musical there may be as many as 300. Each one of these instruments can be hooked up to a central computer board, and light settings—the level, direction, and color of the lighting instruments—can be stored in the computer. By pushing a single button, an operator can bring about a shift in literally dozens of instruments in a split second. The resulting flexibility and control is a remarkable tool in achieving stage effects.

Objectives and Functions of Lighting Design

Adolphe Appia (1862–1928), a Swiss scene designer, was one of the first to see the vast aesthetic or artistic possibilities of light in the theater. He wrote: "Light is to the production what music is to the score: the expressive element in opposition to the literal signs; and, like music, light can express only what belongs to the inner essence of all vision's vision." Norman Bel Geddes (1893–1958), an imaginative American designer who was a follower of Appia, put it in these words: "Good lighting adds space, depth, mood, mystery, parody, contrast, change of emotion, intimacy, fear."

Gordon Craig (1872–1966), an innovative British designer, spoke of "painting with light." The lighting designer can indeed paint with light, but far more can be done; on the deepest sensual and symbolic level, the lighting designer can convey something of the feeling, and even the substance, of the play.

PAINTING WITH LIGHT.
This scene from a production of Ibsen's Peer Gynt *at the Hartford Stage Company demonstrates the dramatic effect of light. Note the bright foreground, the spot of light in the background, and the bright whip which Richard Thomas circles in the air. The actress is Patricia Conolly, and the lighting was designed by Pat Collins.*

The following are the functions and objectives of stage lighting:

1 Providing visibility

2 Assisting in creating the mood

3 Helping to establish the time and place

4 Reinforcing the style of the production

5 Providing a focus onstage and creating visual compositions

6 Establishing a rhythm of visual movement

7 Reinforcing a central visual image

VISIBILITY On the practical side, the chief function of lighting is illumination or visibility. We must be able, first and foremost, to see the performers' faces and their actions onstage. Occasionally, lighting designers, carried away with the atmospheric possibilities of light, will make a scene so dark that we can hardly see what is happening. Mood is important, of course, but obviously seeing the performers is even more important. At times the script calls for the lights to dim—in a suspense play, for instance, when the lights in a haunted house go out. But these are exceptions. Ordinarily, unless you can see the actors and actresses, the lighting designer has not carried out his or her assignment.

MOOD   Light, together with scenery and costumes, can help performers create a certain mood. Rarely can lighting alone create mood. For example, if the stage is filled with blue light, it might be moonlight—bright and romantic—but it could also be a cold, dark, evil situation. The action, scenery, and words, together with light, tell exactly what the mood is. A happy, carefree play calls for bright, warm colors, such as yellows, oranges, and pinks. A more somber piece will lean toward blues, blue-greens, and muted tones.

LIGHTING CREATES MOOD.
In this scene from The Dawns Are Quiet Here, *produced at the McCarter Theater in Princeton, New Jersey, light catches the smoke and mist to create a mysterious effect and establish a somber mood. Light also hits the faces and hands of the performers at a strong angle, clearly defining them, as well as the poles they hold.*

(Cliff Moore)

377

LIGHTING ISOLATES CHARACTERS AND PRODUCES UNUSUAL EFFECTS.

In the three scenes shown on these pages, lighting focuses on key characters and also produces unique visual effects. The first (above) is a production of Kafka's Metamorphosis *in which light sets apart the characters in the center and on the right, while casting deep, elongated shadows in the background. The second (left), from a production of* Crime and Punishment *at the Arena Stage in Washington, isolates one character and also illuminates the figure behind him—all else is in darkness. The third (opposite page), from a production of Martha Clarke's* The Hunger Artist, *shows cross-lighting establishing a sculptural effect on the man, while casting a strong glow of light on the boy lying down.*

(Tom Brazil)

TIME AND PLACE By its color, shade, and intensity, lighting can suggest the time of day, giving us the pale light of dawn, the bright light of midday, the vivid colors of sunset, or the muted light of evening. Lighting can also indicate the season of the year, because the sun strikes objects at a very different angle in winter than in summer. Lighting can also suggest place, by showing indoor or outdoor light.

STYLE In terms of style, lighting can indicate whether a play is realistic or nonrealistic. In a realistic play, the lighting will simulate the effect of ordinary sources—table lamps and outside sunlight. In a nonrealistic production, the designer can be more imaginative: shafts of light can cut through the dark, sculpturing performers onstage; a glowing red light can envelop a scene of damnation; a ghostly green light can cast a spell over a nightmare scene.

FOCUS AND COMPOSITION In photography, the term *focus* means that the lens of a camera is adjusted so that the picture recorded on the film is sharp and clear; in theater lighting, *focus* means that beams of

CHAPTER 19 • LIGHTING AND SOUND

light are aimed at a particular area and therefore focused on that area. Focus in lighting directs our attention to one part of the stage—generally where the important action is occurring—and away from other areas. Lights should illuminate the playing area, not the scenery or some area offstage. Most stage scenery is not painted to withstand the harsh glare of direct light and will not be effective when too brightly lit. Also, if scenery is lit to the exclusion of everything else, spectators will concentrate on it rather than on the performers. Therefore, the first object of focus is to aim the light in the right place. In this regard, designers must be careful to avoid *spill*, that is, allowing light from one area to fall into an adjacent area.

Here is on example of a positive benefit of focus: on a *split stage*, with half the action on one side of the stage and half on the other, the lights can direct our attention from side to side, as they go down in one area and come up in another.

By means of focus, light can create a series of visual compositions onstage. These can vary from turning the stage into one large area to creating small, isolated areas.

RHYTHM   Since changes in light occur on a time continuum, they establish a rhythm running through the production. Abrupt, staccato changes with stark blackouts will convey one rhythm, whereas languid, slow fades and gradual cross-fades will convey another. Lighting changes are coordinated with scene changes for timing. The importance of this is recognized by directors and designers, who take great care to ensure the proper changes—"choreographing" shifts in light and scenery like dancers' movements.

REINFORCEMENT OF THE CENTRAL IMAGE   Lighting, like scenery, costume, and all other elements, must be consistent with the overall style and mood of the production. The wrong lighting can distort, or even destroy, the total effect of a play. At the same time, because lighting is both the most flexible and most atmospheric of the visual elements of theater, it can aid enormously in creating the theater experience.

Achieving the Objectives: The Lighting Designer

The person responsible for creating, installing, and setting controls for stage lighting is the lighting designer. It is important that he or she have a background in the technical and the mechanical aspects of lighting as well as a broad, creative visual imagination. The ability to translate words and actions and feelings into color, direction, and intensity comes only after much training and experience.

THE PROCESS OF LIGHTING DESIGN   Following is an example of the process a designer uses to light a show.

First, the lighting designer reads the script and begins to form some rough ideas and feelings about the play. He or she meets with the director and the scene designer to discuss visual concepts for the show. The lighting designer next receives copies of all the scenery plans from the set designer and usually consults with the costume designer to learn the shape and color of the costumes.

The lighting designer then makes a careful and complete script analysis to determine most of the lighting requirements. The designer will see one or perhaps several rehearsals to get the feel of the production, to see the exact location of various pieces of furniture and stage business, and to consult with the director about possible effects. Following this, the lighting designer draws a plan of lighting called a *light plot*. This includes the location and color of each lighting instrument. Also indicated is the kind of instrument called for and the area of the stage on which it is focused.

When lighting instruments are moved into the theater and *hung* (that is, placed on pipes and other supports), the designer supervises the focusing. During technical rehearsals, the lighting designer works with the director to establish light *cues*, that is, when lights go on and off. The designer also sets the length of time for light changes and the levels of intensity on the dimmers.

QUALITIES OF STAGE LIGHTING   When working on the design for a production, the lighting designer knows what qualities of light will achieve the objectives discussed above.

Intensity   The first quality of light is brightness, or *intensity*. Intensity can be controlled by devices called *dimmers*, which make the scene the lights illuminate brighter or darker. A dimmer is an electric or electronic device that can vary the amount of power going to the lights. This makes it possible for a scene at night to take place in very little light and a daylight scene to take place in bright light.

Color   The second quality of light is *color*. Color is a very powerful part of lighting, and theater lights can very easily be changed to one of several hundred colors by putting a colored material similar to colored cellophane (usually called a *gel*—short for *gelatin*) in slots at the front of the lighting instruments. Color is mixed so that the strong tones of one shade do not dominate, giving an unnatural appearance. The lights beamed from one side are *warm* (amber, straw, gold) and from the other side, *cool* (blue, blue-green, lavender). Warms and cools together produce depth and texture, as well as naturalness. The exception to mixing angles and colors of light would be a scene calling for special effects; we expect stark shadows and strange colors, for example, when Hamlet confronts the ghost of his father.

Direction The third quality of light that the designer can use is *direction*, that is, the way the light is placed on or near the stage so that the light comes from a particular direction. In earlier days, *footlights*—a row of lights across the front of the stage—were popular. Because the light source was below the performers, however, footlights had the disadvantage of casting ghostly shadows on their faces. Footlights also created a kind of barrier between performers and audience. With the development of more powerful, versatile lights, footlights have been eliminated. Today, most lighting hits the stage from above, coming from instruments in front of the stage and from the sides. The vertical angle of light beams is close to 45 degrees, to approximate the average angle of sunlight. Generally, too, light on an area of the stage comes from several sources: from at least two lights above a proscenium stage and from at least four above an arena stage. The lights converge from different sides to avoid the harsh shadows on the face which result when light hits only one side of the face. Once performers are properly illuminated by lights from the front and above, other lighting is added—*down lighting* from directly overhead and *backlighting* from behind—to give further dimension and depth to the figures onstage.

Form The fourth quality is the shape, or *form*, in which the light comes. Is it a single shaft of light, like a single beam of moonlight through trees or a nightclub spotlight? Or is the light in a pattern, such as the dappled light of sun through the leaves of trees in a forest? Are the edges of the light sharp, or soft and diffused? Light can be shaped by special shutters that close in at the edges—an additional tool for the designer.

Movement The last quality of light the designer can work with is *movement*. With various types of dimmers, the light can shift focus from location to location and from color to color. Also, time of day, sunsets, and so on, can help provide information for the audience.

For an example of how these qualities function, consider the lighting for a production of *Hamlet*. To emphasize the eerie, tragic quality of *Hamlet*, with its murders and graveyard scene, the lighting would be generally cool rather than warm. As for angles, if the production took place on a proscenium stage, there would be down lighting and back lighting to give a sculptured, occasionally unreal quality to the characters. In terms of movement, the lights would change each time there was a shift in locale. This would give a rhythm of movement through the play and also focus attention on particular areas of the stage.

THE LIGHTING DESIGNER'S RESOURCES Among the resources of the lighting designer are various kinds of lighting instruments and other kinds of technical and electronic equipment.

PART FIVE · THE DESIGNERS: ENVIRONMENT AND VISUAL ELEMENTS

Types of stage lights   Basically, lights are of three types:

1   *Spotlights,* which throw a sharp, concentrated beam. (A mobile spotlight, which an operator can shift to follow a performer across the stage, is called a *follow spot.*)

2   *Area lights,* or *floodlights,* which cover a small area with general light.

3   *Strip,* or *border, lights,* a row of lights which bathe a section of stage or scenery in light.

Lighting controls   We have already considered some of the advances in lighting. In technical terms, lighting is easily the most highly developed aspect of theater. Lighting instruments can be hung all over the theater and beamed at every part of the stage; and these many instruments can be controlled by one person sitting at an electronic panel, or switchboard.

Lighting changes—or *cues,* as they are called—can be arranged ahead of time. Sometimes, in a complicated production (a musical, say, or a Shakespearean play), there will be from 75 to 150 light cues. A cue can range from a *blackout* (where all the lights are shut off at once), to a *fade* (the lights dim slowly, changing the scene from brighter to darker), to a *cross-fade* (one set of lights comes down while another comes up). Moreover, with today's modern equipment, the changes can be timed automatically so that a cross-fade in lights will take exactly the number of seconds called for; guesswork is eliminated.

Cues can be prearranged by computer so that during a performance, the operator at the console pushes a button, and the entire change occurs automatically. As an illustration, Strindberg's *A Dream Play* has innumerable scene changes—after the manner of a dream—in which one scene fades into another before our eyes. At one point in the play, a young woman, called the Daughter, sits at an organ in a church. In Strindberg's words, "The stage darkens as the Daughter rises and approaches the Lawyer. By means of lighting the organ is transformed into a wall of a grotto. The sea seeps in between basalt pillars with a harmony of waves and wind." At the light cue for this change, a button is pushed, and all the lights creating the majesty of the church fade as the lights creating the grotto come up.

New technology in stage lighting   Stage lighting will doubtless benefit from the technological advances made in lighting for rock music groups and other performers who present acts to vast audiences and for whom light and sound are the essential technical elements. Huge banks of lights are focused on the stage; sometimes there are banks of lights behind the performers, forming part of the stage picture. To get maximum flexibility and control, new instruments have been developed. One, called *Vari-lite,* has amazing versatility. With this new product it

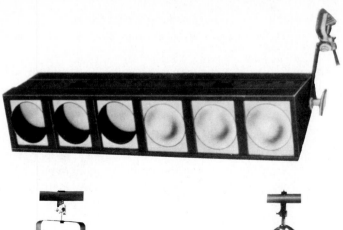

DIFFERENT LIGHTING INSTRUMENTS FOR DIFFERENT PURPOSES.

Shown here are three instruments to light the stage. Most stage lights have three key elements: a lamp that is the source of light, a reflector, and a lens through which the beams pass.

The instrument at the top is a borderlight. *A row of borderlights is hung above the stage on a pipe, or* batten, *to provide general illumination to the stage or scenery. It can blend light in acting areas or "tone" the settings or costumes.*

Hanging below the borderlight to the left is a small spotlight known as a fresnel *(pronounced "freh-NEL"). Spotlights illuminate restricted or limited areas of the stage with a concentrated beam of light. They can carefully define the area that is to be lighted and leave other areas in darkness. The fresnel spotlight has a spherical reflector and a special lens that is flat on one side and has ridges of concentric circles on the other. This arrangement allows the lens to be thinner and lighter than other lenses and softens the edges of the beam. The fresnel spotlight is generally used in positions near the stage—behind the proscenium opening, or mounted close to the action on arena or thrust stages.*

The larger spotlight on the right, hanging from a U-shaped yoke, is more powerful; it is known as an ellipsoidal reflector spotlight. *It is a more efficient instrument and therefore can throw a stronger light farther than the fresnel. It differs from the fresnel by having an ellipsoidal-shaped reflector that partially surrounds the lamp and sends a strong beam through two plano-convex lenses. It is used when the distance between the instrument and the stage area is greatest—for example, from positions outside the proscenium opening in the auditorium. It might be mounted on the balcony rail, in a beam position above the audience, or on vertical booms along the side walls of the auditorium.*

**LIGHTING CUES
ARE COMPUTERIZED.**
In today's theater, complex, sophisticated changes in stage lighting have been made possible by advances in electronics and computerization. Numerous instruments can be cued by computer for subtle, instantaneous changes in the direction, focus, intensity, and color of lighting. In this scene, a technician operates a computer light board at the South Coast Repertory at Costa Mesa, California.

is no longer necessary to change color by putting a gel over the beam by hand; color can now be changed automatically on the instrument—and as many as 1,000 color variations are possible. The instrument can also be tilted, forward or backward and from side to side, to change the angle of the beam and therefore the focus onstage. Moreover, the sharpness and width of the beam can be changed in each instrument. This is all done electronically from a central control, which means there is an almost infinite range of possibilities in terms of color, focus, and the rest—controlled from a central computer panel by operators pushing switches. The various settings can be preset, so that the changes can occur instantaneously.

THE LIGHTING DESIGNER'S COLLABORATORS   As in virtually every aspect of theater, in lighting too, there is collaboration. A number of people collaborate with the lighting designer. These include the people who assist in drawing up the light plot, and lighting technicians who hang and position the lights (often climbing on catwalks and ladders to inaccessible areas above, behind, and in front of the stage). Lighting technicians also assist in focusing the lights on the proper areas and in making certain that the correct color gels and hoods for the lights are in place. Finally, experts run the lighting boards or computers that control the lights during the running of a show, taking cues from the stage manager and coordinating their efforts with other technical aspects of a production.

(Weinhold Adam, The Darkroom)

SOUND EFFECTS.
Sound effects cover a wide range of items, from musical underscoring to recorded airplanes and locomotives to thunder to such basic sounds as a gun firing. In this production of Chekhov's play Uncle Vanya *at the Pittsburg Public Theater, the title character fires a pistol at a professor.*

✳ SOUND IN THE THEATER ✳

Although not one of the visual elements, a technical aspect of theater that must be coordinated with light and scenery is sound.

In recent years, sound has become an increasingly important element in theater productions. It may be said to include all sound effects, recordings, and electrical enhancements used in the theater—all sounds, that is, except spoken words and music which have no amplification. Audiences have become increasingly aware of a variety of sounds because of concerts by musical groups in which microphones are attached to musical instruments as well as used by performers and in which huge banks of speakers project the sound to the audience.

Sound effects can be defined as any sound produced by mechanical or human means to create for the audience a noise or sound associated with the play being produced. Aside from electronic amplification, various devices have been developed through the years to create these sounds. A wind noise, for example, can be produced by a wooden drum made from slats. The drum is usually 2 or 3 feet in diameter and covered with a muslin cloth. When the drum is turned, by means of a handle, it makes a noise like howling wind. For door slams a miniature door or even a full door in a frame can be placed just offstage and opened and shut. Two pieces of wood slammed shut can also simulate the sound of a closing door. In some cases this effect can sound like a gunshot. A gunshot can also be created by firing a gun using blank cartridges (live ammunition should never be used onstage; and in some states there are laws forbidding the purchase of blank guns). The sound of thunder can be simulated by hanging a large, thick metal sheet backstage and gently shaking it.

In the area of electronic sound, there are two means of sound reproduction: records and tape recorders. In professional productions, all the nonlive sound effects are recorded on magnetic tape and played back on tape recorders. These tapes are created in professional sound studios by sound engineers. Some shows require two or more tape recorders. The refinement of cassette players and home tape recorders has allowed many small theater groups, especially at schools, to take advantage of the new electronic techniques. Small groups (as well as large ones) often can get excellent sound effects on records that are either bought singly or found in a sound cue library.

The process of assembling sound tapes is similar for both the professional and the nonprofessional. First, a list is made of all nonmusical sound effects required for the show. This list may come from the director or the stage manager. On shows with a great deal of sound or music, there may be a separate sound designer and music consultant. Once the list is decided upon, a master tape is made, and the sounds are arranged in the order that they appear in the script. This process is called *editing.* When the production moves into the theater, there is a technical rehearsal without performers, during which each sound cue is listened to and the volume level is set. When the rehearsal starts with the performers in the theater, more changes will be made. Depending on the action and the timing of scenes, some cues will be too loud and others too soft, some will have to be made shorter and others made longer.

For speech reinforcement—using a microphone to pick up dialogue and songs—several types of microphones are used. A *shotgun mike* is highly directional and is aimed from a distance at a specific area. A *general mike* picks up sounds in the general area toward which it is aimed. A *body mike* is a wireless microphone attached to a small radio transmitter fastened to the performer's clothing. When the performer speaks or sings, the sound is transmitted by a type of small radio system to a receiver offstage where it is relayed to the sound mixer where all sound is coordinated. All types of microphones must be hooked to an amplifier that increases the electronic energy in the sound and sends it through speakers.

Microphones are placed in various locations. One position is alongside the downstage edge of the stage where the footlights used to be located. Another position is hanging in the air near the lights. In the case of the body mike, the placement is on the performers themselves.

In addition to microphones, speakers which send the amplified sound into the auditorium must be placed in various parts of the theater. This is both an art and a science: to secure the correct speakers for the size and shape of the theater, and to position them so that they carry sound evenly into the auditorium—to the upper reaches of the balcony, to the side seats, to areas underneath the balcony.

Placing microphones and speakers in a theater and on the stage is a complicated process. The goal is to get clear and unobtrusive sound. When electronic sound is not properly modulated, it can become an artificial barrier between the performers and the audience and can seriously interfere with the actor-audience relationship.

Lighting and sound, like scenery and costumes, are means to an end: they implement the artistic and aesthetic aspects of a production. The colors, shapes, and lines of lighting effects and the qualities of sound interact with other elements of theater and contribute to the overall experience.

In Part Five we have looked at the environment and the visual elements of theater. In Part Six we show how all the elements we have studied—the work of the playwright, director, performers, as well as the designers—are brought together for a total experience for the spectators.

✳ SUMMARY ✳

1 Stage lighting, like other elements of theater, has an equivalent in the planning of lighting in homes, department stores, restaurants, etc.

2 Lighting—historically the last of the stage elements to be fully developed—is today the most technically sophisticated of all. Once the incandescent electric lamp was introduced, it was possible to achieve almost total control of the color, intensity, and timing of lights. Lighting controls have also benefited from computerization with extensive light shifts being controlled by an operator at a console.

3 Lighting design is intended to provide illumination onstage, to establish time and place, to help set the mood and style of the production, to focus the action, and to establish a rhythm of visual movement.

4 Lighting should be consistent with all other elements.

5 The lighting designer uses a variety of instruments, colored gels, and control dimmers and panels to achieve his or her effects.

6 Related to visual effects is sound in the theater. Sound effects are created by mechanical means—pieces of wood slapped together for a door closing—or on tape. Microphones are used to enhance speaking or singing.

✳ TOPICS FOR DISCUSSION ✳

1   When artificial lighting became available, playwrights no longer had to use words to suggest time of day or other conditions of light. Defend or attack one of the following statements: (*a*) "The language of the theater is poorer today at least partly because playwrights need not use it to convey such information." (*b*) "It is true that Shakespeare and other playwrights of the past often used language beautifully to convey information which today is provided by lighting; but they were simply making a virtue of necessity, and if they were writing now they would be glad not to have to do it. If the language of plays is poorer today, it is for other reasons."

2   Lighting is described in this chapter as the "most flexible and most atmospheric of the visual elements of theater." What makes the other elements less flexible and less atmospheric?

3   Several qualities of stage lighting are described—intensity, color, direction, form, and movement. Would the relative importance of these qualities be likely to change from situation to situation in a production? If so, what aspects of a situation might bring one quality or another to the fore?

4   "Speech reinforcement" or "miking"—that is, electronic amplification of dialogue and songs—is a source of considerable controversy in the theater today. Leaving aside the question whether it is generally done skillfully or clumsily, make out a theoretical (that is, an aesthetic) case for doing it or not doing it at all.

PART

SIX

THE TOTAL
EXPERIENCE

COMBINING THE ELEMENTS IN A FINISHED PRODUCTION

Every theater production is a collaboration among the writer, the director, the performers, and the designers. When the production is completed, the audience becomes a collaborator too. Chapter 20 re-creates the original production of Arthur Miller's Death of a Salesman, *which was a particularly successful collaboration. Shown in Al Hirschfeld's drawing on the following pages is a revival of the play that starred Dustin Hoffman (left center) as the chief character, Willy Loman.*

20

BRINGING THE
ELEMENTS TOGETHER

THE ELEMENTS COME TOGETHER IN DEATH OF A SALESMAN.

The talents of many people come together to create a stage production. This is especially true when a new script is presented for the first time. A memorable collaboration occurred for the premiere of Death of a Salesman *by Arthur Miller. The chief character of the play, Willy Loman, is a salesman who has inculcated in his sons a false sense of success. Willy himself is near the end of his rope in terms of his career, no longer able to complete even the meager sales of past years. Seen here in the original production are Lee J. Cobb (center) as Willy and Arthur Kennedy (left) and Cameron Mitchell (right) as his sons, Biff and Happy.*

Theater is a remarkable convergence of human and artistic endeavors. This is underscored by the many elements that must come together to produce a theater event: the writing of a play and the planning of a production, which may take weeks, months, perhaps even years; the rehearsal period; the designing and building of scenery and costumes; the technical coordination of light changes, scene shifts, and performers' activities; the adjustments made as a result of the responses of preview audiences. All these contribute to the moment when members of the audience see the performance itself.

The excitement which comes to a group of performers working together or to a crew working backstage on scenery or lights is difficult to describe adequately, as with any human endeavor in which a group has trained for weeks before it has its moment of triumph. Any group which works for a common purpose—to win an election or an athletic contest, to accomplish some scientific breakthrough, or to organize a neighborhood to make it better—has the same sense of group achievement. Each member knows that he or she could not have accomplished the task alone.

Theater is a supreme example of this phenomenon, because, with the possible exception of opera, it is the most complex of the arts. A theater event passes through many hands, and the contribution of each person is essential to its success. When the people creating it work effectively together, they share with one another the deep satisfaction of having collaborated on a difficult but eminently rewarding task. And when the work is performed onstage, the audience senses this achievement and, through its response, becomes a part of the collaboration.

✳ PRODUCING DEATH OF A SALESMAN ✳

It will be easier to understand this process if we examine how a single production was brought together—in this case, the original Broadway production of *Death of a Salesman* by Arthur Miller.

The Playwright and the Play

The play concerns a salesman, Willy Loman, who had hoped to be a big success, in the way that he felt men could succeed in business in America, but has managed only to make a bare living. Nevertheless, he remains eternally optimistic, and he has shifted much of his hope for success to his sons, Biff and Happy, though they too have been unsuccessful. In the play we see Willy during the final hours of his life, at a point when his older son Biff has returned home to Brooklyn, New York, after spending time in the west. The play moves back and forth from the present time to scenes from the past when the boys were growing up and to Willy in the office of his employer. We also see scenes with his Uncle Ben that are apparently taking place only in Willy's imagination.

In his autobiography, *Timebends,* the playwright, Arthur Miller, tells us a great deal about how *Death of a Salesman* was composed. We know that Miller's own father was very much caught up in the idea of business success but had gone bankrupt in the depression of the late 1920s and early 1930s, an experience that was to have a lasting effect on Miller and all the members of his family. When he was in college, Miller had begun a play about a salesman which he later abandoned and even forgot, but obviously the idea stayed in his mind.

Miller had an uncle, named Manny Newman, who, he tells us, was one of the models for Willy Loman. Manny was small in stature and given to gross exaggerations and inconsistencies in conversation. He was a traveling salesman who covered the New England territory for his company, driving an old car with an inadequate heater and sleeping in cheap hotels. Like Willy Loman, Manny had two sons, Miller's first cousins, of whom he was inordinately proud. When Miller asked one of his cousins what Manny wanted in life, the cousin answered, "A business for the boys." Miller says that when he heard this, many pieces of the play fell into place. Here was a proud man, working all his life, hoping to leave a legacy for his sons, but unable to do so.

Just at the time the play was taking shape, in 1948, Miller and his wife had bought an old farm in Connecticut. Miller tells us that before he could actually sit down to write *Death of a Salesman,* he decided he had to build a 10- by 12-foot cabin on the farm that would be his studio. He built it with his own hands, and when he had finished enough of it to make it usable, he began to write. In one session, lasting most of one day and night, he wrote the first act of the play. Over the next 6 weeks, he wrote the second act.

Miller explains that his uncle Manny had given him more than the character of Willy. When Miller's earlier play *All My Sons* was playing its first engagement in Boston, before it opened in New York, Miller was surprised one day to see Manny outside the theater after a matinee. Miller expected Manny to say something about the play he had just seen, but instead Manny abruptly spoke about one of his sons: "Buddy is doing very well," he said. Miller writes about this:

It was the absence of the slightest transition to "Buddy is doing very well" that stuck in my mind; it was a signal to me of the new form that until now I had only tentatively imagined could exist. I had not the slightest idea of writing about a salesman then, totally absorbed as I was in my present production. But how wonderful, I thought, to do a play without any transitions at all, dialogue that would simply leap from bone to bone of a skeleton that should not for an instant cease being added to, an organism as strictly economic as a leaf, trim as an ant.[1]

CHAPTER 20 • BRINGING THE ELEMENTS TOGETHER

DEATH OF A SALESMAN (1949)

ARTHUR MILLER (1915–   )

CHIEF CHARACTERS:
Willy Loman
Linda—his wife
Biff—his older son
Happy—his younger son
Bernard—Biff's friend
The Woman—Willy's mistress
Charley—next-door neighbor, Bernard's
   father
Uncle Ben—Willy's brother

SETTING: Willy Loman's house in New York and various other locations in New York and Boston.

TIME: The present and flashbacks to the past.

BACKGROUND: Willy is an older traveling salesman who doesn't produce much business anymore. Many of Willy's friends and business contacts are dead, and he has a tendency to daydream, drifting off into a time when things were better. His sons are not the successes that Willy expected them to be— Biff, for example, had been a football star but was not a good student and did not graduate from high school. Linda is a devoted wife and mother, trying desperately to keep the family, and Willy, from falling apart.

ACT I: Willy arrives home unexpectedly, having cut short a sales trip. He tells Linda that he kept driving off the road. Linda tells Willy that he should persuade the company to let him work in New York and not on the road. Willy expresses disappointment about his son Biff, who has just returned home after being a drifter in the west. Meanwhile, in their upstairs bedroom, Biff and Happy discuss their concern about their father. Biff is frustrated because of his inability to find a career, and they discuss an old dream of starting their own business.

Downstairs, Willy moves into a scene from the past in which he brags to young Biff about what a great salesman he is and the important people he knows. Bernard, a neighbor who is the same age as Biff, is a good student. Because he idolizes the athletic Biff, Bernard wants to help Biff study so that he can pass his exams. Willy puts Bernard down as the "studious type" and tells Biff that personality will get him further than studying.

Willy, in a different flashback, is shown in Boston with the Woman, with whom he is having an affair. Back in the present, Willy and his neighbor Charley have a minor confrontation during which Willy speaks out loud to his brother Ben's ghost. In Willy's fantasy, Ben was a successful self-made man who once, years ago, offered Willy a chance to go with him, a chance which Willy refused.

Linda defends Willy to the boys and asks Biff to try to get along better with Willy. Linda confesses to the boys that she thinks Willy is trying to kill himself. Willy enters and confronts Biff about Biff's career and is rude to Linda while Biff stands up for her. Before they retire to bed, they make amends. Later, Biff finds the rubber tubing attached to a gas line in the basement that Willy had planned to use to kill himself.

ACT II: The next morning. Willy seems optimistic about the future: Biff represents Willy's final chance to prove that he has not been a total failure. He believes that Biff's former boss will give Biff a job. Also, Linda thinks that Willy has taken the rubber hose away and is no longer contemplating suicide, but later she finds out that it was Biff who removed it.

The scene shifts to Willy's office, where Willy meets with his boss, Howard Wagner, to ask for an assignment to the New York office. Willy is aggressive but becomes desperate when Howard refuses to give him a New York job and then fires him. Willy leaves in despair and vents his frustration on Ben's ghost.

The scene shifts to Charley's office, where Willy and Charley's son, Bernard, now a successful lawyer, discuss the time when Biff failed mathematics. Willy blames Biff's failures on that one incident. Bernard says that he always wondered why Biff didn't go to summer school, as he had planned, after he had failed. Willy is evasive. Willy asks Charley for a loan; but when Charley offers him a job, as he has in the past, Willy turns it down out of pride.

Biff and Happy are in a restaurant waiting for Willy. Happy is flirting with a young woman in the restaurant. Biff arrives and tells Happy that he had an unsuccessful meeting with his ex-boss; but when Willy comes in, he won't let Biff tell the real story—Willy wants to hear only a manufactured, upbeat story. Willy admits to the boys that he was fired and recalls the time when Biff failed math.

The scene shifts to the past and the hotel room in Boston where Willy is with the Woman; the young Biff shows up unannounced and finds Willy with the Woman. He feels that everything Willy stands for is false, and he returns home a beaten person. Back in the present, Happy and Biff leave Willy alone in the restaurant, distraught and fantasizing.

At home, a bitter Linda accuses the sons of deserting Willy in his hour of need when they left him at the restaurant. Willy, still caught up in fantasies, has returned home to plant a garden at night. He tells an imaginary Ben about his insurance policy—the $20,000 would help Biff get on his feet. Back in the present, Willy accuses Biff of blaming him for his own failure, though Biff denies it. Biff tells Willy that he has finally come to realize the truth about himself, and Biff tries desperately to make Willy see the truth about his own failures. Although Willy cannot, there is a momentary reconciliation between him and Biff. Linda is still afraid for Willy and wants him to come to bed. Alone, he gets into his car, drives off, and kills himself in an automobile accident. At his funeral, Linda expresses her sorrow and confusion.

(New York Public Library at Lincoln Center; Astor, Lenox, and Tilden Foundations)

CHAPTER 20 • BRINGING THE ELEMENTS TOGETHER

The form of *Death of a Salesman* does move back and forth, without transitions, from past to present, from reality to fantasy, and this idea first occurred to Miller when talking to his uncle Manny that day in Boston.

The Director

As soon as Miller finished the manuscript of *Death of a Salesman*, he sent it to the director Elia Kazan (1909–   ), the man who had directed *All My Sons* so successfully and had also recently directed *A Streetcar Named Desire* by Tennessee Williams. In his autobiography, *A Life*, Kazan tells us that when he read the play, it affected him more deeply than any other play he had ever read. Although his usual practice was to wait a few days to see what his second thoughts were, he knew immediately that this was a powerful play and called Miller to tell him so.

One reason Kazan was so caught up in the play was that his own father was a salesman, selling carpets, who had many of the same contradictory features as Willy Loman. Kazan's father was autocratic, a perpetual con man trying to seduce customers, and an eternal optimist. The combination of tragedy and absurdity, of sadness and humor that Kazan could see in his own father had been perfectly captured by Miller in *Death of a Salesman*.

The Producer

The next step after Kazan had agreed to direct the play was to find a producer. Kazan and Miller first approached Cheryl Crawford, whom Kazan knew, but she turned it down. They next went to Kermit Bloomgarden (1904–1976), a man who had been an accountant for other producers but now wanted to become a producer himself. Bloomgarden agreed to produce the play, though he urged that the name be changed—the word "Death" in the title, he had been assured by his friends, would mean death at the box office. But Miller and Kazan held firm.

The Designers and the Composer

Once the director and producer were in place, designers and a composer were chosen to work on the production. For the scenery and lighting, Kazan chose Jo Mielziner (1901–1976), with whom he had worked previously on the production of *A Streetcar Named Desire*. For costumes, Julia Sze was selected; and to compose the incidental music, Alex North.

One of the most important steps in the development of the play was the decision to use Jo Mielziner as the scenic and lighting designer. As noted above, Mielziner had worked on *A Streetcar Named Desire* with Kazan, and Kazan wanted him for this play too. In his book, Kazan

THE DESIGNER, PLAYWRIGHT, AND DIRECTOR CONFER.
Discussing the production of Death of a Salesman *are (left) Jo Mielziner, the designer of the original Broadway production; (center) the playwright Arthur Miller; and (right) the director Elia Kazan. As their individual accounts relate, these three worked closely together to create the work finally seen onstage.*

emphasizes what a collaborative art theater is; and nowhere, he says, was this more apparent than in Mielziner's contributions. Miller knew that he wanted the play to move with great fluidity, from present to past and back again, but he had not indicated in the original script how this could be done directorially or scenically.

Mielziner tells us, in a diary he kept at the time, that he was given the script to read on September 24, 1948.[2] As he read the script, he realized what Bloomgarden, Kazan, and Miller had all told him: that this was a "tough" play in terms of its scenic demands. There were over forty scenes in many locales—some in the past, some in the present. The next day, September 25, 1948, Mielziner wrestled with

THE DESIGN OF DEATH OF A SALESMAN.

*Jo Mielziner, the designer of the original production, had the idea of creating a skeletal set
for Willy Loman's home— the kitchen, a bedroom, and an upstairs bedroom—and allowing
space at the side and front of the stage for scenes from the past and scenes taking place in
Willy's imagination. The background consisted of apartment houses closing in on Willy's
house; but by means of projections, this background could appear to be a forest of green
leaves--indicating the open spaces that existed when the family first moved into the neighborhood. In the picture at top left, the director Elia Kazan (right) shows a model of Mielziner's
set to Mildred Dunnock, who played Willy's wife; Lee J. Cobb, who played Willy; and
Arthur Kennedy, who played his older son, Biff. The picture at top right is Mielziner's
sketch of the set, showing the skeletal outline of the house and the apartments in the background. The sketch at bottom left is the way the scene would look when the leaves were
projected onto a scrim. The picture at bottom right is of the actual set after it was completed.*

ideas as to how the play could be accommodated on a stage. During the course of the morning, he gradually evolved the idea that Willy's house would always be onstage, at least in outline, and that the other scenes and flashbacks would take place to the side of the setting for Willy's house and on the forestage. Finally, he decided to use as a background the apartment houses that now surrounded Willy's house, but to add light projections to create an effect of leaves and green trees over the entire set—taking both Willy and the audience back to the time when there were open spaces and to the hope symbolized by springtime and growing things.

When he presented the concept that afternoon to Miller, Kazan, and Bloomgarden, there was a long silence. Mielziner feared that they did not like his idea, but in fact they were stunned by it—they accepted it, and it became a crucial element in the eventual success of the play. In Kazan's words, the design "was the single most critically important contribution and the key to the way I directed the play."[3]

Mielziner's design included a skeleton of Willy's house, outlining the kitchen, Willy's and his wife's bedroom, and their sons' upstairs bedroom. By the use of lighting, the action could move instantaneously from the house, surrounded by oppressive apartment buildings, to a scene in the past on the bare stage.

During the planning and rehearsal period, many adjustments were made in the setting, mostly in the direction of greater simplicity. For example, the script called for two offices, each with a set of furniture. Mielziner convinced Kazan that they could use only one desk and one chair and, by changing the telephones and other elements, convince the audience that these were two different offices. They decided that a hotel room could be created without walls by projecting a pattern of wallpaper onto the set; and in the final scene they dispensed with a gravestone, which would have been technically complicated to bring onstage.

Casting the Performers

The next step for Kazan and Miller was to cast the play. For Linda, Willy's long-suffering wife, Kazan cast Mildred Dunnock (1904–); for Biff, the older son, he decided to use Arthur Kennedy (1914–); and for Happy, the younger son, he chose Cameron Mitchell (1918–). For the part of Willy, Miller had called for a small man, but Kazan had in mind a large, hulking actor, Lee J. Cobb (1911–1976). Cobb had worked with the Group Theater, with which Kazan had been associated, and Kazan felt that Cobb had just the right combination of bravura and vulnerability to make a perfect Willy. And Cobb, once he had read the script, insisted that he was the only one to play the part. At first Miller objected, but he came to see the same qualities in Cobb that Kazan saw, and it was agreed that Cobb would play Willy.

403

The Business Side of the Production

At the same time that Kazan was preparing rehearsals, Bloomgarden and his associate Walter Fried began work on all the business and advertising arrangements. They signed up a rehearsal space in New York City, a theater in Philadelphia for the tryout run, and the Morosco Theater in New York, where the play would actually open. They also made arrangements for advertising in the newspapers and elsewhere and hired an agent to handle press releases and other forms of public relations. They signed contracts with all the actors, the designers, the stage manager, and others working on the production. They were as busy on their side as Kazan, Mielziner, and the performers were on the artistic side.

The Rehearsal Period

Rehearsals for *Death of a Salesman* were held in a small, seldom-used roof theater above the abandoned New Amsterdam Theater on Forty-Second Street in New York City. During the course of rehearsals, Kazan worked very closely with performers, as he always did, encouraging them, challenging them, taking them aside to confer with them about their characters, about motivations, about actions. At one point, for example, he required Mildred Dunnock to deliver an important speech faster and faster: first twice as quickly as she ordinarily did, and then again twice as fast as that. He eventually allowed her to slow down a bit, but the exercise had eliminated the self-pity which he felt was creeping into the role and which he did not want.

In terms of revisions in the script, one of the most important came in a scene in a restaurant near the end of the play. Biff has been to a job interview and has realized in the process what a fraud his life has been. He is determined to confront his father with this realization, but when Willy arrives at the restaurant, Biff learns that Willy has been fired from his own job and is devastated. In the original script, there were many twists and turns in this scene; and although the actors rehearsed it for an entire day, they could not make it work. Miller went home and worked all night on a revision, which was rehearsed the next day and is the version found in the final script.

The chief worry during the rehearsal period was Lee J. Cobb in the part of Willy. For the first 10 days or so, he moved through his role without conviction or emotion. The other performers had learned their lines and were beginning to give life to their characters, but Cobb seemed listless and uninvolved. Miller was extremely worried, and so were the others. Then, on the twelfth day of rehearsals, something happened. On the line "There's more people now . . . ," Cobb turned upstage and bawled the words out, incorporating defiance, rage, and humanity. From then on, the performance that day became larger than life. It was so moving that the press agent who was watching the run-through, the stage manager, and the one or two other people in the auditorium began to weep.

Design and Technical Elements

Throughout the rehearsal period, the other artistic collaborators were supervising the work which was their responsibility. The scenery was being built in a scene shop; the costumes were being bought or sewn; Alex North was composing, arranging, and recording the music; and the lighting instruments were being selected and prepared.

The Out-of-Town Tryout

In discussing the way *Death of a Salesman* was brought together, Kazan wrote: "Although the play script is the essentially important element, after that is finished, actors, designers, directors, technicians 'write' the play together."[4]

At the theater in Philadelphia, the elements of the production were brought together: Mielziner's scenery and lighting, Julia Sze's costumes, and the performances under Kazan's guidance. All these aspects combined to bring the words of Miller's script to life. Many theater people from New York came down to see the production, and both they and the audiences from Philadelphia were deeply affected. During this tryout, the performances were perfected, the necessary adjustments to lighting and scenery were made, and other steps were taken to ensure that the production worked smoothly.

It was clear even in the Philadelphia tryout that *Death of a Salesman* had a powerful effect on its audiences. Miller writes that when the curtain came down at the end, often there was silence rather than applause because the audience members were so stunned. "People stood to put their coats on and then sat again," Miller notes, "some, especially men, were bent forward covering their faces, and others were openly weeping."[5] Kazan adds in his book: "It was the only play I ever directed where men in the audience cried."[6]

The Opening

Death of a Salesman opened at the Morosco Theater on February 10, 1949. Everything went perfectly except that Lee Cobb made a mistake when describing the death of a salesman on the New York, New Haven, and Hartford Railroad: he said "New Haven" twice instead of saying "Hartford." But the audience did not seem to notice. The audience, just like audiences in Philadelphia, was deeply affected, and the critics in their reviews were equally enthusiastic. The play, through this initial production, entered the ranks of American classics.

(Culver)

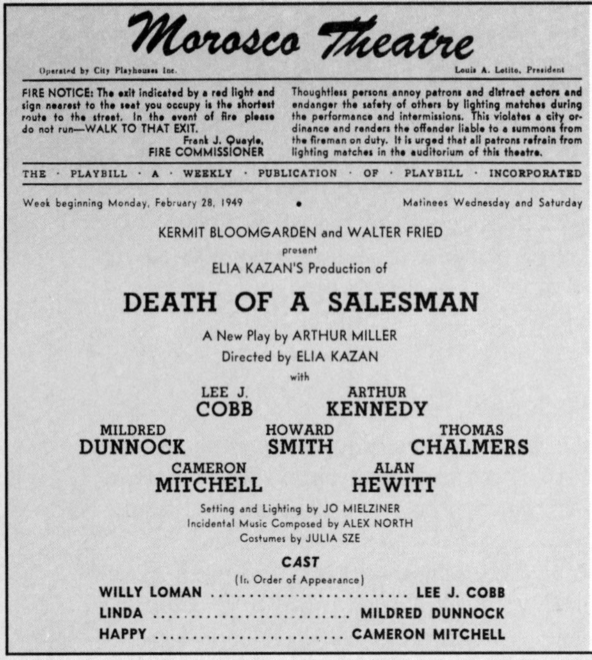
Morosco Theatre

Operated by City Playhouses Inc. Louis A. Lotito, President

FIRE NOTICE: The exit indicated by a red light and sign nearest to the seat you occupy is the shortest route to the street. In the event of fire please do not run—WALK TO THAT EXIT.
Frank J. Quayle,
FIRE COMMISSIONER

Thoughtless persons annoy patrons and distract actors and endanger the safety of others by lighting matches during the performance and intermissions. This violates a city ordinance and renders the offender liable to a summons from the fireman on duty. It is urged that all patrons refrain from lighting matches in the auditorium of this theatre.

THE · PLAYBILL · A · WEEKLY · PUBLICATION · OF · PLAYBILL · INCORPORATED

Week beginning Monday, February 28, 1949 • Matinees Wednesday and Saturday

KERMIT BLOOMGARDEN and WALTER FRIED
present
ELIA KAZAN'S Production of

DEATH OF A SALESMAN

A New Play by ARTHUR MILLER
Directed by ELIA KAZAN
with

LEE J. COBB · ARTHUR KENNEDY
MILDRED DUNNOCK · HOWARD SMITH · THOMAS CHALMERS
CAMERON MITCHELL · ALAN HEWITT

Setting and Lighting by JO MIELZINER
Incidental Music Composed by ALEX NORTH
Costumes by JULIA SZE

CAST
(In Order of Appearance)

WILLY LOMAN	LEE J. COBB
LINDA	MILDRED DUNNOCK
HAPPY	CAMERON MITCHELL

THE PLAY OPENS.
After all the preparation—the work on the script, the development of the designs, the casting, the rehearsals, and the out-of-town tryouts—the play finally opens on Broadway on February 10, 1949. The audience, seeing it, completes the circle of the production. Shown here is the title page from a program of the original production.

✻ ASPECTS OF THE TOTAL EXPERIENCE ✻

The Creators: Risks and Opportunities

As we have seen in this description of the first production of *Death of a Salesman*, a great many people must work closely together to create a stage production. One danger in a collaborative art like theater is that the greater the number of people involved, the greater the chance of failure. And any one link in the creative chain can affect the outcome. The opportunity for a mistake is much greater, for example, than it is with a painting on which just one artist works with only a canvas and paint. In theater a stagehand can destroy an entire scene by a miscue; so can a lighting technician. A performer can forget his or her lines, negating much of the work that has gone into a special moment. In other words, any one person can interrupt or short-circuit the final effect.

Furthermore, because so many creative people are involved, there is always the possibility that divergent points of view will be at war with one another. The director and the playwright may not see eye to eye on the interpretation of the script. A creative actor or actress is another vital force who may be at odds with either the playwright or the director, or with both. When we add the ideas of the scene designer, the lighting designer, and the costume designer, and perhaps others involved—a music composer, for example—we can see the possibilities for conflict. The risk we run when we go to the theater is that the inconsistencies arising from these conflicts will mar the outcome.

Generally, however, everyone working on a production is doing his or her best to make it successful. The great opportunity in theater is that many people working together can produce results which no one person working alone could ever achieve; the audience, too, has a chance to share in this unique collaborative effort.

Fortunately, we do not need to encounter the ideal each time we go to the theater for the experience to be meaningful. A production can fall short of perfection and still be exciting. In a production of *Salesman*, for example, if the performance of the actor playing the younger son Happy is not quite as strong as that of the other performers, it need not destroy the overall effect. And if a member of the audience does not understand every subtlety and nuance in the text, it will not lessen the basic impact of the production. As long as those who create a theater event present the audience with a reasonably clear and cohesive vision onstage, they will have provided the basis for a genuine theater experience. The rest is up to the audience.

The Audience: Integrating the Elements

OBSERVATION AND ASSIMILATION   The ultimate integration of a theater event takes place in each spectator's mind, as it did at the opening of *Death of a Salesman*. No matter how closely the people who produce a theater event work together, and no matter how well the director coordinates the various elements, individual audience members must eventually bring the parts together. So many elements make up a theater production that we might wonder how a spectator can combine them. The answer lies in our ability to handle many kinds of information and bring this information together to form a complete picture. Our everyday activities suggest that human beings have a great capacity to absorb data and stimuli and to integrate them into a single experience.

A good example is what happens when someone drives an automobile. The person at the wheel is aware, first of all, of the parts of the car itself: the steering wheel, the accelerator, the brakes. He or she concentrates on the road, anticipating turns in the highway or stoplights ahead. There are also other cars and pedestrians to consider; the driver is aware of automobiles to the left and right, and glances in the rearview mirror to see what is behind. In addition, the driver might be listening to the radio or to the conversation of other passengers in the car. While dealing with these mechanical or personal details, the driver might also be daydreaming—thinking of some past event or imagining a future one.

THE ELEMENTS COME TOGETHER FOR THE AUDIENCE.

The climax of all preparation in the theater is the performance before an audience, whose members bring all the elements onstage together in their own minds and imaginations. Shown here is a scene from the first production, with Mildred Dunnock as Willy's wife, Linda; Lee J. Cobb as Willy; and Arthur Kennedy and Cameron Mitchell as his two sons.

This same ability to absorb and deal simultaneously with an abundance of activities and thoughts can be brought to bear on every kind of undertaking; it applies to emotional and intellectual as well as physical tasks. Without it we would not be able to survive.

Our powers of assimilation make it possible to form a cohesive whole out of the fragments we see before us on the stage: we watch individual performers in action and tune into their personalities; we observe the costumes, scenery, and lighting effects; we note the progress of the action as characters confront one another; we hear the words of the playwright; and we associate ideas and emotions in the play with our own experiences.

Along the way we relate each present moment with the past. Two kinds of memories contribute to this process. First, we have a lifetime of personal memories—experiences which an event onstage might trigger in our mind—linking our individual past with what is happening onstage. Second, we have the memory of what has just occurred in the play itself. When we attend the theater, our attention is sharply focused on the stage; we have come for the express purpose of seeing one event, and everything centers our attention on that event. The lights converge on the playing area, and the audience becomes abnormally quiet in order to hear what is being said. The ability of spectators to pick up clues is heightened as they become keenly aware of what every character does or says. If the audience sees someone hide a gun in a desk drawer in the first act, and a character goes to the drawer in the third act, the audience knows that the gun is about to be used.

Not only do we connect the past with what is happening at each moment in a performance; we also anticipate the future. People have immense curiosity about what lies ahead; they are fascinated by prophecies and predictions of future events, in everything from religion to horse racing. Again, this is a human activity which comes into play in the theater. We ask ourselves: How will Electra react when she finds that the brother she thought was dead is actually alive? What will Willy do when Howard fires him? We constantly speculate on the fate of characters and look forward—with both fear and excitement—to their encounters with one another.

Each moment in the theater forms a "mini-experience" of its own, resulting from a series of collisions or intersections on many levels: the past meets the present, the present meets the future, performers interact with their roles, ideas combine with emotions, sights fuse with sounds, and so forth. If the playwright, director, performers, and designers have worked together to present a single vision, these impressions and collisions do not result in a fragmented experience; rather, because of the audience's ability to integrate a number of stimuli, they are pulled together to form a rich, multilayered experience.

OBSERVING THE ELEMENTS AS PARTS OF A WHOLE   In different sections of this book, we have seen how separate elements contribute to the overall theater experience. By using the extraordinary powers of perception described above, spectators can focus on specific areas in a production without losing sight of the total effect. They can also relate individual elements to one another. If members of the audience learn to use these powers to the fullest, their enjoyment and understanding will be enhanced.

We can concentrate for a time on acting, for instance, and ask ourselves whether a particular performer is giving the proper interpretation to the role. We can ask, too, how well the performers are playing with one another. Do they look at each other when they speak, and do they listen to the other actors and actresses and respond? As we watch a play unfold, we can also take a moment to observe the visual elements. Do the costumes suit the play? Does the scenery make a statement of its own consistent with the theme and concept? Is the setting symbolic, and if so, what does it symbolize? Do the colors in the scenery convey a particular mood or feeling?

Although such elements as structure and point of view are not as visible as acting or scenery, it is possible to pause during a performance and consider them as well. As events occur onstage, we can determine what structure is being developed and whether it is maintained. If the play is climactic in structure, we can ask whether the events in the play are plausible and whether they follow one another logically.

In looking at separate elements of theater in this fashion, we need not fear that we will lose sight of the whole. If we set our minds to it, our power to absorb and integrate data can pull the experience together for us. The more we become aware of distinct elements, the more we can fit them into the overall picture. In watching a light comedy, for instance, we can observe how the acting underlines and points up the humor of the script; we can note how the costumes assist the performers in creating comic characters—perhaps with an exaggeration of style— and, at the same time, observe how the costumes present a visual image of their own, appropriately bright and lighthearted; we can observe, too, how lighting reinforces the comic spirit of the costumes and the performers. In short, we can see how the various aspects fuse and combine, how they heighten, underscore, and collaborate with one another to create the final experience.

The Overall Effect: What Does Theater "Mean"?

The overall effect of a play raises the question of what a play "means." In a discussion of a play we might hear someone ask: "But what does it mean?" The reply frequently is a catchphrase or brief summary: "The meaning of this play is that love conquers all," or "He who hesitates is lost," or "All's well that ends well." Someone might say, for instance, that the meaning of Shakespeare's *Othello* is that people should not be too hasty to believe gossip and should trust those they love. Certainly one can conclude that *Othello* contains ideas which could be interpreted this way. But is this really what *Othello* means? Isn't this a simplistic and incomplete idea of what *Othello* is about? Can we ever summarize the meaning of a play in one sentence?

There are two ways to look at meaning when we are discussing drama. Some plays specifically underscore a meaning in the text. They seem almost to have been written to point toward a moral or to teach a lesson. The title of Lillian Hellman's *The Little Foxes* comes from the "Song of Solomon" in the Bible; the verse reads, "Take us the foxes,

(Chris Bennion)

WHAT DOES THEATER MEAN?
Some plays, such as The Little Foxes, *shown here in a production at the Intiman Theater in Seattle, Washington, attempt to embody a specific meaning; the audience is told what the playwright wants the play to convey. The vast majority of plays, however, do not attempt to transmit a single meaning or lesson. Instead, the meaning is the entire experience in its manifold aspects, with all the spoken and unspoken communications, the implications, the various levels of meaning. This is true of most art—it is a metaphor for life, for beauty, for some truth about existence.*

the little foxes, that spoil the vines: for our vines have tender grapes.'' The idea of the quotation is that the foxes are evil because they spoil the vines and ravage and destroy the grapes. The title, therefore, introduces a theme of plunder and exploitation, and this theme is carried out in the action. At the close of the play the theme is summed up by a young woman, Alexandra, who has come to realize what has been happening in her family. Recognizing that her mother is one of the greediest and most cunning of the foxes, she confronts her with this knowledge. Alexandra says to her mother: "Addie said there were people who ate the earth and other people who stood around and watched them do it. And just now Uncle Ben said the same thing. . . . Well, tell him for me, Mama, I'm not going to stand around and watch you do it. Tell him I'll be fighting as hard as he'll be fighting someplace where people don't just stand around and watch."

In a play like *The Little Foxes* the author invites us to find a "meaning" which can be expressed in a few straightforward sentences. Most plays, however (such as *Death of a Salesman*), do not contain such direct statements of their meaning. Their substance resides, rather, in their total effect on the spectator. Even the relatively few plays like *The Little Foxes* which have clear-cut themes are far more complex than a few sentences suggest.

In the final analysis, a theater event does not "mean"; it *is*—its existence is its meaning. The writer Gertrude Stein (1874–1946) once said, "Rose is a rose is a rose is a rose." On the face of it, this seems to be a simple, repetitive statement; a reiteration of the obvious. As far as art is concerned, though, there is a great truth hidden in Stein's words. She is telling us that a rose is itself, not something else. In any other form it ceases to have its own existence and thus loses its unique quality. The depiction of a rose in a poem, an oil painting, or a color photograph might have a certain beauty and give us a notion of a rose, but none of these can take the place of the real thing. Only in its presence can we see the texture of the petals and smell the fragrance of the rose. If our direct experience of a rose is irreplaceable, how much more irreplaceable is our experience of a complex art like theater.

The Modern Theater: Different Purposes, Different Experiences

Each theater event has its own meaning and impact, but in today's theater these vary widely from one event to another. The elements we have examined in the various sections of this book can be combined in so many different ways that the results offer a variety of experiences. The same play might be performed in one instance in an outdoor theater with nonrealistic acting and in another instance in a small, indoor theater with realistic acting. Conversely, the same space might serve two quite different productions: a bare stage with no scenery can be the setting for a stark tragedy or an intimate musical comedy. The combination of the play itself with the way it is presented will determine the final outcome.

As we have seen, in a given historical period or within a given society, the kinds of plays presented and the ways in which they were produced were frequently limited. During the past hundred years, however, there have been marked changes in society and consequently in theater. In the past half-century we have witnessed an acceleration of these changes with the result that in the post-World War II era we have experienced a rapid shift in moral and social mores. Long-held beliefs and customs—in dress, in attitudes toward women and minority groups, in family structure—have been challenged and changed.

This breakdown of traditional attitudes and customs, along with the introduction of new ideas, was reflected in theater. No longer was the proscenium stage the chief architectural form for presentations. There was a proliferation of arena and thrust stages, as well as the use of created or found space. No longer, either, were the episodic and climactic forms of structure the only ones considered by playwrights and directors; the absurdist form emerged, as did multifocus, unstructured forms and performance art.

The result of these changes was a multiplicity of theater offerings. It is probably safe to say that never in any culture, at any time in history, has there been such a diversity of theater events available to the public as is available today to audiences in metropolitan centers throughout the western world. This same diversity also reaches into areas outside the major cities.

Not only do conditions vary widely in today's theater, but the intentions of writers, directors, and producers vary too. Audience members should keep in mind when they attend the theater that different productions are presented for different purposes. Some plays—farces like *Charley's Aunt* or comedies like *The Odd Couple*—are intended to entertain us and make us laugh. The intention of serious dramas, on the other hand, like *King Oedipus* or *Long Day's Journey into Night,* is to make us feel deeply about the human condition and identify with the people who are suffering. Some plays are presented for the express purpose of giving us information about a person or an event; others are little concerned with facts—their purpose is to have us lose ourselves in the experience and let sounds and images wash over us without regard for literal truth. Some plays show us horror and violence—not to celebrate or exploit horror and violence but to make us hate them so much that we will rebel against them and do everything in our power to prevent them in the future. This kind of theater hopes to shock us into recognition and awareness. Other types of theater—such as melodrama— show us horror and violence mainly for the thrill of it. Still other plays attempt to inspire us or raise our spirits.

In the end, we come to the fact that while there are common denominators in theater—the actor-audience encounter being chief among them—each theater experience is unique. It has its own combination of elements and its own particular aim or intention. In turn, audience members have their individual responses to each event. With so much variety in contemporary theater, we cannot expect every production to be equally satisfying to every spectator. What we can look forward to are many kinds of experiences in the theater, some of which bring us a sense of fun and some of which arouse in us thoughts and emotions we never knew were there.

The Future: What Lies Ahead?

What of the future? Given the many facets of theater, what can we expect in the years ahead? For one thing, we can expect the variety to continue, with plays of all kinds presented under different conditions. We can also expect continuing realignments in the institutions which

413

produce plays. The past 35 years have seen the development of permanent professional theater companies in major cities throughout the United States. There has also been a marked growth in productions at colleges and universities. Off-Broadway and off-off-Broadway theaters have emerged not only in New York but all across the country. At the same time, the commercial theaters of Broadway have been presenting fewer and fewer productions—especially in the area of serious new plays. There has thus been a shift from the profit to the nonprofit theater and from Broadway to other parts of the country. One problem with the diminution of Broadway is that it becomes more and more difficult for a dramatist to make a living writing plays, and so increasingly these writers are turning to films and television. How far these trends will extend, no one knows.

With nonprofit theaters coming more to the fore, the question of support for these theaters becomes increasingly important. Such subsidized theaters can never expect to earn all their expenses from ticket sales and thus depend on grants and subsidies from governmental agencies, foundations, and corporations. The National Endowment for the Arts, which gave important moral as well as financial support to theaters in the years after its formation, has been cutting back on aid recently. State arts agencies have begun to make grants, but most of these are modest. In the early days of regional professional theaters, the Ford Foundation, particularly, made generous grants to help these theaters become established; more recently, however, not only Ford but other foundations have cut back. For a time, corporations contributed more, but not nearly enough to make up for losses in other areas, and recently that support has leveled off. Again, just what will happen in the area of financial support for nonprofit theaters is not clear, but it will vitally affect the future of theater in this country.

No one can predict the exact shape of the theater of the future, though experiencing it should be an exciting adventure for everyone concerned—those creating it as well as those watching it. The one thing we do know is that theater will continue; it has already demonstrated this in the way it has met the challenges of film, television, and other electronic innovations. The reason is that when we go to the theater, we become part of a group with a common bond: an audience sharing an experience. In the exchange between performers and audience, we take part in a direct, human encounter. And from the stage, we hear the dark cry of the soul, we listen to the joyous laughter of the human spirit, and we witness the tragedies and triumphs of the human heart. As long as people wish to join together in a communion of the spirit or share with one another their anguish and suffering, the theater experience will provide them with a unique way of doing it.

✳ SUMMARY ✳

1   Ultimately, the goal in theater is to bring all the elements together to create one, integrated whole.

2   How this process occurs can be illustrated by looking at the development of an actual production, such the original Broadway production of *Death of a Salesman*. *Death of a Salesman* began with a script by Arthur Miller. When he had completed the script, Miller showed it to the director Elia Kazan, who agreed to direct it. These two found a producer in Kermit Bloomgarden. Designers were chosen, with Jo Mielziner being entrusted with both the scenery and the lights. Kazan selected the performers for the various roles. Designs were completed; rehearsals were held; and all the production elements were brought together in a tryout in Philadelphia and finally at the opening in New York City.

3   Theater is a gamble. The many steps leading to a production, and the great number of people involved in bringing it about, increase the chances for error along the way. Fortunately, we do not need perfection in a theater event for it to be meaningful; a small miscalculation or mistake will not necessarily mar the overall effect.

4   Human beings have an enormous capacity to absorb and integrate data. In the theater this allows us to take the images and stimuli we receive and merge them into a single experience. The ultimate integration of a theater event takes place in each spectator's mind.

5   While watching a theater event, we should be aware of the separate elements of a production and of what each contributes to the whole. We must also note how they relate to one another and synthesize them in our minds.

6   ''Meaning'' in the theater is sometimes understood to consist of the ideas expressed in the text. Some plays stress this aspect of meaning by emphasizing lines which present the author's position; but in the final analysis, meaning is the sum total of the theater experience. It includes the emotional and sensory data as well as the intellectual content. Any attempt to summarize the meaning of a play in a few words, or to reduce it to a formula, robs it of its full meaning.

7   Each theater event forms a complete experience; but in today's theater, experiences can vary widely. Different kinds of theater buildings and environments, many performance styles, and variety in the plays themselves ensure a diversity of theater productions.

8   Because of its complexity, and because it is so people-centered, theater affords audience members a particularly rare experience—especially when the elements of a production come together successfully.

✳ TOPICS FOR DISCUSSION ✳

1   The chapter notes that for the production of Arthur Miller's *Death of a Salesman*, the collaboration among the writer, the director, and the scenic and lighting designer worked well. Describe a situation in which two of these collaborators, or all three, might have disagreed and not worked cooperatively. What might have been points of disagreement? What could have been the results of these disagreements?

2   Suppose that the actor Lee J. Cobb, playing the central role of Willy Loman in the first production of *Death of a Salesman*, had not suddenly emerged as a dynamic performer. What might the director (Elia Kazan) and the playwright (Arthur Miller) have done about this? What might have been the consequences?

3   From the synopsis of *Death of a Salesman*, would you say that Willy Loman was a well-meaning but misguided optimist who only wanted the best for his family; or would you say that he was a selfish, foolish man who had the wrong values and put much too much faith in material success? Discuss.

4   Audiences must observe individual events as parts of a whole and combine those events into a full picture. Which of these do you think presents the greater intellectual challenge?

5   The chapter describes several trends that may indicate what the "theater of the future" will be like. Can you add anything to this list? Do you foresee a different future for the theater? Comment.

APPENDIXES

1

✳ ───────────────────────────────── ✳

REALISM AND NONREALISM

✳ ───────────────────────────────── ✳

The distinction between realism and nonrealism in the theater becomes clearer when the two approaches are placed side by side. They are present in all aspects of theater, as the following table illustrates.

REALISM	NONREALISM
STORY	
Events which the audience knows have happened or might happen in everyday life: Blanche DuBois in Tennessee Williams's *A Streetcar Named Desire* goes to New Orleans to visit her sister and brother-in-law.	Events which do not occur in real life but take place only in the imagination: Emily in Thornton Wilder's *Our Town,* after she has died, appears alive and returns to visit the earth for one day.
STRUCTURE	
Action confined to real places; time passes normally as it does in everyday life: in *The Little Foxes* by Lillian Hellman, the activity occurs over several days in Regina's house as she takes control of her family's estate.	Arbitrary use of time and place: in Strindberg's *The Dream Play,* walls dissolve, characters are transformed, as in a dream.

REALISM	NONREALISM

CHARACTERS

Recognizable human beings, such as the family—mother, father, and two sons— in O'Neill's *Long Day's Journey into Night*.	Unreal figures like the Ghost of Hamlet's father in *Hamlet*, the Three Witches in *Macbeth*, or the people who turn into animals in Ionesco's *Rhinoceros*.

ACTING

Performers portray people as they behave in daily life: Nora Helmer in Ibsen's *A Doll's House* leaves her husband and an unsatisfactory marriage in a believable, forthright manner.	Performers act as ghosts and animals; they also engage in singing, dancing, acrobatics, and gymnastics in musical comedy or performance art.

LANGUAGE

Ordinary dialogue or conversation: the Gentleman Caller in Williams's *The Glass Menagerie* tells Laura about his future in the language of an optimistic young salesman.	Poetry such as Romeo speaks to Juliet in Shakespeare's play, or the song "Tonight" sung to Maria in the musical *West Side Story*.

SCENERY

The rooms of a real house, as in Chekhov's *The Cherry Orchard*.	Abstract forms and shapes on a bare stage—for a Greek play, for example, such as Sophocles's *Electra*.

LIGHTING

Light onstage appears to come from natural sources—a lamp in a room; or sunlight, as in Ibsen's *Ghosts*, where the sunrise comes through a window in the final scene.	Shafts of light fall at odd angles; also, an arbitrary use of colors in the light. Example: a single, blue spotlight on a singer in a musical comedy.

COSTUMES

Ordinary street clothes, like those worn by the characters in August Wilson's *Fences*.	The bright costumes of a chorus in a musical comedy; the strange outfit worn by Caliban, the half-man, half-beast in Shakespeare's *The Tempest*.

MAKEUP

The natural look of characters in a domestic play such as Hansberry's *A Raisin in the Sun*.	Masks worn by characters in a Greek tragedy or makeup such as that worn by performers in the musical *Cats*.

2

THEORIES OF
TRAGEDY AND COMEDY

❋ THEORIES OF TRAGEDY ❋

From classical Greece to the present day, there has been a search for a definition of tragedy. One of the earliest and most influential definitions is found in Aristotle's *Poetics* (ca. 335 B.C.):

> Tragedy, then, is an imitation of an action that is serious, complete, and of certain magnitude; in language embellished with each kind of artistic ornament, the several kinds being found in separate parts of the play; in the form of action, not of narrative; through pity and fear effecting the proper purgation of these emotions.[1]

While there is no scholarly consensus on the meaning of Aristotle's definition, his description of classical Greek tragedy provides insight into the genre. Aristotle defined the tragic hero or heroine as one of noble birth, who is neither all good nor all bad but who suffers a major reversal in fortune (*peripeteia*) because of a tragic flaw in character (*hamartia*). The hero or heroine must learn from this downfall. Aristotle pointed out that the classical tragedies focused on one main action. He was later misinterpreted as requiring the unities of time, place, and action; but he had merely observed that classical tragedy "endeavors, as far as possible, to confine itself to a single revolution of the sun, or but to slightly exceed this limit" and had a single action. He never mentioned the unity of place.

Horace, whose *Art of Poetry* (24–20 B.C.) is the only complete piece of dramatic theory from the Roman period, prescribed rules for tragedy. He stressed consistency in character and the exclusion of comic relief. For Horace, the function of tragedy was to teach. He also dictated a five-act structure.

The Italian Renaissance critics devised rigid criteria for tragedy that were debated for centuries. Among these critics were Julius Caesar Scaliger (1484–1558) and Lodovico Castelvetro (1505–1571). For these men, tragedy dealt with individuals of high birth. Mixture of genres was forbidden. The unities of time (24 hours), place, and action were inviolable. The tragic playwright, they indicated, should strive for an illusion of reality (verisimilitude). Tragedies were to be didactic.

In Elizabethan England, Sir Philip Sidney (1554–1586) in *The Defense of Poesy* (1583), supported the Italian neoclassical ideals. In Spain, Lope de Vega defended his breaking of the neoclassical rules for tragedy in his essay *The New Art of Writing Plays* (1609).

During the eighteenth century, there was a movement away from strict adherence to the Italian ideals. Dr. Samuel Johnson's *Preface to Shakespeare* (1765) is a defense of Shakespeare's tragic style. Gotthold Ephraim Lessing, in *Hamburg Dramaturgy,* suggested that the neoclassical critics had misinterpreted Aristotle. He also called for critical acceptance of domestic tragedy, which dealt with lower social classes. In the late eighteenth and early nineteenth centuries, the German romantics, among whom were Johann Wolfgang von Goethe and Friedrich von Schiller, began writing tragedies that followed Shakespeare rather than the Greeks.

Throughout the nineteenth century, philosophers attempted to determine the relationship of tragedy to contemporary life. Samuel Taylor Coleridge, like most of the romantics, emphasized the need for tragedy to transcend mundane existence. Later, the naturalists, such as Émile Zola (1840–1902) suggested that tragedy should mirror daily life. Friedrich Nietzsche's essay *The Birth of Tragedy* (1871) was probably the most important theoretical essay of the century. For Nietzsche, a German philosopher, tragedy was born out of the fusion of the Dionysiac and the Apollonian, the primitive and the rational.

During the twentieth century, writers have incorporated discoveries about ritual and other past theatrical practices into theories of Greek and Elizabethan tragedy. Recent notions of the tragic universe suggest more comprehensive causes for the disorder reflected in these plays than a single factor such as the *tragic flaw.*

As for tragedy in the present day, the twentieth century has seen the breakdown of generic definitions and differentiations. Arthur Miller, in his essay "Tragedy and the Common Man," argues that "the common man is as apt a subject for tragedy in its highest sense as Kings were" because "the tragic feeling is evoked . . . when we are in the presence of a character who is ready to lay down his life . . . to secure . . . his sense of personal dignity."[2] Francis Ferguson, in *The Idea of a Theatre* (1949), argued that in tragedy the hero is committed to a *purpose,* that is, a goal which may lead to his or her destruction; that the purpose is carried out with *passion;* and that the quest results in a *perception* of the tragic actions. The critical disillusionment with definitions of genre is reflected in Georg Steiner's title *The Death of Tragedy* (1961). Similarly, the Swiss playwright Friedrich Duerrenmatt (*The Visit,* 1956) has suggested that tragedy may no longer be possible in the "Punch and Judy show of our century."

✳ THEORIES OF COMEDY ✳

If tragedy has proved to be difficult to define, comedy seems to have been even more problematic for theorists. In the seventeenth century, Dr. Samuel Johnson's bewilderment led him to exclaim that "comedy has been particularly impropitious to definers."

Aristotle's *Poetics* contains very few references to the lighter genre. According to the Greek philosopher, "comedy is an artistic imitation of men of an inferior moral bent; faulty, however, not in every way, but only insofar as their shortcomings are ludicrous." In comedy, he noted, these shortcomings cause no real pain or harm.

The Renaissance critics took a very rigid and academic approach in their attempts to define comedy. For these critics, comedy dealt with trifling matters. But, more important, they suggested that the comic genre dealt with characters of the lower social strata. Thus, class became a key factor in defining the genre. The use of class to define comedy was probably derived from the character types who roamed through Greek New Comedy as well as from Horace's insistence that each genre observe consistency in character. The Roman critic stressed that the tragic character must be noble and the comic character foolish. (For a description of Greek and Roman New Comedy, see the entry *Comedy* in Appendix 4.)

Comedy of characters, developing out of the Renaissance commedia dell'arte, and comedy of manners flourished in the seventeenth and eighteenth centuries. The French playwright Molière believed that his audiences could learn from dramatizations of ridiculous universal types. The English Restoration playwrights focused primarily on comic sexuality and social pretensions; hence John Dryden emphasized that comedy should portray the eccentricity of character. William Congreve, the author of *The Way of the World* (1700), also subscribed to this theory of comedy.

APPENDIX 2 • THEORIES OF TRAGEDY AND COMEDY

In the nineteenth century, the social functions of comedy intrigued theorists. The English critic George Meredith, in *An Essay on Comedy* (1877), pointed to the corrective function of comedy. Comedy, he suggested, is "the fountain of sound sense" and the "ultimate civilizer." The French critic Henri Bergson, in *Laughter* (1900), viewed the basis of comedy as "something mechanical inlaid on the living." Bergson also saw personal and social values in comedy: "At its most triumphant moments," he wrote, "comic art frees us from peril without destroying our ideals and without mustering the heavy artillery of the puritan. Comedy can be a means of mastering our disillusions when we are caught in a dishonest or stupid society. After we recognize the misdoings, the blunders, we can liberate ourselves by a confident, wise laughter that brings a catharsis of our discontent."

In our century, some theorists have continued to search for definitions and explanations of the comic, among them the psychoanalyst Sigmund Freud who proposed that comedy is "the last laughter of childhood" and a means of releasing tensions. Critic Susanne K. Langer in her book *Feeling and Form* (1953) wrote of the celebratory quality of comedy: "Comedy is an art form that naturally arises wherever people are gathered to celebrate life, in spring festivals, triumphs, birthdays, weddings or initiations. For it expresses the elementary strains and resolutions of animate nature, the animal drives that persist even in human nature, the delight man takes in his special mental gifts that make him lord of creation; it is an image of human vitality holding its own in the world amid the surprises of unplanned coincidence."

Most twentieth-century commentators, however, seem to be in agreement with the Swiss playwright Friedrich Duerrenmatt's disregard for differentiation between the types. Tragicomedy and the theater of the absurd have proved how blurred the distinctions between genres have become. The absurdist playwright Eugène Ionesco went so far as to say: "I never have been able to understand the distinction between the comic and the tragic."

3

TECHNICAL TERMS

Above Upstage or away from the audience. A performer crossing *above* a table keeps it between himself or herself and the front of the stage.

Acting area One of several areas into which the stage space is divided in order to facilitate blocking and the planning of stage movement.

Ad lib To improvise lines of a speech, especially in response to an emergency, such as a performer's forgetting his or her lines.

Aesthetic distance Physical or psychological separation or detachment of the audience from the dramatic action, regarded as necessary to maintain the artistic illusion in most kinds of theater.

Amphitheater A large oval, circular, or semicircular outdoor theater with rising tiers of seats around an open playing area; an exceptionally large indoor auditorium.

Antagonist The chief opponent of the protagonist in a drama. In some cases there may be several antagonists.

Apron The stage space in front of the curtain line or proscenium; also called the *forestage*.

Arena A type of stage which is surrounded by the audience on all four sides; also known as *theater-in-the-round*.

At rise An expression used when describing what is happening onstage at the moment the curtain first rises or the lights come up at the beginning of the play.

Backdrop A large drapery or painted canvas which provides the rear or upstage masking of a set.

Backstage   The stage area behind the front curtain; also, the areas beyond the setting, including wings and dressing rooms.

Basic situation   The specific problem or maladjustment from which the play arises; for example, Romeo and Juliet come from families with a strong mutual rivalry and antipathy.

Batten   A pipe or long pole suspended horizontally above the stage, upon which scenery, drapery, or lights may be hung.

Beam projector   A lighting instrument without a lens which uses a parabolic reflector to project a narrow, nonadjustable beam of light.

Below   Opposite of *above;* toward the front of the stage.

Blackout   To plunge the stage into total darkness by switching off the lights; also the condition produced by this operation.

Blocking   The arrangement of the performers' movements onstage with respect to each other and the stage space.

Book   (1) The spoken (as opposed to sung) portion of the text of a musical play. (2) To schedule engagements for artists or productions.

Border   A strip of drapery or painted canvas hung from a batten to mask the area above the stage; also, a row of lights hung from a batten.

Box set   An interior setting using flats to form the back and side walls and often the ceiling of a room.

Business   Obvious and detailed physical movement of performers to reveal character, aid action, or establish mood (e.g., pouring drinks at a bar, opening a gun case).

Catharsis   A Greek word, usually translated as "purgation," which Aristotle used in his definition of tragedy. It refers to the vicarious cleansing of certain emotions in the members of the audience through their representation onstage.

Catwalk   A narrow metal platform suspended above the stage to permit ready access to lights and scenery hung from the grid.

Center stage   A stage position in the middle acting area of the stage or the middle section extended upstage and downstage.

Chorus   In ancient Greek drama, a group of performers who sang and danced, sometimes participating in the action but usually simply commenting on it. Also, performers in a musical play who sing and dance as a group rather than individually.

Complication   The introduction in a play of a new force which creates a new balance of power and makes a delay in reaching the climax necessary and progressive. It is one way of creating conflict and precipitating a crisis.

Conflict   Tension between two or more characters that leads to crisis or a climax. The basic conflict is the fundamental struggle or imbalance underlying the play as a whole. May also be a conflict of ideologies, actions, etc.

Counterweight   A device for balancing the weight of scenery in a system which allows scenery to be raised above the stage by means of ropes and pulleys.

Crew   The backstage team assisting in mounting a production.

Cross   A movement by a performer across the stage in a given direction.

Cue   Any prearranged signal, such as the last words in a speech, a piece of business, or any action or lighting change that indicates to a performer or stage manager that it is time to proceed to the next line or action.

Cue sheet A prompt book marked with cues, or a list of cues for the use of technicians, especially the stage manager.

Curtain (1) The rise or fall of the physical curtain, which separates a play into structural parts. (2) The last bit of action preceding the fall of the curtain.

Cyclorama A large curved drop used to mask the rear and sides of the stage, painted a neutral color or blue to represent sky or open space. It may also be a permanent stage fixture made of plaster or similar durable material.

Denouement The moment when final suspense is satisfied and "the knot is untied." The term is from the French and was used to refer to the working out of the resolution in a well-made play.

Deus ex machina Literally "the god from the machine," a resolution device in classic Greek drama. A term used to indicate the intervention of super-natural forces—usually at the last moment—to save the action from its logical conclusion. Denotes in modern drama an arbitrary and coincidental solution.

Dimmer A device which permits lighting intensities to be changed smoothly and at varying rates.

Dim out To turn out the lights with a dimmer, the process usually being cued to a predetermined number of seconds or counts.

Director In American usage, the person who is responsible for the overall unity of the production and for coordinating the efforts of the contributing artists. The director is in charge of rehearsals and supervises the performers in the preparation of their parts. The American director is the equivalent of the British producer and the French *metteur-en-scène*.

Downstage The front of the stage toward the audience.

Drop A large piece of fabric, generally painted canvas, hung from a batten to the stage floor, usually to serve as backing.

Ensemble playing Acting which stresses the total artistic unity of the performance rather than the individual performances of specific actors and actresses.

Entrance The manner and effectiveness with which a performer comes into a scene as well as the actual coming onstage; also, the way it is prepared for by the playwright.

Epilogue A speech addressed to the audience after the conclusion of the play and spoken by one of the performers.

Exit A performer's leaving the stage, as well as the preparation for his or her leaving.

Exposition The imparting of information necessary for an understanding of the story but not covered by the action onstage. Events or knowledge from the past, or occurring outside the play, which must be introduced for the audience to understand the characters or plot. Exposition is always a problem in drama because relating or conveying information is static. The dramatist must find ways to make expositional scenes dynamic.

Flat A single piece of scenery, usually of standard size and made of canvas stretched over a wooden frame, used with other similar units to create a set.

Flood A lighting instrument without lenses which is used for general or large-area lighting.

Fly loft, or flies The space above the stage where scenery may be lifted out of sight by means of ropes and pulleys when it is not needed.

Follow spot A large, powerful spotlight with a sharp focus and narrow beam which is used to follow principal performers as they move about the stage.

Footlights A row of lights in the floor along the edge of the stage or apron; once a principal source of stage light, but now only rarely used.

Forestage See *Apron*.

Freeze To remain motionless onstage; especially for laughs.

Fresnel ("fruh-NEL") A type of spotlight used over relatively short distances with a soft beam edge which allows the light to blend easily with light from other sources; also, the type of lenses used in such spotlights.

Front of the house The portion of the theater reserved for the audience, as opposed to the stage and backstage areas; sometimes simply called the *house*.

Gauze See *Scrim*.

Gel A thin, flexible color medium used in lighting instruments to give color to a light beam. Properly speaking, the word applies only to such material made of gelatin, but it is often applied to similar sheets made of plastic.

Grid A metal framework above the stage from which lights and scenery are suspended.

Hand props Small props carried onstage or offstage by actors during the performance. See *Props*.

Inner stage An area at the rear of the stage which can be cut off from the rest by means of curtains or scenery and revealed for special scenes.

Irony A condition the reverse of what we have expected or an expression whose intended implication is the opposite of its literal sense. A device particularly suited to theater and found in virtually all drama.

Kill To eliminate or suppress, as to remove unwanted light or to ruin an effect through improper execution (e.g., to "kill a laugh").

Left stage The left side of the stage from the point of view of a performer facing the audience.

Mask (1) To cut off from the view of the audience by means of scenery the backstage areas or technical equipment, as to mask a row of lighting instruments. (2) A face covering in the image of the character portrayed, sometimes covering the entire head.

Masking Scenery or draperies used to hide or cover.

Mise-en-scène The arrangement of all the elements in the stage picture, either at a given moment or dynamically throughout the performance.

Multiple setting A form of stage setting, common in the Middle Ages, in which several locations are represented at the same time; also called *simultaneous setting*. Used also in various forms of contemporary theater.

Objective Stanislavski's term for that which is urgently desired and sought by a character, the desired goal which propels a character to action.

Obstacle That which delays or prevents the achieving of a goal by a character. An obstacle creates complication and conflict.

Offstage The areas of the stage, usually in the wings or backstage, which are not in view of the audience.

Onstage The area of the stage which is in view of the audience.

Open To turn or face more toward the audience.

Orchestra The ground-floor seating in an auditorium.

Pace The rate at which a performance is played; also, to play a scene or an entire play in order to determine its proper speed.

Period   A term describing any representation onstage of a former age, as *period costume, period play.*

Platform   A raised surface on the stage floor serving as an elevation for parts of the stage action and allowing for a multiplicity of stage levels.

Platform stage   An elevated stage which does not make use of a proscenium.

Plot   As distinct from *story*, the patterned arrangements of events and characters for a drama. The incidents are selected and arranged for maximum dramatic impact. The plot may begin long after the beginning of the story (and refer to information regarding the past in flashbacks or exposition).

Point of attack   The moment in the story when the play actually begins. The dramatist chooses a point in time along the continuum of events which he or she judges will best start the action and propel it forward.

Preparation   The previous arranging of circumstances, pointing of character, and placing of properties in a production so that the ensuing actions will seem reasonable; also, the actions taken by a performer getting ready for a performance.

Producer   The person responsible for the business side of a production, including raising the necessary money. In British usage, a producer is the equivalent of an American director.

Prologue   An introductory speech delivered to the audience by one of the actors or actresses before the play begins.

Prompt   To furnish a performer with missed or forgotten lines or cues during a performance.

Prompt book   The script of a play indicating performers' movements, light cues, sound cues, etc.

Props   Properties; objects used by performers onstage or required to complete the set.

Proscenium   The arch or frame surrounding the stage opening in a box or picture stage.

Protagonist   The principal character in a play, the one whom the drama is about.

Rake   To position scenery on a slant or angle other than parallel or perpendicular to the curtain line; also, an upward slope of the stage floor away from the audience.

Raked stage   A stage which slopes upward away from the audience toward the back of the set.

Regional theater   (1) Theater whose subject matter is specific to a particular geographic region. (2) Theaters situated in theatrical centers across the country.

Rehearsal   The preparation by the cast for the performance of a play through repetition and practice.

Repertory, or repertoire   A kind of acting company which at any given time has a number of plays which it can perform alternately; also, a collection of plays.

Reversal   A sudden switch of circumstances or knowledge which leads to a result contrary to expectations. Called *peripeteia* or *peripety* in Greek drama.

Revolving stage   A large turntable on which scenery is placed in such a way that, as it moves, one set is brought into view while another one turns out of sight.

Right stage The right side of the stage from the point of view of a performer facing the audience.

Scene (1) A stage setting. (2) The structural units into which the play or acts of the play are divided. (3) The location of the play's action.

Scrim A thin, open-weave fabric which is nearly transparent when lit from behind and opaque when lit from the front.

Script The written or printed text, consisting of dialogue, stage directions, character descriptions, and the like, of a play or other theatrical representation.

Set The scenery, taken as whole, for a scene or an entire production.

Set piece A piece of scenery which stands independently in the scene.

Slapstick A type of comedy or comic business which relies on ridiculous physical activity—often violent in nature—for its humor.

Spill Light from stage-lighting instruments which falls outside of the areas for which it is intended, such as light that falls on the audience.

Spine In the Stanislavski method, the dominant desire or motivation of a character which underlies his or her action in the play; usually thought of as an action and expressed as a verb.

SRO Standing room only. A notice that all seats for a performance have been sold and only standees can be accommodated.

Stage door An outside entrance to the dressing rooms and stage areas which is used by performers and technicians.

Stage convention An understanding established through custom or usage that certain devices will be accepted or assigned specific meaning or significance on an arbitrary basis, that is, without requiring that they be natural or realistic.

Stage house The stage floor and all the space above it up to the grid.

Stanislavski method A set of techniques and theories about the problems of acting which promotes a naturalistic style stressing "inner truth" as opposed to conventional theatricality.

Strike To remove pieces of scenery or props from onstage or to take down the entire set after the final performance.

Subtext A term referring to the meaning and movement of the play below the surface; that which is implied and never stated. Often more important than surface activity.

Summer stock Theater companies which operate outside of major theatrical centers during the summer months (usually June through August) and have an intensive production schedule, often doing a different play every week.

Teaser A short horizontal curtain just beyond the proscenium used to mask the fly loft and, in effect, to lower the height of the proscenium.

Technical A term referring to functions necessary to the production of a play other than those of the cast and the director, such as functions of the stage crew, carpenters, and lighting crew.

Theme The central thought of the play. The idea or ideas with which the play deals and which it expounds.

Tragic flaw The factor which is a character's chief weakness and which makes him or her most vulnerable; often intensifies in time of stress. An abused and often incorrectly applied theory from Greek drama.

Trap An opening in the stage floor, normally covered, which can be used for special effects, such as having scenery or performers rise from below, or which permits the construction of a staircase which ostensibly leads to a lower floor or cellar.

Unities A term referring to the preference that a play occur within one day (unity of time), in one locale (unity of place), and with no action irrelevant to the plot (unity of action). *Note:* Contrary to accepted opinion, Aristotle insisted only upon unity of action. Certain neoclassical critics of the Renaissance insisted on all three unities.

Unity A requirement of art; an element often setting art apart from life. In drama, refers to unity of action achieved in a play's structure and story; the integrity and wholeness of a production which combine plot, character, and dialogue within a frame of time and space to present a congruous, complete picture.

Upstage At or toward the back of the stage, away from the front edge of the stage. (The word dates from the time when the stage sloped upward from the footlights.)

Wagon stage A low platform mounted on wheels or casters by means of which scenery is moved on and offstage.

Wings Left and right offstage areas; also, narrow standing pieces of scenery, or "legs," more or less parallel to the proscenium, which form the sides of a setting.

Work lights Lights arranged for the convenience of stage technicians, situated either in backstage areas and shaded or over the stage area for use while the curtain is down.

4

MAJOR
THEATRICAL FORMS
AND MOVEMENTS

Absurdism See *Theater of the absurd.*

Allegory The representation of an abstract theme or themes through the symbolic use of character, action, and other concrete elements of a play. In its most direct form—as, for example, the medieval morality play—allegory uses the device of personification to present characters representing abstract qualities, such as virtues and vices, in an action which spells out a moral or intellectual lesson. Less direct forms of allegory may use a relatively realistic story as a guise for a hidden theme. For example, Arthur Miller's *The Crucible* can be regarded as an allegory of the McCarthy congressional investigation in the United States after World War II.

Avant-garde A French term that literally means the "advance guard" in a military formation. It has come to stand for an intellectual, literary, or artistic movement in any age that breaks with tradition and appears to be ahead of its time. Avant-garde works are usually experimental and unorthodox. In twentieth-century theater, such movements as expressionism, surrealism, absurdism, and the theories of Antonin Artaud and Jerzy Grotowski have been considered avant-garde.

Burlesque A ludicrous imitation of a dramatic form or a specific play. Closely related to satire, it usually lacks the moral or intellectual purposes of reform typical of the latter, being content to mock the excesses of other works. Famous examples of burlesque include Beaumont's *The Knight of the Burning Pestle* and, more recently, such burlesques of the movies as *Dames at Sea*. In the United States the term has come to be associated with a form of variety show which stresses sex.

Comedy As one of the oldest enduring categories of western drama, comedy has gathered under its heading a large number of different subclassifications. Although the range of comedy is broad, generally it can be said to be a play that is light in tone, is concerned with issues tending not to be serious, has a happy ending, and is designed to amuse and provoke laughter. Historically, comedy has gone through many changes. Aristophanic or Greek Old Comedy was farcical, satiric, and nonrealistic. Greek and Roman New Comedy, based on domestic situations, was more influential in the development of comedy during the Renaissance. Ben Jonson built his "comedies of humors" on Roman models. In Jonson's plays, ridicule is directed at characters who are dominated to the point of obsession by a single trait, or humor. The comedy of manners became popular in the late seventeenth century with the advent of Molière and the writers of the English Restoration. It tends to favor a cultivated or sophisticated milieu, witty dialogue, and characters whose concern with social polish is charming or ludicrous, or both. The twentieth century has seen an expansion in the territory covered by comedy as well as a blurring of its boundaries. In the final decades of the nineteenth century, George Bernard Shaw used it for the serious discussion of ideas, while Chekhov wrote plays variously interpreted as sentimental and tragicomic. Since then the horizon of the comic has been expanded by playwrights such as Pirandello and Ionesco, whose comic vision is more serious, thoughtful, and disturbing than that found in most traditional comedies.

Commedia dell'arte A form of comic theater which originated in Italy in the sixteenth century, in which dialogue was improvised around a loose scenario calling for a set of stock characters, each with a distinctive costume and traditional name. The best known of these characters are probably the *zannis*, buffoons who usually took the roles of servants and who had at their disposal a large number of slapstick routines, called *lazzis*, which ranged from simple grimaces to acrobatic stunts.

Documentary See *Theater of fact*.

Domestic drama Also known as *bourgeois drama*, domestic drama deals with problems of members of the middle and lower classes, particularly problems of the family and home. Conflicts with society, struggles within a family, dashed hopes, and renewed determination are frequently characteristics of domestic drama. It attempts to depict onstage the lifestyle of ordinary people—in language, in dress, in behavior. Domestic drama first came to the fore during the eighteenth century in Europe and Great Britain when the merchant and working classes were emerging. Because general audiences could so readily identify with the people and problems of domestic drama, it continued to gain in popularity during the nineteenth and twentieth centuries and remains a major form today.

Environmental theater A term used by Richard Schechner and others to refer to a branch of the avant-garde theater. Among its aims are the elimination of the distinction between audience space and acting space, a more flexible approach to the interactions between performers and audience, and the substitution of a multiple focus for the traditional single focus.

Epic theater A form of presentation which has come to be associated with the name of Bertolt Brecht, its chief advocate and theorist. It is aimed at the intellect rather than the emotions, seeking to present evidence regarding social questions in such a way that they may be objectively considered and an intelligent conclusion reached. Brecht felt that emotional involvement by the audience defeated this aim, and he used various devices designed to produce an emotional "alienation" of the audience from the action onstage. His plays are episodic, with narrative songs separating the segments and large posters or signs announcing the various scenes.

Existentialism   A set of philosophical ideas whose principal modern advocate is Jean-Paul Sartre. The term *existentialist* is applied by Sartre and others to plays which illustrate these views. Sartre's central thesis is that there are no longer any fixed standards or values by which one can live and that each person must create his or her own code of conduct regardless of the conventions imposed by society. Only in this way can one truly "exist" as a responsible, creative human being; otherwise one is merely a robot or automaton. Sartre's plays typically involve people who are faced with decisions forcing them into an awareness of the choice between living on their own terms and ceasing to exist as individuals.

Expressionism   A movement which developed and flourished in Germany during the period immediately preceding and following World War I. Expressionism was characterized by the attempt to dramatize subjective states through the use of distortion, striking and often grotesque images, and lyric, unrealistic dialogue. It was revolutionary in content as well as in form, portraying the institutions of society, particularly the bourgeois family, as grotesque, oppressive, and materialistic. The expressionist hero or heroine was usually a rebel against this mechanistic vision of society. Dramatic conflict tended to be replaced by the development of themes by means of visual images. The movement had great influence because it forcefully demonstrated that dramatic imagination need not be limited to either theatrical conventions or the faithful reproduction of reality. In the United States, expressionism influenced Elmer Rice's *The Adding Machine* and many of O'Neill's early plays. The basic aim of expressionism was to give external expression to inner feelings and ideas; theatrical techniques which adopt this method are frequently referred to as *expressionistic*.

Farce   One of the major genres of drama, usually regarded as a subclassification of comedy. Farce has few, if any, intellectual pretensions. It aims to entertain, to provoke laughter. Its humor is the result primarily of physical activity and visual effects, and it relies less on language and wit than do so-called higher forms of comedy. Violence, rapid movement, and accelerating pace are characteristic of farce. In bedroom farce it is the institution of marriage that is the object of the fun, but medicine, law, and business also provide material for farce.

Happening   A form of theatrical event which was developed out of the experimentation of certain American abstract artists in the 1960s. Happenings are nonliterary, replacing the script with a scenario which provides for chance occurrences. They are performed (often only once) in such places as parks and street corners, with little attempt being made to segregate the action from the audience. Emphasizing the free association of sound and movement, they avoid logical action and rational meaning.

Heroic drama A form of serious drama, written in verse or elevated prose, which features noble or heroic characters caught in extreme situations or undertaking unusual adventures. In spite of the hardships to which its leading figures are subjected, heroic drama— unlike tragedy—assumes a basically optimistic worldview. It has either a happy ending or, in cases where the hero or heroine dies, a triumphant one in which the death is not regarded tragically. Plays from all periods, and from Asia as well as the west, fall into this category. During the late seventeenth century in England, plays of this type were referred to specifically as *heroic tragedies.*

History play In the broadest sense, a play set in a historical milieu which deals with historical personages, but the term is usually applied only to plays which deal with vital issues of public welfare and are nationalistic in tone. The form originated in Elizabethan England, which produced more history plays than any other comparable place and time. Based on a religious concept of history, they were influenced by the structure of the morality play. Shakespeare was the major writer of Elizabethan history plays. His style has influenced many later history plays, notably those by the Swedish playwright Strindberg.

Impressionism A style of painting developed in the late nineteenth century which stressed the immediate impressions created by objects—particularly those resulting from the effects of light—and which tended to ignore details. As such, its influence on the theater was primarily in the area of scenic design, but the term *impressionistic* is sometimes applied to plays like Chekhov's, which rely on a series of impressions and use indirect techniques.

Kabuki The most eclectic and theatrical of the major forms of Japanese theater. It is a more popular form than the aristocratic noh drama and uses live actors, unlike the puppet theater, which is called *bunraku.* Nevertheless, it has borrowed freely from both of these forms, particularly bunraku. Roles of both sexes are performed by men in a highly theatrical, nonrealistic style. Kabuki combines music, dance, and dramatic scenes with an emphasis on color and movement. The plays are long and episodic, composed of a series of loosely connected dramatic scenes which are often performed separately.

Masque A lavish and spectacular form of private theatrical entertainment which developed in Renaissance Italy and spread rapidly to the courts of France and England. Usually intended for a single performance, the masque combined poetry, music, elaborate costumes, and spectacular effects of stage machinery. It was a social event which had members of the court acting as both spectators and performers. Loosely constructed, masques were usually written around allegorical or mythological themes.

Medieval drama There is only meager evidence of theatrical activity in Europe between the sixth and tenth centuries, but by the end of the fifteenth century a number of different types of drama had developed. The first of these, known as *liturgical drama,* was sung or chanted in Latin as part of a church service. Plays on religious themes were also written in the vernacular and performed outside of the church. The *mystery plays* (also called *cycle plays*) were based on events taken from the Old and New Testaments. Many such plays were organized into historical cycles which told the story of humanity from the creation to doomsday. The entire performance was quite long, sometimes requiring as much as 5 days. The plays were produced as a community effort, with different craft guilds usually being responsible for individual segments.

Other forms of religious drama were the *miracle play*—which dealt with events in the life of a saint—and the *morality play*. The morality play was a didactic and allegorical treatment of moral and religious questions, the most famous example being *Everyman*. The medieval period also produced several types of secular plays. Other than the *folk plays*, which dealt with legendary heroes like Robin Hood, most were farcical and fairly short.

Melodrama Historically, a distinct form of drama popular throughout the nineteenth century which emphasized action and spectacular effects and employed music to heighten the dramatic mood. Melodrama employed stock characters and clearly defined villains and heroes. More generally, the term is applied to any dramatic play which presents an unambiguous confrontation between good and evil. Characterization is often shallow and stereotypical, and because the moral conflict is externalized, action and violence are prominent, usually culminating in a happy ending meant to demonstrate the eventual triumph of good.

Mime A performance in which the action or story is conveyed through the use of movements and gestures without words. It depends on the performer's ability to suggest or create his or her surroundings through physical reactions to them and the expressiveness of the entire body.

Musical theater A broad category which includes opera, operetta, musical comedy, and other musical plays (the term *lyric theater* is sometimes used to distinguish it from pure dance). It includes any dramatic entertainment in which music and lyrics (and sometimes dance) form an integral and necessary part. The various types of musical theater often overlap and are best distinguished in terms of their separate historical origins, the quality of the music, and the range and type of skills demanded of the performance. Opera is usually defined as a work in which all parts are sung to musical accompaniment. Such works are part of a separate and much older tradition than the modern musical, which is of relatively recent American origin. The term *musical comedy* is no longer adequate to describe all the musical dramas commonly seen on and off Broadway, but they clearly belong together as part of a tradition that can easily be distinguished from both opera and operetta.

Naturalism A special form of realism. The theory of naturalism came to prominence in France and other parts of Europe in the latter half of the nineteenth century. The French playwright Émile Zola advocated a theater that would follow the scientific principles of the age, especially those discovered by Charles Darwin. Zola was also impressed by the work of Auguste Comte (1778–1857) and a physician named Claude Bernard (1813–1878). According to Zola's theory of naturalism, drama should look for the causes of disease in society the way a doctor looks for disease in a patient. Theater should therefore expose social infection in all its ugliness. Following Darwin, theater should show human beings as products of heredity and environment. The result would be a drama often depicting the ugly underside of life and expressing a pessimistic point of view. Also, drama was not to be carefully plotted or constructed but was to present a "slice of life": an attempt to look at life as it is. Very few successful plays fulfilled Zola's demands. Some of the works of Strindberg, Gorki, and others came closest to meeting the requirements of naturalism. In the contemporary period the term *naturalism* is generally applied to dramas that are superrealistic, that is, those which conform to observable reality in precise detail. Naturalism attempts to achieve the verisimilitude of a documentary film, to convey the impression that everything about the play—the setting, the way the characters dress, speak, and act—is exactly like everyday life.

Noh A rigidly traditional form of Japanese drama which in its present form dates back to the fourteenth century. Noh plays are short dramas combining music, dance, and lyric with a highly stylized and ritualistic presentation. Virtually every aspect of the production—including costumes, masks, and a highly symbolic setting—is prescribed by tradition. (Also spelled *nō*.)

Pantomime Originally a Roman entertainment in which a narrative was sung by a chorus while the story was acted out by dancers. Now used loosely to cover any form of presentation which relies on dance, gesture, and physical movement. (See *Mime*.)

Performance art A type of experimental theater that came to prominence in the 1980s but had its antecedents in previous avant-garde movements of the twentieth century. It may combine elements of dance and the visual arts with theater. At times, video and film are also added. The focus is not on a written text, and the playwright, if there is one, plays a relatively minor role in the overall scheme. A director or an individual performer supplies the vision for the production and coordinates the various elements. When it is the director's vision, performers, rather than playing normal characters, usually function as dancers, acrobats, or parts of a *tableau vivant*—they fit into the visual and choreographic scheme along with music, scenery, and the other aspects of the production. The stress is on picturization, ritual, and choreographed movement. When the performer is the creative force, he or she may tell stories, make political comments, perform acts, or play roles—again, sometimes in conjunction with music, painting, or video.

Play of ideas A play whose principal focus is on the serious treatment of social, moral, or philosophical ideas. The term *problem play* is used to designate those dramas, best exemplified in the work of Ibsen and Shaw, in which several sides of a question are both dramatized and discussed. It is sometimes distinguished from the *pièce à thèse*, or thesis play, which makes a more one-sided presentation and employs a character who sums up the "lesson" of the play and serves as the author's voice.

Poor theater A term coined by the Polish director Jerzy Grotowski to describe his ideal of theater stripped to its barest essentials. The lavish sets, lights, and costumes usually associated with the theater, he feels, merely reflect base materialistic values and must be eliminated. If theater is to become rich spiritually and aesthetically, it must first be "poor" in everything that can detract from the performer's relationship with the audience.

Realism Broadly speaking, realism is the attempt to present onstage people and events corresponding to those observable in everyday life. Examples of realism can be found in western drama—especially in comedies—in the Greek, Roman, medieval, and Renaissance periods. Sections of plays from these periods show people speaking, dressing, and acting in the manner of ordinary people of the time. Certain landmark plays are considered forerunners of modern realism. These include *Arden of Feversham* (ca. 1590), an English play about greed and lust in a middle-class family; *The London Merchant* (1731), about a young apprentice led astray by a prostitute; *Miss Sara*

Sampson (1755), a German version of *The London Merchant;* and *The Inspector General* (1836), exposing corruption in a provincial Russian town. It was in the latter part of the nineteenth century, however, that realism took hold as a major form of theater. As the middle class came more and more to dominate life in Europe and the United States, and as scientific and psychological discoveries challenged the heroic or romantic viewpoint, drama began to center on the affairs of ordinary people in their natural surroundings. The plays of Ibsen, Strindberg, and Chekhov showed that powerful, effective drama could be written about such people. The degree of realism varies in drama, ranging from *slice-of-life naturalism* to *heightened realism.* In the latter, nonrealistic and symbolic elements are introduced into a basically realistic format. Despite frequent challenges from other forms during the past hundred years, realism remains a major form of contemporary theater. (See also *Naturalism.*)

Restoration drama   English drama after the restoration of the monarchy, from 1660 to 1700. Presented for an audience of aristocrats who gathered about the court of Charles II, drama of this period consisted largely of heroic tragedies in the neoclassical style and comedies of manners which reflected a cynical view of human nature.

Romanticism   A literary and dramatic movement of the nineteenth century which developed as a reaction to the confining strictures of neoclassicism. Imitating the loose, episodic structure of Shakespeare's plays, the romantics sought to free the writer from all rules and looked to the unfettered inspiration of artistic genius as the source of all creativity. They laid more stress on mood and atmosphere than on content, but one of their favorite themes was the gulf between human beings' spiritual aspirations and their physical limitations.

Satire   Dramatic satire uses the techniques of comedy, such as wit, irony, and exaggeration, to attack and expose folly and vice. Satire can attack specific public figures, as does the political satire *Macbird,* or it can point its barbs at more general traits which can be found in many of us. Thus Molière's *Tartuffe* ridicules religious hypocrisy, Shaw's *Arms and the Man* exposes the romantic glorification of war, and Wilde's *The Importance of Being Earnest* attacks the English upper classes.

Street theater   A generic term which includes a number of groups that perform in the open and attempt to relate to the needs of a specific community or neighborhood. Many such groups sprang up in the 1960s, partly as a response to social unrest and partly because there was a need for a theater which could express the specific concerns of minority and ethnic neighborhoods.

Surrealism   A movement attacking formalism in the arts which developed in Europe after World War I. Seeking a deeper and more profound reality than that presented to the rational, conscious mind, the surrealists replaced realistic action with the strange logic of the dream and cultivated such techniques as automatic writing and free association of ideas. Although few plays written by the surrealists are highly regarded, the movement had a great influence on later avant-garde theater—notably theater of the absurd and theater of cruelty.

Symbolism   Closely linked to symbolist poetry, symbolist drama was a movement of the late nineteenth and early twentieth centuries which sought to replace realistic representation of life with the expression of an inner truth.

APPENDIX 4 · MAJOR THEATRICAL FORMS AND MOVEMENTS

Hoping to restore the religious and spiritual significance of theater, symbolism used myth, legend, and symbols in an attempt to reach beyond everyday reality. The plays of Maurice Maeterlinck (1862–1949) are among the best-known symbolist dramas.

Theater of cruelty   Antonin Artaud's visionary concept of a theater based on magic and ritual which would liberate deep, violent, and erotic impulses. He wished to reveal the cruelty which he saw as existing beneath all human action—the pervasiveness of evil and violent sexuality. To do this, he advocated radical changes in the use of theatrical space, the integration of audience and actors, and the full utilization of the affective power of light, color, movement, and language. Although Artaud had little success implementing his theories himself, he had considerable influence on other writers and directors, particularly Peter Brook, Jean-Louis Barrault, and Jerzy Grotowski.

Theater of fact   A term which encompasses a number of different types of documentary drama which have developed during the twentieth century. Methods of presentation differ. The Living Newspaper drama of the 1930s used signs and slide projections to deal with broad social problems; other documentary dramas use a more realistic approach. Contemporary theater of fact, as represented by such plays as *The Deputy* and *The Investigation*, tries to portray actual events with an appearance of authenticity.

Theater of the absurd   A phrase first used by Martin Esslin to describe certain playwrights of the 1950s and 1960s who expressed a similar point of view regarding the absurdity of the human condition. Their plays are dramatizations of the dramatist's inner sense of the absurdity and futility of existence. Rational language is debased and replaced by clichés and trite or irrelevant remarks. Repetitious or meaningless activity is substituted for logical action. Realistic psychological motivation is replaced by automatic behavior which is often absurdly inappropriate to the situation. Although the subject matter is serious, the tone of these plays is usually comic and ironic. Among the best-known absurdists are Beckett, Ionesco, and Albee.

Theatricalism   A style of production and playwriting which emphasizes theatricality for its own sake. Less a coherent movement than a quality found in the work of many artists rebelling against realism, it frankly admits the artifice of the stage and borrows freely from the circus, the music hall, and similar entertainments.

Tragedy   One of the most fundamental dramatic forms in the western tradition, tragedy involves a serious action of universal significance and has important moral and philosophical implications. Following Aristotle, most critics agree that the tragic hero or heroine should be an essentially admirable person whose downfall elicits our sympathy while leaving us with a feeling that there has in some way been a triumph of the moral and cosmic order which transcends the fate of any individual. The disastrous outcome of a tragedy should be seen as the inevitable result of the character and his or her situation, including forces beyond the character's control. Traditionally, tragedy was about the lives and fortunes of kings and nobles, and there has been a great deal of debate about whether it is possible to have a modern tragedy—a tragedy about ordinary people. The answers to this question are as varied as the critics who address themselves to it; but most seem to agree that although such plays may be tragedies, they are of a somewhat different order.

Tragicomedy   During the Renaissance the word was used for plays that had tragic themes and noble characters yet ended happily. Modern tragicomedy combines serious and comic elements. Tragicomedy is, in fact, increasingly the form chosen by "serious" playwrights. Sometimes comic behavior and situations have serious or tragic consequences—as in Duerrenmatt's *The Visit*. At times the ending is indeterminate or ambivalent—as in Beckett's *Waiting for Godot*. In most cases a quality of despair or hopelessness is introduced because human beings are seen as incapable of rising above their circumstances or their own nature; the fact that the situation is also ridiculous serves to make their plight that much more horrible.

Well-made play   A type of play popular in the nineteenth and early twentieth centuries which combined apparent plausibility of incident and surface realism with a tightly constructed and contrived plot. Well-made plays typically revolved about the question of social respectability, and the plot often hinged on the manipulation of a piece of incriminating evidence which threatened to destroy the facade of respectability. Although the well-made play is less popular now, many of its techniques continue to be used by modern playwrights.

5

HISTORICAL
OUTLINE

THE ANCIENT WORLD

THEATER		SOCIETY, POLITICS, CULTURE
	EGYPT	
	ca. 3100 B.C.	Old Kingdom (ca. 3100–2185 B.C.)
Ritual drama	ca. 2750 B.C.	
Abydos Passion Play (ca. 2500–550 B.C.)	ca. 2500 B.C.	
	2133 B.C.	Middle Kingdom (2133–1786 B.C.)
	1580 B.C.	New Kingdom (ca. 1580–1085 B.C.)

Note: ca. means "circa," or approximately the date at which the event took place; fl. means "flourished" at the time; r. means "reigned."

THEATER		SOCIETY, POLITICS, CULTURE
	GREECE	
	ca. 800 B.C.	Homer
	ca. 585 B.C.	Thales of Miletus begins natural philosophy (physics)
Play contests begun in Athens	534 B.C.	
Thespis "first actor" fl.	ca. 530 B.C.	
	ca. 520 B.C.	Pythagoras fl.
	510 B.C.	Democracy in Athens
	499 B.C.	Persian wars (499–478 B.C.)
	490 B.C.	Battle of Marathon
Comedy introduced to City Dionysia	487 B.C.	
Aeschylus introduces second actor	ca. 471 B.C.	
Sophocles introduces third actor	ca. 468 B.C.	
	ca. 460 B.C.	Periclean Athens—"golden age" (ca. 460–429 B.C.)
Oresteia, Aeschylus (525–456 B.C.)	458 B.C.	Socrates (ca. 470–399 B.C.)
Prizes for tragic acting awarded	449 B.C.	
	447 B.C.	Beginning of Parthenon; Herodotus fl.
Oedipus the King, Sophocles (496–406 B.C.)	ca. 430 B.C.	Peloponnesian War (431–404 B.C.)
The Trojan Women, Euripides (484–406 B.C.)	415 B.C.	Plato (429–348 B.C.)
Lysistrata, Aristophanes (ca. 450–ca. 388 B.C.)	411 B.C.	
	399 B.C.	Trial and execution of Socrates
	384 B.C.	Aristotle born
	371 B.C.	Theban hegemony (371–362 B.C.)
Poetics (ca. 335–323 B.C.), Aristotle (384–322 B.C.)	335 B.C.	Alexander the Great (356–323 B.C.) occupies Greece
Theater of Dionysus completed	ca. 325 B.C.	

THEATER		SOCIETY, POLITICS, CULTURE
Greek theaters built throughout Mediterranean area (ca. 320–ca. 100 B.C.)	ca. 320 B.C.	Hellenistic culture spreads throughout eastern Mediterranean
Menander (342–292 B.C.) writer of *New Comedy*		
Menander's *Dyskolos*	316 B.C.	
Artists of Dionysus recognized	277 B.C.	

		ROME
	753 B.C.	Traditional date for the founding of Rome
	264 B.C.	First Punic War (264–241 B.C.) Greek influence on Roman culture
Roman farce comedy begins		
Regular comedy and tragedy added to Ludi Romani	240 B.C.	
	218 B.C.	Second Punic War (218–201 B.C.)
Menaechmi (ca 205–184 B.C.) Plautus (ca. 254–184 B.C.)	205 B.C.	
Phormio, Terence (ca. 185–159 B.C.)	161 B.C.	
	147 B.C.	Rome annexes Macedonia
	144 B.C.	First high-level aqueduct in Rome
Vitruvius's *De Architectura*	90 B.C.	
First permanent theater in Rome	55 B.C.	Golden age of Roman literature: Catullus, Cicero, Vergil, Ovid (83 B.C.-A.D. 14)
	44 B.C.	Assassination of Julius Caesar
Horace's *Art of Poetry*	24 B.C.	
Seneca (ca. 4 B.C.-A.D. 65) writes tragedies	27 B.C.	Emperor Augustus Caesar begins reign; rules until A.D. 14
Roman theater and amphitheaters built in first and second centuries	ca. A.D. 30	Crucifixion of Jesus

THEATER		SOCIETY, POLITICS, CULTURE
	A.D. 161	Marcus Aurelius rules until A.D. 180
Theater from first through fourth centuries is mostly mime, pantomime, and spectacle	A.D. 250	Persecution of Christians builds for next fifty years
	324	Emperor Constantine rules until 337
Strong church opposition to theater		St. Augustine (354–430) St. Jerome (ca. 340–420)
Council of Carthage decrees excommunication for those who attend theater rather than church on holy days, actors forbidden sacraments	398	
	410	Sack of Rome
	476	Collapse of western Roman Empire

Note: For almost a thousand years—from the first through the tenth centuries—there was little formal theater in western civilization. We must skip from Rome at the beginning of the Christian era to the Middle Ages to find significant information concerning theater.

MIDDLE AGES

THEATER		SOCIETY, POLITICS, CULTURE
Traveling performers (500–925)	500	
	527	Justinian becomes Byzantine emperor
	570	Mohammed born
	800	Charlemagne crowned emperor of Holy Roman Empire
Quem Quaeritis trope (introduction of choral dialogue into church service)	ca. 925	
Hrosvitha, a nun, writes Christian comedies based on Terence	ca. 970	
(Liturgical drama in Latin, tenth century and later)	1066	Normans conquer England

THEATER		SOCIETY, POLITICS, CULTURE
	1095	First Crusade (until 1096)
Play of Adam, oldest known scriptural drama in the vernacular	ca. 1140	(earliest manufacture of paper in Europe)
(Drama moves out of the church)	1215	Magna Carta
Festival of Corpus Christi established	1264	Roger Bacon (ca. 1220–1292) Thomas Aquinas (1224–1274)
The Play of the Bower, beginning of secular drama in France	ca. 1276	Giotto (ca. 1266–1337), Italian painter
	ca. 1310	*The Divine Comedy,* Dante Alighieri (1265–1321)
	1338	Hundred Years' War between England and France (until 1456) Petrarch (1304–1374)
Vernacular religious drama flourishes; peak of medieval theater (1350–1550)	1350	
	1353	*Decameron,* Giovanni Boccaccio (1313–1375)
Second Shepherds Play, one of a series of *cycle* plays based on Bible	ca. 1375	Geoffrey Chaucer (ca. 1342–1400)
	1378	Urban VI in Rome; Clement VII at Avignon
The Castle of Perseverence	ca. 1425	
	1431	Joan of Arc burned at the stake
	ca. 1450	Gutenberg, invention of movable type
	1453	Constantinople falls to the Turks

RENAISSANCE TO 1700

THEATER		SOCIETY, POLITICS, CULTURE
	1396	Manuel Chrysoloras opens Greek classes in Florence; beginning of revival of Greek literature in Italy
Twelve of Plautus's lost plays rediscovered	1429	

447

THEATER		SOCIETY, POLITICS, CULTURE
	1434	Cosimo de Medici rules Florence
	1440	Founding of Platonic Academy in Florence
	1452	Leonardo da Vinci born
	1455	Wars of the Roses in England (until 1485)
Pierre Pathelin, one of many popular farces in France	ca. 1464	
	1469	Spain united under Isabella and Ferdinand
(Plays in Latin, modeled on Roman drama, written in the academies of Italy)	1478	Lorenzo de Medici controls Florence (until 1492)
		Inquisition established in Spain
(First professional acting companies in Spain; beginnings of secular drama)	ca. 1480	
	1484	*Birth of Venus*, by Sandro Botticelli (1446–1510), Italy
Vitruvius's *De Architectura* published	1486	
(Growth of professional acting troupes)	1492	Expulsion of the Jews from Spain; Columbus discovers America; conquest of Granada
	1494	Italian wars weaken Italy politically but spread its cultural influence
Plays by Aristophanes published by Aldine Press in Venice	1498	
Everyman, morality play	1500	
	1504	*David*, Michelangelo (1474–1564), Italy
	1505	*Mona Lisa*, Leonardo da Vinci (1452–1519), Italy
I Suppositi, Ludovico Ariosto (1474–1533), Italian vernacular comedy based on Plautus and Terence	1509	Henry VIII of England (r. 1509–1547)
(Interest in classical drama in schools and universities in England)		

THEATER		SOCIETY, POLITICS, CULTURE
Mandragola, Niccolò Machiavelli (1469–1527), Italy	ca. 1512	Sistine Chapel ceiling, Michelangelo (1508–1512)
Sofonisba, Giangiorgio Trissino (1478–1550), Italian tragedy based on classic models	1513	*The Prince,* Machiavelli, Italy
	1515	Francis I of France (r. 1515–1547)
	1516	*Utopia,* Thomas More (1428–1535), England
	1517	Martin Luther (1483–1546) posts theses, Germany
Confrérie de la Passion given theatrical monopoly in Paris	1518	
	1519	Hernán Cortés (1485–1547) conquers Aztecs for Spain
	1530	Francisco Pizarro (ca. 1475–1541) takes Peru
	1532	*Pantagruel,* François Rabelais (ca. 1483–1553), France
	1534	Act of Supremacy begins English Reformation
Ralph Roister Doister, English "school drama"	1540	
Serlio's *Architettura* describes scene design and stage effects	1545	
Lope de Rueda (ca. 1510–1565), first important popular dramatist in Spain		
Religious plays prohibited in France; Hôtel de Bourgogne opens; perspective scenery used for first time at Lyon for performance celebrating marriage of Henri II and Catherine de Médicis	1548	
Peak of commedia dell'arte (1550–1650)	1550	
Gammer Gurton's Needle, English "school drama"	ca. 1552	

THEATER		SOCIETY, POLITICS, CULTURE
	1556	Philip II of Spain (r. 1556–1598)
	1558	Elizabeth I of England (r. 1558–1603)
	1560	Uffizi Museum at Florence founded
Gorboduc, Sackville and Norton, first English tragedy; drama at the Inns of Court	1561	
	1564	St. Peter's in Rome (begun 1546)
	1567	Netherlands revolts against Spain
Castelvetro requires unities	1570	
	1572	St. Bartholomew's Day massacre in France, Protestants murdered
The Theater and the Blackfriars, first permanent theaters in England	1576	
Coral de la Cruz, first permanent theater in Spain	1579	El Greco (1541–1614), Spain
	1580	*Essays,* Michel Eyquem de Montaigne (1533–1592), France
Corral del Principe built in Madrid	1583	
Teatro Olimpico, first permanent theater in Italy	1584	(Italy divided politically and largely under foreign rule)
(Commedia dell'arte, improvised popular theater in Italy)		
The Spanish Tragedy, Thomas Kyd (1558–1594), England	ca. 1587	
	1588	Defeat of the Spanish Armada
Alexandre Hardy (ca. 1572–1632) first French professional playwright		
Doctor Faustus, Christopher Marlowe (1564–1593), England	1589	Henry IV (r. 1589–1610) unites France

THEATER		SOCIETY, POLITICS, CULTURE
	1593	*The Faerie Queene,* Edmund Spenser (ca. 1552–1599), England
Alleyn's Lord Admiral's Men and Burbage's Lord Chamberlain's Men the major companies in London	1594	
	1598	Edict of Nantes ends religious wars in France; Philip II of Spain (rules to 1621)
The Globe Theater built in England	1599	
Hamlet, William Shakespeare (1564–1616), England	ca. 1600	
Lord Chamberlain's men become the King's men	1603	James I of England (r. 1603–1625)
	1605	Cervantes, *Don Quixote,* Part I, Spain
Volpone, Ben Jonson (1572–1637), England; Aleotti uses flat wing, England	1606	
	1607	Jamestown, Virginia, founded
	1610	Henri IV of France assassinated; Louis XII (rules to 1643)
	1611	King James Bible, England
The Duchess of Malfi, John Webster (1580?–?1625), England	1613	
The Sheep Well, Lope de Vega (1562–1635), Spain	ca. 1614	
The Cave of Salamanca, Miguel de Cervantes (1547–1616), Spain		
	1616	Cervantes, *Don Quixote,* Part II, Spain
Teatro Farnese in Italy, first surviving proscenium-arch theater	1618	

THEATER		SOCIETY, POLITICS, CULTURE
Inigo Jones (1573–1652), court masques in England, Jacobean playwrights: Beaumont, Fletcher, Webster, Shirley, and Ford	1620	*Novum Organum,* Francis Bacon (1561–1626), England
	1621	Philip IV of Spain (rules to 1665)
(Italian commedia popular in France)	1624	Administration of Richelieu consolidates power of the king in France (until 1642)
	1625	Charles I of England (r. 1625–1649)
	1629	Charles I dissolves English Parliament
'Tis Pity She's a Whore, John Ford (1586–1639), England	ca. 1633	
The Cid, Pierre Corneille (1606–1684), France	1636	
Life Is a Dream, Calderón de la Barca (1600–1681), Spain		
	1637	French Academy founded; *Discourse on Method,* René Descartes (1596–1650)
The Opinions of the French Academy on The Cid establish the rule of neoclassicism in France	1638	Galileo Galilei (1564–1642), Italy
Theaters in England closed by Parliament; theatrical performances banned (until 1660)	1642	English Civil War (until 1646)
		Rule of Cardinal Mazarin in France (until 1661)
	1643	Death of Louis XIII; Louis XIV of France (rules to 1715)
New Marais Theatre in Paris with proscenium arch	1644	
Torelli brings Italian scenery to France	1645	
Invention of chariot-and-pole system of scene shifting permits rapid change of scenes		
	1649	Charles I of England beheaded; Commonwealth (until 1660)

THEATER		SOCIETY, POLITICS, CULTURE
	1651	*Leviathan,* Thomas Hobbes (1588–1679), England
Italian scene designers (Sabbatini, Torelli, Parigi) famous throughout Europe		
	1659	Peace of the Pyrenees; decline of Spanish power
English theaters reopened; royal patents establish theatrical monopolies	1660	Restoration of the English monarchy; Charles II r. 1660–1685)
	1661	Louis XIV, the "Sun King," absolute ruler of France (r. 1643–1715)
Thomas Betterton (ca. 1635–1710), foremost English actor	1662	Royal Society founded in England, dedicated to science
Molière's troupe given Palais Royal; *The Misanthrope,* Molière (1622–1673), France	1666	
	1667	*Paradise Lost,* John Milton (1608–1674), England
	1669	*Pensées,* Blaise Pascal (1623–1662), France
Drury Lane Theater, England	1674	
The Country Wife, William Wycherley (1640–1716), England	1675	
All for Love, John Dryden (1631–1700), England; *Phaedra,* Jean Racine (1639–1699), France	1677	
Comédie Française, first national theater company in France	1680	
	1687	Isaac Newton (1642–1727) formulates laws of universal gravitation
Comédie Française gets new theater, to be used until 1770	1689	"Glorious revolution" in England of William and Mary (r. 1689–1702)

THEATER		SOCIETY, POLITICS, CULTURE
	1690	*Essay Concerning Human Understanding,* John Locke (1632–1704), England
Jeremy Collier publishes attack on the immorality of the English stage	1698	
The Way of the World, William Congreve (1670–1729), England	1700	

EIGHTEENTH CENTURY

THEATER		SOCIETY, POLITICS, CULTURE
(Bibiena family dominates scene design throughout century—"baroque," lavish, and ornate)	1701	War of the Spanish Succession in France (until 1714)
		Peter the Great (r. 1682–1725) begins westernization of Russia
(French and Italian influence in the court theaters of Germany, Scandinavia, and Russia)	1702	Queen Anne of England (r. 1702–1714)
Ferdinando Bibiena introduces angle perspective	ca. 1703	
	1711	*The Spectator* begun by Addison and Steele in England
	1714	George I of England (r. 1714–1727), House of Hanover Baroque music: Johann Sebastian Bach (1685–1750) and George Frederick Handel (1685–1759)
	1715	Louis XIV of France dies
	1719	Daniel Defoe's *Robinson Crusoe*
	1721	Robert Walpole, first English prime minister (1721–1742)
Jeppe of the Hill, Ludvig Holberg (1684–1754), beginning of Danish drama	1722	

THEATER		SOCIETY, POLITICS, CULTURE
Johann Gottsched (1700–1766) and Caroline Neuber (1697–1760) begin reforms of German theater		
	ca. 1724	Baroque music flourishes (Bach and Handel)
The Conscious Lovers, Richard Steele (1672–1729), rise of sentimental comedy in England		
	1726	*Gulliver's Travels*, Jonathan Swift (1667–1745), England
The Beggar's Opera, John Gay (1685–1732), England	1728	
The London Merchant, George Lillo (1693–1739), English bourgeois drama	1731	
Zaire, Voltaire (1694–1778), French neoclassical tragedy	1732	(Italy remains divided throughout century)
Licensing Act imposes severe censorship on theater in England	1737	(French painters Jean Antoine Watteau, François Boucher, and Jean Honoré Fragonard stress rococo sensuality in painting)
(First permanent theaters in Germany	1740	Frederick the Great of Prussia (r. 1740–1786), "enlightened despotism"
Charles Macklin's Shylock— an attempt at costume reform		
David Garrick (1717–1779) becomes actor-manager at Drury Lane	1747	
Garrick, innovations in English acting	1748	*Clarissa*, Samuel Richardson (1689–1761), England
Encyclopedia (1748–1772) in France, edited by Denis Diderot (1713–1784), advocates more realistic drama and staging		
P. J. DeLoutherbourg (1740–1812), realism and "local color" in English scene design	1749	*Tom Jones*, Henry Fielding (1707–1754), England

THEATER		SOCIETY, POLITICS, CULTURE
Hallam acting troupe in Virginia	1752	
The Mistress of the Inn, Carlo Goldoni (1707–1793), Italy	1753	
Voltaire's *Orphan of China*	1755	*Dictionary,* Samuel Johnson (1709–1784), England
	1756	Seven Years' War (until 1763); loss to France of much of colonial empire
The Father of a Family, Diderot, bourgeois drama, France	1758	
		Joshua Reynolds (1723–1792), English painter
Spectators banished from French stage	ca. 1759	Voltaire's *Candide*
"Boulevard" theaters built in Paris; growth of popular drama; Gozzi's *Turandot*	1762	*Social Contract* and *Emile,* Jean-Jacques Rousseau (1712–1778), France
		Catherine the Great (r. 1762–1796) expands Russian power
	1765	Watt's steam engine, England
Drottningholm in Sweden completed; Southwark theater in Philadelphia	1766	
Hamburg National Theater (to 1769)	1767	
"Storm and stress" movement (to 1787)		
Minna von Barnhelm, Gotthold Lessing (1729–1781), Germany		
Hamburg Dramaturgy, Lessing; first major German dramatic criticism		
She Stoops to Conquer, Oliver Goldsmith (1730–1774),	1773	Thomas Gainsborough (1727–1788), English painter
	1775	American Revolution (until 1783)

THEATER	SOCIETY, POLITICS, CULTURE
"Storm and stress" playwrights in Germany. Friedrich Schröder (1744–1818), major German actor	
	1776 Declaration of Independence (American Revolution 1775–1781)
	Wealth of Nations, Adam Smith (1723–1790), England
The School for Scandal, Richard Brinsley Sheridan (1751–1816), England	1777 (Rise of English colonial power; industrial revolution)
	1781 *Critique of Pure Reason,* Immanuel Kant (1724–1804), Germany
The Marriage of Figaro, Pierre-Augustin Caron de Beaumarchais (1732–1799), France	1783
(Impulse toward national theater and drama grows in Europe. Beginnings of German romanticism)	1787 *Don Giovanni,* Wolfgang Amadeus Mozart (1756–1791), Austria
	1789 French Revolution (until 1797)
(Attempts made at greater realism in costumes and scenery)	1793 Painting, *Death of Marat,* Jacques-Louis David (1748–1825), France
Johann Wolfgang von Goethe (1749–1832) "directs" Weimar Court Theater; Friedrich Schiller (1759–1805) assists	1798
	1799 Consulate of Napoleon
Mary Stuart, Schiller, Germany	1800

NINETEENTH CENTURY

THEATER	SOCIETY, POLITICS, CULTURE
	1803 Louisiana Purchase
François-Joseph Talma (1763–1823), foremost French actor	1804 Napoleon I becomes emperor of France

THEATER		SOCIETY, POLITICS, CULTURE
Faust, Part I, Goethe, Germany	1808	Fifth Symphony of Ludwig van Beethoven (1770–1827), Germany
René C.G. de Pixérécourt (1773–1844) rise of French melodrama	1810	Mme. de Staël (1766–1817); German romanticism brought to France
The Broken Jug, Heinrich von	1811	
	1815	Battle of Waterloo; "Metternich system" imposes strict censorship and impedes growth of liberalism in Germany
Chestnut Street Theater in Philadelphia becomes first totally gas-lit theater	1816	
The Cenci, Percy Bysshe Shelley (1792–1822), England	1819	
	1822	Eugène Delacroix (1798–1863), painter, France
Charles Kemble's (1775–1854) production of *King John* in England; historical accuracy in costumes and sets	1823	Monroe Doctrine
Boris Godunov, Alexander Pushkin (1799–1837), Russia	1825	"Decembrist rising" in Russia
	1829	Andrew Jackson, president of United States (until 1837)
Edmund Kean (1787–1833), romantic acting in England		
Hernani, Victor Hugo (1802–1885); "romantic" rebellion against neoclassicism in France	1830	In France, revolution establishes "July monarchy" of Louis Philippe (r. 1830–1848); *The Red and the Black,* Stendhal (1783–1842); Auguste Comte founds positivism
	1832	Upper-middle class enfranchised in England
Lorenzaccio, Alfred de Musset (1810–1857), France	1834	

THEATER		SOCIETY, POLITICS, CULTURE
The Inspector General, Nikolai Gogol (1809–1852), Russia; *Woyzeck*, Georg Büchner (1813–1837), Germany	1836	
	1837	Victoria of England (r. 1837–1901)
William Charles Macready (1793–1873), reforms in English acting and staging		
	1838	*Oliver Twist*, Charles Dickens (1812–1870), England
	1839	Chartist agitation in England to improve condition of working classes
The Glass of Water, Augustin-Eugène Scribe (1791–1861); well-made plays, France	1840	
Theater Regulation Act abolishes monopoly of patent theaters in London	1843	
Maria Magdalena, Friedrich Hebbel (1813–1863), Germany	1844	
	1848	Italian War of Independence in France (until 1849)
		Revolution in Germany and Austria (until 1849)
Astor Place Theater riot in New York	1849	
A Month in the Country, Ivan Turgenev (1818–1883), Russia	1850	
	1851	*Moby Dick*, Herman Melville (1819–1891), United States
		Rigoletto, Giuseppe Verdi (1813–1901), Italy
Camille, Alexandre Dumas fils (1824–1895); "thesis" plays, France	1852	Second French Empire, Napoleon III (r. 1852–1870)
First production of *Uncle Tom's Cabin*, most popular American play of century; use of touring companies		

459

THEATER		SOCIETY, POLITICS, CULTURE
	1853	Crimean War (until 1856)
	1857	*Les Fleurs du Mal,* Charles Baudelaire (1821–1867); *Madame Bovary,* Gustave Flaubert (1821–1880), France
The Thunderstorm, Alexander Ostrovsky (1823–1886), Russia	1859	*Tristan and Isolde,* Richard Wagner (1813–1883), Germany
		Origin of Species, Charles Darwin (1809–1882); *Idylls of the King* (1st vol.), Alfred, Lord Tennyson (1809–1892); first oil well
M. Perrichon's Journey, Eugène Labiche (1815–1888), France	1860	
Victorien Sardou (1831–1908), *A Scrap of Paper*		
	1861	American Civil War (until 1865)
		Liberation of the serfs in Russia
	1862	Bismarck becomes minister-president of Prussia
Edwin Booth (1833–1893) plays Hamlet for 100 nights in London; long "runs" become common	1864	
George II, Duke of Saxe-Meiningen (1826–1914) begins reforms in staging; beginning of modern director, Germany	1866	*Crime and Punishment,* Fyodor Dostoevsky (1821–1881), Russia
	1867	*Das Kapital,* Karl Marx (1818–1883), Germany
Booth's Theater in New York	1869	*War and Peace,* Leo Tolstoy (1828–1910), Russia
	1870	Franco-Prussian War (1870–1871); Paris Commune; Third Republic established; unification of Italy complete
	1871	German Empire founded
Thérèse Raquin, Émile Zola (1840–1902); naturalism in drama, France	1873	

THEATER		SOCIETY, POLITICS, CULTURE
Paris Opera built, epitome of nineteenth-century theater architecture	1874	French impressionist painters
Wagner's Bayreuth theater, innovations in theater architecture, Germany	1876	*Tom Sawyer,* Mark Twain (1835–1910); telephone patented
H.M.S. Pinafore, W. S. Gilbert (1836–1911) and Arthur Sullivan (1842–1900), England	1877	
A Doll's House, Henrik Ibsen (1828–1906), Norway	1879	Invention of the incandescent lamp
Savoy Theater employs electricity in London	1881	
The Vultures, Henry Becque (1837–1899), France	1885	
Henry Irving (1838–1905), first English actor to be knighted, established role of the director in commercial theater		
The Power of Darkness, Leo Tolstoy, Russia	1886	
French actress Sarah Bernhardt (1844–1923), most famous "star" of the century		
Antoine's Théâtre Libre founded in Paris; electricity replaces gas in theater lighting	1887	
The Father, August Strindberg (1849–1912), Sweden	1888	William II (r. 1888–1918), emperor of Germany
Freie Bühne Theater, formed in Germany	1889	
Independent Theater of London	1891	
The Second Mrs. Tanqueray, Arthur Wing Pinero (1855–1934), England	1893	
Shaw's *Arms and the Man*	1894	Dreyfus affair in France (until 1906)

461

THEATER		SOCIETY, POLITICS, CULTURE
The Importance of Being Earnest, Oscar Wilde (1854–1900), England	1895	
The Sea Gull, Anton Chekhov (1860–1904), Russia	1896	
King Ubu, Alfred Jarry (1873–1907), precursor of absurdism, France		
Moscow Art Theater founded	1898	

TWENTIETH CENTURY

THEATER		SOCIETY, POLITICS, CULTURE
	1900	Freud's *Interpretation of Dreams,* Austria
Riders to the Sea, John Millington Synge (1871–1909), Ireland	1901	Theodore Roosevelt (until 1909), Open Door policy
	1903	Wright brothers make successful airplane flight
The Art of the Theater, Gordon Craig (1872–1966); *Major Barbara,* George Bernard Shaw (1856–1950), England	1905	Einstein's theory of relativity; insurrection in Russia
		Separation of church and state in France
	1907	*Les Demoiselles d'Avignon,* Pablo Picasso (1881–1973), cubist painting
Adolphe Appia (1862–1928), pioneer in nonillusionistic scene design		Marcel Proust (1871–1922)
Justice, by John Galsworthy (1867–1933), England	1910	
Théâtre du Vieux Columbier (1879–1949), France	1913	*Le Sacre du printemps,* Igor Stravinsky (1882–1971), Russia, United States
	1914	World War I (until 1918)
Provincetown Players organized, United States	1915	

THEATER		SOCIETY, POLITICS, CULTURE
	1916	Easter Rebellion in Ireland
	1917	United States enters war; Bolshevik Revolution in Russia
Theatre Guild founded, United States	1918	Spengler's *Decline of the West* predicts fall of western civilization, Germany
	1919	Eighteenth Amendment begins prohibition (until 1933), United States
	1920	Nineteenth Amendment extends suffrage to women, United States
Man and the Masses, Ernst Toller (1893–1939), German expressionism	1921	Irish Free State founded
Six Characters in Search of an Author, Luigi Pirandello (1867–1936), Italy		
The Circle, Somerset Maugham (1874–1965), England		
	1922	*Ulysses,* James Joyce (1882–1941); Mussolini's fascists take power in Italy
Yevgeny Vakhtangov (1883–1922), Oleg Yevreinov (1879–1953), Alexander Taïrov (1885–1950), Vsevelod Meyerhold (1874–1940): period of postrevolutionary creativity and innovation in Russia (until 1972)		
	1923	Hitler's "beer hall putsch" in Munich
My Life in Art, Constantin Stanislavski (1863–1938), revolution in acting, Russia	1924	*The Trial,* Franz Kafka (1883–1924), Czechoslovakia; death of Lenin, Russia
First Surrealist Manifesto, André Breton (1896–1966), France		

463

THEATER		SOCIETY, POLITICS, CULTURE
Desire under the Elms, Eugene O'Neill (1888–1953), United States; *Juno and the Paycock,* Sean O'Casey (1884–1964), Ireland		
	1925	*The Dehumanization of Art,* José Ortega y Gasset (1883–1955), Spain
		The Magic Mountain, Thomas Mann (1875–1955), Germany
Meyerhold's production of *The Inspector General,* "constructivist" staging, Russia	1926	Arnold Schoenberg (1874–1951), "twelve-tone" music, Austria
The Three-Penny Opera, Bertolt Brecht (1898–1956), "epic theater," Germany	1928	
Max Reinhardt (1873–1943), foremost director in Europe	1929	*Look Homeward Angel,* Thomas Wolfe (1900–1938); *The Sound and the Fury,* William Faulkner (1897–1962); stock market crash
Private Lives, Noël Coward (1899–1973), England	1930	
Group Theater (until 1941); brought Stanislavski methods to the United States	1931	Collapse of Spanish monarchy
	1933	New Deal legislation begins; Nazis take power in Germany
Brecht and other writers and artists leave Germany		
"Socialist realism" declared official Soviet style	1934	
The Infernal Machine, Jean Cocteau (1889–1963), France		
Brecht and other German artists emigrate; Gielgud's *Hamlet*		
Tiger at the Gates, Jean Giraudoux (1882–1944), France;	1935	Italy attacks Ethiopia
House of Bernarda Alba, Federico García Lorca (1898–1936), Spain		Nuremberg laws deprive Jews of German citizenship; purges in Russia

THEATER		SOCIETY, POLITICS, CULTURE
Federal Theater Project (until 1939); *Waiting for Lefty,* Clifford Odets (1906–1963), United States; *Murder in the Cathedral,* T. S. Eliot (1888–1965), England		
	1936	Spanish Civil War (until 1939)
Tyrone Guthrie (1900–1971), director of Old Vic, England	1937	
The Theater and Its Double, Antonin Artaud (1896–1948), France	1938	
	1939	World War II (until 1945)
	1941	*For Whom the Bell Tolls,* Ernest Hemingway (1899–1961)
The Skin of Our Teeth, Thornton Wilder (1897–1975)	1942	
Antigone, Jean Anouilh (1910–1987), France	1943	*The Myth of Sisyphus,* Albert Camus (1913–1960), France
No Exit, Jean-Paul Sartre (1905–1980), France	1944	Liberation of France
Compagnie Madeline Renaud-Jean-Louis Barrault, founded in France	1946	Nuremburg trials
The Maids, Jean Genet (1910;–), France	1947	
A Streetcar Named Desire, Tennessee Williams (1911–1983); Actors' Studio founded, United States		
The Bald Soprano, Eugène Ionesco (1912–), France	1949	Creation of East and West Germany
Brecht opens Berliner Ensemble in East Berlin		*1984,* George Orwell (1903–1950)
Death of a Salesman, Arthur Miller (1915–), United States		
	1950	Korean war (until 1953)
The Queen and the Rebels, Ugo Betti (1892–1953), Italy; Jean Vilar (1912–1971) made director of Théâtre National Populaire	1951	

THEATER		SOCIETY, POLITICS, CULTURE
Waiting for Godot, Samuel Beckett (1906–1990), France	1953	Death of Stalin
	1954	McCarthy-Army hearings Hydrogen bomb tested
Separate Tables, Terence Rattigan (1911–), England	1955	
Look Back in Anger, John Osborne (1929–), England	1956	Russia crushes Hungarian revolt; Khrushchev denounces Stalin
The Visit, Friedrich Duerrenmatt (1921–), Switzerland		
	1957	*Sputnik I*, first artificial earth satellite
Biedermann and the Firebugs, Max Frisch (1911–), Switzerland; *The Birthday Party*, Harold Pinter (1930–), England	1958	Fifth Republic of France
Marat/Sade, Peter Weiss (1916–); Polish Theater Laboratory founded by Jerzy Grotowski (1933-)	1959	
The Zoo Story (American premier), Edward Albee (1928–), United States	1960	
Tyrone Guthrie Theater opens in Minneapolis, Minnesota	1961	Berlin Wall
Cafe LaMama opened, off-Broadway theater	1962	Cuban missile crisis
Albee's *Who's Afraid of Virginia Woolf?*	1962	
National Theater established (England's first state-subsidized theater)	1963	John F. Kennedy, president of the United States, assassinated; John Glenn orbits earth
		Warfare escalates between North and South Vietnam; Martin Luther King arrested in Birmingham
Dutchman, LeRoi Jones (Amiri Baraka) (1934–), United States	1964	Resignation of Khrushchev

THEATER		SOCIETY, POLITICS, CULTURE
Tango, Slawomir Mrozek (1930–), Poland	1965	
Viet-Rock, Megan Terry (1932–), United States	1966	
Hair, Ken McDermott, United States	1968	Robert Kennedy and Martin Luther King, Jr., assassinated
Towards a Poor Theater, Jerzy Grotowski, Poland		
Ceremonies in Dark Old Men, Lonne Elder III (1931–), United States	1969	Neal Armstrong walks on the moon, United States
Peter Brook's (1925–) interpretation of Shakespeare's *A Midsummer Night's Dream*		
	1970	*The Female Eunuch,* Germaine Greer, England
Sticks and Bones, David Rabe (1940–)	1971	
N.Y. Shakespeare Festival (Joseph Papp) produces *Two Gentlemen of Verona, Sticks and Bones,* and *That Championship Season* in New York City	1972	
Equus, Peter Shaffer (1926–), England	1974	Watergate scandal; President Richard M. Nixon resigns
A Chorus Line	1975	Francisco Franco dies; Helsinki agreement, recognizing the postwar status quo in Europe, signed
For Colored Girls Who Have Considered Suicide, Ntozake Shange (1948–)	1976	Mao Tse-tung, leader of Communist China, dies; Jimmy Carter becomes president of United States
American Buffalo, David Mamet (1947–)	1977	Camp David accords reached between Israel and Egypt; the novelist Vladimir Nabokov dies
Buried Child, Sam Shepard (1943–), wins Pulitzer Prize	1979	Soviets invade Afghanistan; American hostages taken in Iran
Harold Clurman, (1901–1980) Group Theater founder and director, dies	1980	Ronald Reagan elected president of United States

THEATER		SOCIETY, POLITICS, CULTURE
A Soldier's Play, Charles Fuller (1939–) wins Pulitzer Prize	1982	Workers' union Solidarity outlawed in Poland
'night, Mother, Marsha Norman (1947–) wins Pulitzer Prize	1983	
Fences, August Wilson (1945–)	1985	Mikhail Gorbachev comes to power in Soviet Union
Serious Money, Caryl Churchill (1938–) *Burn This*, Lanford Wilson (1937–)	1987	Chernobyl nuclear accident in Soviet Union
M. Butterfly, David Hwang (1957–)	1988	George Bush elected president of the United States
	1989	Political freedom gained in many parts of eastern Europe

Note: The preceding historical survey follows the development of theater in western civilization, but another important theater, the Asian theater, was evolving along a path of its own. The following section traces theater in India, China, and Japan. Theater emerged also in such places as Cambodia and Indonesia.

ASIA

THEATER		SOCIETY, POLITICS, CULTURE
INDIA		
Natyasastra, principal critical work on Sanskrit drama	ca. 50–100	
	ca. 320	Gupta dynasty reunites northern India after 500 years division; golden age of classical Sanskrit
Sanskrit drama highly developed		
The Little Clay Cart		
Shakuntala, Kalidasa, best-known Sanskrit playwright	ca. 400	
	ca. 600	Earliest known use of the zero and decimal
Bhavabhuti, highest-ranked playwright after Kalidasa	ca. 730	

THEATER		SOCIETY, POLITICS, CULTURE
Decline of Sanskrit drama	ca. 1150	
Indian dance drama, puppet and folk plays	ca. 1192	Beginning of Muslim rule
	1526	Mogul Empire (until 1761)
	1790	British power established in India
King of the Dark Chamber, Rabindranath Tagore (1861–1941)		

CHINA

THEATER		SOCIETY, POLITICS, CULTURE
	618	T'ang dynasty founded (until 907)
Academy of the Pear Orchard, school for dancers and singers established by Ming Huang	712	Emperor Ming Huang (r. 712–756), brief flourishing of arts and literature
	ca. 850	Advent of block printing
Development of "northern" and "southern" schools of drama during Sung dynasty	960	Sung dynasty (until 1279), flowering of arts, literature, and scholarship
Development of professional theater companies and urban audiences		
Scholars and artists move south during Yüan dynasty, but a vigorous popular drama flourishes in the north	1260	Yüan dynasty, China ruled by Mongol Khans until 1368
Southern drama becomes predominant during Ming dynasty and develops highly literary and romantic drama	1368	Ming dynasty, Mongol rulers expelled
Gradual decline of southern drama; Peking eventually replaces Soochow as cultural capital	1644	Ch'ing dynasty, Manchu rulers (until 1912)
	1839	Beginning of Opium wars
"Peking opera," a less literary and more theatrical form, becomes dominant	ca. 1875	
	1900	Boxer Rebellion

469

THEATER		SOCIETY, POLITICS, CULTURE
	JAPAN	
	645	Beginning of great period of cultural infusion and cultural growth (until ca. 800)
Development of traditional dance forms		
	ca. 1020	*The Tale of Genji,* classic Japanese novel, by Murasaki Shikibu
	ca. 1100	Civil strife encourages the rise of military government and feudalism
Zeami Motokiyo (1363–1444), development of the noh drama	1395	Rule of Yoshimitsu (r. 1395–1408), stable period of artistic and literary creativity, but followed by civil wars
	ca. 1542	First Europeans to visit Japan
	1568	Period of national unification (until 1600)
First appearance of kabuki, a more popular and theatrical form than noh	ca. 1600	
	1640	Friction with foreigners and religious disputes leading to cultural and political isolation
Noh drama becomes associated with the aristocracy, and its conventions are rigidly standardized	ca. 1650	
Kabuki becomes most popular form of theater	1675–1750	
Japanese "doll theater" established in Osaka (bunraku)	1685	
Chikamatsu Monzaemon (1653–1724), Japan's most famous playwright, wrote for the bunraku and the kubuki	ca. 1700	
Kubuki becomes the most popular form	ca. 1853	Japan open to the west, beginning of continuing western influence

THEATER		SOCIETY, POLITICS, CULTURE
	1868	Meiji restoration; new rules in Japan sanction exchanges with west
Noh, kabuki, and bunraku continue, but modern realistic theater (Shingeki) begins	1910	
Spoken drama, based on western models, becomes important	1920	

NOTES

✳ INTRODUCTION ✳

Opening photograph: Bob Marshak.

1   Bernard Beckerman, *Dynamics of Drama: Theory and Method of Analysis,* Knopf, New York, 1970, p. 129.

2   Eugene O'Neill, *Long Day's Journey into Night,* Yale University Press, New Haven, Conn., p. 108. Copyright © 1955 by Carlotta Monterey O'Neill. Reprinted by permission of the Yale University Press.

3   Robert Edmond Jones, *The Dramatic Imagination,* Theatre Arts, New York, 1941, p. 40.

✳ CHAPTER 1 ✳

Opening photograph: Jack Manning: NYT Pictures.

1   Jean-Claude van Itallie, *The Serpent: A Ceremony,* written in collaboration with the Open Theater, Atheneum, New York, 1969, p. ix.

2   Walter Kerr, "We Call It 'Live' Theater, but Is It?" *The New York Times,* January 2, 1972. Copyright 1972 by The New York Times Company. Reprinted by permission.

3 Gustave Le Bon, *The Crowd: A Study of the Popular Mind*, 20th ed., Benn, London, 1952, p. 23.

4 Ibid., p. 27.

5 Lawrence S. Wrightsman, *Social Psychology*, 2d ed., Brooks/Cole, Monterey, Calif., 1977, p. 579.

6 Ibid., p. 559.

7 B. F. Skinner, *Science and Human Behavior*, Macmillan, New York, 1953, p. 312.

❋ CHAPTER 2 ❋

Opening photograph: Ron Stone.

1 Carl G. Jung, *Man and His Symbols*, Aldus, London, 1964, p. 21.

2 J. A. Hadfield, *Dreams and Nightmares*, Penguin, Baltimore, Md., 1961, p. 8.

❋ CHAPTER 3 ❋

Opening photograph: Gerry Goodstein.

1 Notes on *King Lear* are from G. K. Hunter's edition of Shakespeare's *King Lear*, Penguin, Baltimore, Md., 1972, pp. 243–244.

❋ CHAPTER 4 ❋

Opening photograph: Artificial Intelligence.

❋ CHAPTER 5 ❋

Opening photograph: Joan Marcus.

1 From Arthur Miller, *Death of a Salesman*, Viking, New York, 1968, pp. 100–103. Copyright 1949 by Arthur Miller. Reprinted by permission of Viking.

2 Erving Goffman, *The Presentation of Self in Everyday Life*, Anchor, Doubleday, Garden City, N.Y., 1949, p. 72.

3 Robert Ezra Park, *Race and Culture*, Free Press, Glencoe, Ill., 1950, p. 249.

4 Theodore Shank, *The Art of Dramatic Art*, Dickenson, Belmont, Calif., 1969, p. 36.

❋ CHAPTER 6 ❋

Opening photograph: Gerry Goodstein.

1 Richard Findlater, *The Player Kings*, Weidenfeld and Nicolson, London, 1971, p. 25.

2 Constantin Stanislavski, *An Actor Prepares*, Theatre Arts, New York, 1948, p. 73.

3 Constantin Stanislavski, *My Life in Art*, Meridian, New York, 1946, p. 465.

4 Stanislavski, *An Actor Prepares*, p. 92.

5 Ibid., p. 88.

6 Ibid., p. 38.

7 Ibid., p. 136.

8 Harold Clurman, *On Directing*, Macmillan, New York, 1972, pp. 261 ff.

9 Walter Kerr, drama review, *New York Herald Tribune*, January 10, 1961.

❋ CHAPTER 7 ❋

Opening photograph: Peter Cunningham.

1 Harold Clurman, *On Directing*, Macmillan, New York, 1972, p. 27.

2 Ibid., p. 221.

3 Ibid., p. 30.

4 Ibid., p. 30.

❋ CHAPTER 8 ❋

Opening photograph: Martha Swope/Roundabout.

1 Kenneth MacGowan, *A Primer of Playwrighting*, Dolphin, Doubleday, Garden City, N.Y., 1962, p. 62.

2 E. M. Forster, *Aspects of the Novel*, Harcourt, Brace, New York, 1927, 1954, p. 13.

✳ CHAPTER 9 ✳

Opening photograph: T. Charles Erickson.

1 Jean Anouilh, *Antigone,* Lewis Galantiere (trans. and adaptor), Random House, New York, 1946, p. 36. Copyright 1946 by Random House.

2 John Gassner, *A Treasury of the Theater (From Henrik Ibsen to Arthur Miller),* Simon & Schuster, New York, 1959, p. 457.

✳ CHAPTER 10 ✳

Opening photograph: Nina Krieger/Williamstown Theater.

1 Albert Camus, *Le Mythe de Sisyphe,* Gallimard, Paris, 1942, p. 18.

2 Eugène Ionesco, *The Bald Soprano,* in *Four Plays,* Grove, New York, 1958, p. 39.

3 Samuel Beckett, *Waiting for Godot,* Grove, New York, 1954, p. 28b.

4 Martin Esslin, *The Theatre of the Absurd,* Doubleday, Garden City, N.Y., 1961, p. 149.

5 Ibid., p. 159.

✳ CHAPTER 11 ✳

Opening photograph: Michael Cooper.

1 "You're the Top" 1934 Warner Bros. Inc. (renewed). All rights reserved. Used by permission.

✳ CHAPTER 12 ✳

Opening photograph: Joan Marcus.

1 From Eric Bentley (ed.), *Naked Masks: Five Plays by Luigi Pirandello,* Dutton, New York, 1922, pp. 266–267. Copyright, 1922, by E. P. Dutton. Renewal copyright, 1950, by Stefano, Fausto, and Lietta Pirandello. Reprinted by permission of the publishers.

✳ CHAPTER 13 ✳

Opening photograph: Ivan Kyncl.

✳ CHAPTER 14 ✳

Opening photograph: David Cooper.

1 Arthur Miller, *The Theater Essays of Arthur Miller*, Viking, New York, 1978, pp. 3–5.
2 Friedrich Nietzsche, "The Birth of Tragedy," from Nietzsche, *Works in Three Volumes*, Carl Hanser Publishers, Munich, vol. 1, pp. 19, 92.

✳ CHAPTER 15 ✳

Opening photograph: T. Charles Erickson.

✳ CHAPTER 16 ✳

Opening photograph: George E. Joseph.

1 The Performance Group, *Dionysus in 69*, Noonday, Farrar, Straus & Giroux, New York (n.p.).
2 Material on the first three types of stages was suggested by a booklet prepared by Dr. Mary Henderson for the educational division of Lincoln Center for the Performing Arts.
3 Antonin Artaud, *The Theater and Its Double*, Grove, New York, 1958, pp. 96–97.

✳ CHAPTER 17 ✳

Opening photograph: T. Charles Erickson.

1 Robert Edmond Jones, *The Dramatic Imagination*, Theatre Arts, New York, 1941, p. 25.
2 Ibid., pp. 23–24.
3 Reprinted from *The Dramatic Imagination*, Theatre Arts, New York, 1941, pp. 71–72. Copyright 1941 by Robert Edmond Jones, with the permission of the publishers.

✳ CHAPTER 18 ✳

Opening photograph: Joan Marcus.

✳ CHAPTER 19 ✳

Opening photograph: Robert C. Ragsdale.

✳ CHAPTER 20 ✳

Opening photograph: Eileen Darby/New York Public Library Theater Collection; Astor, Lenox, and Tilden Foundations.

1 Arthur Miller, *Timebends*, Grove Press, New York, 1987, p. 131.
2 Jo Mielziner, *Designing for the Theatre*, Atheneum, New York, 1965.
3 Elia Kazan, *A Life*, Alfred A. Knopf, New York, 1988, p. 361.
4 Ibid., p. 362.
5 Miller, p. 191.
6 Kazan, p. 358.

✳ APPENDIX 2 ✳

1 S. H. Butcher, *Aristotle's Theory of Poetry and Fine Art*, 3d ed., Macmillan, London, 1902, p. 23.
2 Arthur Miller, *The Theater Essays of Arthur Miller*, Viking, New York, 1978, pp. 3–4.

✳ CREDITS FOR COLOR PHOTOGRAPHS ✳

Following page 76:

A Doll's House—Joan Marcus/Arena Stage
Uncle Vanya—Richard Feldman
The Piano Lesson—Gerry Goodstein
Anna Christie—T. Charles Erickson/Long Wharf Theater
Kiss Me, Kate—Michael Cooper/Stratford Festival
The Glass Menagerie—Bob Marshak
Kabuki—Bob Huntzinger/Stock Market
Electra—Donald Cooper
Much Ado about Nothing—Martha Swope

Following page 236:

Macbeth—Pioneer Theater
A Flea in Her Ear—T. Charles Erickson/Long Wharf Theater
Spunk—Martha Swope
Uncle Vanya—Richard Feldman
Waiting for Godot—Will Gullette/Old Globe Theater
The Phantom of the Opera—Bob Marshak
The Good Woman of Setzuan—Richard Feldman
Twelfth Night—Richard Feldman

Following page 332:

A Midsummer Night's Dream—Gerry Goodstein
Twelfth Night—George E. Joseph
Happy Days—Chris Bennion/Seattle Rep
Alcestis—Richard Feldman
Miss Saigon—Michael Le Poer Trench/RDR Productions
Serpent Woman—Richard Feldman
The School for Scandal—Will Gullette/Old Globe Theater
Woyzeck—Jennifer Lester/Hartford Stage
Makeup for Chinese theater—Bruno J. Zehnder/Peter Arnold, Inc.
A Midsummer Night's Dream—Robert C. Ragsdale/Stratford Festival
Into the Woods—Martha Swope
Life Is a Dream—Richard Feldman
The School for Wives—Jennifer Lester/Hartford Stage
Grand Hotel—Santo Loquasto
Six Degrees of Separation—Tony Walton

SELECT
BIBLIOGRAPHY

Allen, John: *Theatre in Europe,* J. Offord, Eastbourne, England, 1981.

Aristotle: *Aristotle's Poetics,* S. H. Butcher (trans.), Introduction by Francis Fergusson, Hill and Wang, New York, 1961.

Artaud, Antonin: *The Theater and Its Double.* by Mary C. Richards (trans.), Grove, New York, 1958.

Atkinson, Brooks: *Broadway,* rev. ed., Macmillan, New York, 1974.

Bay, Howard: *Stage Design,* Drama Book Specialists, New York, 1974.

Beckerman, Bernard: *Dynamics of Drama: Theory and Method of Analysis,* Drama Book Specialists, New York, 1979.

Benedetti, Jean: *Stanislavski: An Introduction,* Theatre Arts, New York, 1982.

Benedetti, Robert: *The Actor at Work,* Prentice-Hall, Englewood Cliffs, N.J., 1971.

Bentley, Eric: *The Life of the Drama,* Atheneum, New York, 1964.

——— (ed.): *The Theory of the Modern Stage,* Penguin, Baltimore, 1968.

Bradley, David: *Modern French Drama, 1948–1980,* Harvard University Press, Cambridge, 1984.

Brecht, Bertolt: *Brecht on Theatre,* John Willett (trans.), Hill and Wang, New York, 1965.

Brockett, Oscar G.: *History of the Theatre,* 4th ed., Allyn & Bacon, Boston, 1982.

——— and Robert R. Findlay: *Century of Innovation: A History of European and American Theatre and Drama Since 1870,* Prentice-Hall, Englewood Cliffs, N.J., 1973.

Brook, Peter: *The Empty Space*, Atheneum, New York, 1968.

Burns, Elizabeth: *Theatricality*, Harper & Row, New York, 1973.

Carlson, Marvin: *Theories of the Theatre*, Cornell University Press, Ithica, N.Y., 1984.

Chambers, Colin, and Mike Prior: *Playwrights' Progress*, Blackwell, Oxford, 1987.

Clark, Barrett H. (ed.): *European Theories of the Drama*, rev. ed., Crown, New York, 1965.

Clurman, Harold: *On Directing*, Macmillan, New York, 1972.

Cohen, Robert: *Acting Power*, Mayfield Publishers, Palo Alto, Calif., 1978.

Cole, Toby: *Playwrights on Playwriting*, Hill and Wang, New York, 1961.

———, and Helen Krich Chinoy: *Actors on Acting*, Crown, New York, 1970.

Corrigan, Robert (ed.): *Comedy: Meaning and Form*, Chandler, San Francisco, 1965.

——— (ed.): *Tragedy: Vision and Form*, Chandler, San Francisco, 1965.

Corson, Richard: *Stage Makeup*, 6th ed., Prentice-Hall, Englewood Cliffs, N.J., 1981.

Dukore, Bernard: *Dramatic Theory and Criticism: Greeks to Grotowski*, Holt, New York, 1974.

Emery, Joseph S.: *Stage Costume Technique*, Prentice-Hall, Englewood Cliffs, N.J., 1981.

Esslin, Martin: *The Theatre of the Absurd*, rev. ed., Doubleday, Garden City, N.Y., 1969.

Felner, Mira: *Free to Act*, Holt, Rinehart, & Winston, New York, 1990.

Fergusson, Francis: *The Idea of a Theater*, Princeton University Press, Princeton, N.J., 1949.

Gassner, John: *Masters of the Drama*, 3d ed., Dover, New York, 1954.

——— and Edward Quinn: *The Reader's Encyclopedia of World Drama*, Thomas Y. Crowell, New York, 1969.

——— and Ralph Allen (eds.): *Theatre and Drama in the Making*, 2 vols., Houghton Mifflin, Boston, 1964.

Goffman, Erving: *Presentation of Self in Everyday Life*, Overlook, New York, 1973.

Goldman, Michael: *The Actor's Freedom: Toward a Theory of Drama*, Viking, New York, 1975.

Grotowski, Jerzy: *Towards a Poor Theatre*, Simon & Schuster, New York, 1968.

Heilman, Robert G.: *Tragedy and Melodrama: Versions of Experience*, University of Washington Press, Seattle, 1968.

Hodge, Francis: *Play Directing: Analysis, Communication, and Style*, Prentice-Hall, Englewood Cliffs, N.J., 1971.

Izenour, George: *Theatre Design*, McGraw-Hill, New York, 1977.

Jones, Robert E.: *The Dramatic Imagination*, Meredith, New York, 1941.

Kerr, Walter: *Tragedy and Comedy*, Simon & Schuster, New York, 1967.

Kirby, E. T.: *Ur-Drama: The Origins of Theatre*, New York University Press, New York, 1975.

Kirby, Michael: *Happenings*, Dutton, New York, 1965.

Lahr, John, and Jonathan Price: *Life-Show*, Viking, New York, 1973.

Langer, Susanne K.: *Feeling and Form*, Scribner's, New York, 1953.

Miller, Arthur: *The Theater Essays of Arthur Miller*, Robert Martin (ed.), Viking, New York, 1978.

Mitchell, Loften: *Black Drama*, Hawthorn, New York, 1967.

Nagler, Alois M.: *Sourcebook in Theatrical History*, Dover, New York, 1952.

Novick, Julius: *Beyond Broadway*, Hill and Wang, New York, 1968.

Oenslager, Donald: *Scenery Then and Now*, Norton, New York, 1936.

Parker, W. Oren, and Harvey K. Smith: *Scene Design and Stage Lighting*, 4th ed., Holt, New York, 1979.

Pilbrow, Richard: *Stage Lighting*, rev. ed., Van Nostrand and Reinhold, New York, 1979.

Roberts, Vera M.: *On Stage: A History of the Theatre*, 2d ed., Harper & Row, New York; 1974.

Schechner, Richard: *Environmental Theater*, Hawthorn, New York, 1973.

Schevill, James: *Breakout! In Search of New Theatrical Environments*, University of Chicago Press, Chicago, 1972.

Southern, Richard: *The Seven Ages of the Theatre*, Hill and Wang, New York, 1961.

Stanislavski, Constantin: *An Actor Prepares*, Elizabeth Reynolds Hapgood (trans.), Theatre Arts, New York, 1936.

Wilson, Edwin, and Alvin Goldfarb: *Living Theater*, McGraw-Hill, New York, 1983.

——— and ———: *Theater: The Lively Art*, McGraw-Hill, New York, 1991.

Young, Stark: *The Theatre*, Hill and Wang, New York, 1963.

INDEX

498